D0305332

THE ALPINE JOURNAL 2016

Nick Bullock climbing the third pitch of Night Fever (M8, 250m) on the west wall of the Tour Ronde, taken during a first attempt on this new winter route in early 2015 with Tim Neill. Bullock returned on 8 January to complete the route with Matt Helliker, finishing late and in bad weather. Winter conditions offer a good freeze on a route with significant loose rock. *(Tim Neill)*

THE ALPINE JOURNAL 2016

The Journal of the Alpine Club

A record of mountain adventure
and scientific observation

Editor: Ed Douglas

Production: Jane Beagley

Volume 120

Number 364

Supported by the
MOUNT EVEREST FOUNDATION

Published by
THE ALPINE CLUB

THE ALPINE JOURNAL 2016
Volume 120 No 364

www.alpine-club.org.uk

Address all editorial communication to the Hon Editor:
Alpine Club, 55 Charlotte Rd, London, EC2A 3QF
email: journal.editor@alpine-club.org.uk

Address all sales and distribution communications to:
Cordee, 11 Jacknell Rd, Dodwells Bridge Ind Est, Hinckley, LE10 3BS

Back numbers:
Apply to the Alpine Club, 55 Charlotte Rd, London, EC2A 3QF or, for 1969 to date, apply to Cordee, as above.

First published in 2016 by The Alpine Club
Typeset by Jane Beagley, Vertebrate Publishing
Printed and bound by Novoprint SA, Barcelona

A CIP catalogue record for this book is available from The British Library

ISBN 978-0-9569309-5-8

Front cover: Sunset high on Link Sar West, with the summit of K6 behind. (*Jonathan Griffith Photography*)

Endpapers
Front: Andy Inglis styling up the third ascent of *Pfugga-lule* (VIII,9) on the impressive Happy Tyroleans wall on No3 Buttress in Coire an Lochain. This superb shot was taken during an ascent of Savage Slit. (*Dave Riley*)
Back: Jon Bracey under the Pyramide du Tacul before setting off on the first ascent of *Mastabas*. (*Matt Helliker*)

Foreword

At the time of writing, it is still more than a month before the 2016 Olympic games open in the Brazilian city of Rio de Janeiro. Given the ominous sequence of negative stories that have cast a shadow in the run-up to this year's Olympics, we can only hope that things have gone better than expected. The people of Brazil and those athletes who have prepared fairly deserve success.

Mountaineering has had a distant and tangential relationship with the Olympic movement. Former president Alan Blackshaw and Roger Payne, the long-serving general secretary of the British Mountaineering Council, wrote a paper for the UIAA on this subject that was published in 2005. They explained that alpinism had been included in the Olympic programme when the modern games were started in 1896. While it wasn't possible to hold an event, a medal could be awarded for an outstanding ascent, just as one could for 'aeronautics'.

The first prize wasn't made until the Chamonix winter games of 1924, when medals were awarded to the British 1922 Everest expedition and its Sherpas. Baron de Coubertin suggested the British should try to put one of them on the summit. This was something Kenton Cool finally achieved 90 years later, although it's worth noting Blackshaw and Payne suggested it might be done in 2008 for the Beijing Olympics. Given the disheartening politicisation of Everest that year, with Chinese security officers working inside Nepal to make sure no foreign climbers went near the summit to interrupt China's 'Olympic' ascent with unsightly protests about Tibet, it's probably for the best this symbolic gesture had to wait.

There were other awards of Olympic medals: the Schmid brothers for example, for the north face of the Matterhorn in 1932, and for Günther and Hettie Dyhrenfurth in 1936, following their 1934 exploration of the Karakoram, particularly the Gasherbrum peaks and the first ascent of Sia Kangri. Both these achievements were admirable, but it's worth asking: why them? Why not, say, the first ascent of the Eiger's north face, or the discovery of the Nanda Devi Sanctuary? It illustrates, to the satisfaction of many of us, how indefinably unique alpinism can be. Perhaps it was for this reason that the IOC dropped alpinism from its programme in 1946.

How things change. Since writing this, not only will the Olympics have been and gone, we will know for certain whether climbing will be included at the 2020 Olympics held in Tokyo. In many ways this is the logical conclusion to the decades-long process of a growing interest in and commitment to performance. Sport climbing and bouldering have become increasingly popular in the last 25 years, activities where it is much easier to make direct comparisons between individuals and the things they climb. It's hardly surprising, given how popular these branches of climbing are, that this process should lead first to competition and then to the Olympics. It's what those involved want to see happen – and good luck to them.

Yet the decision does have implications for alpinism, the long ago rejected but much older version of climbing. Competition climbing has already caused one schism, with the splitting off in 2007 from climbing's international body the UIAA of its competitions committee to form the International Federation of Sport Climbing (IFSC). Under its bullish leader Marco Scolaris, the IFSC's first and only leader, Olympic status has been a long-cherished dream. Yet the UIAA also has Olympic ambitions, having developed its own ice-climbing world cup circuit. It wants to see ice climbing included in the 2022 winter games held in Beijing. (I won't even mention the International Ski Mountaineering Federation.)

None of this seems necessarily a bad thing to me. If that's what people want to do, and it doesn't limit the freedoms of others, then why not? Climbing is a broad church. Personally, I'm a huge fan of bouldering competitions; Shauna Coxsey is an immensely inspiring climber. What is still uncertain is the impact Olympic status could have on organisations that represent all of us: the influx of money, the bureaucratic demands, anti-doping campaigns, the rules and regulations. Will all this deflect attention from issues that are of increasing concern to alpinists, like freedom of movement and increasing regulation, particularly in the Greater Ranges?

One person who would have revelled in such 'jockeying for position' was Ken Wilson, who died in June. John Porter had already written his memoir of working for Ken in the 1970s at *Mountain* magazine, which is included in this year's *Journal*. It captures Ken's extraordinary energy 'at the flood'. Although some perceived him as overly keen to protect tradition, it's worth noting that Ken was always very supportive of young climbers doing interesting new things. He would have been encouraged then to see the current generation of alpinists enjoying success last year on hard new routes with a strong bias towards exploration, like Andy Houseman and Jon Griffith's ascent of Link Sar West in the Karakoram, and Ben Silvestre and Pete Graham's first ascent in the rarely visited Revelation Mountains in Alaska, both of which are covered in this volume.

This ability of the *Alpine Journal* to offer perspective on past, present and future, on extreme deeds and high art, is only possible through the support of the writers, photographers and artists who fill its pages and share our passion for the world's high places. I would like to offer them my thanks, and mention in particular Catherine Moorehead, who has once again done such an able job editing the Obituaries section. This year's includes Roger Chorley, in its long history one of the Club's most distinguished members, whose influence stretched from the National Trust, to the Ordnance Survey and a host of other public bodies – and of course a past president of the Alpine Club.

Ed Douglas

Contents

This year's frontispiece art, which divides the different sections of the *Alpine Journal*, illustrates the work of the Scottish artist Rob Fairley. An introduction to Fairley and his career appears in AC Notes, written by Robin Campbell, who curated these works.

West Nepal

Andy Perkins and Andy Cave at Advanced Base Camp, Annapurna III.
Rob Fairley, 1989. Watercolour. 30cm x 21cm. Private Collection.

MICK FOWLER

The First Ascent of Gave Ding

The north face of Gave Ding in far western Nepal.
(All photos: Mick Fowler/Paul Ramsden/Berghaus)

'My bags are missing.'

This was not the best possible start to the British Far West Nepal Expedition 2015. Miraculously Paul Ramsden's missing bags appeared on the next flight but by this time we were late and our driver was fretting about driving to the town of Nepalgunj – so good they called it Nepalgunj – in order to catch our meticulously pre-booked flight to the airstrip at Simikot.

Northern Humla remains one of the least travelled and least developed corners of Nepal. Mules crossing a bridge on day three of the walk-in.

'I've never driven through the night before,' he explained. I couldn't recall ever having a driver who spoke good English before and contemplated that this is not always a bonus. 'But I think we have enough fuel to get there,' he added in an appropriately reassuring tone. His concern sprang from India's blockade of fuel supplies to Nepal; queues at the pumps were so long that it had taken him 17 hours to gather enough fuel to fill the tank.

A few hours later we were stuck in a queue behind a fatal accident in which two policemen had been squashed by an overturned lorry. As the lorry was lifted by a rather out of control JCB the throng of youths taking photos on their mobile phones was such that riot police had to be called to restore order. Less than an hour after driving past the spread-eagled bodies laid out at the side of the road we stopped and somehow ended up joining in celebratory dancing at what seemed to be a child's birthday party. Yet despite our driver successfully completing his first overnight drive we were gutted to arrive late at Nepalgunj airport. Happily our plane was delayed and so all was well. We would arrive in Simikot as planned. Seldom has a trip started with such a concentrated number of ups and downs. As we waved goodbye to our driver he said he was pleased to have only dozed off a couple of times on the drive and had no idea how he might find enough fuel to return to Kathmandu.

Our plan was to try and climb a 6,541m unclimbed mountain called Gave Ding in the Humla region of north-west Nepal. This is not the easiest of spots to get to which is great for keeping the crowds away but does add a whole raft of uncertainties to any trip. It also means the area is

Weaving a way through the Eiger-like walls on the lower section of the face.

relatively unexplored, so much so that the valley we planned to visit had not previously been visited by westerners. Our decision to visit was based on distant shots from unhelpful angles and Google Earth searches. A key factor influencing us was that by setting Google Earth at the right time of day we spotted that the shadow of the north face of Gave Ding was longer than any other shadow in the area. That presumably meant it was bigger and steeper that anything else around. And an unclimbed big face in a valley not previously visited by westerners seemed to offer such good ingredients for adventurous action that the British Far West Nepal Expedition came into being. Steve Burns and Ian Cartwright joined us, Berghaus and the Mount Everest Foundation gave support and we could but keep our fingers crossed that we had made a good decision.

With only eight people on board the Twin Otter flight from Nepalgunj to Simikot an airhostess seemed an unnecessary luxury. Mind you, she was delightfully friendly and offered us boiled sweets and earplugs served in the same tray. With a population of around 2,000, Simikot is the administrative centre of Humla district. The fact that it is marked on many large-scale maps only emphasises how sparsely populated this area is. There are almost no roads and while the straight-line distance from Nepalgunj is just over 200km, the overland journey takes just under a week. Flights are totally weather dependant and there is always a risk of being stuck for days. Roads are being built from the south and also from Tibet to the north but driving hereabouts is so tortuously slow that flying willbe the only realistic access option for most mountaineers and trekkers for some time to come.

Paul Ramsden on day two.

Frustratingly, even though the aircraft flies at little more than 4,000m, the carriage of gas cylinders for our stoves was prohibited. Knowing this, we paid for cylinders to be portered in weeks in advance.

'How long did it take to get them here?' we asked our supplier.

'Oh, not long. They came on the plane,' he explained. Knowing the right people here is clearly very important.

Back in Kathmandu our liaison officer had decided he might join us later and so our team at Simikot consisted of six of us: four climbers, our cook Prem and his son Lakpa. We also had a porter to carry kerosene and ferry kit to base camp if our mules couldn't make it all the way. Somehow we ended up with far more mules than we needed but the muleteers did an admirable job of spreading the load in such a way that it was not immediately obvious how lightly loaded they were.

After Simikot we were to see no westerners at all. The good mule tracks of this part of the world took us through ethnically pleasing villages on day one and occasional shepherd huts on day two. After day two we were to see no more humans at all until the walk out.

It was on day four from Simikot that the real adventure started. This was the day we left the main valley leading to Tibet and turned into the left branch of the Lachama *khola* where we hoped to have a base camp by a prominent lake we had spotted on Google Earth at 5,000 metres. Our friends Julian Freeman-Attwood, Nick Colton and Ed Douglas had been up the right branch in 2011 but we had no real idea how far we might be able to make it up the left-hand branch. It didn't take long for us to find out.

'The mules can go no further.' Prem was interpreting for the muleteers who were acting in a way that left little room for doubt. We were at about

Mick Fowler on the 'whoop-with-joy' pitch on day two. Hauling the sack up later was not so pleasurable.

Above: Mick Fowler exiting from a steep mixed section on day two.

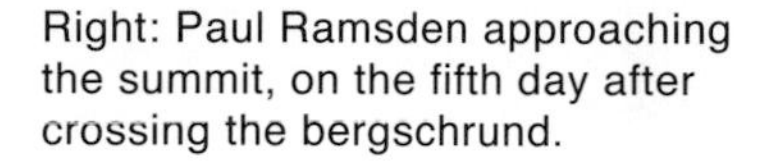

Right: Paul Ramsden approaching the summit, on the fifth day after crossing the bergschrund.

4,500m and a long way horizontally from our intended base camp. Using our one porter to ferry loads was out of the question. Prem and Lakpa offered to help but ultimately we decided it would be easiest to have our base camp where we were. And so after a day sorting ourselves out at base camp, and nine days after leaving the UK, the four of us ventured into the upper valley to find out whether our gut feeling had been right and exciting objectives were to be found here. After all the planning, preparation and anticipation it was a tense day.

We need not have feared. The north face of Gave Ding reared up in a complex line of Eiger-like walls crowned by a Peuterey-like ridge leading to a short but sharp headwall. Ice cliffs threatened both sides but in the centre there looked to be a single safe line.

First though some acclimatising was necessary and that became more than usually problematic. Our plan was to spend time up high in the unexplored side valley immediately opposite the north face of Gave Ding; this was ringed by unclimbed 6,000m peaks. But as we gained a better overall sense of the area it became increasingly clear that the contrast between the north and south sides of the mountains here is extreme. We were told it had been a weak monsoon and perhaps that was a significant factor but just about every face that was not truly north facing was snow-free loose rubble up to a height of 5,600m or so.

Water was a real problem. Above the lake where we had originally planned to have our base camp we could find no water at all. The glacier

was completely covered in sun-baked tortuous moraine and no streams at all came down from the mountains above. All in all we decided that the valley was one of the most dry and desolate glacial basins we had ever seen, we didn't spend as much time as high as we would have liked and it was not our most successful acclimatisation outing. Paul and I could but hope that our bodies were ready for the altitude gain involved in climbing the 1,600m mixed face that towered above the far side of the glacier. At least it looked hard so we would gain height slowly and thereby stand a chance of acclimatising on the route. Positive thinking is important in Himalayan climbing.

After waiting out a couple of days of indifferent weather at base camp we camped under the face with seven days' food and four gas cylinders for the stove. Our plan for the first day was to move together up a snow couloir and then traverse easily to a possible bivouac spot on a col between a pinnacle and the face. The traverse line turned out to be powder snow on slabs and very tricky in places but even so by early afternoon we were at our planned bivouac spot.

The sharp crest sported no good spots for our little tent so we used a snow hammock to hold back as much of the powdery snow as possible and urinated on it in the vague hope that would help freeze everything together. This sort of worked and we ended up with the tent floor draped over a 50cm-wide crest. Boots and other heavy stuff hanging in the fabric on either side vaguely stabilised matters but the ever-present prospect of the whole show slipping off to one side did not make for the most relaxing of nights.

Above us the wall reared up in a series of blank walls broken by discontinuous white streaks. After much discussion, we had a plan and various fall-back plans for this section. Plan A was a curling line of weakness leading to a distressingly steep section. If we failed on this plan B was to abseil diagonally out of the steep section to a parallel line further right. Plan C was to traverse a long way back left to a line that looked harder, making plan C not much of a plan at all. A morning of awkward work on powdery mixed ground followed by delicate traversing put us above a huge drop below the main difficulties of plan A. As I arrived at the stance Paul was hanging out from the belays craning his neck to get a good view of the tenuous line of weakness above.

'Looks hard. Might just go.'

The position had become outrageously exposed. The ground below overhung for several hundred feet so that abseiling into plan B was clearly a non-runner. That meant we really had to get up the near-vertical mixed ground above. Oh dear. There was only one option and it was my lead.

Much as I derive enormous amounts of retrospective pleasure from technical Himalayan climbing it is not often that the Fowler body yelps with delight at the time. Here though the situation was exceptional. Snow and ice conditions were now perfect, the protection reasonable and the climbing just within my limit.

'Absolutely brilliant!' I heard myself shouting to no one in particular.

It soon became apparent that the improvement in conditions was due to the consolidating effect of the large quantities of spindrift that intermittently poured down this part of the face. But nothing was going to detract from my enjoyment here and on the plus side the spindrift waves made for an excellent opportunity to test the neck and hood design of the prototype jackets we were testing for Berghaus.

Three fantastic pitches, including a memorable descent from a disturbingly unexpected cul-de-sac, led to an easing of the angle and a snow crest on top of a buttress which, almost uniquely in my experience, was soft and deep enough for us to quickly clear a platform that was only a little short of the size of our tent. It did collapse a bit in the night, bending the poles, but we had expected a sitting bivouac and a bent pole seemed a small price to pay for the relative luxury of tented accommodation.

Above us steep mixed ground led to another rock band cleaved by another difficult-looking line of weakness. By now we were fully appreciating the fact that the face is very truly a north face. We had had no sun whatsoever since crossing the bergschrund three days earlier and the temperature was stubbornly low. Paul persevered out of sight as I shivered. Soon he reported that he was leaving his rucksack hanging on a runner. Never a good sign. We both like to avoid the faff of hauling if at all possible. The problem was ice too thin for secure protection stretching a long way up a near vertical groove. Seconding on a single 7mm rope I couldn't help but be aware that the rope looked very thin and the sack being hauled on the other rope was making much smoother progress than I was. It was a pity I couldn't get any

Mick Fowler in the bivouac tent on descent just below the summit. Temperatures were lower than either had previously experienced on expeditions together.

photos of Paul leading such a spectacular pitch. But I did manage to snap a shot of his sack.

By now we were well up the face and excitement levels were growing. We seemed to be correct in our judgement that the line was completely safe from objective dangers and the climbing was turning out to be even better than we had expected. And to end an excellent day we found a perfect tent ledge on top of an ice cliff just as we were resigned to a sitting bivouac.

Not far above us was the start of the Peuterey-like section. The Peuterey ridge on Mont Blanc is a classic of its genre with a sharp icy crest in a superb position and this bore many similarities to my experience of the upper section of that route. And here we welcomed the sun for the first time in four days, although it seemed to have very little warmth in it and we were already commenting that the conditions were among the coldest we had experienced on our climbs together.

At the end of the ridge, a 20m wall of ice gave access to a small hanging glacier below a 150m headwall of cornice-fringed, hard blue ice. This looked challenging but with gathering clouds our first priority was to get the tent up. Thus far the weather had been good with afternoon snow showers clearing by nightfall. Now though darkness fell with snow falling heavily. Soon the wind picked up and the snow accumulated so that the walls of the tent pushed heavily against us. I lay awake deep into the night listening to the sound of the wind and snow. I didn't sleep well.

It was a relief when morning dawned clear and calm but bitterly cold. We guessed the temperature could be as low as minus 30°C. Around 75cm of new snow had fallen and the snowline was way below base camp. In places the powder snow was chest deep and it was a fine, energy-sapping effort by Ramsden to trail-break a trench to below the headwall.

Fowler and Ramsden arrive back at base camp eight days after leaving.

The hard blue Himalayan ice here was of the kind that only those who have experienced it can fully appreciate. By now our axes and crampons were blunt and bounced ineffectually off the ice. At one point the enormous effort required to get secure placements saw me reduced to clipping into the base of my axe and hanging sack-like against the ice. Exhausting stuff this Himalayan climbing. And the cold was so intense that this turned into the only climbing day ever that Paul, who seems largely immune to cold, wore a down jacket all day.

The summit crest came suddenly. After five days of hard climbing on the steep and inhospitable north side it felt like something of a release to pull into the sun, have a whole new panorama open up and be able to walk about freely on the relatively amenable southern slopes. The summit was easily reached and a firm summit hug felt to be in order.

We pitched our tent in a good spot just below the top and enjoyed spending the last few hours of daylight soaking in the wonderful view of unexplored terrain and relishing the feeling of having completed the climb that we had dreamed of for the last year. We wondered how close the nearest other climbers were and concluded that it was a very long way. The remote grandeur of our position felt very special.

All we had to do now was get down. That took a further two days involving complex glacier travel on the south-west side, 25 abseils from abalakov threads on the north side and four absolutely exhausting hours crossing the glacier and descending to base camp. Once down I soon fell asleep and spilled my dinner in my lap. Before that, we agreed it had been one of the very best climbs we had done together. And as we walked down through the changing seasons of old growth deciduous forests I knew already that the retrospective pleasure of such a fine trip would stay with me for many years. Adventures in the remote Himalaya are difficult to beat.

TOM RICHARDSON

Mukot Peak

Mukot Peak from base camp during the expedition puja. *(Tom Richardson)*

Not having made the first ascent of a Himalayan peak since 1979, I decided the time had come to do another. I say 'first ascent', but unless someone builds a cairn, sticks a flag on it or writes about it somewhere, you never know whether you are really the first and I'm not sure that it matters all that much anyway. It's not a competition.

These days the Nepali government are keen to encourage climbers to visit new areas and have consequently opened up new peaks of moderate height and difficulty, trying to tempt people away from the honey pots of the busy Khumbu area into the rest of the country. It's a good policy.

KE Adventure Travel, one of my several employers, has always had the spirit of mountain exploration at their heart, and for autumn 2015 they made a plan to make the first official ascent of Mukot Peak (6087m), located in a remote and wild corner of western Nepal, nestling on the flank of the rarely seen but phenomenal Dhaulagiri 2 (7751m), in Lower Dolpo.

The plan was to have three groups, A, B and C, attempt the peak. Using Sherpa support, we would fix ropes on the steepest section leading to the summit ridge. I was to lead group B and while excited at the prospect some-

The magnificent Dhaulagiri 2 from high on Mukot Peak. *(Tom Richardson)*

how doubted that following group A, with leader Ade and sirdar Phanden having done the reconnaissance, we would get to make the first ascent.

They left a week ahead of us and we followed in their footsteps. The approach to Mukot Peak is quite complex. The first stage is a flight from Kathmandu to Nepalgunj, the regional airport hub on the Terai, close to the Indian border and very hot. Next day is another flight, nearly as impressive as the famous flight to Lukla that takes you to the landing strip at Juphal. It's a sharp contrast, set amid steep wooded hills with just a dusting of snow on them. Unusually though, the trek begins by descending to the valley bottom at a mere 2,510m and after four hours walking in the heat we made camp at Dunai, the last village where there is a shop.

After five days of wonderful trekking along the river valley, encountering wide sandy plains, narrow trails above huge drops, spectacular bridges and mountain vistas, we reached the final settlement of Mukot village. People here have a very tough life eking a living from their animals and fields in the high cold atmosphere. Here we also learned that four out of 12 members of group A had climbed the mountain with Sherpa support but none of the summiteers were English or American. We were, so first English and American ascents were still available.

Next day our camp was on a flat strip of land called Nani Goth, the view dominated by one of the most truly dramatic and rarely seen peaks in the world, Dhaulagiri 2, the Dhaulagiri range containing not just an

Looking down at base camp, just visible, from the summit ridge of Mukot Peak. *(Tom Richardson)*

8,000m peak, Dhaulagiri, but five other family members, which, though slightly lower, are equally breath-taking.

Base camp at 5,000m was another dramatic spot right at the base of the north face of Mukot Peak. It's traditional to have a Buddhist ceremony of blessing before setting off up a mountain and fortunately one of our Sherpas, Dawa, was an ex-monk so could oblige with the formalities. Base camp was a cold place, especially at 3am the following day when the whole team – Pasang, the sirdar, climbing Sherpas Dawa and Dorji and seven members, including Janet, my wife, and myself – all headed off to the mountain. We had planned to climb as two roped parties. At the point where we needed to put on crampons, one member turned back and returned to base camp with Dawa. The rest of us continued. Snow conditions were good and we made good progress on the easier-angled slopes. At two-thirds height the terrain steepened considerably as did the exposure. Fortunately we were able to use the fixed ropes set up for group A.

The wind picked up as we closed in on a col from which we would ascend the ridge to the summit. On the ridge it accelerated, sapping energy and breath from the already tired team. We moved slowly along to reach a small col. The summit lay just above us but the cold and wind were fierce. Some of the party decided they couldn't go on. It was out of the question for anyone to hang around in the conditions so we began our descent. It had taken six hours from putting our crampons on.

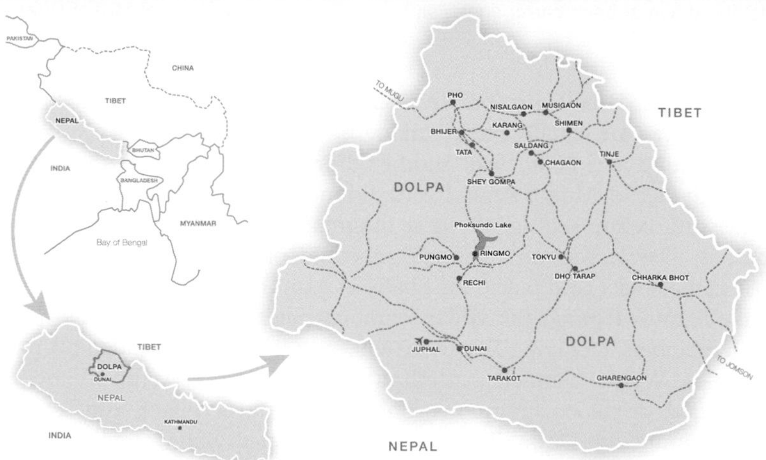

The following photographs are taken from Gerda Pauler's new book *Dolpo: People and Land*. Pauler, who wrote a charming account of her trek along the Great Himalaya Trail, explores the individuals, communities and culture that make Dolpo one of the most fascinating regions of the Himalaya. It includes compelling interviews with local people that reveal a complex world which retains much of its traditional allure while facing up to the changes, good and bad, imposed by an encroaching world, as well as setting Dolpo in its historical and ethnic context. This photograph above shows the old part of Chharka Bhot, located on the map in eastern Dolpo. Mukut Peak and Dhaulagiri 2, which feature in Richardson's article, are roughly to the south of here. *(Gerda Pauler)*

Though the dangerous trail described by Karna Sakya, Peter Mathiessen and other travellers no longer exists as such, it still demands courage in some places. *(Gerda Pauler)*

Descent was, initially, a bit quicker; we were able to use the fixed ropes and descend with prusiks and slings as a back-up. When the angle eased things became more tiring as adrenalin abated and real exhaustion set in. We finally reached base camp after nine and a half hours of climbing. The team was done in. Some members had given everything and just collapsed in the doorway of their tents still wearing their boots, stirring only to endure spasms of coughing brought on by the effort and breathing thin cold air.

Next day we descended from base camp with the aim of carrying on the trek, crossing several high passes, including the first one at over 5,700m. It would be a tough challenge to any trekking party but we were severely weakened by our climb. Kala Pattar, the well-known highpoint above Everest Base Camp is only 5,545m. Many of the team were struck down with coughs, sickness, bad stomachs and exhaustion too.

The camp below the pass was at 5,000m, cold and windy. I was concerned we would have a lot of difficulty getting over this first col, let alone the subsequent ones. We had been blessed with the weather up to now. It hadn't snowed. But if it did, we could be left stranded or at least late in making our rendezvous at Kagbeni from where we would trek to Jomsom and fly to the regional hub of Pokhara.

In the morning my decision became easier, but not in a good way. One of the mule men who had been with us all the way from Juphal was in a state

Right: A yartsa gunbu collector's camp at Danigar. This caterpillar, *Ophiocordyceps sinensis*, infected with a fungus is highly prized in Chinese medicine and commands huge prices. Increasing wealth in China has driven demand, causing environmental problems and sometimes violence. *(Gerda Pauler)*

Below: Handmade felt boots replace modern sneakers from China as soon as winter arrives in Dolpo. *(Gerda Pauler)*

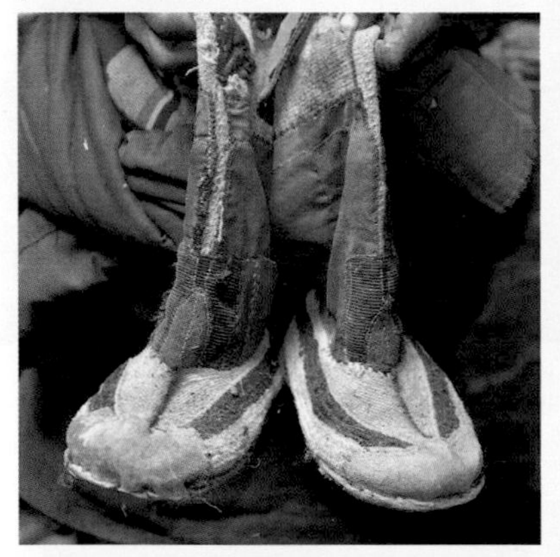

Pupils from Crystal Mountain school. *(Gerda Pauler)*

of distress. One of his precious mules had died from the cold in the night. Everyone was upset. It would have been unfair to ask him to go on. We attempted at least to recompense him financially for his loss, sorted out tips for the staff, and I called up a helicopter to take the sick and their partners to hospital. The remaining members flew out too. Conflicting feeling of slight disappointment and relief were overridden by the ride of a lifetime in the helicopter, passing our route on Mukot Peak and the Dhaulagiri range and down to the airstrip at Jomsom.

Back in Kathmandu, officials in the ministry of tourism weren't bothered we were just below the summit and handed out certificates accordingly. We may have been the second ascent and first English and first American ascents. It doesn't matter much, what is certain is we had a hell of an adventure.

If you are wondering what happened to group C, they followed us but as soon as they reached base camp, an enormous storm blew in. Overnight they had more than a metre of snow. It was all they could do to evacuate base with all their equipment and retreat back along the trek towards Juphal from where they flew back to Nepalgunj and Kathmandu.

If the outcome was certain, it wouldn't be an adventure and would be hardly worth doing.

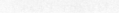

Pakistan

Everest from Rongbuk Glacier, Tibet.
Rob Fairley, 1987. (Watercolour. 36cm x 55cm. Private collection.)

SIMONE MORO

The First Winter Ascent of Nanga Parbat

The Diamir face of Nanga Parbat. Moro switched from the Messner route to the Kinshofer due to unusually risky conditions on his favoured line. *(All photos courtesy of Simone Moro)*

It was a cold dream, one almost 30 years in the making, on an epic mountain, the biggest in the world even if it isn't the highest. In the course of those three decades I spent a whole year either under or on the slopes of Nanga Parbat before finally realising my ambition of climbing to the summit in winter, and with a unique group of people. To realise big dreams you have to accept long waits and numerous defeats; rework strategies, teams and tactics. In a nutshell, you have to be willing to be mentally very strong as well as physically.

A winter expedition to an 8,000er is not the cold version of a spring or summer expedition. It's another world, a way of doing alpinism that's completely different; one that has to be learned, understood and experienced. Cold is certainly one of the elements with which you have to cope, but there is also the constant wind, freezing and damn loud, a wind that can force

Jumaring a fixed line on the summit bid.

you to stay in your tent at base camp even if the sky is clear and the sun is shining. Good weather windows are very rare and brief so acclimatisation phases are often irregular and incomplete; staying on the mountain for gradually increasing periods is incredibly difficult. Days are also very short and so the potential period for active climbing is reduced.

The times you leave and reach camps or for a summit bid are very different from those in summer. You can't be out in the dark, out of your tent and sleeping bag. Gas cans used to melt snow and provide water often freeze and must be kept warm. You never leave high camps up; tents are taken down and packed every time you leave them to return to the valley. There are so

many technical details and protocols that must be respected when climbing an 8,000er in winter. Our climb of Nanga Parbat this winter was all this, but with a human drama and a sequence of events spread over nearly three months, which eventually focused on six days and five nights spent on the mountain in late February, days that were unforgettable and ultimately historic.

There were so many of us this year dreaming of the first ascent of the penultimate winter summit of an 8,000er. These dreamers formed six expeditions, four on the Diamir side, totalling nine climbers, and two on the Rupal side, with 10. Routes chosen were the *Messner-Eisendle-Tomaseth* and *Kinshofer* for the Diamir side and the *Schell* for the Rupal. These were the three lines along which our dreams ran last winter; all had been attempted before in the years since the first winter attempt in 1988-89, when a Polish team led by that brilliant expedition leader Andrzej Zawada made the first winter attempt on Nanga Parbat, on that occasion via the *Kinshofer*.

But there was something different this year to all my previous winter expeditions. I felt something in my soul, in my heart and mind. I've never wanted a mountain like I did this year and this desire was sweet: it was love. I didn't think about defeating the mountain, I never thought like that; I wanted instead to have a good relationship with her, I wanted to court her, to take things gently. I was already prepared to accept a third failure in winter following those of 2012 and 2014, but this time I was sure, really strongly confident that Nanga Parbat would be granted me after so many years.

I had learned a bit about the Himalayan giants; I had the experience of 15 winter expeditions. Although I had already climbed three 8,000ers in winter, both in the Himalaya and the Karakoram and always with several companions, I realised that for a special dream like Nanga we wanted a special team and a special atmosphere. For this reason I chose Tamara Lunger:

we had shared some mountaineering projects since 2009, but only recently, in the last year, had we become climbing partners, following my long association with Denis Urubko. In 2015 Tamara and I attempted Manaslu together in winter, and although we didn't make the summit, we climbed two smaller peaks via two new routes alpine style, and I realised that Tamara was the right one, even for an adventure in winter. She is strong at altitude [*Editor's note:* Lunger was the second Italian woman to climb K2 without oxygen and is a highly regarded ski mountaineer], stronger than most I've met in my 25-year career, she is always in a good mood, and most of all she was also in love with Nanga Parbat and high altitude.

As a team of two people of different sexes, taking a different approach from usual made sense; we decided not to communicate with the outside world for the whole of the expedition. We weren't in a hurry, we had more than three and a half months, all of the winter season, and we knew we wouldn't be back home until 21 March. We chose not to report anything, not to update websites or have a dedicated blog; that was the second surprise, and I knew this decision was at odds with others on the mountain.

It was 6 December when we flew from Milan to Islamabad and as always happens on any expedition, especially winter, things did not go as expected. We wanted to acclimatise on the 7,000m peak Spantik, before going to Nanga Parbat, but our local agent did not respect our agreement, and tried to quadruple our fee; we knew there would probably be further increases when we got back from base camp, and that we had no other option but to accept. So we cancelled the first part of the expedition and headed to Nanga Parbat base camp, which we reached on 27 December.

Two months passed, intense, beautiful and fascinating months, before the day arrived when all our waiting and efforts paid off. Before that, however, Tamara and I tried for a month to climb the *Messner* route, more dangerous this year than usual. That month was spent going backwards and forwards up the Diama glacier, always briskly, and then going as high as possible on Ganalo Peak while still getting down during the day to the base of our route. It was nearly 15km to base camp from that quiet and wild place. The Pole Tomek Mackiewicz and his expedition partner Elisabeth Revol had the same goal but with different methods and strategies from our own, although with the same belief in the beauty and appeal of the *Messner* route.

In the course of a month Tamara and I weren't able to get beyond 6,000m and spent just two nights at 5,800m. That was too little gain in altitude for any valuable acclimatisation and any realistic hope of success in winter on that route. Constant serac collapses and a dangerous maze to work through the initial part of the route made us realise we had to change. Tomek added weight to our decision; his last desperate attempt ended at 7,400m. He and Elisabeth decided to return home.

It was a similar story with the Poles Adam Bielicki and Jacek Czech, who returned home, the first after a fall and the other for health problems. Time was moving on; the large Polish expedition attempting the Rupal Face stopped hoping and fighting and went home, as well as the Brazilian-

At camp 2 the four climbers discovered that two of their sleeping mats had blown away. They were forced to share for the next five nights.

born American Cleo Weidlich and her team of Sherpas. Of the original expeditions, there remained just me and Tamara and the team of Alex Txicon from Spain, who had invited us to join him and his group on the *Kinshofer* at the start of the expedition.

After we gave up on the *Messner*, we accepted his offer and were both happy and excited; I was always convinced that this was the year. I kept repeating to Tamara and later also to Alex and his climbing partner, the Pakistani Muhammad Ali Sadpara: this year we would go to the top. However, Alex's invitation caused a strange reaction from his expedition partner Daniele Nardi. For complex reasons and personal relationships, we split them apart, and Daniele took the decision to abandon base camp.

So it was a case of those who were left, those who were stranded on Nanga Parbat to carry on to the summit in the teeth of the winter cold. Despite this, we were for sure the most resilient and optimistic team I'd ever experienced, able to move every day over the course of two months, even in cold weather, keeping fit and active. True, we were also the least acclimatised we had ever been; although Tamara and I were very fast, we hadn't once slept high in almost three months of the climb. Finally, having switched to the *Kinshofer*, we had an opportunity to spend a night at camp two. With Alex and Ali, we tested our engines, going in less than 10 hours from base camp, around 4,300m on Nanga Parbat, to camp two at 6,100m; we passed a good night and worked beautifully with our two new fellow adventurers.

We had made the most of a single sunny day to make that flying visit to altitude and now prepared to wait for the right window, a period of good weather sufficiently long and stable to allow us a try. There was a little less than a month to go before the end of winter but I kept repeating like a mantra that this was the year I would get to the top, we will go to the top, the top… It was not an obsession, but a clear conviction. I felt it. I knew it.

It was a cold and frosty morning when Tamara, Alex, Ali and I set off on 22 February 2016 on snowshoes to the base of the *Kinshofer* route. The window of good weather had arrived, and with it the clear intention of attempting the summit even though I knew that on paper both Tamara and I had insufficient acclimatisation for a big jump of more than 4,000m in altitude.

We reached camp two in about nine hours, fast, smiling, happy, despite the bitter cold and the shady steep gully we climbed. But when we arrived we had a nasty surprise that would cost us for the next five nights. Two sleeping mats had been blown away by the wind in the preceding few days; the four of us would have to share the remaining mats in the incredible cold of winter nights high on Nanga Parbat. We spent two nights in the tent at camp two because of strong winds that arrived next day. Four sleeping on two mattresses wasn't very comfortable, but at least we found a solution to this setback that would see us through the attempt.

The weather remained stable, albeit with wind and cold, and we climbed first to camp three at 6,750m and then camp four at 7,150m, striking and packing the tent each morning with all the other gear. The last camp we deliberately located lower than usual, 1,000m below the summit. We could feel our obvious failure to acclimatise and so had to come up with a new strategy as well as being determined. Tamara and I were already 1,000m higher than the maximum altitude we had reached in the previous three months, and now we had to climb another 1,000m.

We had divided the work with Alex and Ali, but now we needed to decide how best to deal with the summit day. We left the tent at different times, to allow everyone to get ready comfortably and not all four of us at the same time. I wasn't using battery-heated insoles like the others, so I left the tent last. First were Ali and Alex, at 6am on 26 February; half an hour later it was Tamara's turn to leave the haven of the tent. I got myself ready, warming my feet over the stove and then left at 7.45am. I kept up a strong and steady pace, with regular breaks, and reached first Tamara and then my companions. It was cold, very cold, minus 34°C with a strong wind of 45km/h, so it felt more like minus 58°C.

It was only at around 10.30am that we saw the first rays of the sun transform the mountain's harsh appearance and lift our mood, even though the unceasing wind seemed now to spread everywhere as we gained altitude and became more exposed to its exhausting effects. Our hypoxia was becoming more pronounced; I could manage only around five steps, sometimes ten. It was past 2pm when we passed the 8,000m mark, spread out but in visual contact. Ali, in that last stretch, climbed a little to the right of the usual line of ascent, while Alex, Tamara and I stuck to the regular route, becoming increasingly fatigued as we strove towards a summit that seemed never to arrive.

Moro had to persuade his two fellow summit climbers Alex Txicon and Muhammad Ali Sadpara to pose for a photograph in the face of intense cold.

In the morning, just after she left the tent, Tamara had been sick, vomiting the little breakfast she had managed to eat. She continued to vomit every time I offered her liquid or food. It was also the start of her menstrual cycle, adding to her fatigue. Clear-headed and rational, she took the decision to abandon the summit at around 8,040m, only 80m or so in altitude from the top. The decision probably saved her life. The three of us, a little ahead, took the last few steps to the summit at 8,126m. It had taken 27 years since the first attempt in winter, generations of alpinists passing on the baton to keep alive a project that seemed almost impossible.

We hugged on top, exhausted, incredulous but sharing an ecstatic joy. It was already 3.30pm. Now in the last hours of daylight and coping with the obvious exhaustion, we hurried to start our descent. Not seeing Tamara, we realised that something had happened and she was already on her way down. Ali had seen her from the summit and waved a few minutes before. I insisted that we stop to take a photograph on the top; Ali and Alex weren't fussed because of the cold, but I managed to capture this historic moment not only for us.

I wanted to look once again to the Rupal side. I imagined it was almost 50 years ago, and those two lads from the South Tyrol, Reinhold and Günther Messner, were climbing up towards me. As a child they had made

The four climbers back at base camp: left to right Alex Txicon, Tamara Lunger, Simone Moro and Muhammad Ali Sadpara. Ali became the first Pakistani to climb an 8,000er in winter. Only one woman has reached the summit of an 8,000er in winter, the Swiss Marianne Chapuisat on Shishapangma in 1993, despite Lunger's best efforts.

me dream. Reading about them, realising that their strength was in the co-operation and understanding they shared, I developed the ambition to one day become a man capable of climbing mountains, to try to do it my way, finding my own path with a close companion as they did. With Tamara I found that connection again, and with Ali and Alex we established a unique and almost unrepeatable bond. If the dedication of my fourth first winter ascent was to Günther Messner, I must also acknowledge the team with whom I lived for five nights and six days on Nanga Parbat, as well as all those who for 30 years kept the flame of this dream alight.

Summary

On 26 February Simone Moro, Alex Txicon and Ali Sadpara reached the summit of Nanga Parbat via the *Kinshofer* route to make the first winter ascent. Nanga Parbat was first attempted in winter in 1988-89 by a Polish team and more than 30 expeditions have tried since. Moro has now climbed four 8,000-metre peaks in the winter: Shishapangma in 2005, Makalu in 2009, Gasherbrum II in 2011, and Nanga Parbat in 2016. Only K2 remains to be climbed in winter.

ANDY HOUSEMAN

Fever Pitch

The First Ascent of Link Sar's West Summit

Misty conditions on the lower part of the north-west face of Link Sar, located between K6 and K7 in the Karakoram's Charakusa valley. *(All images Jonathan Griffith Photography)*

We approached the face in wet sleet and knee-deep sodden snow. Ignoring the enormous faces and the gaping crevasses, it was like walking into Stob Coire nan Lochan in typical Scottish weather: nothing is frozen, you get soaked and you really start to wonder why you are there.

Yet we were far from Scotland. Jon Griffith and I had travelled to the Charakusa valley in the Karakoram to attempt the unclimbed Link Sar (7041m). The Charakusa is one of the more developed valleys in Pakistan. Dominated by the towering golden granite spires of the K7 massif and the huge complex north faces of the three K6 peaks, it's like Chamonix on steroids. Link Sar sits in the back corner, almost forgotten.

A bivouac high on the north-west face with K7 behind. The climbers spent a day here to let snow conditions on the face improve.

It's name means merely 'Linking Peak' but it is far more than just a bump on the chain between better-known neighbours. Not much is known about the peak; it's hard to see the mountain in its entirety to plan an ascent or know what to expect, so it remains a complex mountaineering puzzle waiting to be solved. But that's the draw for Jon and I, the unknowns, a guarantee of adventure whether or not the summit is reached.

We didn't make it all the way to the base of the face as we had hoped that day, the lack of an overnight freeze on the glacier slowing us down

A photo diagram of the route Griffith and Houseman took up Link Sar, reaching the summit of Link Sar West (6938m) before descending.

at the end of the 8km approach from base camp; as the temperature rose the mountains came alive. We picked a small island of safety tucked under a rock buttress to hack out a ledge and escape the weather.

It was still snowing hard later that afternoon and everything was soaked. It wasn't meant to be like this: it should be cold and dry. We pretty much decided to bail there and then before we'd even seen the face. I am not an overly confident climber; everything needs to be right to set off up an unclimbed 7,000m peak, and it felt like everything was against us. But this isn't Chamonix either; you can't wait for perfect conditions and blog posts to give you all the beta. Decisions are made on the weather; everything else you just have to deal with. It was a tight one, but we did have the window we needed.

Approaching mixed ground halfway up the north-west face of Link Sar.

Yet stepping back onto the north-west face of Link Sar left me with mixed emotions. Two years ago, fighting off a virus, my mind had been willing but my body not. It shattered my confidence and it was a long time before I wanted to pick up ice axes again and even longer for my body to properly heal.

Next day the glacier still hadn't refrozen but more post-holing finally got us to the base of the face. Our concern now wasn't our wet gear but the amount of snow yesterday's bad weather had put down. We were later on the face than we'd hoped and the sun would soon swing round. The east face of K7 was already bathed in morning light and was fully alive with avalanches as the intense sunlight heated up the snow.

Linking lines of snow we managed to avoid most of the black ice and made steady progress up the face. The returning clouds made it a lot safer but also added to the fresh snow from yesterday. Our first bivy on a snow arête was one of the more exposed places I've ever put up a tent. It was one of those scenes I'd seen in pictures before I was a climber, stared at in awe, wondering how they'd perched a tent there. Feeling pretty tired after the last couple of days it was a massive relief to find the ledge Jon and Kevin Mahoney had spent hours hacking out of black ice during their attempt the year before. Half an hour of easy shovelling and we had a tent-size platform ready.

In the morning we stayed put. We'd been thankful of the afternoon weather rolling in the day before, sparing us from the torture of the intense and powerful sun. But climbing the next section of the face before it had had a full day in the sun to shake off its latest layer of snow would have been suicidal. We lost a day but I could think of worse places to hang out, losing myself in the Karakoram vista.

Above the mixed section, closing in on the summit ridge in energy-sapping conditions – and large cornices above the climbers.

Above: Topping out of the north-west face of Link Sar, with K6 in the background. Griffith, suffering from a virus, experienced mental confusion at the bivouac. Hence the route's name: *Fever Pitch*.

Below: Sunset on the summit of K6.

Houseman approaching the summit of Link Sar West with a bright halo around the sun signalling a change in conditions.

It was just after 11pm when I pressed the snooze button for a second time. The warmth and relative safety of the tent make it too easy to put off committing ourselves to climbing higher on the face. Besides, we'd got used to our tiny exposed perch on the side of Link Sar. Yet eventually we coaxed ourselves out of the tent. While Jon climbed up into the blackness, retracing his steps from last year, I savoured the spacious and flat platform with the faint flicker of his headlamp occasionally visible as he slowly climbed up the steep ice face above. The rope came tight and I followed on behind him.

Separated by 60m of rope we slowly climbed upwards, moving together, lost in our own worlds of thought. Soon darkness had been replaced by the dawn of a new day. The sun we would soon be hating slowly rose behind us with the vast shapes of the Karakoram stretching out before us. In moments like this you truly appreciate how small we are and the scale and beauty of your surroundings.

The mixed pitches that followed flowed well; they were even fun. I'd taken the lead from Jon and found myself in a steep *goulotte*, tapping the picks of my axes into a narrow and brittle seam of ice. Steep granite walls rose either side, with the remnants of Jon and Kevin's stuck rope from last year just to my left reminding me that I wasn't the first and reminding Jon of last year's suffering. This was my second attempt on Link Sar, but for Jon it was his fourth: the history was much deeper.

We were in the central gully line of the face now, looking up at relentlessly steep black ice and gravity-defying cornices above. Before the trip Jon had tried to describe these; terrifying was a term he kept coming back to. Looking back at the photos now I can stare mesmerized at how nature has sculpted these features, but at the time, knowing we had, at some point, to climb under them, I agreed with Jon: terrifying. They were gargoyles peering down on what was to become our hell.

I hate black ice, and we had hundreds of metres of it ahead. Like a child's pencil joining the dots in a drawing book I'd gone from one protruding rock to the next. No matter how small, they offered us the tiniest relief from the calf-burning front-pointing. The buttress we were climbing under offered a little protection from the cornices above but otherwise we were fully exposed. By now we were pitching it, and on one of the most exposed sections, where we would normally have gunned it, we had little left and had to let fate take it hand as we crawled our way up. We'd been completely destroyed by the altitude, sun, the black ice and our heavy packs.

Traversing vertical but surprisingly solid névé with my sack trying to pulling me down, it was a relief finally to join Jon at his belay on the ridge and escape the face. But Link Sar wasn't letting us have it easy yet. Jon dug his way through unconsolidated snow and honeycomb ice along the ridge for an hour until he eventually found a spot to dig a tent platform, 17 hours after leaving the last one. Hacking away into the ice we were treated to some of the most surreal light you can imagine. It was magical and for a brief moment we even let ourselves forget about the turmoil of the day. The sun we had cursed for hours was now rewarding us with a view I'll cherish for a lifetime.

Beginning the descent of Link Sar West.

Then reality returned. Back in the relative safety of the tent Jon's drive for survival to escape the face, that raw instinct that keeps you going when your body wants otherwise, had gone. He'd given it everything. We'd given it everything. But now the cold he'd been suffering from won and turned into a chest infection. Collapsed in the tent, full of fever and in a complete state of delirium, he mumbled gibberish in an unintelligible mixture of English and French. I couldn't get him to eat or drink. Apart from a few slices of *saucisson* he touched nothing. I was scared. I couldn't sleep but summit aspirations were the last thing on my mind. Instead, I was constantly running through every scenario of how I was going to get us both off the mountain safely the next day.

Next day Jon had to rest, slowly rehydrate and refuel his weakened body. Descending would have been the sensible option but he felt he could at least reach the west summit. Besides, we had got that far and given it so much that we knew neither of us would be back for another go. In the morning, Jon wanted to lead straight off, to test himself. We left the north face line of retreat and committed to descending the south face of the mountain. More unknowns, more adventure, more uncertainty. There were steep sections of unconsolidated snow, big run-outs, easier but still awkward climbing, but we were moving, making progress. The enjoyment and fun was back after the horrors and pain of the north-west face two days ago.

We looked across at a view we'd dreamt of for years. Only 100m higher but nearly a kilometre away and protected by a mess of convoluted cornices and granite gendarmes, the main summit of Link Sar would have to be for someone else. We were out of time and weather; we'd pushed it far enough.

The giant sun halo we'd be climbing under all day was spectacular but a sure sign the weather was changing; our window was gone, the next storm front slowing moving in in the distance, black and ominous.

Yet standing on the 6,938m west summit, we were not disappointed; the dreamlike vista was breathtaking, unforgettable, worthy of all the pain and hard work of the last five days. We were satisfied and happy; we'd done what we could, gambled as much as we were willing on this adventure. It was too dangerous to descend during the day so we put the tent up right next to the summit, another wild place to spend the night with amazing views over the Karakoram giants: K2, Broad Peak, Masherbrum, and the Gasherbrums to the north-west and a bird's eye view down into the closed off Kondus valley to our east.

Jon's fever had returned during the afternoon, inevitably I suppose. I worried again, the situation even more serious than before if he continued to deteriorate. The snow that had started briefly during the night was even more worrying. Link Sar was not a mountain to be descending in bad weather; it would quickly become a torrent of avalanches, a fight for survival as the steep slopes struggled to hold the snow. We were both scared now.

By 3.30am the snow stopped and Jon was feeling better. The descent, down a large gully on the south side, went quickly, Jon keen to do his bit again, leading the way. I post-holed down the unfrozen glacier, every step a tentative one, expecting to fall through into some unseen crevasse as the powerful sun weakened the snow bridges. The icefall we had naively thought to be okay took hours to navigate, turned back by one dead end after another.

At one point I was crawling on my stomach to spread the weight as I crossed over yet another weak bridge, holding my breath expecting it to break. We stopped at one point, not entirely sure we'd find a way out this maze of towering ice blocks and crevasses. How one of us didn't take a ride into one of the many dark bottomless holes we crossed I really don't know. Maybe, at last, after pushing us to the limit for the last seven days since leaving base camp, the mountain was showing us a bit of respect. Finally sitting down in the relative safety of the dry Charakusa glacier, I hoped we had earned it.

Summary

First ascent of the west summit of Link Sar (6938m) via the north-west face. Starting in mid July, Griffith and Houseman made their first bivouac on the face at 6,100m and waited a day to allow snow to clear. After 17 hours, the pair reached the top of the face at around 6,800m, having climbed consistently steep ground and several mixed pitches up to M4. That night Griffith came down with a fever and the two decided to stay put the following day. On 17 July, with Griffith improved, they set off up the remaining ridge and by midday reached the west top. They bivouacked close to the top, and next morning made a committing and blind descent of a couloir on the south-west face, which led to an unnamed glacier and through a time-consuming icefall to reach the main Charakusa the same day. They named their route *Fever Pitch*.

WALTER POLIDORI

Khane Valley, Karakoram

Peaks on the north side of the Khane valley in the Karakoram.
(All images courtesy of Walter Polidori)

Our expedition in August 2015 was to celebrate the 40th anniversary of the mountaineering and ski mountaineering school Guido Della Torre of the Italian Alpine Club (CAI). Five different sections of CAI support the school: Busto Arsizio, Castellanza, Legnano, Parabiago and Saronno. All are located in Lombardy, northern Italy. In line with the school's tradition and ethical spirit, the aim of the expedition was mountaineering's original feature: exploration, with, obviously, full awareness of its risks and dangers. These requirements seemed to be met in the rather unexplored Khane valley, where only three summits have been climbed so far.

The relatively limited descriptions of this valley were collected from three recent expeditions: two from Bulgaria between 2011 and 2012, the first purely exploratory followed by a more mountaineering-oriented second one, and a climbing expedition from the USA in 2012. Other information included Jerzy Wala's 2012 map 'Karakorum Masherbrum Mountains: Tagas Group – The Khane valley' (Swiss Foundation for Alpine Research, 1990). The map has no contour lines but is nevertheless useful for a broad understanding of the features of the valley.

KARAKORAM Masherbrum Mountains - Tagas Group

The Khane Valley

Prepared by Jerzy Wala Kraków 1st Edition 2012

The orographical sketch map presenting the Khane Valley an images (supplied by Grzegorz Głazek CDW-PZA Warszawa General Štab Map USSR 1:200 000 I-43-V, edition 1985; orogr edition 2006; Topography of the Tagas Mountain Group, edition 1:100 000, 1st Edition 2004; Google Eart Image – Bulgarian Expedition 2011.

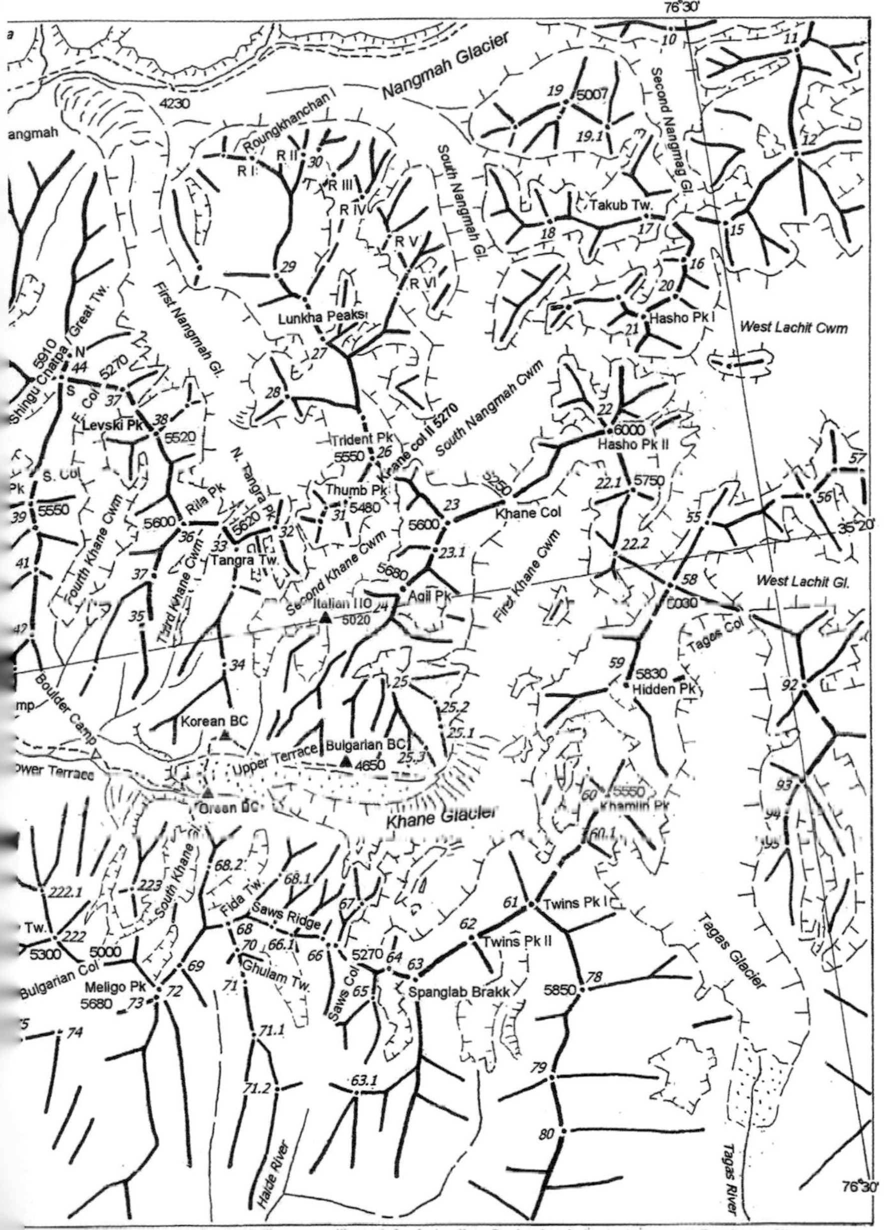

Jerzy Wala's 2012 edition of his map of the Khane valley with the Italians' notations in red.

Mountaineering History of Khane Valley

The Khane valley remained unexplored until a few years ago for the simple reason that the valleys close to it, such as Nangma and Charakusa, were more famous. The large majority of peaks in the Khane remain unclimbed and unnamed. Only a small number of them, visible from villages along the Hushe river, from the Nangma valley or from high pastures along the Khane river, were given a name by local people. According to locals from Khane village, the first foreigners to visit the valley were Koreans in 2001 and in the two subsequent years. They probably attempted, unsuccessfully, to climb the west face of Agil. During their second expedition they successfully climbed a 250m rock route on a satellite of a ridge close to their base camp, located at 4,450m. After them, an American visited the valley to trek after taking part in an expedition to The Ogre. She reached the base of the Great Tower, passing through a lateral valley located between the Rila Peak on the east side and Sofia Peak on the west.

In 2009 two locals, Ali Mehmed and his son Ruhal Ali climbed a graceful tower located above Khane village, calling it Nauri Brakk (c3250m). Other ascents were attempted before 2011 from the Nangma valley: Black Tower or Sarigo) and Singu Chapta, also named Singu Charpa as well as Great Tower. As already mentioned, a Bulgarian expedition visited the valley for the purposes of exploration in September 2011. The Khane valley first came to the attention of Doychin Boyanov and Nicolay Petkov in 2005 and 2006 when they crossed the valley from north to south descending from the Gondogoro pass and then, in 2009, when they returned to the valley after an expedition to Gasherbrum I. In August 2012 Tervel Kerelov and Michail Michailov joined them for the Bulgarian Khane expedition. Together they made first ascents of Levski Peak (5733m) and Grey Tower (5435m). In September 2012 Anna Pfaff and Camilo Lopez attempted Peak 25 via the west face to within 200m of the summit but were forced to retreat because of the poor quality of the rock.

Italian Expedition 2015

While our main goal was unclimbed summits, the expedition's other aim was to explore the valley and produce a detailed description of the area through photo and video documentation. Our team included Walter Polidori, national instructor and expedition leader; Emanuele Nugara, regional instructor; Luca Monfrini and Matteo Filippini, sectional instructors, all of them part of the school. Finally, Tommaso Lamantia, alpine rescue member, took part in the expedition.

The Khane valley is located in north-east Pakistan, in the Tagas group of the Baltistan-Karakoram region. Perpendicular to the Hushe valley, which gives access to Masherbrum, and parallel, towards the south, to the more popular Nangma valley, the Khane valley spreads east. Still further north of the Nangma valley, the small Khridas valley and the much more popular Charakusa valley, thanks to K6 and K7, are located. The Halde valley is south of the Khane valley, while a mountain ridge divides

The Grey Tower (5435m) at the south-west corner of the Khane valley.

Khane from the Tagas valley. Khane village, set at 2,800m, is the last place reachable by vehicle.

The main entrance to the valley is from Skardu, connected to Islamabad by a short flight when weather conditions allow or by a two-day drive on the Kakakoram Highway. From Skardu it is possible to get to Khaplu thanks to a gravel road alongside the Shyok river; from there, a bridge on the true right bank gives access to Hushe valley. After driving through Machulo, a small bridge standing at the entrance of the village of Khane is reached in five hours. Due to the frequency of landslides, the road is often closed to the traffic; we experienced some troubles approaching this area due to flooding at the end of July.

A path runs up the true left bank of the valley above a gorge characteristic of the region; the Khane river here is pretty wild. The start of the path is marked with cairns to reach slopes on the left bank, a gorgeous path alongside which runs walls holding a water channel. Unfortunately numerous landslides have damaged this as well as the path, which crosses steep screes in many places. The path eventually disappears and we crossed the river on a temporary bridge made of a tree trunk. Then we climbed along a poorly marked path on the true right side of the river. The path angled back approaching the ruins of a few stone shelters; finally we reached a large flat area at 4,000m three or four hours from Khane where we put base camp. We called this the First Terrace. Pastures here explain the paths, and we frequently encountered flocks of goats and sheep, as well as yak and cattle herds guarded by a local shepherd, named Ismail.

Khane valley is oriented from west to east. After the First Terrace, heading east, the Khane river goes over a cliff to form a pretty waterfall. The path crosses this step to the Second Terrace (c4500m). From here, above a moraine,

The Italian high camp in the Second Khane cwm on the north side of the valley. The climbers reported unusually high temperatures resulting in serious rock fall, which limited their activities.

the dry glacier appears at the head of the valley. A little before it, there's a good spot for an ABC, a useful starting point for climbs in the upper section of the valley. The Bulgarians had their base camp here. From this point the valley changes its orientation, running south to north, and after a steep icefall (c4900m) reaches a col at 5,250m giving access to the Nangma valley.

Khane Valley Peaks

The most significant peaks are in the main valley, starting from base camp towards Khane col on the true right bank. Peak 46, named Shorsa Tower II by our expedition because of a name used by locals, is characterised by its graceful and long rocky south-east ridge. Peak 41 is located south of the massive Sofia Peak and is characterised, on its east side, by huge hanging slabs. Peak 42 is a wide and stocky mountain; Peak 35 is attractive, part of a ridge leading to Peak 37. Peak 34 is probably the first mountain climbed in the valley, thanks to a Korean team; it is located close to the waterfall. Peak 25 was attempted by the American team; they climbed most of it, but were unable to reach the summit due to poor rock quality. Agil is an impressive mountain with its west wall facing the North Khane glacier in the second Khane cwm (see map) and its east wall facing the main valley above the icefall; its upper slopes are snow-covered. Peak 23 can be reached from a second Khane col above the North Khane glacier but is difficult to find. Mixed ground and snow characterise this mountain.

On the true left bank are Peaks 226 and 225, small but attractive mountains at the end of debris channels. Peak 224 is a difficult shoulder of the Grey Tower; the Grey Tower itself was first climbed by the Bulgarians

The final pitch on Shorsa Tower I (4900m), at the north-west end of the Khane valley.

in 2012. Peak 223 divides the snow gully below Bulgarian col. There are two towers, Peak 68.2 and 68.1, under the north face of Meligo, an impressive and complex mountain, visible from the Hushe valley. A huge serac connects the main summit to the south peak. Meligo Ridge runs through Fida Tower, Ghulam Tower and then the different summits of Saws Ridge up to Saws col. Spanglab Brakk is particularly pretty viewed from the Hushe valley, with a sharp pyramidal shape. The Twins is a remarkable mountain, with a severe mixed wall overlooking the Khane valley. Khamlin is also an impressive mountain while Hidden Peak is characterised by huge seracs. Peaks 22.2 and 22.1 are mainly rocky and mixed on the Khane valley side but snowy on the opposite one. Hasho Peak II is a huge mountain reaching 6,000m adjacent to the Nangma valley with a snowy side probably reachable from the Tagas valley side; the Khane col is located between Hasho Peak and Peak 23.

Side Valleys

Starting from the west on the true right or northern side of the Khane valley, there is a debris channel that starts on the right side of Shorsa Tower II; from this it is possible to reach a col at 4,780m that we named 'Hope col', wanting an easy climb of Sofia Peak. The col offers a view of a secondary valley (fifth Khane cwm) that starts at a much lower altitude in the Khane valley to reach the base of Sofia and Great Tower. Beyond the col, on the left side, it is possible to reach a small terrace at 4,800m from where we could see a chaotic ridge reaching rocky towers. Sofia is located beyond these towers. Shorsa Tower II is located on the right side of the channel at its entrance and is connected to the higher Shorsa Tower I (c4900m) by a grassy rock ridge. A little below Hope col, the east ridge reaches the summit of Shorsa Tower I, which we climbed for the first ascent.

Next, a lateral valley rises toward the Great Tower and Levski Peak in the fourth Khane cwm, located shortly before the waterfall up to East col (5270m). On the true left side of the valley, starting from the bottom, Peak 35, Peak 37 and Rila Peak form a stunning ridge leading, eventually, to Levski Peak, a snowy rock summit climbed by the Bulgarians in 2012. On the true right or western side, the wide face of Peak 42 is followed by Peak 41, Sofia, with its impressive and complex shape, and the Great Tower, already climbed from the Nangma valley side.

The Meligo group from the north, across the Khane valley.

The third valley, leading to the third Khane cwm, is located between Rila Peak and Tangra Tower. This is a narrow gorge, close to the waterfall, between the east face of Peak 37 and west face of the Tangra Tower. In its upper part it becomes snowy forming a couloir. Right at its start, a route along the true left or east side most likely allows you to reach a small rocky col from which the east ridge of the Tangra Tower begins; this is an impressive ridge with evidence of a recent landslip in its lower part.

A final valley on the northern, true right side of the Khane valley leads to the North Khane glacier in the second Khane cwm. This is the first side valley after the waterfall and is truly gorgeous. It rises up to a col (Khane col II) giving access to the Nangma valley. The peaks from the bottom up on the west side are Peak 34, Tangra Tower, an amazing granite tower with a beautiful south-east face, North Tangra Peak, South Tower, a rocky mountain presenting a smooth buttress, Central Tower and Thumb Tower. These last three mountains, close to each other, together form a stunning sight. Between Trident and Peak 23 lies Khane col II. On the east side, Peak 25 is followed by Agil and Peak 23.

On the southern, true left side of the Khane valley, there are gullies before the Grey Tower leading to Peaks 225 and 226, which are fairly unattractive due to poor rock. The first gully on the right of Grey Tower is the likely route to Peak 224. There is a snow gully reaching the col between Meligo and Grey Tower (Bulgarian col, c5000m). This was used by the Bulgarians to climb Grey Tower. A gully and ramp between The Twins and Meligo leads to Saws col, dividing Peak 64 from Peak 66 at an altitude of 5,270m. We couldn't find a col or route that easily crossed the mountain chain from the west side to get to the Tagas valley; from this valley an easy

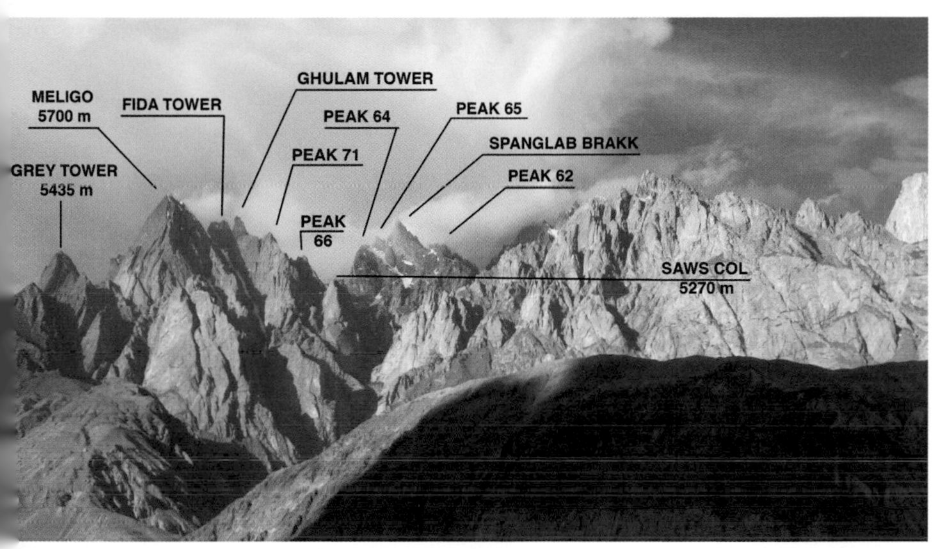

The Meligo group from the south, in the Hushe valley.

ascent to some summits dividing it from the Khane valley might be possible up snowy slopes.

Italian Exploration and Climbing

Using GPS for heights and tracking, as well as photographs, we explored and surveyed the main Khane valley and the Khane glacier up to the icefall at 4,900m. Unfortunately, the icefall was not practicable due to very poor ice conditions caused by high temperatures resulting in frequent ice and stone falls from its slopes. We explored the second Khane cwm, where the Tangra Tower is located, up to the moraine and the beginning of the upper glacier cirque at 5,020m. We climbed up the valley leading to Levski Peak, the fourth Khane cwm, almost to East col that connects with the Nangma valley at 5,270m. We also climbed up the gullies beside Peaks 45 and 46, up to the col we named Hope (4780m), to figure out whether an attempt on Sofia was possible, and the gully behind Peak 42 and two other minor satellites we named The Nails.

As far as climbing went, we climbed Peak 45 via its east ridge (VI+, 300m). We used this mountain's local name Shorsa Tower I (c4900m). Descent was by abseil, first down the route and then the south face with independent stances. Although of good quality, the rock was blocky, except for the last pitches where it appeared much more compact. We attempted the south face of Peak 42. The rock seemed attractive with many cracks; however, the presence of dirt, grass and strange concretions in the cracks made climbing unappealing. Only the first pitch, 35m long, was climbed with difficulties of VI/A2; poor quality of rock persuaded us to abandon the attempt. The exploration of the lower portions of the other towers led to the same conclusion.

The Tangra peaks above the Second Khane cwm.

An attempt on the col between Twins and Meligo (Saws col, 5270m) from an ABC at 4,780m near the head of the glacier was abandoned at roughly 5,000m due to frequent stone falls from the west face of the Twins. We attempted Peak 23 from the North Cirque glacier from an advanced camp, named Italian high camp (5020m) in the upper glacial cirque. The climbing was glacial and mixed terrain through the unvisited Khane col II. Again, we gave up due to poor ice conditions. Stones fell continuously from the overhanging face of Agil throughout the night; furthermore, a snow and rock fall missed our camp by only 80 metres the night before our attempt. Finally, we attempted a satellite peak near base camp close to Peak 42. Unfortunately, poor rock quality prevented us from reaching its summit by only 30m; the climbed section was roughly 300m with difficulties up to III+. The peak was named The Nail I (c4500m).

Conclusions

Weather conditions were favourable throughout the expedition. However, high temperatures all over the region made it dangerous, even impossible to climb on snow and mixed terrain and to approach some of the walls. Even attempts to climb peaks above 8,000m in the area were abandoned due to exceptionally high temperatures. Despite its appearance, the quality of rock in the Khane valley turned out to be very poor. We experienced frequent rock and snow falls even on mountains with snowy summits or partially covered by snow. Due to such poor conditions, the majority of the team chose to abandon our mountaineering attempts after the exploration phase.

Acknowledgements
On behalf of the expedition, I would like to thank instructors at the Guido della Torre mountaineering school and the presidents of the CAI sections of Busto Arsizio, Castellanza, Legnano, Parabiago and Saronno for their support. My gratitude goes to the city of Castellanza, Legnano and the Banca Popolare di Milano Bank for funding. Particular thanks go to Maurizio Pinciroli, the school president, who enthusiastically helped us, and to Susanna Martinelli, a school instructor and friend, who continuously pushed us towards our objective. On behalf of Tommaso, thanks go to Salomon and Suunto for their technical support. Finally, I would like to thank my family members for their patience in all these months of work.

Translation from Italian by Vittorio Bedogni, director of the Guido della Torre school.

Alaska

Building in a Landscape
The CIC Hut and Tower Ridge, Ben Nevis.
Rob Fairley, 1982. (Pencil. 130cm x 80cm. Private collection.)

WILL SIM

Degrees of Faith

A New Route on Mount Deborah

The north-west of Mount Deborah (3761m) in the eastern Alaska range. The line taken by Sim and Griffith climbs the ice and snow slope towards the central gully before breaking right under a line of overhangs towards the north-west ridge. *(All images by Jonathan Griffith Photography)*

'If you get it in, it's any drink for free, go on, no cheating!' The barmaid twitched a little, suggesting too many years spent in too many end-of-the-road Alaskan dives like this one. I perched forward on my bar stool, got a good grip on my screwed-up dollar bill and faced the jar on the far side of the bar, trying to visualise the arc of my arm. As soon as the paper left my fingers it was obvious I'd missed. What did this mean for our trip? I'd told myself that getting the dollar bill into the jar would be a good omen. Now it lay between bottles of spirits among some dead flies. I felt betrayed. Since arriving in Alaska a week ago, most of our time had been spent drinking, playing with Jon's drone and pondering how we would get to the bottom of Mount Deborah.

Finding a pilot prepared to fly us in had led us to this dark, seedy hole of a pub somewhere on the Alaska Highway: a place where people looked suspiciously happy given their bleak, stale surroundings. We were here to

Looking down the initial snow and ice slope.

A different angle on the same problem. An aerial view of Mount Deborah, a far more remote and lonely challenge than peaks in the central Alaska range. This angle shows the north-west ridge that forms the route's upper portion.

After the storm: within hours of arriving, the team's base camp was flattened in a storm. They dug the snow cave and continued after waiting out the weather in their bivouac tent.

meet a man from Fairbanks called Alex who said he could take us in to the notoriously isolated Hayes range, although not before we helped him fix a helicopter whose rotor blade had been dented with a dart meant for a caribou.

After hundreds of days tied together on big mountains, Jon and I have an almost synergetic partnership. But it's now, in the high-tension, boredom-filled downtime that a partnership is truly tested. I'd lured Jon north once again with a grainy image from Google Earth of a 2,000m spiky face protruding from an icy range he had never heard of. Now, with our chances of even seeing the mountain looking slimmer and slimmer, I could sense his irritation, even through the cloudy IPA that had fuelled us this far.

Finally, in the last week of April, Alex dropped us on the inhospitable Gillam glacier. A storm immediately engulfed us, almost destroying our base camp. For three days we struggled to meet each other's gaze as we sat in our bedraggled bivy tent, bracing the walls and wincing every time we heard the roar of the wind accelerate from down the valley. With our main tent lost and all our gear now buried under metres of snow, I was half expecting to call Alex for a pickup once the winds abated. Failing on expeditions is something you have to accept, but calling it a day before even putting on our harnesses would be hard. Instead we spent two days digging a palatial snow cave and regrouped. The climb was still on.

Crossing a bergschrund is always meaningful. It's the first level of commitment: a symbolic act. You're showing intent, making the first move. It's normal to have butterflies. Jon's hesitant movements were telling me all

The band of overhangs on the right of the picture that split the face to the right of the gully. Threatened by avalanches, the climbers moved right here to the north-west ridge.

I needed to know. A few minutes ago two avalanches had swept either side of the couloir we were now entering. I was scared; it felt too much like looking down the barrel of a loaded gun. It was at least reassuring to know Jon was on the same level. 'It's not worth it, let's head down,' was on the tip of both our tongues. Yet an urge was working away at both our minds, stoking that inner fire you can't explain, a vacuum pulling us upwards. Two long strides and I was over the bergschrund. It was time to climb.

Steep, plastic ice reared up above us. 'The first third looks skiable,' I'd said days earlier when studying this section through binoculars. What an idiot. Commenting on difficulties before you get to them is a fool's game. Thankfully the ice was squeaky and friendly, despite our big bags levering against our Achilles tendons, trying to snap them. Standing at a belay for more than five minutes was unpleasant. We were both wearing down trousers underneath our hard shells, which means it was cold, even by Alaskan standards.

My mind retreated to a phone call a month earlier. I'd listened reluctantly as my friend talked of faith: a voice, a feeling. It made me angry she was happy to shape her life around a belief she knew defied rationality. Right then, I could kid myself that I was different: that my life was structured around logic, black and white decisions and a pragmatic consciousness; that I didn't

Sim caught against a cloud of spindrift as avalanches continue to threaten the face.

have an inner voice which you can't quite explain; and that I never handed my life over to an urge or unaccountable feeling. But now, a third of the way up the face, as we entered a coliseum of black shale, my own carefully weighed thoughts began to move away from pure reason to a deeper current of consciousness: one where reason and logic give way to a more primal instinct.

Where we'd expected to climb low-angled ice were huge roofs, 10m across, barring entry to the upper face. To the left a beautiful steep gully arced upwards; it was a fine line and I could tell we were both tempted. But as we reached the upper section of the face, the snowfields above had come alive, shedding their weight straight down our line. The beautiful gully, which had tempted us only hours earlier, was now a raging river of avalanches. My imagination got the better of me as I visualised what could have been. The couloir above us – our planned escape through the headwall – was in a similar state of chaos and I wouldn't let my imagination go there.

So after a swerve of indecision I chose right. Thin smears through rotting black rock were the more attractive option. Taking over for a block of easy-angled ice, I climbed like shit. I couldn't do more than three moves before craning my head back and taking in the view upwards. Don't look up. Looking down is more comforting. In the distance our snow hole that saved the day during the storm is now in full sun. We have bacon and eggs there, whisky and music. Looking upwards is terrifying. Keep bluffing. Keep bluffing.

Emerging from the north-west face, the two climbers bivouacked before reaching the summit next day.

From nowhere, our world erupted in a deep, ear-splitting bang. I cowered and made myself small as I anticipated the unknown event heralded by this terrifying sound. It was a sonic boom, caused by an object compressing sound waves as it passed through the speed of sound at 768mph. Alex had told us the US air force used the hundreds of miles of tundra to our north for F16s on training exercises. It seemed wrong that our only other human interaction had to be so violent, shaking our already frazzled nerves.

I crawled the last few metres on to the crest of the north-west ridge as the sun skimmed the horizon. Sugary snow on top of black ice had soaked up the last energy from our fading bodies in a way that steep technical climbing never does. We'd been on the run for hours, since we made the decision to escape the apex of the face, leaving the dream line to seek shelter. Even though we were on the ridge sooner than we wanted, the traverse had been exhausting with an unexpected thin crux gully.

It was the early hours of the morning by the time we were both inside our little bivy tent, perched precariously yet securely on the ridge. Trying to sit up and tend the stove was the new challenge, as cramps attacked my back and stomach. Jon did an amazing job as usual, organising and sorting our perch as we fought to keep our eyes open. Although pleased with our progress we were also in disbelief that we were here. An inexplicable decision to carry on, when rationality was saying no, had found us halfway up this beautiful cold mountain. The short, still, Alaskan night was now upon us; you could hear a pin drop, and the wafer thin layer of

Pertex encasing us allowed us to forget our precarious situation and descend in to a careless trance.

'Should we take the poles down? Will! Shall we take the poles down?'

The roar was back, thunderous and full of fury. I woke from my short, intense sleep to see the walls of the tent being tested to their limit once again. The fabric against the poles looked like a shopping bag caught in a fence. The difference was that we weren't on the security of the glacier anymore, but a thousand metres up a 2000 metre unclimbed bit of mountain. Before I could answer I must have fallen back in to my coma, as this is all I can remember.

Once again the pure beauty of the Alaskan wilderness was startling. We straddled the crest of the north-west ridge like ants clinging to a writhing animal, a reptilian spine of ice thrust from the subarctic tundra. Two weeks earlier we'd stood on a hill near Fairbanks and seen this razor ridge piercing the skyline some hundred miles distant, and now it thrilled me to think we were on it. To our south the Yanert glacier, an anarchic mess of seracs, crevasses and freshly fallen debris, was an unsettling sight. This was our way down and the first time we'd seen it in the flesh. I could see Heinrich Harrer, Fred Beckey and Henry Meybohm weaving their way through this maze, making the first ascent of Deborah. On the other side of the Yanert, the south summit looked tantalisingly close in the eye-watering clear air I've only experienced in such cold, high-latitude places. I imagined what it would be like to see some dots top out over there from the huge unclimbed south face. Then I stopped dreaming. There was no one else here.

Getting going had been hard work; it always is. But with the summit nearly visible we felt the grab of success drag us back into the current – upwards. We climbed 500m of easy mixed ground, moving freely. When only hours earlier each step had to be forced from us by an act of will, now we moved over friendly ground, the first on the route, with ease.

I've done it again. Got carried away thinking I can make the next level section of the ridge, but we're now moving together with no screws between us – our umbilical cord of trust no longer has those comforting doglegs of protection along its length, hanging almost freely for 20 metres. It's snow climbing, what's the fuss? Yet these horizontal corniced beasts are where bad things happen; give me some water ice any day. 'Don't fall Jon, don't trip, not now,' I pray.

'Let's call this the summit,' I said to Jon when we were close enough yet far enough from the summit cornice. Six almost horizontal 100m pitches had drawn us along the most involved part of the upper north-west ridge. The wind was back, stinging our eyes and sending impressive swirls of ice crystals into shining vortices, like breaking surf on a windy day. Clinging to the rocks on the south side we avoided the house-sized cornices and 2,000m drop to the north. It hadn't let up, extending in to the blue horizon every time we reached a levelling. I imagined Dakers Gowan and Charles Macquarie popping their heads over the cornice from their tenacious 12-day epic on the north face in 1977. Times change. If we now spent a total of 15 days on a route, as they did, it would be because something went wrong. Back then they just knuckled down, it was normal. [*Editor's note:* Macquarie's account of their climb is the *Alpine Journal* for 1978. The final paragraph reads: 'By the time we got back to our base camp, two days later, we had been out for a total of 15 days. When we arrived there we found it occupied by another team who had come to try the north face. They thought we were dead. We were not sorry to be able to disillusion them.']

Sometimes a summit can be an elative experience, but more often than not there are other things on your mind. I was anxious about the descent: 500m of abseiling and down-climbing a steep, sun-baked slope would see us over what looked to be a large bergschrund and on to the Yanert icefall. The Yanert would have to be navigated to a point where we could re-ascend a few hundred metres to gain our bivy on the north-west ridge.

The purr of our stove was as good a soundtrack as any. The backdrop of a thousand jagged peaks under a setting sun needed no superlative to describe it. Content, but shattered, we sat at our bivy, pleased that the south-facing summit slope hadn't parted the mountain taking us with it, pleased that the bergschrund beneath it had provided no complication, and the Yanert had proved navigable. In the morning we would then have a ridge about a mile long to traverse, before 800m of abseiling down to the Gillam glacier on a nastily cross-loaded face. Once down, we would walk for a few kilometres to the base of the route and collect our skis before gliding down to our snow hole, for food and satisfaction.

'What do you think?' I asked Jon, scrolling the screen of my camera, enlarging shots of the ridge we now stood on taken from base camp days earlier. Having identified a gully that seemed to have the least objective hazard, we were now trying to find it from above. Committing to the best of some bad options, Jon lowered himself into the void beneath. Large cornices drooped like wet grass as we set up one inventive rap after another: V-threads in névé; a cam in a decomposing crack. 'Don't weight this one too much.' The end was in sight; we were riding the fine line between fast and careless. 'Let's shed some weight, just leave it all.' Alarm bells were ringing. 'Keep it together, slow down, play the long game,' I told myself.

Back at the snow cave, I wait for the euphoria, the elation-pitched scream, the joy, the glee and the party. Then I remember what I always forget about these experiences, that they're not a quick fix or an innocent high, but a deep thoughtful process, one that slowly rewards you with time and contemplation. Collapsed in a heap outside our snow hole, we stare up at our face, its top half bathed in amber light. We know a hundred times more about it than we did three days previously, and see it with different eyes. Our minds turn to a cloud of lazy happy thought with each sip of whisky.

That irrepressible feeling we felt when first stepping on the face three days previously, which by-passed our rational thinking, was now a distant memory. A memory which we could let slide, pretend hadn't happened and

Sim closing in on the summit of Mount Deborah. The descent involving down-climbing on the opposite side of the ridge before re-crossing it to descend.

attribute success to fine-tuned decision-making. Yet that would miss a fascinating part of climbing in the big mountains, an arena in which you would rarely climb anything if you didn't hand yourself over to something else.

As climbers, we like to talk about calculated risk and margins of safety. This is what keeps us alive and coming back for more. But I also think we gloss over the times when we listen to something else. Call it intuition, an inner fire or just stubbornness. It's not all black and white, maths and science; there are those rare moments we tap into when it's nothing more than a blind belief that takes control. The more I climb the more I wonder: is it possible to have success in the big mountains, without having a degree of faith?

Summary

First ascent of *Bad to the Bone*, the 2,000m north-west face and north-west ridge of Mount Deborah (3761m). They crossed the bergschrund at 2am on 23 April and reached the summit the following day from their bivy tent on the north-west ridge. The pair reported very poor rock and a high avalanche risk, prompting them to escape the face earlier than planned. Asked for a grade, Griffith said: 'We ended up having to simul-climb thin and delicate technical sections with a big pack on and at times just a couple of bits of pro, on a mountain that kept threatening to sweep us off it. I can't really give that a grade.'

BEN SILVESTRE

The Trouble with Happiness

All alone: base camp below Jezebel East Summit (2880m) in the rarely visited Revelation mountains. *(All images Ben Silvestre)*

The line of *Hoar of Babylon* on Jezebel's east face.

'I think it's so foolish for people to want to be happy. Happy is so momentary – you're happy for an instant and then you start thinking again. Interest is the most important thing in life; happiness is temporary, but interest is continuous.'
Georgia O'Keeffe

Tentatively, Peter Graham weights the V-thread he's just made in a two-foot-square patch of ice, the only patch solid enough to trust in the eight metres of ice we've both just climbed. Lowering, he strips the ice screws from below and joins me at the belay. We look up a final time, photograph the pitch in our minds, and descend. Already our thoughts are fixed on a single thing: when will we get another chance?

From the glacier, vast and featureless and giving nothing to measure or gain perspective from, the pitch we have just failed to climb had looked short and easy. We'd expected an ice step a few moves long, making the novice error of assuming that mountains are as small as they look. Instead we found overhung sweeps of icicle insanity, too hard to be a reasonable proposition with the lightweight rack we're carrying. We both got as close as we dared though, both let the idea of climbing a pitch like that in a place like this get under our skin. I, less skilled on ice, was ready to admit defeat. An ice-filled winter has made Pete ready, however, and he accepts the challenge, he votes to carry the gauntlet. We will be back.

We ski slowly back to our tent, turning to look, enjoying what is now a sunny morning. A week and a half in Alaska and this is our first bright day. Hopefully it won't be the last.

Skiing to the base of the route.

We are in the Revelation mountains, attempting the east summit of a peak called Jezebel. This summit could well be considered the highest unclimbed peak in the range, as it is a distinctly separate point from Jezebel's true top. Having landed on the Fish glacier on 25 March, directly below the east face, not having seen a photograph of it before, we became incredibly excited and changed our plans from the north face, a day's skiing away, to this incredible challenge. For our first attempt, we took eight ice screws and a day and a half of food; it wasn't nearly enough. We have learned our first lesson: things in Alaska are bigger than they seem.

It took months to plan this trip, to make it happen. Expeditions are like that; even when the line to be climbed is unknown, the climb itself begins months before crampons touch snow. The will to be there, to keep going, to struggle onward and upward is seeded and seated for a long time beforehand. Some people can't stand the planning, but I love it. Searching for maps, looking on Google Earth for any possible beta, reading reports and booking transport: it's all part of the process and I lap it up gladly. It comes with its own special stress, of course; we found out last minute that we'd have to change our objective, and almost failed to get to our range at all, but it all came together in the end. Even with such worries, the chosen stress of working towards an objective has a different nature than that of daily life. It feels somehow worth it.

A few stormy days later we wake before sunrise, glad we retreated; glad we didn't have to descend from high in a blizzard. This time we're armed

The overhanging ice pitch that proved the crux of the climb.

with a large rack, food for more than a day, and a burning will born out of having tasted the unknowable, the invisible. We follow footsteps blown to a blur and all of a sudden the days that have passed seem distant. Pete wears 'the gauntlet' well and when the time is right I wear it too, rising together and knowing and seeing. The pitch above also needs care, an overhanging section up a fin of ice, like the wing of an aeroplane tilted 95°. Screws go in one side and re-appear on the other.

A steep chimney follows, filled with overhanging snow, and it takes a good two hours of stubborn excavation, precarious back-and-footing and convoluted aid from Ben, and then we're in the couloir proper; after a few hundred metres of easier gully climbing we find an excellent bivy on a prow to the right. Next day a couple of easy pitches land us at the base of an excellent steep ice chimney, like *Exocet* in Patagonia. A few more pitches and we reach a tower, jokingly dubbed the tower of commitment when scoping the route, where we discover a steep wall separating us from the continuation of our couloir. We fix one of our ropes as an emergency exit and reach the top as dusk falls. Descending a few pitches, we chop out a bivy ledge. We're right that we can and we do, until all that remains is to come down. We do this too; slowly, painstakingly, gladly.

Back on the flat we gorge and drink and talk in our palace of a tent, and within days or perhaps hours we peer towards the mountain once again. Joy, so transitory, has passed. But interest, the eternal, remains and makes itself well known. For what little we have seen, a mass remains undiscovered, and we wonder at what else we might find. But unknown it will stay: good weather is elusive in the Revelation mountains and to climb two routes in three weeks seems a bit of a big ask. But we couldn't ask for more.

It would be a lie to say that I didn't value the whispers of happiness that we met along the way, but the true reward was coloured otherwise. It was gratifying to climb our route but all the while the mountain stayed itself, uncaring stone subject of awe and aspiration that it is, a summit a symbol; of completion and little else. It doesn't always go as it did, but uncompleted climbs aren't necessarily unsuccessful. In climbing or otherwise, true success can be measured in the journey, the reward hides in the tale.

Approaching the steep *goulotte* that barred access to the upper mountain.

If climbing was just brief moments stood shivering on summits we probably wouldn't bother, but climbing is discovery and so we do. We discover that the world holds far more unknown than we could ever begin to uncover. We discover that sometimes we can, and that sometimes we can't. But most of all we discover that being interested in something and pursuing that interest breeds more of it, and that therein lays our purpose.

Storm or sun I want to be in the mountains, peering around corners that hide small truths, always searching for bigger corners. Whether I reach the top or not means a lot less to me than seeing what lies in the middle. I am interested in what lies ahead, and that is reason enough to go there. As the artist Georgia O'Keeffe said. 'Whether you succeed or not is irrelevant, there is no such thing. Making your unknown known is the important thing – and keeping the unknown always beyond you.'

Summary

First ascent of the east face of Jezebel East Summit (2880m) in the Revelation mountains, Alaska, via the *Hoar of Babylon* (VI, WI6, M6, A0, 1200m), by Ben Silvestre and Peter Graham in late March and early April 2015. The team had originally planned on climbing the central couloir of Pyramid Peak but the climbers were advised that landing an aircraft on the Revelation glacier wasn't possible so they switched to attempting the north face of Jezebel from the Fish glacier via the col north-east of Jezebel. They then switched to the east face of Jezebel East Summit as a more interesting objective closer to base camp. They left base camp on 2 April and reached the summit next day, returning to base camp on 4 April.

Revelation Mountains Information

The best time for climbing is from the middle of March to late April. Temperatures before the middle of March can reach minus 40°C but then quickly rise to 20°C. We had no thermometer but the coldest nights reached minus 18°C on the forecast. Most days were cloudy and thus considerably warmer, and we could often relax in base camp without gloves. It snowed a lot. From 19 days spent on the glacier there were only two when it didn't snow at all. This is normal weather in the Revelation.

Climbing the *goulotte*.

The granite on the east face of Jezebel is of the highest quality and there would be countless rock objectives, but getting there in summer would necessitate a long and expensive helicopter flight as the glaciers dry up. The most reliable glaciers to land on are the east facing ones, due to snow conditions. Talkeetna Air Taxis no longer land on the Revelation glacier due to dryness in recent years. Rob Jones seemed more confident in that respect; he has a smaller plane.

We were camped in a sheltered north-east-facing valley, and except for a few violent days experienced next to no wind. Clint Helander, at a similar time, was buffeted almost constantly by violent winds. He was camped in an adjacent north-west-facing valley, south of Jezebel. We were told the prevailing wind was westerly but the evidence suggests otherwise. We may just have been lucky.

The Revelation are outside the Denali national park and so no permit is necessary for climbing there. We downloaded some very accurate and free maps from *http://www.usgs.gov*.

Acknowledgements
The Mount Everest Foundation, the British Mountaineering Council, the Alpine Club, the Austrian Alpine Club (UK) for their financial support; Rab and Mountain House UK for equipment and supplies; Talkeetna Air Taxi, especially Paul Roderick, Rob Jones, for reporting on the condition of our landing site; Clint Helander, Darren Vonk, Pedro Angel Galan Diaz and Tad McCrea for general beta for climbing in the area; Malcolm Scott, Tom Ripley and Rick and Jenny Graham for texting weather reports.

Acknowledgements

Off the Beaten Track

Mal Duff at Annapurna Base Camp (North Side). Rob Fairley, 1992.
(Watercolour and coloured pencil. 36cm x 50cm. Private collection.)

GEORGE CAVE

Trying Tajikistan

Looking out across the stunning ridgeline of the Ak Baikal valley. *(Clay Conlon)*

At 5,200m, in the middle of Tajikistan, I was panting hard. James Monypenny, on the other hand, strolled nonchalantly beside me. He was feeling the benefit of six weeks trekking in India whilst I had been sat at my office desk in Warwick a mere four days earlier. Over the past few years I have perfected the art of convincing my friends to fly out ahead of me on expeditions to shop and prepare, enabling me to push the limits of what I can acceptably squeeze into a two-week holiday. Pausing for a moment, I sat down on the glacier and breathed in the consequence of my rapid ascent to altitude. It's never ideal when your only method of pre-trip acclimatisation is the flight from the UK.

Our team of five were on expedition in central Tajikistan with eyes on an unclimbed ridgeline in the Muzkol range. We spanned the whole gamut of mountaineering lifestyles, from committed climbing bum to nine-to-five office worker. When Clay Conlon and I stepped off the plane at Osh airport, we all stood together for the first time. It would be glamorous to write of how we had been dreaming of this great traverse from the start, but in reality we had simply planned a trip to the valley on a hunch and only later learned more of its mountaineering potential. An email from a Latvian climber led to a book from 1940 in the RGS library, which included the quote that came to define our objectives:

Clay Conlon leading onto steeper ice of a new route at the end of the ridgeline above the Ak Baikal. *(George Cave)*

'Five of the peaks on the ridge create a traverse. The passage of this route would have done credit to any master mountaineer.' We arrived in the valley 75 years to the day after Soviet military officer V S Yatsenko had penned that description in his book *In the Pamirs: Travel Notes of a Participant in the Pamir Alpine Expedition of 1940*. His tantalising tagline lured us in. Who wouldn't want to become a master mountaineer, given the opportunity?

Clay and I had travelled from the UK on a Saturday, before meeting Emily Ward, Al Docherty and James in Osh, Kyrgyzstan's second city, on the Sunday, and immediately beginning our journey to the mountains. Osh was chaotic, bustling and baking hot as we meandered our way through the dusty suburbs of the town. Our first driver, Alek, passed us on to his brother, Momo, who then swung by his father's before running various errands for friends and family on our way out of the city. As we drew closer to the land crossing into Tajikistan, we thought the hitchhiking border guards we had collected would ease our passage. We were wrong.

From inside the truck we watched as Momo worked his way methodically through the bureaucratic faff of seven separate checkpoint bribes, hilariously insisting on driving the 20m between each office. Until now the road had climbed quite quickly but instead of crossing a col and dropping back down as we entered Tajikistan, it continued to rise further still to around 4,300m. Finally, after twelve hours of driving, we turned off and headed into the Ak Baikal valley.

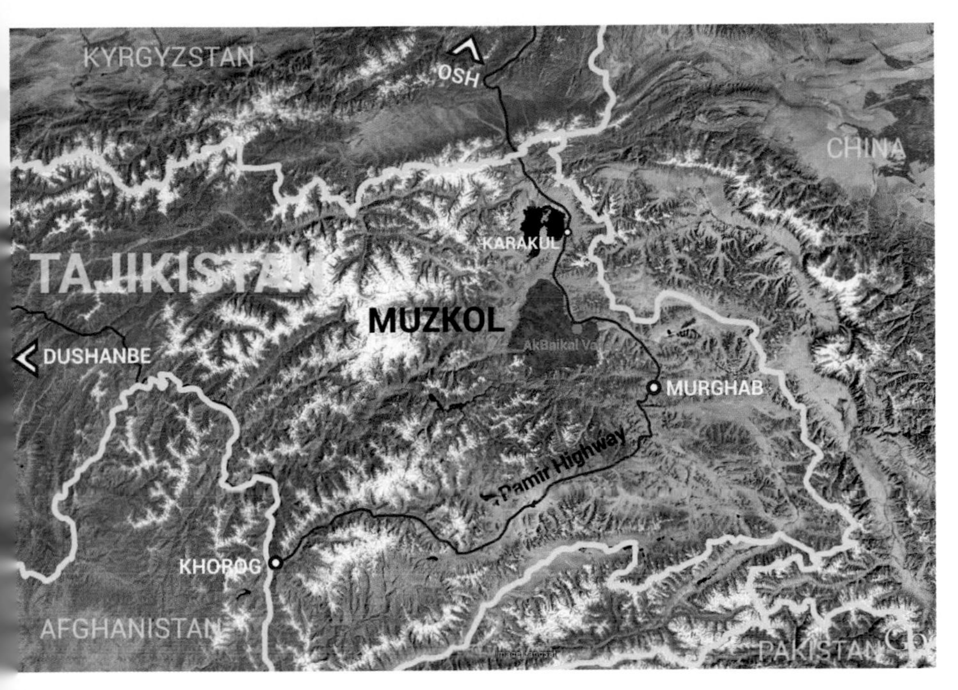

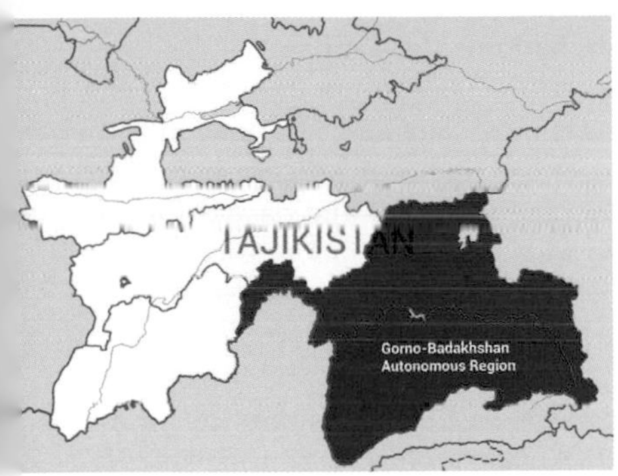

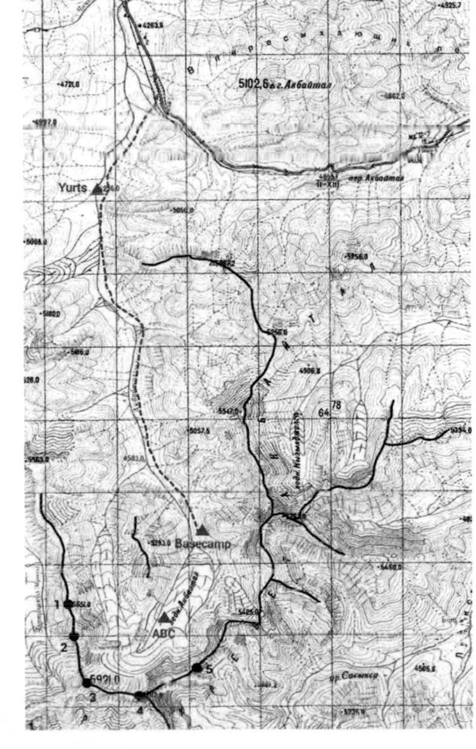

One of the biggest gambles of the trip had been whether the valley would be inhabited, thus offering the potential to recruit help to avoid a depressing 13km load carry at altitude into the basin. Inhabited it was, for which we were immediately thankful, since our driver's parting act was to manoeuvre our 4x4 slowly into the river and leave it stranded there. I climbed onto the roof to watch the river flowing in one door

A panorama shot of the ridgeline of Ak Baikal showing the team's ascents and attempts. The traverse remains to be done. The peaks have been numbered in keeping with V S Yatsenko's original numbering. See summary for key. *(George Cave)*

and out the other and then waded across, leaving the recovery of the vehicle to the locals, for whom this river crossing is a part of their daily lives.

Our impromptu host, Akilbek Zhanybaev, was a 39-year-old yak herder, living in the valley's yurt village during the summer months with his family, which included an army of incredibly mischievous children. He generously let us into his home, fed us, and laughed loudly as he posed for a photo, joking with us to tell our mothers that we had met the Taliban.

Our rapid ascent to altitude in the valley had compounded the gut infection Al had acquired in Osh, and was now causing him some considerable grief. For him, the scenic and stunning ride into Muzkol had been an unpleasant mix of uncomfortable sleeping positions and dashes for the roadside gutter. We made the decision to split and left Emily to keep an eye on Al whilst Akilbek drove us up the valley towards our planned base camp. Momo also stuck around, bailing out his truck and trying in vain to interpret the German engine manual. Next day Al had had enough and hitched his way back home to Osh. Not long afterwards he flew to Antarctica for an 18-month stint working with the British Antarctic Survey and it's slightly surreal to think that in two years' time when I see him again, it will be our first meeting since I left him asleep on the floor of a yurt in Tajikistan.

With our team reduced to four, Emily borrowed a donkey and rode to base camp whilst James and I sat on the glacier to rest, unaware of her approach. I'd had enough of the climb and turned back, leaving James to summit the route solo; a great early effort putting up a new route on a peak first climbed just the previous year.

A few days later Emily and James headed up to the main glacial basin for a good sleep before their climb, yet when we spoke the next day by radio they told us how in the centre of a large, flat glacier they had spent the night awake with fear and hadn't managed to leave camp. Both confused and bemused, Clay and I hiked up over the moraine to join them and admire James's choice of campsite. Hunting for a flat piece of ground he

Emily Ward soloing new ground in the Pamirs. *(James Monypenny)*

had pitched the tent on a large boulder perched atop a much thinner ice pillar. It looked ideal for a photo-shoot, but less ideal for a relaxing night's sleep given the frequency with which the ice pillars collapse, unceremoniously dumping their loads onto the glacier beneath. We moved camp, settled in and scanned the serac-guarded faces for a first objective.

Shortly after first light the next morning, Clay and I abseiled off the face on abalakov threads and breathed a sigh of relief. We had risen early and spent the morning traversing on brittle ice beneath a large and threatening serac band, which had loomed above us all the more menacing in the early morning darkness. Clay's technical ability on steep ice was questionable, but in contrast to me at least he had *some* ability. After I had floundered

Left: James Monypenny, a small dot in the centre of the frame, makes the first of many abseils following his solo first ascent of Peak 4, the highlight of the expedition. *(Clay Conlon)*

Below: The small mouse that terrorised base camp. *(Emily Ward)*

along in fear behind him for several hours we called it quits and retreated to the cold, comforting safety of the glacier beneath.

A familiar pattern was emerging in which I, and my rucksack of excuses, would bail on a route, leaving James to solo on ahead. Yet looking up, I couldn't help but stop and smile. Sat surrounded by the majesty of this ridgeline, bathed in orange from the rising sun, it was our own private alpine retreat far from the lifts, queues and bureaucracy of life in the Alps. How could I not enjoy the adventure of being here, even if that adventure didn't actually involve much climbing? Or is that just what climbers who bail early say?

James's route up the unclimbed mountain was the crowning moment of the expedition, a superb 12-hour solo push that represented the first ever

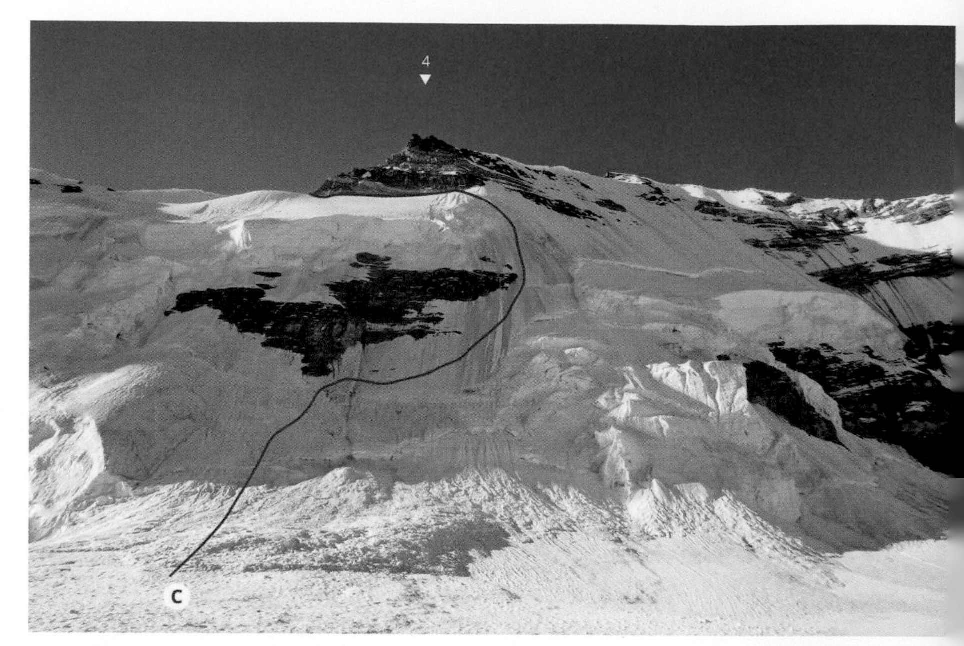

The north-west face and north-east ridge of Pik 5792m, 'Mt Emily', the first summit on the chain to be reached (D, 75°, 800m) solo by James Monypenny. *(George Cave)*

ascent of any of the peaks on the ridgeline. From the comfort of our camp we watched as he rappelled the couloir to the ground: a tiny, insignificant speck, dwarfed by the vast white canvas of ice on which he danced. We finished our time in the valley with two further routes. James and Emily made another foray up onto the ridgeline to confirm once again that it was a chossy, fractured mess requiring the skills of a master levitator, let alone a master mountaineer, to traverse. Clay and I finally summited too, repeating the line climbed by James at the beginning of our trip.

While packing up base camp we discovered the enterprising mice, which had tunnelled under our tent to eat our oats and plague me with sleepless nights. We chased them away, cleared the camp and hitched a lift down the hill on Akilbek's donkeys. To repay the children for brightening our lives with their cheeky misdemeanours, Emily and I taught them a few games drawn from the heights of western culture. A generation of Tajik children will now grow old well versed in the dance moves of the Macarena.

There comes a time on any expedition when you let your guard down and tell yourself the trip is over. The route back is obvious and the mental drain of life far from home has worn its course. Sadly, this happened a little too early in Tajikistan. Not far into our drive back, a bogus national park official flagged us down. He asked to speak with our chief or director. For some reason everyone pointed at me. A few tense moments followed as we refused to be extorted for our stay in his park and our new friend was less amused still by James's cunning sleight of hand to steal back our passports. He followed us to the next town where we hopped out of our truck and promptly watched our driver disappear with all of our belongings. Setting off in pursuit, we caught up with him to discover that he was fortunately not unloading our possessions but instead simply pumping up the spare tyre. He didn't like our new friend either and we quickly climbed back in and drove away to evade payment. One mile down the road he turned to me and smiled: 'National park, no good'.

Our next run-in with a government official was somewhat more serious. We had celebrated in Osh with a big night out and, hung over, pushed our way through the queues at check-in for our flight home via Russia. Check-in at Osh was a very low-budget affair, the passenger manifest was written on a sheet of lined paper, boarding cards were blank save for a hand-written seat number and a good knowledge of Manchester United was all I needed to bypass any fees for our overweight baggage.

Landing in Novosibirsk we were denied boarding onto our connection to Moscow; we discovered a Russian visa is required to transit through Russia. An assembly of airline and security officials gathered, including one with a Taser, and feeling bold I demanded we were upgraded and flown home immediately by the next available route. The representative from S7 Airlines simply smiled and told us to buy a new flight or be deported back to Kyrgyzstan.

Four hours of negotiation ensued before we could finally agree upon an alternative route and an airline that would take our overweight luggage for free. With no visa to enter Russia, and no way to buy tickets airside, our passports were confiscated and the guard with the Taser escorted us through security like VIPs to a ticket desk in the foyer. Negotiations complete, it was all smiles as we checked in our baggage for Kazakhstan and I asked the guard what he had planned to do with the Taser. He grinned and pointed to the ceiling; it was in fact a fluorescent bulb for the strip lighting overhead. The title of master mountaineer remains to be claimed, but our little adventure was finally over.

Summary

The panorama photograph illustrates the various forays of the team. A and D: *DofE Bronze* (PD+, 50°, 500m), north face of Pik 5560m, soloed by J Monypenny on 11 August 2015, and repeated on 16 August by G Cave and C Conlon. A Latvian made the first ascent of this peak in 2014 via the north-east ridge at the Russian grade of 2b. B: Pik 5560m, west face and south-south-west ridge (F, 500m), Emily Ward on 14 August. C: *DofE Silver* (D, 75°, 800m), north-west face and north-east ridge of Pik 5792m ('Mt Emily'), J Monypenny on 14 August. E: *Pie Josh Horrorshow* (AD, 55°, 500m), Pik c5700m, E Ward and J Monypenny on 18 August 2015.

DEREK BUCKLE

Hidden Zanskar

Exploration of the Korlomshe Tokpo[1]

Hidden Zanskar: the team named Peak 5916, left, 'Kusyabla', the Ladakhi word for monk. The peak on the right is Peak 5947, called 'Temple'. *(All images Derek Buckle)*

For our 2015 expedition to India, we were again attracted to the Zanskar region of Ladakh, drawn by its relative remoteness, opportunities for exploration and the chance to attempt high, hitherto unclimbed mountains. A further potential advantage was that Zanskar, blocked as it is by the Himalaya to the south, is largely protected from the impact of the monsoon, with an arid terrain similar to that of Tibet. Having previously climbed in Zanskar's Pensilungpa valley, the source of the Suru river[2], we were keen to travel further south to investigate one or more of the valleys closer to Padam, situated at the junction of the Doda and Zanskar rivers. Padam is currently accessed via a single road from Kargil, on the main road between Leh and Srinagar. The Padam road initially follows the Suru to the Pensi La and then the Doda river from the pass.

1. Buckle, D, *Alpine Journal* 118, 2014, pp15-23.
2. Sakamoto, K, *American Alpine Journal* 84, 2010, pp286-287.

Knut Tønsberg on the first ascent of Temple (5947m).

This arduous journey involves some 236km of backbreaking unmade track that is often washed out, although the need to maintain access to Padam ensures it is kept navigable. Everything is likely to change when the embryonic direct road from Leh, following the Zanskar river itself, is completed. The likely impact of this new road is already evident in Padam, where hotels and other new buildings are under construction, although it may be several years yet before the expected increase in visitors becomes a reality.

An annotated panorama of the view from the summit of Kusyabla showing the peaks around the Korlomshe Tokpo valley in Zanskar.

While trekkers and mountaineers have visited several of the major valleys south of Padam, large swathes of this relatively inaccessible area have received little attention. The Raru or Reru valley in particular has become popular following an exploratory visit in 2009 by a senior Japanese team led by Kimikazu Sakamoto.[3] More recently, Sakamoto has made other trips to Zanskar, but we were especially interested to read the account of his 2012 expedition to the Temasa *nala* and subsequent exploration of the lower Korlomshe Tokpo[4]. His was the first party to enter this tributary valley where he identified and assigned major peaks in the vicinity of the Temasa *nala* based on an alphanumeric notation. Twenty-one hitherto unclimbed peaks were identified and photographed. Following extensive correspondence with Kimikazu Sakamoto we selected several potential objectives in the Korlomshe Tokpo cirque for which he generously provided information and photographs.

After reviewing the commercially available terrestrial maps in combination with Google satellite images we hoped to establish camps high on the Korlomshe glacier during late August to early September from which to explore its upper reaches and attempt one or more of the unclimbed peaks of the high cirque. The absence of readily available high quality maps was a distinct disadvantage during our early planning, but Sakamoto's detailed, annotated sketch map of the topography surrounding the Temasa *nala* was extremely helpful.[4] While satellite pictures indicated that most, if not all, the major peaks had rocky summits guarded by precipitous walls, extended glacial fingers appeared to offer several weak points in the cirque's upper bastions. Only close inspection would establish whether or not this was the case.

First we had to transfer the team – myself as leader, Drew Cook, Gus Morton, Knut Tønsberg and Stuart Worsfold – our support staff and

3. Sakamoto, K *Himalayan Journal* 68, 2012, pp125-137.
4. Altitude and position recorded by GPS.

assorted food and equipment to a suitable base camp. Initially everything went to plan as we drove the short distance from Padam via Bardan Gompa to Pibchu, where we had arranged to pick up horses. It was here the first problems began. Miraculously, the eight horses we had requested morphed into ten rather small donkeys that one of the locals had managed to borrow from other villagers. Since donkeys have only about half the capacity of horses, it was immediately evident that we had insufficient carrying capacity. By sheer chance, however, we managed to recruit five extra horses that were coincidently returning to the village as we left. Without these additional animals the interminable ascent to an impromptu camp at the Chokmetsik springs, just 6km up the Temasa *nala*, would have been impossible. Laden donkeys are not suited to the terrain of the Temasa *nala* and they struggled under their 40kg loads, frequently dislodging them on projecting boulders and having to have them removed on less stable ground. Being taller, and stronger, the horses performed considerably better. As it was, we lost a day with the interim camp and were obliged to locate base camp near the confluence of the Temasa *nala* and Korlomshe Tokpo at only 4,153m, rather than at 5,000m in the latter valley as anticipated.

Exploration of the Korlomshe Tokpo

With base camp situated beside the Temasa *nala*, several trips up the Korlomshe Tokpo were necessary in order to both locate and stock an advance base camp (ABC) from which we could explore and climb the upper reaches. (See map overleaf.) This was not helped by yet another setback when one of our high-altitude porters (HAPs) became unwell and wasn't able to carry loads. As a result we did much of the early carrying ourselves, although Malkeet 'Maly' Singh, our liaison officer, helped enormously by transporting more than his fair share of the equipment and food needed for an extended stay above base camp. The first two forays explored a variety of options to optimise the route through a kilometre of boulder-fields, and to limit the number of lateral moraine crossings we had to make, but rarely

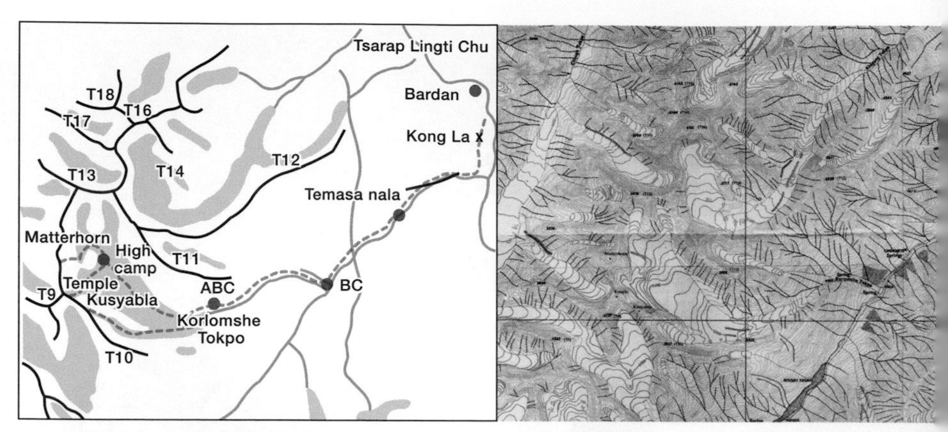

Sketch map of the Korlomshe Tokpo with routes followed in red.

was the same path followed in its entirety. After establishing two high gear stashes we eventually located ABC at 5,135m close to a small fresh-water tarn fed by glacial melt-water. This was undoubtedly the site used by the 2012 Japanese team since it fitted their description with fair accuracy.

The views from ABC were impressive. Dominating the southern aspect was the impressive north wall of T10 (5957m) and to the north loomed the equally steep south face of T11 (5908m). Neither looked attractive propositions from this position. What did appeal to us was a prominent snow peak to the northwest of T10 that we felt was approachable via a glacial tongue running east-south-east towards the main glacier. Closer inspection showed that this tongue was continuous and offered a viable proposition.

After precariously crossing the icy Korlomshe Tokpo early on 1 September, Drew, Gus and I soloed the easy but *penitente*-covered tongue until it turned left and steepened. At this point we roped up before climbing the consistently angled slope – up to 40° – to the south-east ridge. The north-west ridge of T10 rose impressively on our left as we continued rightwards to climb a steep, 40° corniced ridge to a small rocky summit to make the first ascent of Peak 5916 at Alpine AD).[5] In addition to the obvious feature of T10, the view west overlooked the awesome east face of T9 (6107m), the peak that we had designated as one of our primary targets. It was immediately clear that we would not be attempting this peak, separated as it was from us by a long and difficult knife-edged ridge. To the north-west, however, was another attractive option that we considered might be approachable from a camp higher up the main glacier. We subsequently named Peak 5916 Kusyabla, the Ladakhi word for monk.[5] As we had seen few crevasses, and found it easier to climb the ultimate ridge un-roped, we retraced our path back to ABC solo. Three days later Knut made the second ascent of Kusyabla with Maly following the same route.

5. We chose to call the mountain 'monk' for two reasons. First, Pemba, one of our HAPs, had spent 14 years training as a monk and only left the monastery three months before our expedition. He spent one intriguing evening recalling the experience. Second, we likened the scenery to that of the Mönch in the Bernese Oberland.

With little more that we could hopefully achieve at ABC, we spent a day trekking up the main glacier to the upper headwall, intending eventually to establish a high camp within reasonable reach of some climbable objectives. It was soon evident, however, that no straightforward access to either T11 or T13 (6436m) lay within the capabilities of our team. Nonetheless, we were drawn to the Matterhorn-like peak (6050m, on the Olizane map, but probably much higher) that formed the centrepiece of the headwall cirque. But first we had to carry enough gear and provisions to establish a high camp at 5,500m directly beneath the 'Matterhorn'.

By 7 September, with Stuart having earlier decided to return home for personal reasons, the remaining team were together again at the high camp. Drew, unfortunately, was now suffering from a disconcerting dizziness of unknown origin so reluctantly decided to rest rather than climb higher. On 8 September, therefore, Gus, Knut and I reached the east face of the 'Matterhorn' via a broad glacial spur before roping up when the face steepened to 45° or 50 ° – Alpine D. Five or so long pitches later, with the ice fan narrowing as it approached the rocky ridge, it was evident the summit was still some way off. Unfortunately, despite the lack of technical difficulty, time was no longer on our side. After reaching c5,900m, we reluctantly agreed to descend. Four full-length abseils, one off an impressive natural ice thread, led to easy ground and a relatively quick return to high camp.

Next day Gus returned to base camp to investigate rock-climbing possibilities in the Temasa *nala* while those left behind rested at high camp. A quick stroll to the medial moraine convinced us that a viable route did indeed exist to the peak we had earlier identified from Kusyabla, and we planned to attempt this next. With Drew still concerned about his dizziness he wisely decided to descend on 10 September while Knut and I crossed the Korlomshe glacier to the peak's east-north-east face. Solo climbing on continuous 45° corrugated ice led ultimately to a narrow col, right of an impressive cornice at c5,800m, that offered superb views of the north-west ridge of Kusyabla. Keeping right, we then climbed steeply (50°) towards the north-west to stay left of an obvious short rock tower on the summit ridge.

Some 4h 30m after leaving camp we arrived on the compact summit of Peak 5947 to make the first ascent (Alpine AD). As on Kusyabla, the views were far-reaching and magnificent. Kusyabla dominated the foreground to the south-east, with T10 close behind, but it was the imposing bulk of T9 to the south-west that caught the eye. To the north was the 'Matterhorn' and beyond that was T13, the valley giant. More distant were peaks to the south of the Temasa *nala*, with the glaciated face of R3 (6036m) standing out. Resisting the urge to linger we returned to the high camp by the route of ascent. We chose to call this peak Temple to reflect the characteristic pulpit-like structure on its summit ridge and to retain a tenuous link with the choice of 'monk' for our earlier peak.

With time now running out we evacuated high camp next day, with Knut and I carrying excessively heavy loads as far as ABC. Here we left all but essential items to be collected by Maly and the HAPs the following morning

The peak T9 (6107m) seen from Kusyabla.

and then rejoined the rest of the team to enjoy base camp before returning home. Having base camp low down in the main Temasa *nala* should have made its dismantling on departure a straightforward affair, but again we encountered unexpected problems. After much checking and confirmation, eight horses were 'guaranteed' to arrive late on 13 September, but when we looked out of the tents the following morning lo and behold they too had metamorphosed. This time it was into one donkey and four porters, one of whom was well into his prime. In no possible way would this be adequate to transport our gear back to Bardan.

The solution was to carry down our personal gear and leave camp equipment and two support staff to descend later when the horses did eventually arrive. Needless to say the horses failed to materialise, obliging the residual support team to return empty-handed just as we left for Padam. It necessitated a night hike with 11 local porters to retrieve what had been left behind and some serious negotiation over how much they were to be paid. Fortunately, once we reached Padam there were no further significant problems. The two-day drive to Leh, the flight to Delhi and a meeting with the Indian Mountaineering Federation were still ahead of us, but these were unavoidable, and in the euphoria of success passed uneventfully.

Morton and Tønsberg descending from the c5,900m highpoint on the east face (D) of the 6,000m+ Matterhorn-like peak due west of their high camp. This is marked as 6050m on the map, but is likely much higher.

Acknowledgements

The team gratefully acknowledges the invaluable financial support of the Mount Everest Foundation, the Alpine Club Climbing Fund and the Austrian Alpine Club. They would also like to thank Bergans and Duffler/Primus/Snigel-Design for their generous gift of clothing and equipment.

Summary

In August and September 2015, Derek Buckle, Drew Cook, Gus Morton, Knut Tønsberg and Stuart Worsfold explored the Korlomshe Tokpo valley in the Zanskar region of India. From an advance base camp at 5,130m Buckle, Cook and Morton made the first ascent of Peak 5916 ('Kusyabla') via the south-west ridge (AD) on 1 September. Three days later Tønsberg and liaison officer Malkeet Singh made a second ascent by the same route. After establishing a high camp at 5,500m on the Korlomshe glacier Buckle and Tønsberg successfully made the first ascent of Peak 5947 ('Temple') via its east-north-east face and south-east ridge (AD) on 10 September. From the same high camp Buckle, Morton and Tønsberg also climbed to c5,900m on the east face (D) of the 6,000m+ Matterhorn-like peak due west of the camp.

References and Notes

For more details see: Buckle, D R, '2015 Temasa *nala* Expedition', *Mount Everest Foundation Report*, 2015

EVELIO ECHEVARRÍA

Cordillera Santa Vera Cruz, Bolivia

Panoramic view from the north of the main group of peaks of the Santa Vera Cruz. Left to right: Pico (or Cerro) de la Fortuna (5493m), Cerro Chupica (5100m, the reddish dome), Nevado Cunocollo or Santa Vera Cruz (5560m), Cerro Huariananta (5400m). *(Javier Sánchez)*

Its name was typical of the invading *Conquistadores*: Range of the True and Holy Cross. It only reflected the intense Christian faith of 16th century Europe and not the spirit of the relief itself. The Santa Vera Cruz seems to be the smallest range in the immense mountain world of Bolivia, but several of its scant eight or ten rock and ice peaks did merit the attention of unusual mountaineers at unusual times. Its story has so far been only partially told. This brief contribution purports to tell the rest.

Briefly, it is a conglomerate of very alpine, granodioritic peaks rising to over 5,500m, with an ice field in their midst. It is located some 125km north-north-west of the mining city of Oruro and south of the larger and higher Cordillera Quimsa Cruz, from which it is separated by the wide 4,300m Abra Tres Cruces: Pass of the Three Crosses. The range rises above the Bolivian high plateau, often likened to a Tibetan landscape. Wide, barren valleys, scant pastures and some occasional lakes or lagoons are found below the peaks. Natural life is limited to the *huallatas* or wild geese (*Chloephaga melanoptera*) that alight on lagoons. Pastures are used by small flocks of llamas and sheep belonging to a few local villagers, mostly of Aymara descent.

Climbing the south-west ridge of Pico de la Fortuna in 1999. The terrain to the east is unclimbed. *(Javier Sánchez)*

Few peaks make up the range but they are imposing. Official Bolivian maps at 1:50,000 do not clearly show them. It is better to describe them one by one as travellers would face them from their only known point of access so far, the Huariananta valley and lake, rising above the Huañacota village and close to the Abra Tres Cruces.

Starting place for mountaineering is the large Huariananta lake area, some 6km south of the Huañacota village. At 4,500m it offers good campsites and access into the map's Campo de Nieve or ice field. The bold, enormous pyramid of Pico (or Cerro) de la Fortuna (5493m) rises almost above village and lake. Its southern gap, quite wide, connects it to the south with Nevado Cunocollo (Aymara: 'ice peak'), also locally called Nevado Santa Vera Cruz. At 5,560m it is the highest in the range. Nestled under it is unmapped Cerro Chupica (Aymara: 'red blood'), about 5,100m high. The ice field yields access to the flanks of the steep rock peaks of Huariananta (5400m), Trinidad (5360m) and to the south, San Roque (5300m). The latter rises above a small cluster of mines and hamlets. West and north-west of these major elevations are scattered groups of unglaciated, milder rock heights, around 4,600m. Several may be unnamed – see sketch-map.

Unknown to mountaineers is the eastern side of the range. It is constantly cloud-covered. I myself gained a brief sight of a very sharp pyramid of glaciated rock, about 5,100m high, situated east of the Fortuna gap. The official Bolivian chart shows contour lines for three heights, c5200m high, in that location. Access to the eastern flank of this range has not been

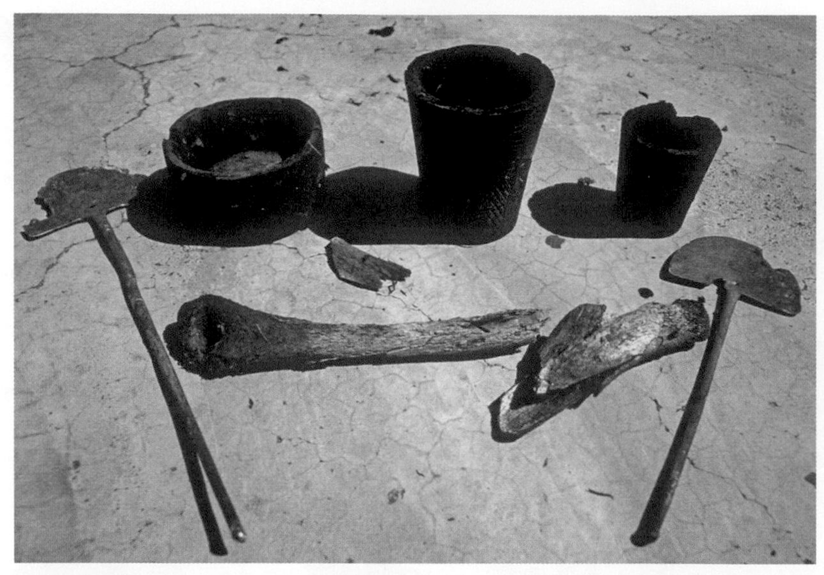

Aymara relics found on summit of Cunocollo (5560m) by the Spanish expedition of 1999. *(Javier Sánchez)*

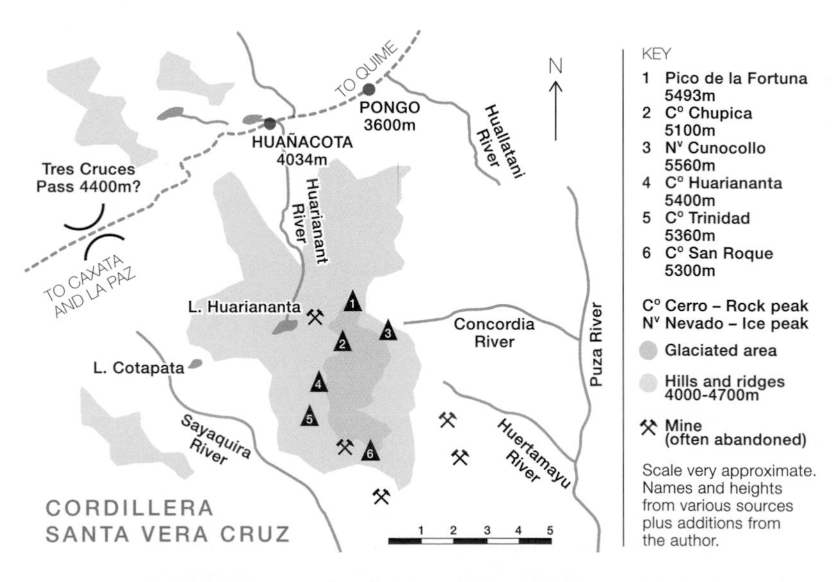

determined. Likewise, its southern flank is unknown. The entire massif appears to be around 12km north to south and some 10km wide. Incidentally, it carries the southernmost glaciers in the Bolivian Andes.

The brief mountaineering history of this small range complements the above. In 1939 the active Austrian mining engineer Josef Prem ascended Cunocollo. He was a major figure in the history of Bolivian climbing having made, besides other good ascents, the first of Nevado Sajama (6542m),

Ice slope of up to 55° on the west face of Nevado Cunocollo, climbed by the Spanish in 1999. *(Javier Sánchez)*

highest in the country. (A German engineer and traveller, Hermann Reisach, is at present researching the mountaineering career of Josef Prem.) On Cunocollo, Prem was followed in c1942 by the German-Bolivian scientist and explorer Friedrich Ahlfeld. Both had climbed the exposed north ridge, all rock.

Thereafter the Santa Vera Cruz was forgotten. In December 1983, out-of-season, and with local hill-man Pantaleón Calisaya I made the first ascent of Cerro Calacala (Aymara: 'rock-rock', c4600m), situated on the north shore of lake Huariananta. I returned in June 1991, entered the edge of the Campo de Nieve or ice field and ascended the dome of Cerro Chupica (5100m?), but stopped short below the three sharp needles of smooth granite that crown the peak. I did not dare to tackle them, feeling that instead of my rather big boots I needed light, tight sneakers to negotiate the smooth granite. Whether through common sense or pusillanimity, I left the summit needles unclimbed.

The true year for Santa Vera Cruz mountaineering was 1999. Three young Madrid climbers led by Javier Sánchez climbed the bold Pico de la Fortuna as well as Cunocollo, the latter by its icy west face. Sánchez narrated in *AJ 2001* the climbs he led and also an incredible, unexpected find on the summit of Cunocollo. Rescued from the top was Josef Prem's card, proof of his 1939 ascent. And the Spaniards also found proofs of hitherto unsuspected forerunners:

'...archaeological remains dating from the last period of Tiwanaku culture. Apart from several silver brooches and the remains (teeth) of a sacrificial rat, the artefacts included ceremonial objects such as wooden pots and goblets, a hawthorn's needle and a human collarbone, which would have been used as a spoon. Although this cordillera is within easy reach of La Paz these treasures had been kept from the human eye for centuries.'[1]

Within the context of international summit archaeology, that is, unknown mountain ascents by Pre-Columbian peoples, the discovery of that material by Sánchez bears a double importance. He introduced the new field of summit archaeology, already practised in other Andean countries, to Bolivia. And after the Aymara summit objects had been analysed and dated in Spain, it was learned that they had been buried on the high ground between 900 and 1030, which preceded by some five centuries all Inca ascents believed to have taken place around the year 1400.

It will never be known which route the Aymaras took on Cunocollo. They either followed the exposed north ridge, as Prem and Ahlfeld did,

1. Editors, 'Renewed Interest in the Santa Vera Cruz', *High Magazine* 206, 2000, pp53-4.

Above: Josef Prem's calling card, recovered from the summit of Nevado Cunocollo in 1999. *(Javier Sánchez)*

Left: The highest peak in the Santa Vera Cruz: Nevado Cunocollo or Cerro Santa Vera Cruz (5560m). On the left is the north ridge taken by Prem in 1939 and Ahlfeld in the early 1940s. On the right is the top of the ice face climbed by the Spanish party. *(Javier Sánchez)*

or they scaled the west ice face. Sánchez stated that on this face 'one has to climb.' He estimated that it starts at an angle of 55° and is about 40° in the upper part of the mountain.[2]

Leading a joint Spanish-Bolivian party to conduct archaeological studies, Javier Sánchez re-ascended Cunocollo a year later. But no other party has visited the Range of the True and Holy Cross again. To approach the north and west flanks of the area, the only ones so far used by mountaineers, is easy and not costly. From the capital city of La Paz one can use any of the two bus companies operating between La Paz and Quime, located at the city's bus terminal. A ride of some eight to 10 hours will take travellers through Caxata town and the Tres Cruces pass to the hamlet of Huañacota (4034m). This place is devoid of resources but there a herdsman and his donkeys could be hired to carry loads up the Huariananta valley and its large lake, which yields access to the north side of the main group of peaks. The climbing season runs between late April and September. Weather is then normally dry and clear but cold.

2. Sánchez, J, 'Bolivia: Cordillera Santa Vera Cruz', in *Desnivel* 157, 1999, pp32-40.

South-west face of Pico de la Fortuna (5493m). *(Javier Sánchez)*

For prospective visitors three options are obvious: open new routes, probably quite difficult, on the different flanks of Pico de la Fortuna and on the east and south sides of Cunocollo; explore the unknown east side of the range, with the aim of identifying the unnamed peaks that are shown on maps; explore and attempt unclimbed Huariananta (5400m), Trinidad (5360m) and the summit needles of Chupica (5100m). Acclimatisation could be gained on the lower, c4400-4700m high peaks around the north and west sides of lake Huariananta.

Quick access, low cost and simplicity characterise mountaineering in this range. It seems to be indicated for light expeditions or small groups of climbing friends.

Background

Ahlfeld, F, 'Las Altas Cordilleras y el Andinismo en Bolivia', *Boletín de Ski y Andinismo (La Paz)* 1, 1945, pp6-19.

Editors, 'Renewed Interest in the Santa Vera Cruz', *High Magazine* 206, 2000, pp53-4.

Ekkehard, J, *Die Gletscher der Bolivianischen Anden*, Stuttgart, Franz Steiner Verlag, 1991, pp229-30.

Mesili, A, *Los Andes de Bolivia*, La Paz, Producciones Cima, 1996, pp295-8.

Prem, J, 'Climbing in the Bolivian Andes 1939', in *American Alpine Journal* 5, 1945, pp322-32.

Rivera, O, 'Un Santuario Tihuanacota de Altura', in *Revista Cultural* (La Paz) 39, 2006, pp7-13.

Sánchez, J, 'Bolivia: Cordillera Santa Vera Cruz', in *Desnivel* 157, 1999, pp32-40.

Sánchez, J, 'Bolivia 2000', *Alpine Journal* 106, 2001, p284.

Sánchez, J, 'Andinistas Aymaras', *Desnivel* 169, 2001, pp94-5.

Maps

Instituto Geográfico Militar of Bolivia, 'Carta Nacional', 1:50,000, *hojas* (sheets) Ichoca 6142-I and Yaco 6142-IV, 1991. The Ekkehard Jordan work listed above includes a glaciological sketch-map.

Greenland

Annapurna, Camp One, North Side Looking toward Nilgiri.
Rob Fairley, 1992. (Ink wash drawing. 23cm x 32cm.)

REV BOB SHEPTON

Tilman Must Never Die

Climbs in West Greenland

Climbing on the Starter Walls, Hamborgerland. *(Rob Beddow)*

There were two main aims for this 'Tilman 2015: Sail and Climb' expedition. One was to climb new routes from my 10m, or 33ft, Westerly 33 Discus sloop *Dodo's Delight* in various locations as we wended our way south down the west coast of Greenland from Sisimiut where I had left the boat for the winter. The other was to sail the boat back across the Atlantic home to Scotland after three years in the Arctic.

The team this year were not the 'Wild Bunch', those talented professional climbers, including Nico and Oli Favresse, who came in 2010 and 2014 and made those superb climbs in Greenland and Baffin, but the 'Mild Bunch' – that is to say ordinary non-professional climbers doing more ordinary routes. Our team comprised Rob Beddow, Patrick Deacon, Mark McKellar and Trystan Lowe. Rob left us in Nuuk where Martin Doble joined as mate.

I was quite happy that they were going to climb at a lesser standard, but I have to confess to becoming a little disappointed on occasion that they were not more ambitious and did not push themselves harder, tending to stick to shorter routes within their comfort zone. But at least this did show that there is scope for first ascents in Greenland to be made by 'holiday' climbers doing ordinary routes.

Routes on Afternoon Sun Wall, Starter Walls, Hamborgerland. Six routes were done here, ranging from 25m to 155m and from VS to E3. *(Bob Shepton)*

The east face of Shark's Fin, Maniitsoq, where the team climbed the expedition's most substantial lines. *(Bob Shepton)*

A glorious exception to this were two fine routes on the dramatic Shark's Fin as I dubbed it, alias Kin of Sal, a sudden and strangely British name on the Danish maps and charts (we were unable to discover why), where the team really worked themselves to climb well above their standard on steep, sometimes loose, rock at E4 6a (280m). I had hoped this was a prelude to them continuing to stretch themselves for the sake of making new routes, but then I have always been fanatical when it comes to the chance of making first ascents, and maybe I had been spoilt by sailing and climbing – and rapping on subsequent lecture tours, oh dear! – with the Wild Bunch.

And the team did make a number of first ascents on the west coast of Greenland. We went down the long Evighedsfjord, an old stamping ground of Tilman's and where Denise Evans had climbed Mt Attar, the second highest summit in Greenland, some years ago. At the far end, from the offshoot fjord of Sangmissoq, Patrick and Trystan walked 3km up the edge of the glacier to the south-east to a rock buttress at the far end and climbed a route on the right hand side: *The Rocky Road to New York*, just E1 because of the last pitch, 5a, 100m. There was plenty more potential here but a lot of the rock was wet for reasons that will be explained in a moment.

Already in this fjord we had been brought up against another difficulty which became even more apparent when we moved south to the Hamborger land/Maniitsoq area with its tremendous potential for climbing new routes: the mountains were still in winter mode with snow right down to sea level. As the manager of the Maniitsoq hotel put it: 'this year in Greenland winter has lasted longer than in the previous 47 years.' We had only brought rock climbing gear expecting it to be summer.

One of the results of the late winter was that snow beginning to thaw at the top of rock walls made some potential routes wet. All the same the lads found a wall, which we named 'Starter Wall', quite close to the convenient anchorage of Agpamiut off Hamborgerland Sund, some of which was dry. Here they put up six new routes from E1 to E3, 25m to 120m, a good introduction to rock climbing in the area, on two different walls of the crag. In this category they had also slipped in two shorter routes high up on the back of the second summit of that Kin of Sal after their glorious sally on the main wall, *The Invisible Werewolf* (E3 6a, 100m) and *Rotten Rabbit* (E1 5a, 100m), on 'the best rock so far'.

But many of the potential walls were up glaciers and with limited alpine gear they felt reluctant to thread their way up the snow-covered glaciers, with possibly concealed crevasses, to potential climbs. We did go off 30 miles south to another potential crag as it appeared on the rather inadequate (for climbing) Saga map, which turned out to be a dramatic looking ridge. They set off from the boat to attempt it with enthusiasm but again it turned out to be guarded by a huge snowfield and they aborted. I was initially disappointed, but when I saw the pictures later I saw their point! So the alpine-type ridge of Finnefjeld remains inviolate as far as I know.

On the way south to Nuuk there was some tricky pilotage through islands and rocks in the by now dusky night to examine yet another fjord which might yield some climbs. It didn't but on the way out we discovered a fine anchorage in sand, unusual in rocky Greenland, which we duly wrote up for the *Arctic and Northern Waters* pilot book. Discovering and making a note of suitable anchorages along this huge coastline where there is still so much to be explored could almost be added as a third aim of the expedition.

Arriving at Nuuk we investigated the network of fjords to the north and east for climbing but again the team were put off by the fact most walls were long, big and sheer for at least some of their length. To abort halfway would have been complicated. But Rob and Patrick did tackle the long ridge that included Nakaigajutoq (1180m), requiring five pitches of roped climbing to get up its narrow, if not quite knife-edge start. Boat to boat it took them 25 hours. We thought this might have been a first ascent but they had found some tat and it turns out some Norwegians had completed the ridge previously. It was probably the first British ascent then, and at around TD.

It was ironic that when we searched the fjord immediately east of Paamiut and they found a crag a little inland from a subsidiary fjord which they liked, the mist stayed obstinately over the area even though it was clear elsewhere. It obscured the climbs and after waiting two or three days and re-visiting Paamiut because we were short of loo rolls, we finally gave up and motored south in mist and no wind a hundred miles to the Kap Desolation area (Nunarssuit). Here we made an intriguing anchorage in the channel between Kap Thorsvalden and the line of islands at its foot, which had the advantage that the numerous icebergs in the area had not found their way in, except for one which was fortunately stretched too deep under water to reach us. The lads also found a rock slab/wall round the back of the big headland

Above: Trystan Lowe on the first ascent of *Midnight Sun* (E4), east face of Shark's Fin, Maniitsoq. *(Mark McKellar)*

Below: Lowe nearing the top of *Midnight Sun. Dodo's Delight* can be seen below. *(Rob Beddow)*

Sailing in the beautiful Evighedsfjord, where both Tilman and Denise Evans visited and where plenty of climbing potential remains. *(Bob Shepton)*

and put up two routes, *The Lost World* (E1 5b, 170m) and *McKellar's Pilates Masterclass* (HVS/E1 5a, 100m). An attempt on The Thumb, a prominent spire we had sighted across the other side of the fjord to the west was aborted owing to loose rock and them 'freezing', climbing in cold mist all day!

The Atlantic crossing back to Scotland was also successfully accomplished, but not without its usual stormy adventures. A depression just

A shot of Hamborgerland, illustrating the climbing potential. *(Mark McKellar)*

south of Iceland threw a spider's web of isobars right across the Atlantic from Greenland to Scotland and beyond. We went south to get round and hopefully to pick up some west winds to the south. We hove-to for 26 hours at one occasion because of stormy conditions, on another a huge wave hit the side of the boat and burst open a repair I had previously effected, shooting water into the cabin. The wind instrument gave up the ghost and the crew had to sail by the feel of the wind. Two of them had not sailed before; if I was slightly disappointed in some of the climbing, I was impressed with their endurance, good humour and sailing.

Routes Summary
Though winter conditions lasted longer this year than in the 'previous 47 years' on the west coast of Greenland, a team on Bob Shepton's yacht *Dodo's Delight* made first ascents of rock climbs in various areas on the west and south coast of Greenland.

Evighedsfjord
Or 'Eternity Fjord', an old stamping ground of Tilman's. Denise Evans climbed Mt Attar (2190m) here a while back. There are some rock walls with glacier approaches off this long fjord. Many 'alpine' peaks still require first ascents, though it is difficult to discover what has and has not been done.

Sangmissoq Buttress (N65° 48' W52° 14')
The Rocky Road to New York (E1 5a, 100m, Deacon, Lowe, 10 June). The buttress is visible 3km up the glacier to the SE of the end of Sangmissoq Fjord off the main fjord. The start is on far right (east) side of crag, a short scramble up loose grey rock leading to red rock.

Hamborgerland/Maniitsoq Area
To my knowledge no rock walls have been climbed here to date. All routes were pioneering adventures. There are a number of rock walls to be climbed including north faces. Also much scope for alpine ascents of prominent peaks, 1,000m to 2,000m from sea level, when equipped with suitable gear for glacier approaches. We only touched the edges of the huge potential

Patrick Deacon climbing *The Rocky Road to New York* (E1) on Sangmissoq. *(Trystan Lowe)*

Hamborgerland: Starter Walls (N65° 40' W53° 06')
Not far east of Agpamiut anchorage, an obvious extensive but relatively low buttress (100m), with a smaller buttress to the right. Or from the first inlet east of Agpamiut (N65° 39.6' W55° 09.7') go right – less distance to walk! Six new routes, VS to E3, 25m to 155m, give a good introduction to climbing in this area. Further details are available on request. Climbing team of Beddow, Deacon, Lowe and McKellar.

Shower Head (E1 5a, 40m)
Welly Welly Flaky (VS 4c, 55m)
Saucy Badger (E3 5c, 40m)
Friday Night Fever (E2 6a, 25m)
Chimney Sweep (E2 5bc, 155m)
Hallelujah, It's Raining Moss (E1 5b, 110m)

Maniitsoq: Shark's Fin
Also known as Kin of Sal, or 'Big Heart' in Greenlandic, an island off the SW corner of Maniitsoq Island.

East Face (N65° 26' W53° 04')
Two notable pioneering routes on left side (facing) of this prominent steep wall. Technically challenging and some loose rock. Both teams climbed well above their usual standard to complete these bold climbs.
Midnight Sun (E4 6a, 280m, Beddow, Lowe, 28 June)
Dusk 'til Dawn (E4 6a, 280m, Deacon, McKellar, 28 June)

West Face
This cliff was 'round the back' on the second summit of Kin of Sal. Two routes completed starting high up, above the obvious ramp or slab on the right (south-west) side of the crag. Start just to the right of the deep chimney (not climbed). 'Best rock encountered so far.'

The Invisible Werewolf (E3 6a, 100m Beddow, Lowe 3 July). Takes the crack line immediately right of the deep chimney. Technically exacting, varied route.

Rotten Rabbit (E1 5a, 100m, Deacon, McKellar, 3 July). Takes the right side of the large flake to the right of previous route.

A French group based on S/Y Maewan reported climbing a route on the main west face, mossy and some loose rock. The team failed in an attempt to climb the prominent ridge of **Finnefjeld**, 30 miles south of Maniitsoq, as we had not brought alpine climbing gear expecting the usual summer rock climbing conditions at this time of year.

Nuuk
The prominent ridge between Itossoq and Umanap Suvdlua fjords taking in Nakaigajutoq (1180m) (TD, Beddow, Deacon, 8 July). Second recorded ascent and first British ascent?

Nunarssuit/Kap Desolation area: Kap Thorvaldsen
A wall on the next summit to the north, on the east side gave two routes.
The Lost World (E1 5b, 170m Deacon, Lowe, McKellar 28 July)
McKellar's Pilates Masterclass (HVS/E1 5a, 110m Lowe, McKellar 29 July)

JIM GREGSON

A Polar Bear had Wandered by Unseen

North Liverpool Land, East Greenland 2015

The north-west aspect of Farfarer Peak, North Liverpool Land. *(All photos: Jim Gregson)*

After arriving home in May 2014 from a very successful and rewarding expedition in east Greenland, as my wife Sandy womanfully tackled the pile of fragrant laundry and I worked through a variety of kit repairs and refurbishments, our thoughts turned to the prescient words of Tom Longstaff, a Greenland expeditioner in the 1920s and 1930s.

'It is impossible to overestimate the influence of the arctic regions on the life of man in the habitable globe,' he wrote, going on to outline the origins and persistence of the Greenland icecap. Alarmingly, he continued: 'Once it disappeared it probably could not reproduce itself under present climatic conditions.' This was, of course, before the post-war explosion in our use of hydrocarbons, which has accelerated the rate of climate change and global warming. Further on, Longstaff details the *per* capita cost of twelve weeks 'Spartan holiday' in 1928 at £58, or £3,200 in today's money, of which 'passage money' to Greenland was £37. Longstaff got three months of expedition for that price, whereas the modern climber gets a mere three weeks.

Mount Mighty's north face. The 'S' line is *Snake in the Outback*.

Base camp for 2015, North Liverpool Land.

Having become over the last 25 years something of an arctic specialist myself, climatic conditions and expedition costs are issues that have increasingly affected my own northbound ventures. My earliest trips to Greenland took place in late July and August, constrained by the dates of academic vacations, but it became obvious that Arctic regions were suffering more and more from climatic warming with a more rapid onset of summer ice melt and lessening winter snowfall, so that in later years the optimum times for mountaineering expeditions shifted to the tail-end of winter and very early spring. Fortunately for me, early retirement facilitated this change. The costs of going to Greenland however, continue to escalate, eye-wateringly so, which probably explains the still small numbers of people who actually set foot or ski on Arctic mountains each year.

Still, if you really want an adventure in a remote setting then you are likely to find a way to make it happen. By dint of a lot of research I realised there was a splendid area for mountain exploration in the east Greenland location of North Liverpool Land and I was able to go there, first in 2007 with a ski-touring group, and again in 2014 when my group began to tap some more of the mountaineering potential. The only other teams to climb there, to my knowledge, had been two Australian women in 2012.

So for a return visit in mid April 2015, I began recruiting a suitable group of experienced alpinists before Christmas in 2014. In this endeavour I was aided by the beautiful short film the Australians had made, and by my own large collection of photographs from previous visits which showed the array of striking peaks which abound in North Liverpool Land with ample potential for more first ascents. The proposed duration for the trip and its undeniable expense thinned out the numbers but eventually I had a group

Looking east from the Eastern Ramparts, Castle Peak.

of six keen and experienced climbers signed up: Sandy and myself, both AC, and Geoff Bonney from the Climbers' Club, went as we have done for several years, and we were joined by Ingrid Baber (Edinburgh SC), Richard Toon (AC) and Roger Gott (Lancs MC).

Using my longstanding links with the excellent logistics services provided by Paul Walker of Tangent Expeditions International, I was soon able to organise charter flights, food and fuel, specialised equipment, freighting of cargo. A few problems over insurance were eventually ironed out. As my friends and I get older, but no less active and adventurous, actuaries and underwriters seem to want to make life harder for us. Climbing mountains is the easy bit.

We all assembled in good time at Reykjavik and next day drove north to Akureyri from where a Twin Otter charter would take us across the Denmark Strait and the pack ice to land at Constable Pynt/Nerlerit Inaat where there is an airstrip on a delta projecting into Hurry Fjord in the Scoresby Sund region. Our onward journey was delayed for a day as Tangent's Snow Dragon snowmobiles were away from base dealing with the evacuation of a group from the Stauning Alper who had suffered injuries in an avalanche incident. This minor delay allowed us to begin to adjust to the winter cold, and get our 'baggage train' into order.

Loading all of our stuff into Tangent's heavy-duty Siglin sledges, we set out with four snowmobiles on the 80km journey towards the icecap in North Liverpool Land, the weather improving as we went, taking our minds off the jolts and bangs which accompany travel over sea ice and snow-covered tundra. Once over the watershed of Klitdal we dropped onto frozen Carlsberg Fjord and pulled up by the snout of the glacier that

On the first ascent of Farfarer Peak, by the Dennis Davis Memorial Route.

would give us access to the icecap. After a brief recce to assess safe passage, the snowmobile drivers took us up onto the ice and I was happy to see again the superb mountains I recognised from my two previous visits.

GPS navigation easily relocated our base camp position (N71° 21.679' W22° 07.389') at an elevation of 525m and after waving off the drivers we set about installing our tents just 50m from our 2014 site, a safe enough distance to avoid digging up anything unwelcome. I knew from experience that this camp position would give easy access to the mountains, and importantly keep us in sunshine for as long as possible each day. Camping in winter becomes noticeably less comfortable in shade. We worked to get the camp rigged with a perimeter tripwire attached to alarms to alert us to polar bear intrusion. I distributed an assortment of flares and firearms to our four tents for additional safety.

After a morning usefully spent constructing a durable, deep and stormproof latrine, we held firearms drill both for reassurance and to make sure I was not the only person who could use the rifle should it prove necessary. Then we were good to go. For orientation we went on skis, judging the glacier to be safe enough to travel unroped, over to 3pm Attack Nunatak (so-called after a late start made the original 'Noon Attack' Nunatak unfeasible) a couple of kilometres distant. A short scramble took us to the rocky top,

An array of unclimbed peaks in the north sector of North Liverpool Land.

which gave a very good outlook to learn the lie of the land. Three of us had been here last year so we could show the three first-timers what was where. Advice was also offered about mental adaptation to Greenland perceptions of distance; in my experience gauging heights is not a problem, but getting used to distances for peak approach and return is not so easy. This is probably something to do with clarity of Arctic air and paucity of glacier surface features.

Over the coming days, we climbed and skied in two teams, Richard and Roger together, being regular partners from many other trips, while myself, Sandy, Ingrid and Geoff linked up, with Geoff having the odd day off. We adopted what for me has become the Greenland norm: climbing gear and ropes, first aid and survival kit, shovels, plus, for those of us who ski telemark-style, climbing boots to change into, are loaded onto a pulk, which is then left with the skis at the bottom of the peak. This saves carrying everything and also doubles as a stretcher in case anyone is injured.

Our first ascents and new routes soon began to stack up. Initial forays over to the Seven Dwarfs group saw first ascents of two north faces each giving mixed climbing. The rock quality on the Dwarfs is variable, some of it very solid but in other parts disturbingly loose. After these pipe-openers, we went east towards Neild Bugt where there are many fine peaks. On the

Polar bear tracks and, inset, up close.

same day, on opposite sides of the glacier, simultaneous first ascents were made of Farfarer Peak from the north-west, and Lewty Peak by its shining white south face. Then followed a new route and traverse of Castle Peak, which proved the inspiration for Ingrid to construct a special birthday cake for my own celebrations next day.

We interspersed our climbing days with some ski tours and ascents for variation, allowing us to investigate further afield from camp. These outings were very enjoyable and gave us some superb ski descents on excellent snow, two of the best being 'Pulk-hauler's Plummet' and 'Pulker's Plunge'. Both of these delighted Ingrid, as she had acquired the sobriquet of the 'Big Diesel' due to her prowess in towing the laden pulk. Even with a broken telemark binding held together with wire, I found these ski runs to be great fun.

More climbing was done, including new routes on two peaks first climbed by the Australian ladies in 2012. We climbed *Cryogenic* on Longridge Peak, with Richard and Roger also repeating the Aussie first ascent line, and a very fine outing for a new route on the north side of Mount Mighty, *Snake in the Outback*, completed on a very cold day of climbing in the shade. Richard and Roger had a long, long day going down to and east on the southern branch of Neild Bugt glacier to make the first ascent of Lancstuk, one of the highest peaks in the area, especially from their start point quite close to sea level.

A satisfactory outing, particularly for Sandy and me, was the first ascent of Hvithorn by a route on its south face we called *Blanco*, very good compensation for being thwarted at the lesser top of Varmtind in 2014. On our return to camp from this climb, Roger and Richard reported the discovery, not so far from the tents, of the tracks of a big polar bear, causing them some unease. Next day the rest of us skied over to look at this track. Sure enough, big deep footprints with long trailed claw-marks went right along the glacier. Luckily the camp was out of sight and the bear had probably not picked up any scent. He didn't come back, but while I slept with a loaded rifle, Roger admitted he'd had a couple of nights without deep rest.

We made further ski tours and then completed first ascents of two more north side routes on another two of the Seven Dwarfs to add to our list of successes, with a final group outing to the Eastern Nunatak and excursions over Bird Bone Peak and the Carlsberg Crest. All of our ascents were either on snow and ice, or mixed ground. April and May are on the cold side for more technical rock climbing, but there are good potential lines on more solid rock, such as the impressive 400m Tower of Silence, other exposures on the Seven Dwarfs and several spurs on the north side of Mount Hulya – maybe better done later in the year, although that would exclude snow-mobile access. There are still many spectacular unclimbed peaks in North Liverpool Land so it is far from being fully developed. Approach to some of them would probably require different base-camp locations, which might increase the risk of bear encounters. As to other wildlife, we saw ravens and snow buntings, and a lot of Arctic fox tracks including one almost at the summit of Hvithorn.

As our days ticked towards the end of our month in Greenland, I learned by sat-phone that Paul Walker's snowmobiles had problems. To evacuate us he generously arranged to piggyback us onto a Twin Otter ski-plane charter. We would be spared the bone jarring 'bump and bang' of a three or four-hour surface journey. The aircraft landed right by our camp and an old friend of mine, Icelandic pilot Ragnar Olafsson, gave us a quick 20 minute ride back to Constable Pynt. Next morning he flew us back across the sea to Akureyri in Iceland to round off a splendid expedition with lovely weather, lots of good climbing and skiing, plenty of laughter and friendly company and a great experience of the High Arctic.

Routes

Happy (830m), No4 of Seven Dwarfs: N face (Co-ordinates not recorded)
Disneyland (PD+, J & S Gregson, Baber).

Dopey (820m), No5 of Seven Dwarfs: NE face (Co-ordinates not recorded)
Vanishing Gully (AD+/D-, Toon, Gott). Gully and rock ridge.

Castle Peak (780m): N flank (N71° 20.778' W22° 03.322')
Postern Gate (PD, J & S Gregson, Baber, Bonney,). Second ascent by new route. Descent and traverse over the Eastern Ramparts ridge.

Farfarer Peak (815m): NW face and ridge (N71° 21.839' W21° 54.295')
Dennis Davis Memorial Route (PD+, J & S Gregson, Baber). First ascent of peak. Named for Dennis Davis, a friend who made the first ascent of Nuptse in 1961 and died February 2015.

Twin Otter over base camp.

Lewty Peak (855m): S face (Co-ordinates not recorded)
Memorial Ridge (PD+, Toon, Gott).

Mount Mighty (1005m): NE face (N71° 21.391' W21° 58.850')
Snake in the Outback (PD+/AD-, J & S Gregson, Baber, Bonney.) Second ascent by new route).

Lancstuk (1050m): NE face and N ridge (N71° 19.27' W21° 54.45')
First ascent, (PD+/AD-, Toon, Gott). Co-ordinates nearest from N ridge.

Longridge Peak (960m): E rib and face (N71° 23.031' W21° 58.073')
Cryogenic (PD+, J & S Gregson, Baber) Third ascent of peak by new route. Earlier second ascent of peak via original 2012 Australian by Toon and Gott.

Hvithorn (825m): S face (N71° 23.148' W21° 55.925')
Blanco (PD+, J & S Gregson, Baber). First ascent of peak.

Sleepy (740m), No7 of Seven Dwarfs: N face (N71° 20.974' W22° 01.428')
Nanok (PD+, J & S Gregson, Baber, Bonney). First ascent of peak.

Sneezy (c850m), No2 of Seven Dwarfs: N couloir and E ridge (N71° 21.11' W22° 00.40')
Atisshoo, Atisshoo, All Fall Down (D+, Toon, Gott). First ascent of peak.

Eastern Nunatak (620m): W face (N71° 22.574' W22° 01.876')
Second ascent (F, all except Bonney).

Further Reading

American Alpine Journal, 2009, pp154-5.
American Alpine Journal, 2013, pp184-5.
American Alpine Journal, 2015, pp183-4.
Gregson, J, 'The Really Northern Playground', Alpine Journal, 2014, pp167-176.
Gregson, J, *Exploring Greenland: Twenty years of Adventure Mountaineering in the Great Arctic Wilderness*, Vertebrate Publishing, 2012.
Higgins, A K, 'Exploration History and Placenames of Northern East Greenland', *Geol Surv Den Green Bull 21*, Copenhagen, 2010.
Longstaff, T, *This My Voyage*, London, John Murray, 1950.
www.climbgreenland.com

Letters from Everest

Looking towards Skye from summit of Roisbheinn. Rob Fairley, 1984.
(Watercolour. 75cm x 102cm. Private collection.)

ABBIE GARRINGTON

'Write me a little letter'

The George Mallory/Marjorie Holmes Correspondence

In November 2015, Bonhams auction house of Knightsbridge, London sold for £12,500 a lot comprising 10 letters from the mountaineer George Mallory. Purchased by an as yet undisclosed private buyer, the letters span a single year. They begin in March 1923, during Mallory's return from the US following a lecture tour, having given talks reflecting on the Everest reconnaissance expedition of 1921, and the attempt of 1922. The last is written in March 1924 while Mallory was *en route* to his final attempt on Everest and bears the address 'Anchor Line, TSS California.' While the sale of these original letters prevents access to them until further notice, the Royal Geographical Society does hold photocopies of the set, forming part of the George Mallory Collection, the bulk of which is made up of items recovered from Mallory's body following its discovery in 1999.

The recipient of these letters is Eleanor Marjorie Holmes, known as Marjorie, aged 19 to 20 at the time of writing, living with her family at Bentham, Yorkshire, and working as an unqualified teacher at a local private school. It was Holmes who had instigated the correspondence with an admiring letter of her own – a 'fan letter', as the Bonhams catalogue has it. Her side of the correspondence, believed lost or destroyed, reached Mallory when he was working for the Extramural Studies Department at the University of Cambridge, and he advised caution in addressing envelopes in order to secure their privacy and, we assume, to prevent any implication of scandal. On 13 October 1923, Mallory asks: 'do you realise that I really was damned, no, I mean dreadfully angry with you Marjorie, you naughty girl? You tell me you meant to put 'Personal' on the envelope, [and] I have no doubt you did: but that is not the point.' Mallory's caution seems to have affected his subsequent biographers, and these letters are rarely referred to at any length in accounts of Mallory's personal or professional lives. There is, however, no question of impropriety, since Mallory and Holmes never met, indulging instead in what Mallory's contemporary Virginia Woolf referred to as 'the humane art [of letter-writing], which owes its origin to the love of friends.'

The peculiarity of this arrangement, in which Mallory, despite not knowing his addressee in person, used the intimate setting of the personal letter to explore his thoughts on life, purpose and literature as well as the call to climb, struck him as a matter for wonder, and he observes on 26 May 1923: 'I can never write to you without a delighted surprise that we should have travelled so far together without meeting.' While the circumstances in this

Left: 'My chief feeling is: we've got to get to the top next time or never. We must get there [and] we shall. Here a pause while I imagine myself getting to the top.' A sketch of George Mallory by E F Norton, taken from Vertebrate Publishing's elegant reissue of Norton's classic, *The Fight for Everest 1924*. As well as the full original text and illustrations, this edition reproduces some of Norton's superb pencil sketches and watercolours along with previously unpublished materials from his private archive.

Right: Norton's sketch of Andrew Irvine described by Mallory in his final letter to Holmes as: 'a splendid specimen of a man; he rowed two years in the Oxford boat as a heavy weight [and] yet is not clumsily made at all; [and] he is completely modest and has a nice voice which reminds me strangely of Rupert Brooke's.'

instance were odd indeed, the function of the personal letter, as opposed to the letter of public record, as a space where a man might meet himself, might work out the more philosophical elements of his existence, was less so. In fact, Mallory had earlier written to Holmes regarding their mooted future meeting, not so much in anticipation as in dread: 'Still, we're going to meet one of these days. We shall have the presence of our bodies [and] what we see in each other to embarrass our intercourse, [and] then you'll have to be quite at your frankest to get over my timidity. By the way, are you beautiful? I hope not. [...] if you are beautiful then Heaven help us; I shall shut up like a sea anemone.' Rather than the *lack* of a meeting hampering their discourse, Mallory instead suggests that it is just such a confrontation – one in physical form – that will disrupt the communion that has grown up on the page. They are, he implies, nearer when apart; a fine thought for an expedition participant condemned to spending such stretches of time alone, or in company he has not himself selected.

Woolf, a careful thinker regarding the function of the letter as a form, suggests in a letter of her own to Clive Bell in 1932 that the hurried intimacy of the comparatively cheap missive of the early 20th century is precisely its value. Previous generations were compelled by the expense of postage to make a letter 'count,' writing in a manner which anticipates the circulation of that letter from hand to hand within a household and beyond; those of her own time were an opportunity to speak hastily, without reticence, and with a single addressee in mind. 'I'm encouraged by the fact that since our generation's letters can't be published,' she writes, because as a result 'this can be a wild scribble between the lights.'

Mallory's letters to Holmes are his own 'scribble between the lights': letters written outside the glare of his fame, and with no anticipation that they will form any part of his posthumous reputation (in contrast, say, the travel journal).[1] The letters are certainly passionate, but that passion is diffuse, rather than being directed solely, or even primarily, at Holmes: for the power of letter-writing itself; for mountaineering; for writing; for addressing oneself to a particular challenge, and finding one's place in the world. Mallory's own lines hint at Holmes's passionate replies, a kind of ghost correspondence since we do not have her letters. Yet Mallory's ten are worthy of consideration in themselves, providing as they do an insight into the way that the mountaineer viewed his own life and achievements, laid out here at times with an interlocutor in mind, but at others as if speaking to himself, undertaking what Clare Brant has referred to as the travel letter's 'experiments in subjectivity.' The letters also encourage us to place more centrally in our understanding of Mallory the identity to which he was most wedded: that of a writer.

1. These are not intended as letters of record. The other epistolary form, the traveller's diary or journal, is often written with reputation in mind, and may be carried with the body intentionally as a final testament, or else deposited at the last-left camp, for discovery by a search or trailing party. By contrast, the letter sent to a 'nobody' in expedition terms, forms a private conduit for thinking about one's self, life and aims. R F Scott's journals and their public function may well have been in Mallory's mind when thinking of his own posthumous reputation. We should note that Mallory had visited Scott's widow Kathleen shortly before leaving on this final journey, as Robert Macfarlane amongst others has observed.

If addressed by biographers, these Mallory/Holmes letters tend to be mined for presentiments of Mallory's coming doom or, in the case of the last in particular, for logistical or strategic insight into the approaching attempt on the peak. The final letter expresses a particular liking for Andrew 'Sandy' Irvine, who was to join Mallory for his ill-fated summit bid: 'a splendid specimen of a man; he rowed two years in the Oxford boat as a heavy weight [and] yet is not clumsily made at all; [and] he is completely modest and has a nice voice which reminds me strangely of Rupert Brooke's.' Naval officer and poet Brooke has already received a mention in the letter of 26 May 1923, when his poem 'The Great Lover' is commended, and Mallory remarks that 'he was a friend of mine at Cambridge [and] he had that same love of things' which Mallory ascribes to his own habits of thought, allying himself with Brooke's poetic sensibility.[2]

In the last letter of the Mallory/Holmes correspondence, Sandy Irvine's physical fortitude is of interest to Mallory not only in a spirit of admiration for a significantly younger man, but also with the coming climb in mind. Mallory may already have had Irvine in view as at least a potential climbing partner, anticipating reserves of energy that would last out to a final summit bid: 'You know we've got to do it this time; [and] yet it won't be at all easily done. Nor have we come to a conclusion yet as to the best way of trying to do it,' Mallory tells Holmes. In an earlier letter, written on 7 November 1923, Mallory had stated, perhaps with greater confidence: 'my chief feeling is: we've got to get to the top next time or never. We must get there [and] we shall. Here a pause while I imagine myself getting to the top.' The mountaineer finds a visual correlate for that pause in speech, leaving a section of his page blank, before picking up again. That he needs a pause for imaginative mountaineering is anticipated in Mallory's earlier 'Pages from a Journal,' in which he claims that 'It may be harder to think oneself to the top of a mountain than to pull oneself so far.'

Yet there is much in these letters to draw the attention, beyond their contribution to a thorough history of British efforts in the Himalaya. Not only are they a space in which Mallory forms and plays with a selfhood elsewhere constricted by family and public responsibilities. They also contain a valuable set of speculations about the power of the letter as a literary form, in particular its ability to extend the touch of the writer's hand, stretching across the miles to meet the reciprocal touch of the addressee, and its summoning up of the presence of the other. 'Write me a little letter with a word of affection and I would kiss the hand that wrote it,' as Mallory puts it.

2. Brooke's own letter to Edward Marsh of 1912 is more ambivalent: 'Funny your finding George Mallory, I've known him so many years, discontinuously. I'm rather fond of him: but I never have a warm enough affection – no, it's a sharp enough interest I lack – to see him a great deal – I've meant to go [and] find him at Charterhouse [where Mallory was then teaching], but never done it. I always, or generally, have a vague feeling in his presence – as if I'm, momentarily, dull, not he, especially. But what's one to do? But I like him.' In a final Mallory/Brooke connection, William Edward Arnold-Forster, Labour politician and great grandson of Dr Thomas Arnold of Rugby School, married Katherine 'Ka' Laird Cox, the former lover of Rupert Brooke, in 1918. His second marriage was to the widowed Ruth Mallory. Virginia Woolf makes a passing reference to this second marriage in a letter to Angelica Bell of 16 October 1939: 'we've been seeing Will and Ruth Arnold-Forster [...]. The filling in of that story, and the story of Ruth, of Rupert's letter, of George Mallory's death on Mount Everest would fill oh the whole of the telephone book.' Any such letter from Brooke has been lost.

R W G Hingston, expedition doctor and naturalist, captured in affectionate caricature by Norton, probably early in the expedition.

The north face of Everest from the Pang La, about 35 miles from the mountain, in a watercolour by Norton.

The hand that sends a letter to the mountaineer is revered to the point of a courtly kiss; Holmes' presence, and her touch, is both transferred by a letter which bears the traces of her body, and conjured up in the imagination of the recipient. By contrast, Mallory imagines his own writing hand as disembodied, emphasising that which is missing from an exclusively epistolary relationship: 'Can you love a shadow – a mere hand that spins out lame halting words [and] belongs in some way to a name in the newspapers? But words are thoughts, and thoughts are men and women. Can thoughts love each other? Clearly they must.'

It seems Holmes has declared love in her previous letter, prompting from Mallory not only speculations regarding the capacity of letters to allow such strength of feeling, but also consideration of his fame as a kind of lightning rod for female affection. Whatever his doubts about the validity of Holmes's feelings, and whatever his scruples as a married man about discussing such sentiments, Holmes becomes intensely present to him through her letters, an effect which borders on the marvellous. On 4 October 1923, Mallory asks: 'Why should a letter from you have a strange effect on me? – Strange effect? Well, only this, that after reading it I wanted to kiss you. He wanted to kiss a girl he'd never seen – curiouser [and] curiouser [...]. If she's a scolded child she's a kissed child, spiritually kissed by a man she never set eyes on.' Sending letters, as well as receiving them, could create such a summoning up of the other party, and the fact of never having met appears no barrier: 'Farewell to you now – my holidays all unrelated – but you a figure more distinct, and nearer, and – yes – dearer. So dear Goodbye.'

This process of imagining into being the absent interlocutor is clearest in Mallory's letter to his wife Ruth in 1922, from which Macfarlane quotes at length: 'I am conscious of you at the other end [of this letter-writing process]; and very often dearest one I summon up your image & have your presence in some way near me.' While these are lonely images – the distant adventurer peoples his solitude with imagined loved ones, so vividly that they take on physical form – Mallory is excited by this conjuring power, and repeats the implication of his bashful imagined meeting with Holmes: that this particular form of discourse might be superior to all others. Writing on 31 July 1923, he claims that 'the letter which proceeds from the real desire to tell things or still more which is inspired by some curiosity or excitement in the spiritual presence of the imagined recipient can be the best talk in words, the best of all.'[3]

If letters to Holmes provided a space for Mallory's 'best talk in words,' it was certainly the case that he remained concerned for the other aspects of his literary output as well. Holmes, we gather from Mallory's replies, has stated an interest in becoming a writer, and he formulates his own status as man of letters using the pose of mentor. In that 31 July 1923 letter, Mallory praises William Henry Hudson, and a note in the archives records the fact he sent Holmes a copy of Hudson's *A Shepherd's Life* (1910), a delivery which is somewhere between a gift and an imposed education. 'Have you by the way seen the two Everest books?' he asks on two occasions, 'I should like to think you had read my chapters.'

Yet his concern is not only with passing on his writer's wisdom to a coming generation, but also with establishing a sense of his own influences, placing himself within a genealogy of landscape writers. In the last letter, *en route* to Everest once more, he declares that 'My reading on board so far has been chiefly [André] Maurois' Life of Shelley, or Ariel, he calls it. Ariel is a good name for him for all that he was never so sad as poor Shelley. Do you know Shelley? One of the greatest spirits that have appeared on earth [and] a man of such moral beauty that I feel dazzled in his presence – I can't tell you how profound a feeling I have for Shelley; he has influenced my life more than any one; when I read Shelley I become like the sensitive plant [and] tremble.' The mention of 'spirit' here sticks with the Ariel theme, and nods toward Shelley's 'Spirit of Delight' or 'Rarely, rarely, comest thou', which Mallory had recommended in his letter of 26 May 1923.

It also refers to the only material to which Mallory at time of writing would have had easy access: that contained in poet laureate Robert Bridges' *The Spirit of Man* anthology of 1915, taken on the expedition for common use, which, we should note, is 9.6% Shelley by entry. David Robertson

3. Mallory was himself the subject of conjuring practices the following year. Subsequent to his death alongside Irvine, Britain's mountain fans experienced a revived interest in spiritualist séances, as mediums attempted to contact the pair to ask if they had reached the summit, and where it was they now lay. See Hansen.

has recorded that the expedition party reached for the Bridges collection following a particularly bad night at camp III. It is curious that Mallory again commends the vivid and emotionally affecting qualities of writing, and Shelley is, like Holmes or Ruth, summoned by his imagination; he quakes in Shelley's *presence*. It may be that the two central themes of Mallory's letters to Holmes (the power of the epistolary form; his own literary legacy) are linked, since he suggests in his 31 July 1923 note that 'The act of detachment, of planing [sic] off to some other world from which this one may be viewed, is often the genesis of literary work.' The letter's function as a free space for contemplation might permit just such literary beginnings, and it may be this as well as Holmes's requests for guidance in her writing career, that makes literature a central topic in their correspondence; he works out ideas here he may go on to use elsewhere. However, the shift to another world or plane and its value as a catalyst for literary production, might also be read more straightforwardly as the thought of a literary mountaineer: getting high, either physically or in imagination, will get the literary muscles working.

In the previous letter, 23 July 1923, Mallory adds a disclaimer that clarifies his present status in literary terms: 'you might think from one part of my letter that I am a much experienced writer. That is not the case [and] yet I have constantly had writing in mind [and] have gone on writing at intervals though little has been published.' The ever-sensitive Mallory might have perceived the gap between his ambition and his reputation here, given that his lectures and essays were accused during his lifetime and after of excessive complexity and over-writing: too much Shelley, perhaps?

In reviewing David Pye's memoir of Mallory in 1927, 'E F N', presumably Edward Felix Norton, rehearses the faults in Mallory's literary endeavours but, crucially, identifies his particular talent for letter-writing: 'The book quotes extensively both from Mallory's letters and from his more serious literary work. The former are always preferable: his letters are vivid, picturesque, and discursive – recalling those of a bygone generation when men had time to take letter-writing seriously as a branch of literature. His more serious work is often too verbose, and it is sometimes hard to follow him in all his flights of introspective fancy.' These claims confirm that Mallory's writing was not consistently well thought of, in part explaining his anxieties about his abilities, and his intentions, as outlined to Holmes, to continue to develop his literary skills.

Yet they also suggest that he is one of the last great letter writers, a man allied to earlier generations in this respect, and perhaps Woolf is his companion in this. Uncomfortable with his status as 'a name in the newspapers,' the 'scribble between the lights' of dashed letters, often written on the move, permitted not only speculations about his subjectivity, life achievements and future plans, but also a level of literary skill unencumbered by public expectations. The correspondence with Holmes shows us that Mallory writes best when no one (but Holmes) is watching. Part of his work in these letters, even with the clarity of hindsight taken into account, is surely a loose

E F Norton's watercolour of the hamlet of Rongli-Chu in Sikkim. Now a small town, the old temple bell has an inscription in Nepali that reads: 'Rongli was a dense forest in the early days, which had a small path that lead far to Tibet.'

Mallory and Irvine are conspicuous by their absence in this team photo taken at the end of the 1924 expedition. From left to right, back row: Hazard, Hingston, Somervell, Beetham, Shebbeare; front row: G Bruce, Norton, Noel, Odell.

and easy first attempt at writing his own obituary. Read in this way, we should take seriously the claims set out here for Mallory's status as a writer.

In the letter of 15 January 1924, Mallory binds the two sides of his life, the mountaineering and the writing, by metaphorically linking the written line and the rope line of the belay, suggesting that 'words spelt in ink twist a line as one writes to throw over [and] tie to oneself that other one.' That climbing and writing were, for Mallory, linked at a fundamental level is no surprise. That the exploration of those intertwined ambitions appears most compellingly in the epistolary form is something that is clearest in these ten often-neglected letters. Credit is due to Holmes, who was sufficiently wraith-like and half-imagined to count as a 'between the lights' correspondent, yet vividly present enough to draw out the most philosophical speculations of a reticent man. And as Woolf states in her *Three Guineas* of 1938: 'Without someone warm and breathing on the other side of the page, letters are worthless.'

References

Brant, Clare, *Eighteenth-Century Letters and British Culture*, Basingstoke, Palgrave Macmillan, 2006.

Brooke, Rupert, 'Letter to Edward Marsh, 25 February 1912', *The Letters of Rupert Brooke*, Geoffrey Keynes (ed), London, Faber, 1968, p360.

Hansen, Peter, 'Modern Mountains: The Performative Consciousness of Modernity in Britain, 1870-1940', *Meaning of Modernity: Britain from the Late-Victorian Era to World War II*, Martin Daunton and Bernhard Rieger (ed), Oxford, Berg, 2001, pp185-202.

Macfarlane, Robert, *Mountains of the Mind: A History of a Fascination*. London, Granta, 2008.

Mallory, George, 'Copies of Letters from George Leigh Mallory to Marjorie Holmes', Royal Geographical Society, LMS/M48, 1923-4.

Mallory, George, 'Pages from a Journal', *Peaks, Passes and Glaciers*, Walt Unsworth (ed), London, Allen Lane, 1981, pp171-81.

N, E F, 'Review of *George Leigh Mallory: A Memoir* by David Pye', *The Geographical Journal*, 70.2, August 1927, pp181-2.

Robertson, David, *George Mallory*, London, Faber, 1999.

Woolf, Virginia, 'The Humane Art'. *The Essays of Virginia Woolf* Vol 6, (Ed) Stuart N. Clarke. London: Hogarth Press, 2011, pp225-9.

Woolf, Virginia, 'Letter to Angelica Bell, Monday 16 October 1939', *Leave the Letters Till We're Dead: The Letters of Virginia Woolf* Volume VI: 1936-1941, Nigel Nicolson (ed), London, Hogarth Press, 1980, pp363-4.

Woolf, Virginia, 'Letter to Clive Bell, February 1932', *The Letters of Virginia Woolf Volume V: 1932-1935*, Nigel Nicolson (ed), London, Hogarth Press, 1975, p26.

Woolf, Virginia, *Three Guineas, in A Room of One's Own and Three Guineas*, Hermione Lee (ed), London, Chatto & Windus/Hogarth Press, 1984, pp107-268.

JACK LONGLAND

8 June 1933

Jack Longland was among the most influential figures in British mountaineering in the 20th century and a key player on the 1933 Everest expedition, arguably the best team to have attempted the peak before the Second World War. In this previously unpublished letter he describes to his father the crux period of the expedition and the trials and tribulations of life at altitude.

My dear Daddy,

We are in the middle of a short peaceful interlude – and feel just like troops in comfortable billets, but with the thought of the frontline a day or two ahead present in our minds nearly the whole time. Still, base camp seems quite incredibly civilised and warm and peaceful. We came down two days ago, to find all the snow melted, and a little bathing-pool constructed, and little mosses and saxifrages coming out, and room to stand up in the enormous-seeming Whymper tents, and a mess tent for meals, and, it is not possible for you to appreciate the importance of this: fresh vegetables, and large meals appearing without our having to stir a finger to cook or wash up!

I'd been away from base camp over six weeks, and during that time we've had the hell of a hammering, as you've probably been gathering from the papers. Worse weather than any of the previous expeditions experienced, and lasting over a much longer time. We've simply smashed all records for living at high altitude – I was well over a *month* living at over 21,000[ft] of which over a fortnight was spent at camp IV, 23,000[ft], or above. And every step we've had to fight for; first of all living in blizzards just under the north col, at the exposed camp on the upper glacier plateau at camp III A. From there day after day working the route out to the col, not the easy snow trudge of 1922, but a steep snow and ice climb equal to a difficult Alpine route, and almost every foot of which had to be fitted with fixed ropes to make it safe for porters. And during this period so much new snow fell, that the route had practically to be made again, not once, but half a dozen times. I think I went up to the col five times by this route, before actually going to live at camp IV, either remaking it, or taking up parties of porters to stock camp IV. That was the first phase, 8 to 19 May, when we hoped all the time that the weather would clear and give us the long settled period that previous expeditions had had. And just at the end of this time we got the added shock from weather reports that a very early monsoon was expected, and might be on us almost any day.

Then, on 19 May, Lawrence Wager and I came up to IV to stop, escorting our last lot of porters and loads, quite a long job, as there is an ice cliff, up which we had fixed a rope ladder, just below the camp, and here the porters had to be brought up separately on the rope. We were several days later in coming up than we had hoped, as weather had cut us off, and when communications were reopened with IV, the first thing they wanted up there was food, and not two extra hungry mouths. The plan at that time was that Boustead, Birnie, and Wyn Harris should establish camps V and VI, and then Wyn and one of the others go on to make the first reconnaissance, followed a day later by Frank Smythe and Shipton as the first assaulting party, and then by Lawrence and me as the second. This plan was formed more or less in accordance with the state of the party, Frank and Shipton being by far the best acclimatised at this period, Birnie being a transport officer, supposed to be specially good at handling porters, Boustead something in the same category, and Wyn Harris having acclimatised very rapidly, was chosen to lead the reconnaissance party, being a much more experienced mountaineer than either Birnie or Boustead. I had acclimatised pretty slowly so far, each journey to a new height giving me a good deal of trouble, and so I was put with Lawrence Wager to make up the second assaulting party. All the others mentioned had been at camp IV nearly a week when we two arrived, and so were fairly well in advance of us in acclimatisation. The day we arrived at IV, they had been making an abortive attempt to get the porters up to camp V in a fairly high wind: they only got just over halfway, and then Birnie and Boustead turned the party back, saying conditions were too bad for the porters. This unfortunately caused a fairly serious split, as Wyn, by far the most experienced, was convinced they should have gone on to V – *and*, of course, we had lost a day in the middle of wretched weather, with the loads dumped only half way to V.

Sir Jack Longland's portrait for his presidency of the Alpine Club. *(Alpine Club Photo Library)*

The army 'transport officer' section hasn't been much of a success on this show; Hugh Boustead always playing for his own hand, and would have been a positive danger high up on the mountain, if he'd ever got there, as he's pitifully slow and insecure on ordinary moderate rock and snow, no mountaineer at all. And Bill Birnie, besides being not much use as a climber, has a perfectly appalling dignity and temper, which only develops at high altitudes, and caused a ludicrous series of scenes. This expedition has proved over and over, that this mountain needs mountaineers first and foremost, and that these other specialists are unnecessary, and may be an infernal nuisance. It's been a very happy party, and the *only* trouble we've had at all has been from people like Birnie and Boustead, charming as they both were down at lower levels.

Anyway, next day Hugh Ruttledge came up to IV (Eric and Frank meanwhile failing entirely in a reconnaissance up to V in *really* bad conditions) and there was a rather bad row, ending in Boustead nearly getting sent down the hill, and being put firmly in his place, and Wyn being put in full charge of the camp-pitching and reconnaissance party, so that the sole decision as to turning or going on could be his. And to strengthen his hand Raymond Greene was added to the party, in the hope that he might do the reconnaissance with Wyn, if the latter wanted a mountaineer with him, and not one of the 'soldiers'.

Well, we all set out next day up towards V, Lawrence and I accompanying them for training, and to bring down the unwanted porters. At about 24,000ft one of the porters collapsed completely, and someone had to bring him down, so I volunteered, as being probably slightly less acclimatised than Lawrence at that time. Had a terrific job getting the porter down, as he would go about 30 yards and then collapse completely and say he was dying – having to be persuaded to his feet each time and sent on down. Well, we got down in the end, and shortly after returning porters began to come in with messages that V had been established at about 25,700ft, much higher than in any previous year: so we felt pretty sanguine that next day they would pitch camp VI proportionately higher. Then came the first setback: Raymond Greene came staggering in about six in the evening, absolutely all in, with a badly enlarged heart. That meant he was practically out of the show for good – he had reached V, but the effort had finished him completely. Also it was rather a blow for me, as Lawrence Wager had stayed up at V to take part in the reconnaissance instead, so I had lost my climbing companion for the second assault, with no hope of an effective substitute since Tom Brocklebank could not get fit, Ferdie Crawford could not be expected to get beyond V, and George Wood-Johnson, my one really solid hope, had just been sent down to base camp with a bad gastric ulcer.

Then came three bad days, during which the V party were stuck in their tents by conditions, except that Smythe and Shipton went up to stop on the second day, and Wyn and Lawrence came down to relieve congestion. After the third night, the three of us took a scratch lot of porters out to try and relieve V, and had got up to about 24,500ft when we met the other party on the way down from evacuating V, pretty well all in, and somewhat demoralised. So we turned as well, as weather was awful, and followed them down.

That was the first real reverse, as opposed to mere delays caused by weather. And when we got down to IV, we found of the 10 picked porters who had been three nights at V only about two were fit for further action, three bad cases of frostbite, other ailments and morale collapses. So here were our 'tigers' apparently finished with already. Several of the sahibs had slight frostbite also, and Hugh Boustead had obviously had about enough, and as his leave was now nearly up, he decided to go down to base camp on his way home.

So things didn't look very bright, and now in addition after the new falls of snow, small avalanches began to fall on to the shelf on which camp IV was pitched. So we decided, a little prematurely I think, since Frank Smythe is always scared stiff of avalanches after his Kanchenjunga show, and Ferdie is over-frightened of north col after *his* avalanche experience in 1922 – we decided to evacuate IV, but in an *upward* direction, to put two tents right on the north col itself, and a skeleton force of sahibs and porters in occupation.

So there we were, another scraped together 10 porters, whom we hoped would prove equally 'tigrish', in one arctic tent, and six of us in the other, Frank Smythe, Shipton, Bill Birnie, Wyn Harris, Lawrence Wager and myself – about the windiest and most exposed spot you could imagine, right on the narrow backbone of the pass, propped on the edge of the world. A day's rest, to give our porters a chance, and then up that weary slope towards V again, with all 10 porters and Wyn, myself, and Lawrence. Bill Birnie was supposed to come up with us, as transport officer, to urge the porters on, but he had a damaged leg, and though he started with us, he was soon miles behind, and we thought he had turned back, as indeed we urged him to do, by a note sent down by a porter who went ill.

I got to V pretty tired, my first visit – the other two rather fitter, especially Wyn, as they'd already been up before. We arranged that I should go up with them to help pitch camp VI and bring the porters down safe, and were just turning in when to our consternation Bill Birnie arrived, some five hours after us, indomitable indeed, but extremely foolish, since he could do no possible good up there, only taking up room and food. So, rather disgruntled, I shared a small tent with him that night.

We couldn't start early next morning, high wind and bitter cold, but eventually decided to try our luck and got our porters away at 8am. Very cold, in spite of sun, and I fancy most of us got touched with frostbite in those first hours. We left Bill Birnie, already almost a sick man, in his tent – a curious comment on the alleged necessity for transport officers who can speak fluent Nepalese, for camp V had been pitched almost solely by Wyn's efforts, and here was I going off as transport officer to pitch camp VI!

Lawrence took us rather a difficult route, over those eternally outward sloping slabs that make up this face of Everest – all right as long as you stand up boldly, but no belays at all, and a slip could hardly possibly be checked. I was pretty nervous for the porters, but they came along splendidly, with the occasional encouragement by me at the tail, for the lamer ducks! Hours seemed to go on, and it got a little less cold; I was very tired, but certainly no more so than the day before, in fact I think I went a little better between V and VI than between IV and V! Certainly one was well enough acclimatised not to get the amount of panting that Norton describes, and Wyn was going at what seemed almost Alpine pace. Finally about 1pm, just as I was insisting that the porters must turn back, if they were to be sure to get down safely, we reached a place where a platform for one tiny tent could be dug out of the snow, some 200ft below the ridge, and well on the way towards the First Step – height about 27,300ft or a good 500ft higher than man has ever put a camp before.

I don't remember much about my sensations, as I sat while the tent was pitched – everything is rather dulled, and one's brain certainly not functioning at anything like the usual speed or precision. I do remember looking at the final pyramid, and thinking it looked very close and not very hard, and then round the horizon to see that one was higher than any peak that could be seen on this northern side, and also a feeling of regret that somebody had to take the porters down and that I couldn't join Wyn and Lawrence on their attempt tomorrow.

But I soon had plenty to think about – I'd decided not to take them down our difficult route of the morning, but to strike right across towards the old camp VI, on the north ridge, and down that, the old 1924 route, to camp V. Had to get them down the infernal Yellow Band first, a longish and anxious job, and then, just as were crossing easier ground to the north ridge itself, a blizzard came on, with driving snow and bitter cold, which reduced visibility to about 30 yards – no joke at all as I'd never been on the upper part of the ridge before, and it was broad and ill-defined, and might easily be strayed from. The next hour-and-a-half were pretty nearly the worst I've ever had on a mountain, stumbling down snow-covered rocks and icy screes, trying to keep the porters together, half of them fit, and half very tired and inclined to sit down and give up. And never a glimpse of the big ridge down to the north col, so that I could get my bearings. Then we suddenly hit on Mallory's old camp VI, still quite recognisable, and found his lantern there, and one of those handle-pressing electric torches (which still worked, after nine years exposure!) – and I felt happier for the next bit, until I remembered I had heard that the old 1924 camp VI wasn't on the ridge at all, but on a subsidiary buttress to the east. I pulled a photo of the mountain out of my pocket, and sure enough the camp VI seemed to be marked on a little ridge, which ran out on the appalling ice slopes above the East Rongbuk glacier, and here was I leading a party of porters down it, and never a gap of visibility of more than 50 yards! I tried to keep my head, and edged them over to the left, where I knew I should find a great snow couloir if I was on the wrong ridge. When I couldn't find it I was a bit happier, but I didn't get much rest, what with the uncertainty and the storm, and the fear that the weakest of the coolies might refuse to move at all, until I saw the green tents at V, when I was only about 100ft above them. Lord, that was a relief!

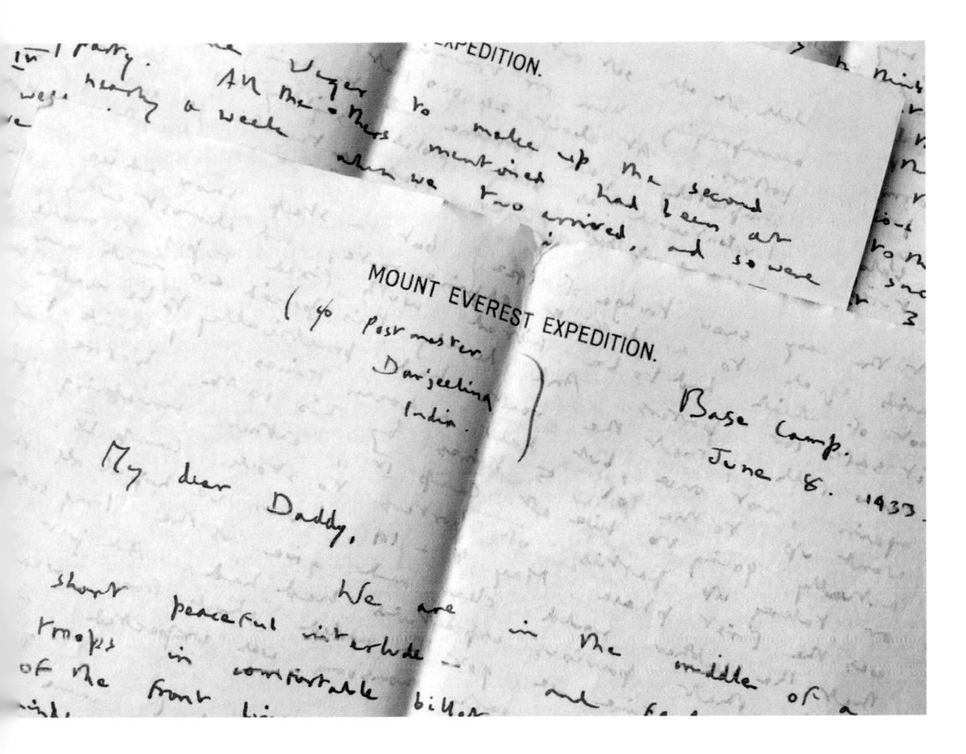

At V Eric and Frank had come up for the next shot, but that silly ass Bill Birnie had stayed on, ill though he was, so there was no room for me, and I had to push on down to IV. With the relaxation of tension, and after the storm all the way down from VI, I was very tired indeed already, and didn't relish the 2,500ft down to the col. But I gave the porters half an hour's start, all except two, who were so done in that they decided to spend the night in the porters' tent at V, and then staggered on down, with the storm still continuing – and cursing Bill Birnie good and proper. I was moving so clumsily that I was frightened of falling off, and it was really a relief to find, some way below Finch's old camp, a porter who was obviously worse tired than I. So I gradually shepherded him down towards IV, encouraging him not to give up, and just before dark, about 6.30pm, the welcome figure of Ferdie came out to meet me: that was a relief too, as I was afraid I was coming down to an empty tent, and would have to cook my own supper – but luckily Ferdie and McLean had come up in support, and I was well and truly looked after that night! It had been a hard day, especially the worry of getting the Tigers down safely in those conditions – but now they *were* down, they were frightfully pleased with themselves: they knew they had carried higher than coolies had ever carried before, and that they had beaten up the *first* lot of chosen Tigers, and that they would now be going down to base camp for a drink and a rest.

Willie McLean, as doctor, soon pounced on me to overhaul me, and I found I had come off pretty lightly: two fingers and a cheek very slightly touched by frostbite, and a heart showing signs of strain, but not actually enlarged – all of which was pretty good.

Then came four rotten days, sitting about in IV, not knowing, or only knowing intermittently, what was going on above, alternating between optimism and pessimism, and confidence and anxiety. I picked up Wyn and Lawrence through the telescope at about 7am next morning, moving well under the First Step – then clouds came down, and we didn't see the mountain for some hours, and all through the afternoon no sign of them, though I searched the mountain pretty thoroughly. And all the next day we waited for news, pretty nervous, till Wyn and Lawrence came in in the late afternoon, very much done in, having stopped at V the night before. We were pretty disappointed to learn they hadn't climbed the thing – they had intended to try along the ridge, but had been lured downwards along easy ledges, and had finally been forced on to Norton's Traverse. Wyn had got across the couloirs, and reached a height a bit above that gained by Norton, only to be stopped by snow lying on very steep rocks. In fact, and we had not expected this, they were turned by actual technical climbing difficulties.

Still we were thankful to see them down, and hoped better things of Eric and Smythe. We saw Wyn and 'Waggers' off down to III next day, both still pretty done in, with enlarged hearts and frostbite and bad throats, and then sat down to wait for the other party. All this time Bill Birnie was lying more or less sick at V, no use to us, since he could not communicate, and precious little use to the parties returning from higher up, since he lay in his tent and did very little as a support. All next day we waited without news, the mountain mostly under cloud, and our nerves suffering pretty badly – we sent Ferdie Crawford down as he was none too well, leaving Willy McLean and myself to wait for the others. Then next morning, a clear one, came the worst moment of all, because I picked up in the telescope a *solitary* figure leaving the tiny tent at VI and slowly moving downwards. So I was prepared to hear of a smash, in which Eric or Frank had been scuppered; then, a couple of hours later, I saw two figures leaving V and coming down – but I still could not make out if the two *included* the figure I had seen leave VI, or whether he was still above V, in which case it meant that all three, Birnie, Smythe and Shipton were safe. I left Willy McLean to cook soups and other comforting things, and went out myself with hot brandy toddy in a Thermos to meet the others coming down. I was much better acclimatised than before, cut about 200 steps in the fresh wind-crest snow to give them a good path in, and found the way up towards V much less laborious than before.

Eric Shipton was the first I met, about three-quarters [of an] hour up the slope – and he explained what had happened. They had lain in the tent at VI one whole day of weather, that on which they had hoped to examine the Second Step, and on which Wyn and Lawrence had come down to us at IV, that cost them a day's reconnaissance and a day's strength, and then yesterday they had made their full shot, by Norton's traverse. Eric Shipton, through lack of sleep and food, had given out only an hour from camp VI, and had returned. Frank Smythe going on by himself, to reach almost the same point as Wyn had reached, on the steep part of the final pyramid beyond the couloirs, only to be stopped, early in the day at 10am by the same technical difficulties, snow on steep loose rocks, as had stopped Wyn. Eric went on down to V that same evening, nearly getting done in by a bad storm on the way down, to leave Frank to have a more comfortable night by himself in the tiny tent at VI. That explained why I had only seen *one* figure leave VI the next morning. I left Eric, after a drink, to get down to IV, and went on up the ridge to meet Bill Birnie, coming down slowly a long way behind, with frostbitten feet, and in a state of pretty general debility! He revived a bit after my magical Thermos, and was able to carry on by himself, while I went on still further up to meet Frank Smythe, whom I had seen a long way behind. He was very tired when we met, having come down all the way from VI in a bad storm, much what I had experienced when getting the porters down – so I escorted him slowly down to IV, very thankful to have all my chickens in at last!

Next day, everybody showing signs of wear and tear, we evacuated the camp on the north col, meeting porters coming up with Shebbeare, and taking a lot of stuff down from the old deserted camp IV on the avalanche-liable shelf below. We had a new patient on our hands that day, since Willy McLean, who had never been comfortable at IV, collapsed almost completely, something to do with lungs and oxygen lack, and had to be shepherded down by Eric Shipton – who himself got sunstroke on the way down, so that by the time I had got Bill Birnie down to camp III A with his bad feet and various ailments, I found Willy McLean lying comatose in a tent, and Eric Shipton, in a state of almost entire aphasia, unable to speak a single full sentence! But we finally got everybody down to III, Willy pretty well carried between two stout porters, and found Hugh there, with Wyn and Lawrence waiting to go on down, still in a state of pretty general tiredness.

On 4 June began a general exodus to base camp for repairs and refitting – Ferdie Crawford and Tom Brocklebank straight through to camp I, Waggers, Wyn, and myself escorting Bill Birnie, whose feet gave him trouble, and who took a coolie's shoulder all the way down, down to II. The glacier had changed extraordinarily, most of our well-known landmarks having gone, and we realised what has been increasingly clear ever since, that if it was storm and frost and wind on the mountain, it has been steadily getting warmer and warmer all this last month down the glacier, until this comparatively balmy climate at the base camp is reached. On 5 June we came right through from camp II to the base [camp], feeling happier and happier the lower we got, till one could almost have wept to see the blue sky over the once desolate seeming Rongbuk valley, and rows of cumulus clouds marching across the distant Tibetan plain, exactly like summer clouds over the plain at Cropthorne. [*Editor's note:* Jack Longland's father, Rev Ernest H Longland, was vicar at Cropthorne from 1927.] Bill Birnie we had to leave behind at II, as he could not stand on his feet any longer, so he arrive with Eric the next day, being carried in turn on the backs of good stout coolies, all the way from II to here.

Jack Longland's camera from the 1933 Everest expedition made by Ernemann of Dresden. A folding camera with a bellows and rising front, it had an aperture of f3.5-f22 and shutter speeds of 1s to 1/250s. The body weighed 750g, and that was without a film pack, which added another 310g. It was donated to the Club by Jack's daughter-in-law Deborah Newman, a former assistant secretary at the Club. *(Alpine Club Photo Library)*

One day later the last of the lame ducks came in, Willy McLean, with a strong man on each side of him, and Hugh to escort him down.

So here's the state of the war, home billets, and a general attempt to fatten up. And we need it – I've lost about two stone, and you know I hadn't much fat on me – I literally never have been so thin in 10 years, and my muscles have simply disappeared. And everybody who has been really high is in comparable state. Well, we hope to gather the cripples together, and put in a last shot after four more days here of recuperation. We hope for a skeleton swiftly moving party, probably Smythe, Shipton, Wyn, Lawrence, and myself (if hearts have gone back into shape by then) with Ferdie and Tom Brocklebank in support, and an attempt to push straight through to IV in as many days, and then launch two attacks in the next week. Much longer we cannot stand, we haven't many porters, or provisions, and we certainly haven't the physical strength for another prolonged attack such as the last. Ferdie Crawford still talks glibly of another attack if this fails, in August, after a period of recuperation in the Kharta valley, but there are limits to what flesh and blood can manage, and I am certain that those who go high on this next attempt will have nothing left in them for any more. I don't think our chances are high this time, but they're certainly not negligible – we shall try first along the ridge towards the Second Step, to see if we can pass there through this wretched vertical grey band which runs all round the mountain, and has so far spoilt our chances. We should be back in Base camp before the end of June – and I hope that means home well before the end of August. Tell Mummy to get in all sorts of fattening food for when I come back – I hope to have all September to eat in! I'm really surprisingly fit, only very tired, and only wanting to get this old mountain finished off this next shot, and to get back. But it's been a very good fight, and I think we've done more than has ever been done before, and against far worse conditions.

With much love to everybody, and in great envy of the heatwave, which the wireless tells us you are enjoying just now.

Jack

PS 9 June.
Very nice to get your last letter, just arrived, describing Cambridge in May, and Charles' linguistic experiments, and everybody going off for picnics in the sun!

No cable arrived about the Adelaide business – but I'm writing to the London Board to turn it down: it was a very tempting amount of money to someone wanting to get married, but I'm getting very good at turning jobs down – seem to have been doing it for the past eight or nine years now! – till someone takes me at my own estimate, I suppose! But Adelaide was a bit too thick [*Editor's note:* Longland had been offered a professorship at Adelaide University on an annual salary of £1,100.]

Two days of regular monsoon weather here, and the mountain showed up last night *completely* coated with new snow and looking quite inaccessible. But we hope our last plan starts tomorrow, Ferdie and Tom going up the glacier in advance to remake the way; then Eric Shipton and myself on 12 June, and Frank Smythe and Wyn on 14 June. Lawrence Wager is out of it, as his heart hasn't come back to shape yet. If monsoon weather allows, that means a couple of shots (Eric and I will have the privilege of first bang at the Second Step!) round about 20 to 22 June. But Lord knows what weather and mountain will do.

The Everest Flight photos have caused some amusement, as quite half of them (including the frontispiece and the main double page of *The Times* special supplement!) are not of Everest at all, but of Makalu and other peaks in the neighbourhood!

I think home before the end of August is a fair forecast at present – may even catch the old [SS] Comorin again, which leaves Bombay on 5 August!

Perhaps Peggy [Harrison, Jack's fiancée] might like to see this long screed eventually, but send it on to the Head first, if he's been seeing my letters to you. [*Editor's note:* Rev Cuthbert Creighton (1978-1963) was Jack's housemaster, and later headmaster, at the King's School, Worcester. Creighton regarded Jack as one of his most outstanding pupils.] Writing this in bed before breakfast, and a much better looking morning – must get up!

Much love to everybody.

Jack.

Editor's note: Jack Longland used this letter as a way of recording his experiences at the climax of the 1933 expedition; his diary finishes in early May before the events described took place. Although supplies for a further attempt were moved up to camp III, the advancing monsoon put paid to further climbing. Expedition leader Hugh Ruttledge asked the Mount Everest Committee for a small group to remain until later in the year but there were no funds. Longland would withdraw from the 1936 expedition on principle, unable to offer his unconditional support to Ruttledge.

Art & Literature

Tibetan Trader
At weekly market in Namche Bazaar.
Rob Fairley, 1998. (Watercolour. 20cm x 14cm. Sketchbook drawing.)

JOHN PORTER

The Mountain World of Ken Wilson

The gospel according to Wilson. Few mountaineering publishers in the English-speaking world have come close to the impact Ken Wilson had in the 1970s. His coverage in *Mountain* of the Cairngorm tragedy in 1971 was influential and exemplary.

'Ken is the most considerate of men: the brash ones usually are. They're hiding their feelings behind the hard words.' Tim Lewis, *Mountain 59*

'[Mountain] captured the profound changes affecting climbing at that period and Ken proved a relentless guardian of the soul of mountaineering – as he saw it.' Doug Scott, *Up and About: The Hard Road to Everest*

In today's media-rich world, suffused with tweets and video footage of the latest Font 8b problem available on Vimeo within seconds of its completion, it is difficult to appreciate how revolutionary Ken Wilson's *Mountain* magazine was when it first appeared in 1969. Bernard Newman, former editor of both *Mountain* and the *AJ*, summed it up:

> *'Gone were the stuffy, cramped journals that hadn't moved on since Victorian times, and in came the glossy, visually stunning, and supremely readable spreads of Ken's vision. Mountain was a crucible for top-quality writing, photography and rigorously accurate information gathering, all powered by Ken's unrelenting attention to detail combined with peerless photo editing. It's often quipped that you haven't climbed a peak in Nepal unless Liz Hawley says you have. Well it was Ken you had to get past in those days, after a thorough grilling to provide a "plausible scenario" for your claims.*[1]'

For six months in 1974-5, I worked for Ken at *Mountain*, on issues 40 to 45 to be precise, over the winter and into the following summer. I knew Ken, had climbed with him on his visits to Leeds, and found him good company, if a bit abrasive, always quick to remind me that I was a 'Yank.' But it was a fluke I ended up working for him.

It wasn't Ken who offered me the job. That was Chris Brasher, who was in the process of buying *Mountain* from Ken in late 1974 and recruited me as editor. As an ambitious journalist, Chris saw opportunities to take the 'new look' magazine to a wider audience. The popularity of the BBC's outside broadcasts featuring climbing and the sport's heightened media profile pointed to new consumer interest.

Ken wanted to offload the magazine to take on a new challenge, creating a publishing company specialising in mountain topics. He had edited *Mountain* for five years and, prior to that, the last two editions of *Mountain Craft*, the only independent climbing magazine in the UK in the 1960s, but looking tired when Ken took over. With the development of *Mountain*, Ken created a media platform that mirrored the changes taking place in climbing, and for that matter, in society as a whole.

At the time of the job offer, I was floundering with my 'PhuD' at Leeds University, having spent more time climbing than researching and writing. It came on the back of my editorship of the *Leeds University Union Climbing Club Journal* in 1974. I was shocked but delighted when Brasher gave me the call. The *Leeds Journal* was clearly amateurish compared to *The Observer* where Brasher regularly appeared as a feature writer.

For a week or so, Brasher and I travelled around the UK, meeting existing correspondents and contributors to reassure them and discuss the direction we should take *Mountain*. Our final call was Ken's local pub in East Finchley to agree final details of the sale over a pint. Ken and Chris went into a huddle in a corner, while I joined the north London climbing regulars,

1. From the Climbers' Club Newsletter December 2011 on Ken being awarded honorary membership to the CC.

Ken Wilson on Everest in 1972. According to Doug Scott: 'He might have seemed trenchant in his views, but Ken was never consumed with self-importance.'

including an old friend from Leeds, Dave Cook, soon to be appointed national organiser of the Communist Party of Great Britain.

As we sat swapping news, there was a sudden altercation. We turned to see Ken lean towards the dapper Brasher, wearing his trademark cravat, and then cup the great man's face in his hands before vigorously slapping him on the cheeks. It was like a scene from the *Three Stooges*. Chris was not about to take part in any slapstick. Turning red with rage, he exited the door, stopping momentarily to throw a few blustery insults in Ken's direction. I wondered whether I could catch the last train that evening to Leeds.

Ken, pint in hand, came over to join us, still chortling. 'I can't let *Mountain* go to someone who thinks it's just another publication to make a bit of money. The deal's off.' Ken paused then turned to me, his watery eyes full of mischief. 'So, Porthole, you might as well come work for me.' The nickname annoyed the hell out of me. Ken knew that, and I knew this was a test. The only way to impress Ken was to stand your ground and not hesitate. I accepted immediately.

Ken had previous with editors of the *Leeds University Climbing Club Journal*. Bernard Newman had come to work for him after his 1973 edition – far better than my 1974 effort. Yet Bernard had survived London for three months. Could I outlast him?[2] Next day, I found a bedsit within walking distance of Ken's office in the back of Ken and wife Gloria's house on Sylvester Road.

'Okay, you'll work fulltime and then some,' he warned. 'Come in at 9.30am, make Gloria and me a cup of tea, leave it on the landing upstairs, then open the post.'

My apprenticeship had begun. By 10.30am every morning, Ken was in the office, going through the articles and news items that had come in the post. Then he would be on the phone, checking facts, commissioning, arguing, demanding, bullying or being amazingly charming, depending on what he was after. He was the consummate journalist. The radio was always tuned to the 'Light Programme' – Radio 2 today. Rock music was the domain of the pirate stations. Ken would occasionally interrupt, either singing along or shouting at the announcer. Lunch was always sausages on white bread with brown sauce, with endless cups of tea throughout the day and well into the night.

My first task was to edit the international news. 'Make the language clear, consistent, factual – key dates and people – capture the drama, but remember *Mountain* readers include climbers in Japan with only high school English. You have to be universal.'

No easy task I thought when it came to obscure outcrops on sodden British moors, but it was great advice. Foreign readers bought the magazine for its international news. No other climbing magazine in the world had correspondents in most major climbing areas on just about every continent but nothing was printed without evidence. The phone was rarely on the hook; the bill was astronomical.

Ken usually collected that day's work at 5pm. We would then have an hour or two on layout and planning future editions, sometimes three issues in advance. The walls, desks and cabinets were papered with A3 sheets amounting to 58 pages with covers. I sometimes walked back to my bedsit at 8pm but it was much later most days. As printing deadlines approached, after midnight, I often drove Ken's car through London's deserted streets, as they were at night in the 1970s, to Waterloo Station, bundles of completed layouts with photos and text attached on the front seat ready to go 'Red Star' down to the printer in Dorset. Most nights, there would be galley proofs to collect for final checks.

In the morning, after making tea and opening the post, I would work through Ken's heavy red underlines, deletions and margin comments on copy I had edited the day before. Then I'd sit down at the typewriter to redo – laborious work. I thought I was getting better with each news item, but the red didn't diminish for the first six weeks. One day I slipped some of Ken's copy into a bundle of my own. Next morning, the red pen had been used equally on both sets of news: 'Sorry Ken. Some of your news on Gogarth seems to have got mixed up with my Himalayan stuff.'

2. Bernard later returned to *Mountain* in 1978 under the ownership of Paul Nunn, Tim and Pat Lewis and became the magazine's longest-serving editor.

Wilson on the last pitch of Tennis Shoe, Idwal, as a young climber. *(Ken Wilson Collection)*

He looked through the items, appearing bemused by his avid use of red pen on his own copy. Then he looked up and smiled with his characteristic mix of inquisition and mockery. 'Well done Porthole – you've learned the first lesson.' The use of the red pen was fully deserved but far less frequent in the months that followed.

Apart from news of developments worldwide, the magazine fed its British audience on a diet of often controversial articles from lead climbers of the time: Pete Livesey, Bugs McKeith, Al Rouse, Alan Fyffe and Joe Tasker, to name a few from those issues. Their articles were not only about new climbs but the development of climbing techniques, grades, ethics, outdoor education, equipment and the use of chalk. Ken called those who used chalk the 'powder-puff kids'. In a notorious headline in *Mountain 43*, he censured John Allen for using the stuff to free Great Wall on Cloggy. He fought the use of expansion bolts to greater effect; their use by Cesare Maestri on Cerro Torre was never far from the pages of *Mountain*. But Ken could change his mind when the tide turned against him; he overcame his distaste for chalk when he discovered why all his mates were using it.

Livesey's piece 'Castaways on Gritstone Island' in *Mountain 42* was a classic example of Ken's ability to gather photos of the key players and new climbs of the day to bring an article to life. Black and white was still preferred for rock climbing in those days and Ken would spend hours in his dark room drawing out minute details and maximizing the chiaroscuro effects of light and shadow.

'If there are no photos, go get them!' was his maxim. 'Photos that give you sweaty palms and make you want to be there: snap, snap, snap!'

Counterpoint and controversy underpinned *Mountain*'s articles and reporting. In the same issue, Livesey was criticised in a letter from Muriel Files for serious errors on Lakeland history. In a subsequent edition, Paul Nunn and Ed Grindley took the criticism further, accusing him of rewriting history for his own glory, and of being unethical: inspecting and practising routes, and pre-placing protection. It is no coincidence that the steadfastly ethical New Englander Henry Barber appears on the cover of *Mountain 42*.

Live issues were fiercely contested and Ken carefully selected what those issues would be: the use of obscenities for example. In *Mountain 41*, for example, under the heading 'Gratuitous Vulgarity', John Shorter wrote:

> *'... I regret that I shall not again renew my subscription unless the magazine ceases to acquiesce in the encouragement of vulgarity. The phrase "creative relevance", which you use to justify the printing of an extraordinarily blasphemous and obscene expletive of eleven syllables, seems to me on a par with the sociological jargon in vogue today, which is used to justify anything which anybody wants to do.'*

This and similar letters received were in response to an excellent if visceral article entitled 'Hands' in *Mountain 37* by Anne-Marie Rizzi.

Ken mined the seam of this controversy for several issues. Here's David Hewett's response in *Mountain 47*:

> *'[previous correspondents] seem to imbue expletives with an almost mystical power. The words themselves are nothing; indeed they are in most dictionaries. Do Messrs Shorter and Langdon... hide dictionaries from their children?'*

Anyone familiar with Ken's passionately egalitarian philosophy will appreciate this debate was not just a question of literary licence. The real issue was the use of expletives by a woman. Ken defended the female voice in climbing with gentlemanly vigour. After Ken joined the Climbers' Club, he immediately took them to task for the club's men only membership. Here's Bernard Newman again[3]:

> *'The club Ken joined was an all-male setup, a concept difficult to grasp in this day and age, but by no means unheard-of back in the Swinging Sixties. Ken proposed that the word "gentlemen" be changed to "persons" in the section on eligibility in the rules. The membership present at that AGM, presided over by John Hunt, naturally thought the change was to dispense with outmoded wording, but Ken explained, honourably, that it meant women would be allowed to join the club. It was voted out. It took several years, several AGMs and Ken's resignation (with others' including Martin Boysen and Ed Drummond) to get it passed, eventually during the presidency of Hamish Nicol in the early 1970s.'*

Despite the strident and serious nature of debates in the pages of *Mountain*, Ken was not the ogre many thought him, and as some prefer to remember him today. He enjoyed telling stories that displayed his own weaknesses and foibles, as capable of laughing at himself as others. *Mountain* regularly featured the sparkling humour of Ian McNaught-Davis; articles such as 'After Dinner Speaking Made Easy' and 'In Memoriam.' The latter examines the vanity of climbers who feel the need to leave a lasting legacy, especially members of the Alpine Club:

> *'Perhaps the final stroke for remembrance is the intended last request of a good friend (happily still climbing) whose ambition was to die at the age of 87, shot by a jealous husband, and to have his ashes ceremoniously flushed down the famous echoing toilet of the Alpine Club.'*

I wonder what Japanese readers made of Mac's esoteric images. Another popular feature Ken introduced was the 'People' column, edited by Audrey Salkeld. Audrey unearthed individuals making contributions away from the headlines in areas like mountain medicine and equipment design, and in the arts and literature. With contributions from Mac, Audrey and sub-

3. Climbers' Club Newsletter December 2011.

editors Mike and Lucy Pearson, *Mountain*'s scope broadened to encompass subjects rarely found in mountain journals, the style always informal, readable and 'newsy.'

A month or two after I arrived, we picked up two 'Yanks' from Heathrow in Ken's new but battered Ford Cortina. Yvon Chouinard and Michael Covington had flown in from Nairobi. Ken stuffed our visitors in the back seat. Yvon was half buried behind a huge sack. They were in the UK for a bit of cragging before going home having just made the first ascent of the *Diamond Couloir Direct* on Mt Kenya. Ken knew Mick and Yvon from a tour of the American climbing scene in 1973 and had stayed in touch.

As the late May dusk brought the sky alive, Ken swung off the A5 and headed for the centre of London. Yvon and Mick were about to be given Ken's famous guided tour. This consisted of crossing six bridges over the Thames, starting with Tower Bridge. When the Houses of Parliament hove into view crossing Westminster Bridge, Ken ranted about the increasing influence of the nanny state. Then Ken fired endless questions about American climbing achievements and ethics over his shoulder at Mick and Yvon. The somewhat wary Americans tried to answer this inquisition as best they could. After Vauxhall Bridge, the car was pointed towards the hospitality of Ken's office and home.

As we drank tins of McEwan's, more or less the only beer you could find back then, we took down their story and then drifted into more general climbing topics: chalk, pre-inspection, use of photo topos and so on. Ken was still vehemently against the use of chalk mainly because it provided a map of the holds but also because it despoiled the look of the crag. But at the same time, Ken also was the first to make use of photos to unveil the secrets of the great faces in the Alps and Himalaya. The following issue, *Mountain 33*, had a centrefold of colour photos from Dick Renshaw's and Joe Tasker's winter ascent of the *North Face* of the Eiger that unveiled its secrets and left little to the imagination for those that followed.

Yvon and Mick engaged politely, but this was Chouinard before political activism on environmental and conservation fronts. And Covington was definitely more interested in going climbing than talking about it. Ken suddenly changed tactics. He began to rant against the government's impending legislation to make wearing of seatbelts a legal requirement. 'The next thing they will impose top-rope climbing only and everyone will have to be insured for rescue, or they might ban climbing altogether,' Ken ranted, quite literally spitting mad.

Ken had a point, and he was not the only one worried. The solicitor Martin Wragg wrote that the seatbelt legislation was indeed the 'thin end of the wedge.' He predicted it would lead to further attacks on personal freedoms. There had been an ominous cloud hanging over the debate on outdoor pursuits following the deaths of six young people in the Cairngorms in the winter of 1971. Odd statements were being made from politicians: 'there are only a handful of people in the world who could survive a night out in Scotland in the winter.'

In the summer of 1960, Wilson hitchhiked to the Tyrol for a Mountaineering Association alpine course. Wilson is on the left and Wilson's childhood friend Dave Cook second from right. Cook, a leading British communist, died in a cycling accident in Turkey in 1993. *(Ken Wilson Collection)*

The UK's disparate club structure had no consistent representative voice, but this was changing as the British Mountaineering Council gathered pace under the able leadership of Dennis Gray. Ken supported the BMC despite general opposition from the majority of climbers who felt the organisation was part of a government conspiracy to impose regulation on climbing through the Sports Council. Ken realised the truth was the exact opposite: the BMC was essential to fend off government interference. Dennis Gray advertised in *Mountain* for a new post, that of national officer, a post soon to be filled by Peter Boardman. Even so, British climbers were sceptical, something which emerged in the letters pages of *Mountain*.

Ken finished his brief history of UK climbing politics and the Americans sat somewhat bemused. With the beer finished, they were no doubt thinking about crawling into their sleeping bags. Suddenly, another light came on in Ken's head, and he turned on the two Yanks. The western world was facing a petrol shortage as OPEC countries turned on America's policy in support of Israel. President Gerald Ford had placed a speed limit on all roads in America to reduce fuel consumption.

'And you Yanks, with your big fast cars and open highways. What the hell are you doing going along with a 55mph speed limit. You ought to be ashamed of yourselves.'

There was a slight pause, then Mick said: 'Well, you know Ken, not everyone wants to drive fast in the States like here. We like to enjoy our big open spaces. When we go on a road trip, we have a case of beer handy, light up a joint and well… 55mph seems just fine.'

We laughed, but Ken turned red, knowing the conversation was not going any further. The Americans set off for Wales next morning.

Ken's obsession with seatbelt legislation reveals his view that risk is an essential driver in climbing, crucial for both creativity and pleasure. I disagreed with him on this, as did many others in later years. The management of risk rather than risk itself is what fascinates most climbers. But there is a misconception that key players in the alpine-style revolution of the 1970s and 1980s blamed *Mountain* for generating a state of competition that led to accidents. Nick Colton, for example, took exception to the idea that climbers thrived on risk, but he never criticised *Mountain* for its policy of reporting where to find 'the last great lines' or for any direct responsibility for accidents. But for reasons known only to Ken, he began to believe that such accusations were being made, even though Ken knew better than anyone that freedom of choice had to be coupled with responsibility for your own actions.

Ken also believed, sometimes obsessively in the early years of *Mountain*, that top-class climbers were driven largely by their competitive nature. I agreed to some extent. Competition is part of the character of many well-known climbers, but not necessarily all the best climbers. Ironically, some of today's most famous 'adventurers' are those who take the least risk. I doubt Ken saw that coming.

His fascination with competition was in part shaped by his early exposure to the North Wales climbing scene and its race to claim the best routes at Gogarth. In the last days of *Mountain Craft*, he even went so far as to create a league table of the best climbers based on the number of new routes they had done there. But as Doug Scott pointed out in *Up and About*, Ken was never afraid to put counterarguments in *Mountain*. His new approach brought some stern and thoughtful reprimands from climbers who saw mountaineering as a way to bring people closer to a natural state, among them Bugs McKeith and Rob Wood who had left the UK to experience the wild spaces of the Canadian Rockies away from the pressure and competition of needing to do more with less in the UK. In Ken's later work as a publisher at Diadem and Bâton Wicks, there was a shift toward encompassing and understanding the complexities of what happens 'when men and mountains meet' with the publication of compilations such as *The Games Climbers Play* and *Mirrors in the Cliff*, and the reprints of Shipton and Tilman.

That attitude, held by the often silent majority of climbers, was perhaps best summed up in a letter to *Mountain* by another Canadian climber, Brian Greenwood: 'to the majority of climbers climbing is still something separate from the crass materialism of everyday life, please try and keep it that way for us.'

Still, you had to read the magazine to know when to protest, and we all did. It was the oracle of modernity and barometer change in mountaineering.

Leader of the gang. Wilson, centre, with from left to right, Wilf Jarvis, Graham Ricketts, Bob Grandfield and Dave Smith in Snowdonia in 1957, when Wilson was 16. *(Ken Wilson Collection)*

Even the purist could not hide under a boulder. As Tom Patey commented: '*Mountain* was the magazine that all climbers were seething about.'

Ken was always looking for the state of the art: nothing else was good enough for him. He believed that to achieve the highest levels of performance in life, as in climbing, required dedication, trial and error and a determination to experiment. He briefly introduced banner-style headlines, beginning with *Mountain 42* but after two issues had modified the layout and largely gone back to the earlier style after complaints that the new graphics made *Mountain* look like the *Daily Express*.

One of my jobs was to do the accounts, pay bills and sort out tax. While processing a bill from our printer, I discovered that all the itemised costs – colour reproduction, 'hot' typesetting, various proofs, paper, ink, shipping, etc. – were sub-totalled and then there was one final item on the bill: the Wilson Factor. This put another 10 per cent on the final total. Ken was not around so I phoned the printer to query this: 'Ah the Wilson Factor... we agreed that with Ken after the first couple of magazines. It is the additional costs of his quest for perfection. We sometimes run off a couple of hundred front covers with Ken overseeing the run, insisting on minor adjustments to the tint and hue until he is satisfied. We have to cover those costs but we always bow to Ken's judgement and want to do the best for him.'

As we moved *Mountain* briefly from six to 10 issues a year, the intensity of the work increased and more of my time was needed on editorial work and copy editing. Ken decided to employ an admin assistant to do many of the basic tasks like accounts, post, and booking appointment and meetings. He duly interviewed and appointed the woman he though best suited but with one firm instruction: 'Don't come in until 10am after John gets here. He'll show you what to do.'

The lady wanted to impress her new boss so decided to come in at 8.30am on her first Monday. She let herself quietly in, collected the post and went to the office. At 9am the phone rang. Ken ran downstairs stark naked, charged into the office and stood shouting down the phone with his back to the corner where the new appointment's desk had been located. The woman froze, and remained frozen for 10 minutes while Ken carried on an animated discussion, buttocks and privates swaying to and fro. Ken only turned around when he banged the phone down. He stood full frontal, shocked by the sight of the now terrified woman before him:

'I told you not to come in before 10am.'

She gathered her bag and was never seen again.

As I gained ability and confidence, the editorial work was not only enjoyable but it brought me close to many people for whom I had a huge respect. I transcribed, edited and laid out an interview with Fred Beckey. It was easy bringing to life such a fascinating character. Chris Bonington's 1975 Everest expedition dominated the Himalayan news for a time, and I travelled to meet some of the team and interview Chris before their departure. Ken, curiously, did not give them much chance. I took a difference stance in my news item, praising them for their excellent preparation, innovative equipment and planning.

Other editorial tasks were more demanding. The copy for a major feature on the Mont Blanc massif by André Contamine arrived as a set of badly translated notes about each mountain. I had to write the article from scratch and learned a huge amount in the process. In *Mountain 41*, we began a series by Oscar and Norman Dyhrenfurth on the world's 25 highest mountains, beginning with Nanda Devi, ending in *Mountain 66* with a major feature on Everest. For a short time, I was in regular communication with Norman.

Perhaps the most harrowing interview we did was with Sir Edmund Hillary. He arrived at Ken's on time and as planned one warm April evening despite the fact that his wife and daughter had been killed when their plane crashed taking off from Kathmandu only a couple of weeks earlier. Ken invited Ed into the dining room and we sat around the large table. Ken came straight to the point:

'Ed, I can't say how sorry I am about your wife and daughter. If this is not a good time, we can just go for a bit to eat and do an interview some other time.'

'Now's as good a time as any,' said Hillary. 'Nothing is going to change the facts and having a good chat about life and climbing might even do me some good.'

With that, Ken produced a tape recorder, a bottle of malt whisky and three glasses. Four hours later, all the tapes were full and the bottle was empty. The interview appeared in two parts after I had left the magazine, but I had the pleasure of transcribing and editing the piece before I left.

I told Ken I was leaving in the middle of July. I explained that while I was writing about climbing, I was not getting much of it done, apart from the occasional days when Ken and I would hare up to the Peak District: eight hours driving for a few hours climbing. I was missing the mountains, especially on those many days when I found myself reading and writing about what my climbing mates were doing. Ken didn't want me to go, and we both became quite emotional. But I was done. I agreed to take a last batch of proofs to Waterloo Station that last night before heading up the M1 in the Mini the job had allowed me to buy. I took the opportunity to say goodbye to London following Ken's guided tour over its bridges before finally turning north.

Ken Wilson died on 11 June 2016 while this article was being prepared for publication. A full obituary will appear in AJ 2017.

Ken Wilson at Tremadog in the early 1960s. *(John Harwood)*

JOHN CLEARE

Some Thoughts on Mountain Photography

The Weisshorn from above Wildi by William Donkin: a powerful composition using the natural geometry. Note how the shape of the mountain is echoed – inverted – by the interlocking spurs, always a good ploy, while the hay huts establish a positive foreground. *(Alpine Club Photo Library)*

Were it not for the pristine Dru, the glacier snout and the undeveloped Chamonix valley, this fascinating picture of Donkin's could well be a contemporary composition. The Montenvers shoulder forms a natural middle-distance while the foreground is anchored by the pine trees, obviously carefully arranged to overlap the dark shoulder; although if my camera position allowed, I'd have moved the tree top slightly more left to avoid the convergence of powerful lines. *(Alpine Club Photo Library)*

'From today painting is dead!' the French painter Paul Delaroche claimed in 1839, taken aback at seeing early Daguerreotype images – the first photographs. But while painting remained as vital as ever, the revolutionary art of photography, essentially painting with light, the offspring of physics and chemistry rather than pigment and artifice, developed apace.

Photographs were taken *on* the mountain, as opposed to of the mountains, quite early on: the first were possibly shot in 1860 on the summit of Mont Blanc, the work of Joseph Tairraz, progenitor of the celebrated dynasty of Chamonix photographers. In 1865 the Rev H B George, editor of the *Alpine Journal* no less, took Ernest Edwards, a London professional, around the Oberland glaciers to shoot pictures for a book. The fledgling *Alpine Journal* was swift to use the new art form, publishing Edwards' work as its first photograph, 'The Jungfrau from Steinberg Alp', in 1865, just two years into the *Journal*'s publication.

Cameras in the second half of the 19th century, though large and heavy, were handsome instruments of mahogany and brass with surprisingly good optics and mechanisms, but the lengthy exposures necessary demanded unwieldy tripods. Lens panels were mounted on leather bellows while

I like this picture. Vittorio Sella shot this on the Songuta Glacier, probably during his 1898 Caucasus foray. It has a casual air about it while still being a useful geographical illustration. Sella has manoeuvred to balance the foreground glacier table with the powerful background shapes and I can just hear him cry: 'Lean on the rock! Relax! Now hold that pose for ten seconds.' *(Alpine Club Photo Library)*

lenses were focused on a ground glass screen with the photographer's head shrouded under a 'dark-cloth'. There was scope for innovation and the Rev George invented his own miniature camera that weighted only 4lb and fitted onto his ice axe; it never caught on.

A major constraint was the 'collodion process', coating a plate in a wet chemical mix of iodide and cellulose nitrate on which the image was recorded. The fragile glass plates had to be coated immediately before exposure and processed immediately afterwards. They also took a long time to absorb light.

Sella's classic 1888 picture on the Glacier Blanc in the Dauphiné: the faultless composition has great depth, holding interest all the way from the foreground to the Écrins massif in the far distance. While the figures are perfectly placed, the leader's inquisitive stance – held for the longish exposure – is the touch of a master, adding a completely new dimension. *(Alpine Club Photo Library)*

In 1879 Vittorio Sella constructed a rudimentary darkroom on the summit of Monte Mars, a notable rock peak of 2,600m near Aosta, in order to shoot a 360° panorama of the Pennine Alps. He used 30cm x 36cm glass plates in a camera weighing over 30lb. However, 'faster' dry plates using a gelatine base were under development, and when Sella shot his 12 plate panorama from the Matterhorn summit three years later, he was able to use them.

Sella (1859-1943) was a master technician with a true artist's eye, adept at placing small figures in just the right place to give scale to his compositions.

His English friend William Donkin (1845-1888), an equally outstanding photographer, was hon secretary of both the AC and the Royal Photographic Society. A dark room wizard, Donkin's superb prints have remained immaculate in the AC's collection, comparing favourably with duotone prints of a century later. On an alpine day Donkin preferred to carry his own camera gear, leaving the essential tripod, the climbing gear and the sandwiches to his guides. He was famed for his speed of operation: 'ten minutes was all he needed to make a shot!' Had Donkin not disappeared on Koshtan-Tau during his second Caucasus expedition, it's likely his fame would at least have equalled that of Sella. But with exposure times of many seconds, minutes even, true action images were beyond even their contemporary equipment.

As mountaineering and rock climbing evolved and more difficult routes were climbed, so too did the technology and performance of cameras and film – and the ambition of photographers to record what they were doing rather than merely what they saw. One of the first action climbing photographs known was shot in 1893 by Lily Bristow showing Mummery fighting his eponymous crack on the Grépon. There's no record of the camera she used, but unable to erect her tripod on the small stance, she relied instead on Geoffrey Hastings' head for support.

After dry plates came the invention in 1884 of flexible roll film by George Eastman; the firm Eastman Kodak was established in 1892. Soon small, simple, highly portable roll-film cameras appeared. Aimed at the general public, initially the cameras had to be returned to Kodak for processing. Eastman claimed: 'You press the button, we do the rest.' It's difficult to make a mundane mountain or crag situation appear dramatic and exciting – should that be your aim – but by the turn of the century there were climbs that were photogenic and cameras and film that could record climbers climbing them. Though the results were pretty rough, by 1900 many alpinists carried such cameras and the two decades before the First World War saw the first climbing photographs to depict action.

In Britain the Abraham brothers, George (1872-1965) and Ashley (1876-1951), professionals based in Keswick, dominated not only the mountain photography scene before 1914, but also played a major role in the exploration of British rock, proving it was possible to be both a dedicated photographer and a leading climber. Their equipment was little different, if rather more sophisticated, from that of twenty years earlier; they still used glass plates and a tripod remained axiomatic. For that reason they were still unable to portray action as we see it today.

Left: The Aiguille Dibona in the Écrins massif, well known for its magnificent south face routes, must boast one of the smaller summits in the Alps. Here Ian Howell is organising the rope before starting down the narrow north ridge, which is the easy way off. The picture is an excellent example of using 'rope out of camera' to involve the viewer in the action, rather than being a mere onlooker. It also gives depth to the pictures, a third dimension to what would otherwise be a figure posed on a shadowed pinnacle. *(John Cleare)*

Nevertheless they managed to shoot real climbers posing in steep and difficult-looking situations, in so doing exposing themselves to singular hazards: twice, emerging disoriented from under the dark-cloth, Ashley stumbled and fell from exposed stances, only to be saved by a belay. Their many pin-sharp photographic 'studies' and their nine books did much to popularise rock climbing in Britain, but I see their work as essentially the successful culmination of all that had gone before, rather than ground-breaking innovation.

Roll film was all very well but there was no means of keeping it perfectly flat behind a camera lens. Yet the fledging movie industry was already using film punched with sprocket holes to ensure constant take-up speed, and in 1908 an English inventor patented a system tensioning 35mm movie film in still cameras, thus solving the problem. Five years later, in Germany, Oskar Barnack, an asthmatic who struggled to carry heavy equipment, developed the Leica to exploit the invention.

Delayed by the war, the first production Leica appeared in 1925 and became the iconic 35mm stills camera. Its rangefinder focusing involved aligning two tiny images while the photographer aimed though a small viewfinder window, seeing only approximately what the lens saw. Yet it was small, compact, swift to use and silent; it could also shoot 36 frames on a single cassette and several interchangeable lenses were available. Leicas, and other German 35mm cameras such as the Contax, remained the workhorse of many notable photographers for over forty years and though the small 24mm x 36mm negatives were considered unsuitable for serious landscape work, photographing climbing action of every kind was now possible.

In a half-century photography had progressed from the alchemy of Donkin and Sella to a popular art form mastered by everyman, though its workings remained magic to most. In the 1930s and after the Second World War, medium-format cameras shooting a 60mm wide negative such as the Rolliflex, and later the Hasselblad, became the preferred option for most professional photographers, giving results comparable to all but the largest glass plates. But though highly portable and often hand-held, they were still rather a handful and not very practical for mountain use. Frank Smythe, pre-eminent British mountain photographer of the 1930s, used a Patent Etui, an innovative folding German camera virtually the same size as a Nikon FM body that 'packed a huge negative into the smallest possible package'. It weighed just 500g and used a pack of 12 sheets of 9cm x 12cm film: 12 times the area of a Leica negative. Despite focus being by estimation and aiming rather arbitrary, the camera was equal to Smythe's artistic vision. He used it to interpret rather than merely record situations and scenes that had never before been photographed.

After the Second World War, handheld light meters were universal and it was no longer necessary to judge exposure from experience. Unfortunately in Britain, unlike in America, most publishers distrusted 35mm photography and the print unions often refused to work from 35mm originals. However, the Japanese had been busy and during the Korean War the

Eliminate 'A' on Dow Crag in the Lake District is an old favourite, an exposed 400ft VS from 1923. Another example of 'rope out of camera', this picture places the viewer quite definitely on the crag as the belayer – hopefully aware from Ian Howell's expression that the move is demanding serious concentration. It is never easy to pay proper attention to the climber and the camera at the same time, and such pictures, however well planned, must be grabbed swiftly. *(John Cleare)*

innovative modern Japanese 35mm SLR was 'discovered' by war photographers picking up a spare camera as they passed through Tokyo. While possessing many of the useful attributes of the Leica, albeit slightly larger and noisier, the versatile Nikons, Canons and others could accept a virtually unlimited range of lenses from very wide angle to long telephoto, and were aimed through the lens itself. You saw exactly what the camera saw. In a few years built-in exposure meters were standard. Advances in film technology allowed properly processed 35mm negatives to equal medium format quality and after years of gestation colour film became a practical medium and almost ubiquitous. By the 1970s several innovative photographers were pushing mountain photography to a high art in both its landscape and action genres. Nothing seemed impossible to photograph.

Since the millennium, photography, as we of a certain age knew it, died a slow death. Automation replaced professional expertise; computers hijacked the mystique of the darkroom. The camera-phone has become the casual plaything of every Tom, Dick and Harriet. Yet a new photography has been born: digital technology has placed exciting tools and incredible creative techniques in the hands of those imaginative enough to use them, and removed much of the hard graft from mountain photography. No more wondering if that difficult picture has worked. No more fumbling for focus with frozen fingers or changing film while dangling on an abseil rope. No more husbanding every exposure during a long expedition. Forget scratched transparencies. Like the painter's brush, the camera is still a tool, as it always has been. It is the eye behind the camera that makes the picture.

This is an illustration from my 1966 book, the 50th anniversary edition of which is reviewed elsewhere in this *Journal*. It shows Pete Crew in a rather precarious position fighting the crux moves of the Direct Finish to Erosion Groove on Carreg Wastad in Snowdonia. It demonstrates how, especially when shooting in monochrome, the colour of the climber's clothing can make or break a picture. Back then, with a couple of white sweaters in my rucksack, I could cope with any such situation. This was a planned picture in as much as the camera position – merely a couple of small footholds – was reached by abseil specifically to shoot down onto the pitch below and then to get in close on these particular moves. *(John Cleare)*

The photograph is a means of communication, no less so than the written word. Before a shoot, before pressing the trigger, one should have a shrewd idea of the purpose of the shot, a straightforward record perhaps, or something more esoteric? Is the picture to be objective, saying merely *this is the Matterhorn*, or whatever, or subjective – evocative – spelling out the tenseness, the fear even, of a difficult move, or the sublimity of moonlight on the icefall. The viewer can identify with a well-placed figure in a landscape, while a rope leading into camera firmly places the viewer actually on the climb. But an 'angel's eye view' from a contrived viewpoint on a space-hung rope or a helicopter, immediately becomes an objective image.

With automation, a viable digital exposure is a given, so photography today is largely about composition – in its widest definition. Many people are born with the 'eye' and recognise instinctively a situation with potential, but are then unable to do justice to its mood and atmosphere in a photograph. Still, the eye can be trained, chiefly though constant analysis of one's work. Despite what the textbooks say, the only rule is that if it looks right, it is right, and that's where the eye comes in.

A picture is essentially an arrangement of shapes, tempered by texture and usually these days also by colour. It is the eye that must select the most appropriate combination of shapes from the scene ahead, and the choice of lens that best frames and records that selection. A pleasing arrangement might communicate tranquillity; a slightly different but perhaps jarring arrangement of the same shapes could suggest the opposite, and so on. It's a choice.

Silhouettes often work well, especially against sky or distant out of focus landscape. Climbing shots looking vertically upwards or downwards can be exciting but rarely work for obvious reasons to do with bottoms and backgrounds, while a vaguely horizontal view is usually fairly safe. A long enough exposure to catch the movement blur of a hand going for a hold is well worth trying.

The fine details in a picture are often overlooked. 'Think before you shoot,' should become second nature. A critical glance through the view finder should avoid such aberrations as horizons balanced on heads, trees protruding from ears, people standing on stalks or even ice axes looking like walking sticks. Ideally every part of a picture, not just the main subject, should impart useful information that helps define the context, the most obvious being clouds that will suggest the prevailing weather. Large areas of blank sky or dull foreground may devalue the main subject, unless, returning to the purpose of the picture, space is required for lettering.

Patience, anticipation and the ability to react swiftly are obvious requirements. Many years ago, when carrying a large sack, two Nikons and my usual gear, I found myself slogging up the Baltoro glacier with a foreign photographer carrying a medium-format camera and followed by a porter carrying his boxes, bags and tripod. The only way to make sense of this incredible avenue of unreal peaks was to provide scale, and luckily several dozen porters were also ascending the glacier. Though perfectly camouflaged against the endless mounds of rubble, every so often as they crested yet another moraine ridge they were momentarily silhouetted. And every time they did so I was waiting in a steady position with a telephoto lens already focused and able to snap off just one frame before they were gone. Then I'd move on to anticipate the next likely crest. Months later we were able to compare notes: I had a dozen sensational pictures of tiny men below towering peaks, he had just one picture of immaculate quality but a reference shot, begging the question, 'So what?'

In a climbing situation anticipation can make all the difference. A little preparation, personal knowledge, a reconnaissance, studying the guidebook, can ensure the camera is in the ideal position to shoot the move that best captures the mood and ethos of the climb and the climber. A lot can depend on the model; one famous climber I knew made every move appear straightforward, another, equally brilliant, always looked like he was struggling. Style is crucial; a baboon-like fluidity is very photogenic.

Some of the best rock-climbing pictures are shot with the climber actually down-climbing a particular move, although that requires cooperative models. While the same principles apply, it is not easy to translate this into an alpine or big mountain setting where safety is more elusive and where one can only take advantage of situations as they present themselves, although with experience one can often anticipate a likely picture and be ready to shoot it as it occurs.

Clothing and colour choice are important. Forty odd years ago, before fashion hit mountain clothing, climbers frequently 'dissolved' into the rock, particularly when shooting in monochrome, so I would dress my climbers in white sweaters knitted specially for the task. Later, on a Himalayan expedition, we were generously given excellent wind-proof suits in an environmental dark green that proved virtually invisible against a black high-altitude sky. Though appealing, yellows can burn out against snow, while navy can lose all detail.

Carrying vulnerable photographic equipment is always a compromise, but cameras don't take pictures inside rucksacks. Early in my career, photographing while clambering around on such locations as the Forth Bridge and the Eigerwand, I found the regular photographer's gadget bag downright dangerous and so developed the first soft camera bags. I believe that weight should be taken on equipment properly designed for the job, such as a rucksack harness or a hip belt, thus on trek or snow plod I often hang the camera from a dog clip sewn to the rucksack harness where it's instantly usable, while a small pouch either side on a hip belt is far more comfortable than one large bag. Though the concept was copied commercially, vital features were missed. The best gear is homemade.

I can still look at a picture I shot 60 years ago and relive the moment. I'll know the place, the mood – even the smell. I'll recall exactly why I pressed the button. Will photography still be as evocative and still magic in another 170 years? I wonder.

A journey up the Baltoro glacier in the Karakoram offers continuous photographic potential, though demanding anticipation and careful selection to do justice to the awesome scenery. This picture, shot on the south bank of the glacier not far from the Liligo camping place, shows the Grand Cathedral with the Lobsang Spires beyond. Purposely lagging behind my friends, I'd noted where the vestigial trail crossed the skyline of the huge lateral moraine and waited, 200mm telephoto in hand. But it was luck that prompted my inadvertent model into a perfect pose as well as silhouetting the small group of porters, just visible on the steep moraine slopes beyond. *(John Cleare)*

TERRY GIFFORD

Step in Stone

An Exhibition at Fairy Cave Quarry, Somerset

The three gabions hanging from the route Halfway to Kansas at Somerset's Halfway to Kansas, the work of artist Catherine Bloomfied. *(Duncan Simey)*

Mountaineers on the *Alpine Ridge* (PD) under full winter conditions, catching the last of the winter afternoon's sun, photographed in close-up, can look very impressive on social media. But this is Fairy Cave Quarry's easiest route to the quarry rim, all 100m of it. When I moved to the Mendip Hills of Somerset four years ago, Stephen Venables was summing up the local climbing for me, adding, 'and there are some over-rated grotty quarries.' A month after I moved into Stoke St Michael, unaware of this particular locked quarry (BMC website for access details) just a lane away from my house, it announced itself in the guise of a Climbers' Club guidebook all of its own. It has since become the best-selling CC guidebook ever. What began as a bit of a joke, a sop to activists down in the lonely south-west from the CC guidebook committee, has become a runaway success going through reprint after reprint.

So what is the secret to Fairy Cave Quarry's popularity that draws climbers not just from Bristol and south Wales, but from all along the M4, from the south coast, and even tempts Iain Peters out of Devon? Most of its climbing is north-facing and has a reputation for limestone looseness and vegetation. But it has the nearest slabs to London. And there's not a bolt or peg in sight. The clean line of the classic *Rob's Crack* (4c), benign beginners' routes on the west-facing *Balch's Slide* (4a) area and the thin steeper challenge of *Withy Crack* (5a), plus plenty of tricky overlapping slabs at higher grades, attract climbers on most dry days of the year. But actually this is a cavers' quarry, owned by a caver, the locked carpark reserved for cavers and its management committee dominated by cavers whose base is the cavers' hut at the top of the lane. Apparently the many locked cave entrances in the quarry give access to some of the best decorated caves in the Mendips, where many cavers are also climbers. *Withy Crack*'s first ascent is credited to Cerberus Speleological Society in 1992. Given that it is also an SSSI (great crested newts; at least two species of orchids; ravens reared three young last year; Western Red Cedar has just been discovered there) climbers need to be aware that Fairy Cave Quarry is a place that we share, like so many of our crags, with other interests.

So what of the three gabions of orange plastic hanging from the diagonal crack of *Halfway to Kansas*? Or the quarry floor littered with strange white tents on wheels in which green shoots grew from teapots? Or a disembodied voice that spoke from somewhere up in the crag's West End? Then over 1,200 people finding all sorts of other oddities around the quarry during the two weeks and three weekends it was open to the public? Actually climbers seemed to have enjoyed sharing the quarry with the 'step in stone' sculpture exhibition for two weeks in October 2015 and may not have realised that they became exhibits themselves in the time-lapse, attention-provoking, photographs of Christina White displayed at the Earth Science Centre down the road. Indeed, climbers were responsible for hanging those gabions at the request of the artist, Catherine Bloomfield, so that their impact (unintended by the artist, apparently) as people entered the quarry was like a parody of three ducks on a wall. Actually, more subtle than that, they were the highest of a line of orange gabions that had colonised the quarry and clearly wanted to join in the climbing.

Poet Ralph Hoyte's voice works were both an echo of the human construction of the quarry and an eerie post-industrial mysterious communication of echoing absence. Sally Kidall's white tents on stick and sisal platforms looked like some post-industrial survivors' attempts at nomadic domesticity that were now abandoned and being reclaimed by nature. From the climbers' perspective on the quarry rim this seemed to be a community that had run its wheels into a dead-end before it simply gave up. Duncan Cameron developed a picture of the quarry site through evening, day and overnight 'expeditions', collecting fascinating found materials (including a wrist watch – but no old pegs!) that he finally mounted in his 'Fairy Cave Cabinet' on the dramatic cliff-edge start of the *Alpine Ridge*. For those climbers who walked around into the West End with their eyes open, a dome set into the ground will have revealed another miniature world of insects, ants and a dead bird. Tessa Farmer's fairy world was a predatory one that certainly suggested 'Alice's unsettling journey down the rabbit hole into Wonderland' as she puts in the excellent catalogue representing all 14 artists who took part in the larger project involving six venues with workshops, walks, talks and performances that attracted 8,114 visitors in total. Amazingly, the curator of all this, Fiona Campbell, found time to make work for at least three sites where ancient sea creatures might have inhabited what is now limestone. Here, her 'Eviscerated Earth' combined rusty steel bits with wax, cloth, paper and wire to evoke, ironically, the strange formations lost in the destruction of caves by quarrying. Actually, what remains was not only the inspiration for the artists, but also for the audience: the natural folds and features of Fairy Cave Quarry itself, especially in the Death Wish Area, attracted a lot of public attention, which should remind us of how lucky we are to have access negotiated by BMC volunteer Ian Butterworth.

So could there be limits to sharing climbing rock with other artists? (Like bullfighting in Spanish culture, rock climbing, we know, is an art form.) Only one climb was made more difficult for only two weeks here. And from the quarry rim climbers still get the benefit of various imitations of the famous Salt Lake land art 'Spiral Jetty'. But on some gritstone boulders in West Yorkshire and Lancashire six poems by Simon Armitage have been carved into the rock to comprise the Stanza Stones Trail of 47 miles. Each poem is about a form of precipitation: 'Rain', 'Snow', 'Mist', etc. These are semi-permanent, although expected by the poet to be mossed over, erased by their subjects and climbed over. Unlike bird-bans, they don't require art-bans. But they have, with a kind of hubris, humanised the natural rock we come to climb. Is it our rock? Of course not, and climbing is still possible. Indeed, you might feel enriched by being reminded of climbing 'up here where the front of the mind distils the brunt of the world' in 'Rain', for example. For years we've shared the crags with ravens and ring ouzels, and now we must share them with conservationists and curators.

My three nuts from which the gabions hung stayed untouched by other climbers for two weeks. When I mistakenly removed them, thinking the exhibition finished, other climbers replaced them with stones so the final weekend show could go on. But at another, open, quarry, a weekend rave of 600 people destroyed one artist's work. There are other people we should resist sharing the crags with – the 'green trail' 4x4 drivers, the destructive trail bike riders, the access improvers, the commercial bolters, the selfish route-hogging groups. Besides these, a few thought-provoking, amusing or distinctly odd fellow artists are life-enhancing presences for which we should be grateful, as many climbers obviously were at Fairy Cave Quarry in 2015.

Science & Nature

Breakfast with Henry

Looking towards Kyashar and Makalu from south side of Kusum Kanguru.
Rob Fairley, 1996. (Watercolour. 30cm x 40cm. Private collection, Switzerland.)

Science & Nature

JAMES S MILLEDGE

Stanhope Speer: Early Alpinist and Pioneer in Mountain Medicine

The Wetterhorn group of peaks from the Mönch. Speer and his three guides made the first ascent of the central peak, the Mittelhorn, in 1845. *(Alpine Club Photo library, Jules Beck c1872)*

Browsing in the Alpine Club Library, I came across a booklet on the shelf devoted to mountain medicine. It was a reprint of an article on mountain sickness by someone called Stanhope Templeman Speer. Dated 1853 and printed by T Richards, the original paper had been published in two parts in successive weeks in the *Association Medical Journal* on 21 and 28 January of that year. The journal was one of a number of titles that were forerunners of the *British Medical Journal*.

I realised that Speer's publication predated a work I did know, most usually regarded as the first description of mountain sickness by a physician: Conrad Meyer Ahrens' *Die Bergkrankheit; oder der Einfluss des Ersteigens grosser Höhen auf den thierischen Organismus* – 'Mountain sickness, or the influence of climbing great heights on the animal organism' published a year later. Yet Speer's contribution was unknown to me. It is the first attempt to offer evidence of the reality of what we now call acute mountain sickness, to define systematically the symptoms and speculate on the causes.

Given what was known about the body in the mid 19th century, Speer inevitably failed with the latter ambition; but his achievements deserve to be recognised.

Speer was born on 20 October, 1823 in Boulogne-sur-Mer, the fishing port and tourist town on the Channel coast of France. He was baptised at the nonconformist British chapel there. His parents were Thomas and Catherine Speer. I could find no information about his boyhood or schooling but he went to Edinburgh and was a member of the Royal Medical Society of Edinburgh. This is a student society – the only one to have the 'Royal' appellation – and so we know that Edinburgh was his medical school. There is a record of his attending a session of the society in 1847 when he would have been about 23 and presumably qualified in medicine. The record implies he was from Boulogne-sur-Mer, where he was born, though whether he was resident there at the time is not obvious.

There is a letter of recommendation from Alexander Peddie (1810–1907) of the Minto House Hospital and Dispensary in Edinburgh, dated 1 August 1848, starting: 'Speer has been an assistant at Minto House since the previous 1 May.' This period might have been equivalent to his intern year after qualifying in medicine.

His climbing career must have started as a student. In his paper, he drew on an ascent of the Wetterhorn made in 1845 when he would have been about 21. He mentions climbing on Mont Blanc, also in 1845, trying to get as high as he could in one day from the valley. He also says he spent 'some months' in 1846 in the Bernese Oberland, but I could find no further information about his climbing. There is no record of his being a member of the Alpine Club, founded in 1857; possibly Speer had by then stopped Alpine climbing. He had married Maria Eves in 1850.

He recorded his first ascent of the middle peak of the Wetterhorn in considerable detail in the *Athenaeum* of 1 November 1846, an account reprinted in the *Alpine Journal* (Vol 17,1884-5, pp104-15). Speer found out that the other two peaks; the Rosenhorn and Wetterhorn had first been climbed the previous year leaving the Mittelhorn, the highest summit, still unclimbed. He started from Interlaken. There, he was told all attempts to climb the Wetterhorn from Grindelwald, the nearest village to the peak, had been in vain. The only possible approach had to be from Grimsel. He hired one of the guides, who gave him this news, Melchior Bannholzer, though he does not name him and, starting at 6pm on 4 July 1845, walked the 20km to Grindelwald, arriving at 10pm.

Next morning he and Bannholzer set off for Grimsel, via Meiringen, where they spent a night at an inn, a walk of about 42km, making an aggregate of 62km in two days. At Grimsel he engaged two more guides, whose names he gives as J Jaun and Caspar Alphanalph. Both had climbed the Jungfrau previously. They set off next day along the Aar valley and then onto the Aar glacier with Jaun as lead guide. The glacier itself was hard going with many crevasses. He writes: 'the vast glacier itself spread out before us for many miles, and surrounded by the gigantic peaks of the

Finstrathorn, Shreckhorn, Oberaarhorn, Vischerhorner and Lauterarrhorn [sic].' As evening fell, they decided to find a spot safe from avalanches for a bivouac and enjoyed a wonderful sunset. It was a cold night and they got little sleep. Around midnight they were woken by the sound of a huge avalanche on the other side of the glacier. They considered further sleep impossible, so decided to set off for their peak. It was early in the morning of 7 July 1845.

On coming down to the glacier from their bivouac they found themselves, as Speer put it, 'at the bottom of a well, round three sides of which walls of ice rose up almost vertically. Up these walls it was necessary to ascend in order to exit from our dismal prison.' Jaun led the way out of this trap and they continued up the long Aar glacier for hours with some difficult crevasse crossings, often in snow up to their knees. The clear air and the vast scale of the landscape made them underestimate the distance to their next goal, a steep snow ascent to the Col de Lauteraar. Speer says this col had 'hitherto been considered impractical'. At its foot was a 'labyrinth of blue and ghastly abysses to the redoubted Col de Lauteraar, which now rose quasi-perpendicularly far above our heads for many hundreds of feet, whilst its ridge we perceived a mass of overhanging snow, which from its threatening aspect caused us great uneasiness.' The lead guide overcame a huge crevasse at the start of the climb, using his alpenstock to excavate a hole on the very steep slope across the crevasse, onto which he then jumped. He helped the others do likewise but when Speer jumped the snow gave way and he came onto the rope. Jaun held him and he scrambled up. Speer wrote: 'the ascent now commenced in earnest, the first guide having been relieved by the second in command, who (hatchet in hand), assiduously dashed holes in the snow in which to place the hands and feet.'

The ascent was slow; it took five hours after leaving their bivouac to reach the col where they were greeted by fantastic views, including their goal of the Mittelhorn. Descending from the col to begin the climb itself needed care, 'great stress being laid on the ropes and hatchets', and once on the Ober Grindelwald glacier, nearing the Mittelhorn, Speer began to wonder. 'I ventured to inquire of the guides whether they expected to attain the summit; to this they replied, that they most assuredly did so. I therefore held my peace, thinking myself in right good company.' The ascent was difficult but after four hours they reached the summit, 11 hours after setting out from their bivouac. Again they had wonderful views, which Speer describes in detail, and were delighted with their first ascent. It was windy and cold, so after twenty minutes they fixed a 'flag-staff' to mark their ascent and started down.

The group descended the opposite side of the Mittelhorn to their ascent. Speer doesn't comment on this decision to go down into unknown territory but it turned out to be a practical route. They glissaded down to the plateau leading to the Wetterkessel glacier and followed this to the Rosenlaui. Here there were again many crevasses and they were on unknown territory. There was some hunting around for the right line, the glacier here being steep and a mixture of rocks and ice, and they were now getting very tired.

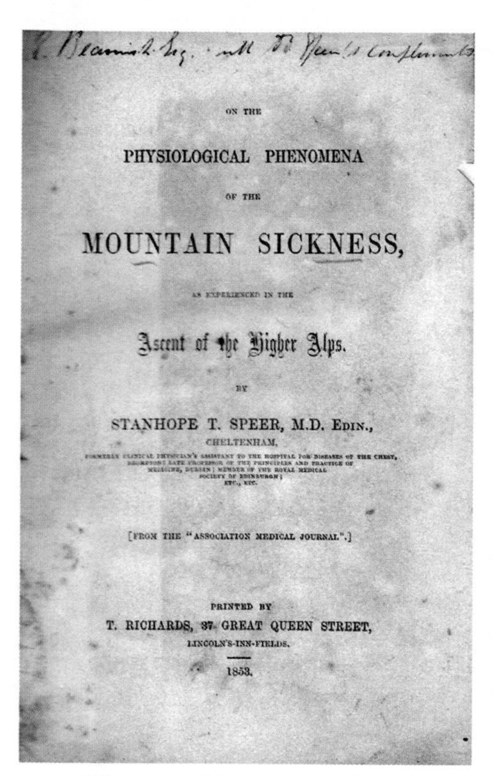

ON THE

PHYSIOLOGICAL PHENOMENA

OF THE

MOUNTAIN SICKNESS,

AS EXPERIENCED IN THE

Ascent of the Higher Alps.

BY

STANHOPE T. SPEER, M.D. EDIN.,

CHELTENHAM,

FORMERLY CLINICAL PHYSICIAN'S ASSISTANT TO THE HOSPITAL FOR DISEASES OF THE CHEST, BROMPTON; LATE PROFESSOR OF THE PRINCIPLES AND PRACTICE OF MEDICINE, DUBLIN; MEMBER OF THE ROYAL MEDICAL SOCIETY OF EDINBURGH; ETC., ETC.

[FROM THE "ASSOCIATION MEDICAL JOURNAL".]

PRINTED BY

T. RICHARDS, 37 GREAT QUEEN STREET,

LINCOLN'S-INN-FIELDS.

1853.

Title page of the reprint of Speer's ground breaking paper on mountain medicine. *(J S Milledge)*

Dr Stanhope T Speer, seated, physician and alpinist, with the medium Stainton Moses and Rector, one of Moses' 'apparitions'. *(Mary Evans Picture Library)*

Eventually, at about 8pm, they got off the ice 20 hours after starting out from their bivouac. The descent over rocks and fallen pines was very tedious and night was falling but at 9pm they reached the baths and hotel of Rosenlaui. (Now, of course, the normal route is from Grindelwald by road to the Wetterhorn Hotel, then a two or three hour walk to the Gleckstein hut, and next day a five or six hour AD climb to the Mittelhorn.)

Speer obtained his medical degree from Edinburgh and he mentions, on the title page of the reprint of his article, that he was 'formerly clinical physician's assistant to the Brompton Hospital for Diseases of the Chest, London.' The hospital is still a leading respiratory diseases institution. He also describes himself 'late professor of the principles and practice of medicine, Dublin'. His publication list, from the *Medical Directory* for 1863, included a translation from the French of an important paper on pathological chemistry and two papers of his own from 1851 on respiratory illness, including tuberculosis and 'pulmonary apoplexy'.

He was professor of medicine at Cecilia Street School of Medicine in 1853. He would have been about 29 then. This was one of a number of private medical schools in Dublin at that time. In 1854, the school became part of the newly formed Catholic University of Ireland, with the future Cardinal Newman as its first rector, although Newman left when he realised that its purpose was more political than educational; its degrees were never recognised by the civil authorities. It would also have had an overtly Catholic bias and it was perhaps for this reason that Speer, baptised a Protestant, resigned his chair in medicine.

The title of his mountain sickness paper was 'On the physiological phenomenon of the MOUNTAIN SICKNESS as experienced in the ascent of the higher Alps.' It ran to 10 pages in the *Association Medical Journal* and to 50 in the reprint. It is written in the style of its time, that is to say, florid and full of circumlocutions, with long sentences and many clauses. (Here is the opening sentence: 'It is, I believe, very generally admitted, that when an individual habitually residing at a moderate elevation above the level of the sea, attains, in a short space of time, a considerable altitude above such level, he will, in all probability, experience a state of indisposition, if not of disorder.')

After the introduction, Speer asks three questions: is there a condition of mountain sickness? Are these symptoms felt by all persons alike and at the same height? What are the causes, and whence the explanation of such phenomena? He sets about answering the first of these by recounting the experiences of the small number of travellers who had been to altitude in the greater ranges and written about it. As a preamble, he also points out that some travellers and climbers may not make much of any symptoms of mountain sickness because such symptoms clear on descending. This is especially true in the European Alps where the climber, having reached the summit, typically descends to the valley the same day.

Also, he claims, the climber is so enthralled with the mountain experience that he dismisses the memory of symptoms and fails to report them. He graphically describes, 'The succession of wonder-striking scenes which they now behold… the rapidity with which marvel succeeds marvel… the glaciers, the feeling of dread occasioned by the ghastly aspect of the gaping crevices… the dreaded sound of the falling avalanche…' and so on. These novel and exciting experiences, Speer argues, may push the memory of symptoms of mountain sickness out of mind.

He does not mention earlier accounts that have been regarded as descriptions of mountain sickness, such as that of the Andean traveller José de Acosta from 1590 or in Chinese documents dating from the 1st century. He might have been unaware of de Acosta's work, though there was an English translation of his book in 1604. Or he may not have considered his experience as being mountain sickness. He would not have been aware of the Chinese reference since it was not translated into English until 1881 and not generally recognized as referring to mountain sickness until 1983.

Speer says that the accounts from travellers such as Alexander von Humboldt, Jean-Baptiste Boussingault, Alcide d'Orbigny, Horace-Bénédict de Saussure, Marc-Auguste Pictet and others are to be trusted. On Chimborazo, Humboldt experienced the desire to vomit and vertigo, which were more trying than the difficulty in breathing, which he also suffered. One companion was more afflicted: 'blood started from his lips and gums in each of us the conjunctiva was distended with blood.' This was at an altitude of 16,724ft. He eventually reached a height of over 19,000ft.

Humboldt does not report headache, but d'Orbigny, a French traveller also in the Andes, does complain of violent headache when crossing a pass of over 13,500ft. d'Orbigny also mentions that his guides used the term soroche for the symptoms suffered at altitude; they considered the symptoms due to 'emanations arising from mines of antimony, which they believed exist in the neighbourhood: the Spanish term for antimony being *soroche*.' In La Paz, d'Orbigny also complained that he had the sensation of suffocation. This problem remained for his entire stay in the city.

Other Andean travellers were very little affected. For instance, Charles de La Condamine and Pierre Bouguer did not suffer much at an altitude of 14,750ft, apart from slight bleeding from the gums, which they attributed to 'a scorbutic condition of the blood due to the cold.'

Many accounts emphasize the need for hyperventilation, which we would not class as a symptom of mountain sickness, since it continues after acclimatization when all other symptoms have cleared and affects all persons including those with no other symptoms of mountain sickness. It is physiological rather than pathological. Another symptom common in these early accounts is the feeling of fatigue, of having to rest every few steps.

Finally, Speer comes to de Saussure and his attempts to climb Mont Blanc. Speer considered de Saussure to have 'described with accuracy, the phenomena attendant upon considerable elevation above the level of the sea' in his book *Voyages dans les Alpes*. Speer recounts de Saussure's experiences on Mont Blanc and symptoms in his guides and porters. Fatigue was a principle symptom, together with anxiety, uneasiness, and in some guides, nausea and vomiting. As they climbed, shortness of breath was the main symptom. Speer then adds accounts of various other climbers on Mont Blanc.

Aldejo and his party, for example, began to suffer at 12,000ft with constriction in the chest, rapid pulse, fullness in the head and thirst. Later, violent headache and palpitations were the main symptoms. Other climbers reported 'a dry rugoes condition of the integuments', or wrinkled skin; one party with a dog noticed it also appeared to suffer the same problems, including vomiting, but nevertheless reached the summit. A French physician, Dr Le Pileur, is quoted at length describing how one of his guides suffered from syncope, or fainting, as soon as he stood up. On his own climb of Mont Blanc, at 9,000ft Speer began to feel a fullness in the head, throbbing of the carotids and palpitations of the heart. He lost his appetite for food but had considerable thirst. At 10,000ft he noticed increased respiration and the taste of blood in his mouth due to oozing from the gums.

Speer then discusses the relative non-susceptibility to mountain sickness of those of his guides who lived at a moderate altitude of around 6,000ft. He cites his experience in climbing one of the Wetterhorn peaks, his first ascent of the Mittelhorn. One of his guides lived on the plains, the other two

Table 1. 'Abnormal sensations'	
Speer writes: 'The abnormal sensations constituting mountain sickness may thus be classes in a tabular form accordingly as they affect the different functions.'	
Of the nervous system	• Vertigo • Cephalalgia [sic – Speer means headache] • Somnolence [sleepiness]
Of the respiratory and circulatory system	• Dyspnoea • Increased rapidity of the respiration • Sense of thoracic constriction • Occasional oozing of blood from mucous surfaces • Syncopal tendency • Cardiac palpitation • Throbbing of the vessel within the cranium • Increased rapidity of pulse
Of the digestive functions	• Anorexia • Nausea and vomiting • Thirst • Constriction below the epigastrium • White tongue
Of the locomotive functions	• Muscular pains • Paralysed sensation in the lower limbs
Of the tegumentary system	• Harsh skin • Suppression of the cutancous [sic] transpiration • Pallor of the surface • Cyanosed appearance of the countenance

lived at over 6,000ft. The latter showed no sign of mountain sickness, though they were breathless and needed to halt frequently near the summit. The man from the plains showed signs of distress at quite an early stage of the climb with nausea and headache. On this climb, two of the guides, who omitted to wear sunglasses, suffered from snow blindness, which lasted two days.

Speer ends the first part of his publication: 'I conclude from these observations that, as a tolerably satisfactory answer to the first question proposed, it may be stated that at great elevations there actually do occur certain manifestations in the natural functions of the body, in no way to be accounted for by admitting the existence of influences to which at an ordinary level it is not exposed.'

Part two, published in the following number of the journal a week later, starts by listing the symptoms of mountain sickness in tabular form, classified into five bodily systems. the Nervous system, Cardiorespiratory, Digestive, Locomotive and Tegumentary system. [See Table 1]

He points out that not all symptoms will be present in every case but claims each one has been noticed while climbing Mont Blanc. These he attributes to mountain sickness, which he compares with seasickness. Like seasickness, some individuals are more susceptible than others.

Some have nausea and no vomiting, others the opposite. Others complain of headache with or without vomiting. He returns to this comparison later in the article and also compares mountain sickness to 'ephemeral fever'. This condition is characterized by languor, distaste for motion, muscular pains, nausea, anorexia, headache, thirst, white tongue, and acceleration of pulse and respiration.

To answer his third question, about the causes of mountain sickness, Speer then explores possible mechanisms. The language in this long section is hard to follow and summarise. It is difficult for us to appreciate the limits of mid 19th century physiology available to Speer. The circulation of the blood and the importance of oxygen for muscular exercise were known, as was the effect of altitude on barometric pressure. But nowhere does he mention hypoxia or the reduction in the partial pressure of oxygen. He does say altitude results in the 'rarefaction of the atmosphere'. But X-rays were not yet discovered and measurement of blood pressure, by Korotkoff sounds, was still over 50 years in the future, not to mention the many other advances in all branches in physiology and pathology.

In discussing the possible causes of mountain sickness, Speer first refers to what he says is the first attempt to explain them, that of de Saussure. He quotes de Saussure as suggesting the symptoms of mountain sickness 'are due, not to the difficulty of breathing in such an atmosphere but to the relaxation of the vessels, which arise from a diminution in the compressing power of the air.'

However, since vessels are filled with a fluid, which is virtually non-compressible, and the effect on bubble formation of slowly reducing the barometric pressure, by even half an atmosphere, is negligible, there is no increase in trans-mural pressure in the vessels. Also, we now know that the plasma volume is quite quickly reduced negating any slight rise in intravascular pressure even if the circulation was a perfectly closed system.

Speer then has a long section comparing the relative heights at which mountain sickness is reported as between the European Alps compared with the Andes and Himalaya and concludes that it seems to come on at higher altitude in the latter two areas compared with the Alps because the snow line – he calls it 'perpetual congelation' – is lower in the Alps. There is then a section comparing mountain sickness with 'ephemeral fever', whatever that is. (It doesn't seem to be related to bovine ephemeral fever.) He finds similarities in symptoms between the two conditions.

Speer then considers whether the rapid drop in temperature on ascent from valley to summit is a factor in inducing mountain sickness. He says: 'The idea suggests itself that, were it was desired to produce such a pathological condition [mountain sickness] there could scarcely be a more efficacious way of doing it than by suddenly removing him from a temperature of between 70 and 80°F to one in which he would be surrounded by fields of snow and masses of ice. This leads to a consideration of the singular fact that the mountain sickness commences only at the limit of perpetual congelation, whatever that limit may chance to be.'

He does not seem to consider that climbers in the greater ranges usually have to spend more time in getting to high altitude because of the geography and remoteness of such areas and therefore usually have more time to acclimatise, although he had noted that people in the Alps who lived or spent time in the higher villages were less susceptible to mountain sickness.

Most of the rest of the article is taken up with reporting results of measuring pulse rates at frequent intervals, with dates and times, while ascending to altitude, together with comments on symptoms. The pulse rate was one of the few physiological measurements that could be made and recorded. The report concludes with a seven-point summary, the first point being: 'That in mountainous districts and upon attaining a certain elevation, a series of physiological phenomena manifest themselves, which differ solely from the standard of health, and exist as long only as the exciting causes are in activity: disappearing upon a return to the ordinary level of human habitation.' The remaining six points may be summarized as: There is great individual variation in susceptibility to the condition and in the actual phenomena suffered.

Speer's retirement was both long and a curious contrast to his professional life. According to E T Bennet, writing in his book *The Physical Phenomena Popularly Classed Under the Head of Spiritualism*: 'Dr Speer practised as a physician at Cheltenham and in London, and at different times held various important hospital posts. He had scientific and artistic tastes, and being possessed of private means, he quitted professional work at the age of thirty-four, and spent his subsequent life in studious retirement.' That would have been in about 1857.

His 'studious retirement' included a powerful interest in spiritualism, then quite popular among the professional classes. He was introduced to this by William Stainton Moses, who had been a Church of England clergyman and later a schoolteacher. He was first Speer's patient, and became a family friend. Moses became a leading figure in the movement and convinced Speer, who was also at first a sceptic. The Speers' house became, for some time, a venue for séances in which Moses was the medium; the author Arthur Conan Doyle, himself a spiritualist, gives a hair-raising account of a séance at Speer's home on the Isle of Man. Moses also became tutor to Speer's son Charlton, a talented musician, who later wrote a biography of his tutor. Stanhope Speer died on 9 February 1889 in Cheltenham, aged 65.

DR NATHAN SMITH

The Exploration Tribe

The right stuff: five of the 20th century's leading adventurers, explorers and mountaineers. Clockwise, starting with the polar explorer Roald Amundsen, the aviatrix Amelia Earhart, Tenzing Norgay and Ed Hillary on Everest and Neil Armstrong with an experimental aircraft.

'These men expanded the realms of possibility. Most of us will never climb Mount Everest, cross Antarctica, or land on the moon, but we know we can. The truth is we are all liberated by the success of others because they show it can be done.' Peter Hillary

Peter Hillary's stirring quotation, equally applicable to women, raises interesting questions about the types of people who climb mountains, traverse vast and desolate landmasses and explore the frontiers of space. I should start, though, with a disclaimer. I am writing this, not as an expert mountaineer, but as a scientist: a scientist with an interest in extreme environments and the people who pursue activities in challenging, stressful, and potentially dangerous conditions.

My fascination with what academics call 'extreme and unusual' environments started a few years ago while following the polar explorer Ben Saunders' Scott Expedition journey. Since then, I have been fortunate enough to study a variety of extreme environment groups, including polar expedition-goers, Antarctic over-winterers, military personnel, Mars simulation participants – individuals who spent 520 days in isolated and confined conditions – and most relevant to the present article, mountaineers. My intention with the following thoughts is not to suggest definitive answers, but to present observations based on the personality and personal characteristics of the mountaineers I have studied, and how they compare to other extreme environment groups and the general population.

To frame the discussion, let me rewind to the summer of 2015. During July and August I spent several weeks in the European Alps, in Switzerland and France, as well as travelling through Austria exploring the Dachstein and Wilder Kaiser. Immersed in these awe-inspiring environments, I often stopped to watch climbing and mountaineering teams working towards their goals. As a psychologist, my question was not 'why', although I still find this interesting, but 'who'. Who are the people striving for summits? Who are the people spending days at a time in tents, battling weather conditions, and following spells of monotony with bursts of danger?

The question 'who?' interests me for several reasons. The first is to do with performance. Past work suggests a vast proportion of the population would not cope and perform well in such conditions. The second is to do with the benefits afforded to those who do opt to take up the challenge.

Clearly I am not the first psychologist to study these questions. However, I do believe that the research my collaborators and I have conducted contributes, at least in some small way, to questions that up until this point have remained unanswered. In George Mallory's early writings he talks a lot about psychological factors and the different types of people undertaking mountaineering activities. Issues of motivation' are also covered at length in *Mountains of the Mind*, Robert Macfarlane's wonderful voyage through mountaineering history. For this article, though, I am going to focus on the work of Jim Lester. Lester accompanied the 1963 American Everest expedition and reached 22,000ft with the group in an attempt to study personality, stress and the compatibility of the expedition team members. He subsequently wrote an article 'Personality and Everest' for the *Journal* charting an extensive study into the personal characteristics of the mountaineers he had observed.

At times, findings from my own work with mountaineers stand in contrast to the observations made by Lester. For instance, based on responses I collected from 83 mountaineers, defined as people who had completed at least one expedition lasting one week or more, results point to a personality profile marked by higher levels of agreeableness and conscientiousness and lower levels of neuroticism compared to the general population. This profile suggests someone who gets on well with other people, plans thoroughly and is not easily anxious. A similar personality profile has been found when studying the performance of other groups operating in challenging environments, such as military settings, astronauts and aviators.

In contrast to our current findings, Lester's results, based on responses from 17 mountaineers, suggest the 1963 American Everest team were generally more introverted and could be defensive, self-centred and less agreeable. However, Lester pointed out that those mountaineers who generated the most positive feelings towards themselves were 'sensitive, considerate, inviting, cheerful and free from anxiety,' which is more consistent with findings from my own work. Clearly when comparing to Lester's work there are a number of factors to take into account, not least the cultural and societal changes that have taken place since the 1960s.

Despite the differences, there were also a number of similarities that emerged when comparing the group studied by Lester with the mountaineers assessed recently, especially when focusing on the motives for taking part in mountain-based ventures. In mountaineering, there is a considerable body of pre-existing work focusing on the reasons for engaging in such activities and popular topics include sensation seeking, risk taking and more recently emotion regulation.

In our recent studies, the focus was on the personal values of mountaineers. Personal values are distinct from personality and provide information on the motivation or reasons for choosing to do something. The mountaineers we assessed over the past two years consistently ranked the personal values of 'self-direction', 'stimulation', 'universalism' and 'benevolence' as high in importance. Interestingly, these same values were also reported a priority by military patrol groups, Antarctic over-winterers and those undertaking a Mars confinement study. It was also notable that mountaineers highlighted 'tradition', 'conformity' and 'power' as low priority values.

Overall, this type of value profile suggests a person that is interested in being in control and making decisions, identifies the importance of group working, enjoys a sense of adventure and appreciates the natural world and 'bigger picture'. These people also place less importance on achieving a position of dominance and esteem, and are not so concerned with maintaining the *status quo*. Lester pinpointed very similar characteristics when identifying the American Everest team as 'planful', 'self-reliant', 'adventurous', 'concerned with personal pleasure' and 'rebellious'.

When reflecting on the present findings, I find myself being drawn back to the mountaineering individuals and groups who have been immortalised in the pages of history. I look at pictures of Mallory and Irvine, Hillary and Tenzing, Bonatti and Bonington and Messner. Do the findings fit? My experience of mountaineers would lead me to say yes. Of course, that is my opinion based on information collected, individuals observed and accounts rendered. I am sure you will have your own perspective. In questioning our findings, and inquiring as to your own personality and motivation, this article will have achieved something.

Moving away from personal characteristics, I want to touch on additional reports that are incredibly striking and worthy of attention. We asked individuals taking part in the study to talk about what their involvement in mountaineering has taught them and the challenges they face when returning from expeditions. While a number of people were stoic in their response, many individuals provided detailed accounts of the benefits of mountaineering. When considered as a whole, several themes were identified. The first was 'personal' strength.

Repeatedly, individuals suggested they had a greater appreciation of their own ability and capacity to overcome difficulties as a result of their endeavours in the mountains. Second was an appreciation for others. Being tolerant of other people is such an important part of life and many of the individuals who took part in our study indicated that mountaineering had taught them to have empathy, consider other peoples' emotions and perspective and support struggling expedition team members. Finally, there were overall reports on the value and appreciation of life. Repeatedly, people indicated that they felt more alive and vital, and could identify the important parts of their life. Such benefits cannot be underestimated and provide a compelling argument for getting outside in an age where it is possible to live without ever needing to leave the house.

Although many positive responses to expeditions were offered, a darker side to the experience should also be acknowledged. When returning to daily life, participants in the present work indicated feeling overwhelmed by demands and pressures, being bored and experiencing low mood. There was sometimes also a type of 'lonely tree' syndrome reported where a person struggled to reintegrate and reported being misunderstood by friends and family. Other work I have conducted would suggest that these feelings will pass, however it would seem pertinent to consider what can be done to manage post return difficulties when preparing for the expedition itself.

The findings reported have been collected from a variety of groups over the past two years. I am incredibly grateful to all of the study participants, the Alpine Club and the British Mountaineering Council for their support. As new projects emerge the focus remains on understanding the 'who' but also questioning the 'why', the 'what' and the 'when'. In asking such questions, we will better understand the psychological factors associated with personality, coping and responses to activities in extreme and unusual environments. It is likely that information gained from mountaineering groups operating in extreme settings could help in some way to preparing and supporting future expeditions into the unknown. For now, I'll end with thoughts from the first American to reach the top of Everest, and one of Jim Lester's subjects, American mountaineer and explorer, Jim Whittaker:

> *If you're not living on the edge, you're taking up too much space. It has nothing to do with thrill seeking. It's about making the most of every moment, about stretching your own boundaries, about being willing to learn constantly and putting yourself in situations where learning is possible – sometimes even critical – to your survival. Being out on the edge, with everything at risk, is where you learn – and grow – the most.*

EUAN MEARNS & ALEX MILNE

The Shrinking Glacier Conundrum

The Glacier de Leschaux meeets the Mer de Glace, which is estimated to have retreated 1.27km since records began in 1878. Currently there is no compelling evidence in the Mer de Glace research for acceleration in the glacier's retreat. More research is needed to unravel the influence of CO_2 emissions, which will be challenging against a background of natural glacier retreat. *(Nicolas Vigier)*

Anyone who has skied or climbed in the Alps regularly over the last 40 years will know that glaciers are retreating. The popular narrative in the media and among energy policymakers is that melting glaciers is due to climate change, which is undoubtedly true. In this article we examine the evidence for the cause of this climate change. Is it down to man and his CO_2 emissions, something widely assumed to be the case, or could glacier retreat be down to natural causes? This article focuses on the latter point.

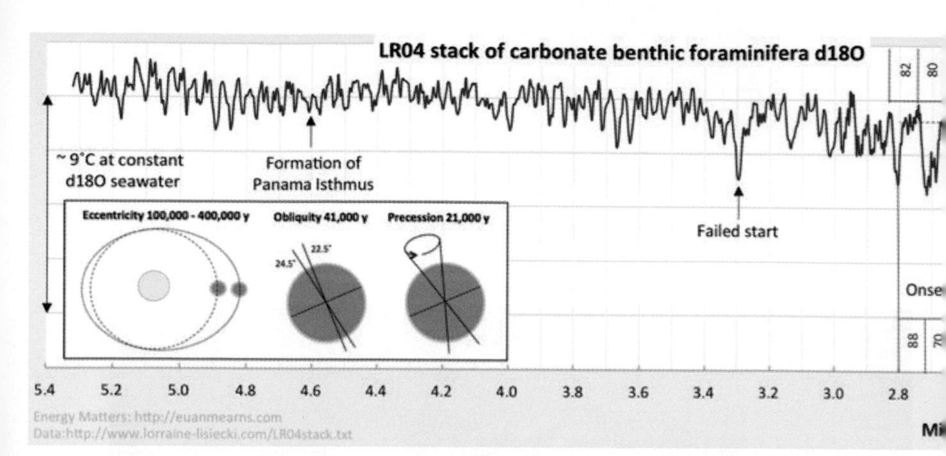

Figure 1 The LR04 stack[1] of ∂[18]O isotope ratios for foraminifera from the ocean basins provides a record of global temperature change. The data are plotted so that warm temperatures are up and cold temperatures are down and time is passing from left to right. 2.8 million years ago there is an abrupt change where cyclical fluctuations in temperature begin to trend towards much lower temperatures. This marks the onset of the Ice Age. The inset illustrates the three orbital cycles that are believed to influence glaciation. In red, the cycle lengths are marked from which it can be seen that glacial cycles appear to be dominated by the 41,000-year obliquity cycle and multiples of it (Figure 3).

We are both geologists, and appreciate more than most that we live on a restless planet that is in a continuous state of flux. The first fact to consider is that Earth is actually in the middle of an ice age that began 2.8 million years ago. That's something easy to forget but is manifest from the ice that covers large portions of the planet in Antarctica, Greenland, the Arctic Ocean and mountainous areas like the Alps where ice caps and glaciers are commonplace. Since the Ice Age began there have been approximately 50 periods of glacial advance and retreat. The glaciations, when ice sheets covered much of Europe and North America, have been punctuated by 'inter-glacials' with a more benign climate. That is where we are now, in an inter-glacial called the Holocene that began between 10,000 to 12,000 years ago.

Ice sheets expand during ice ages and retreat during inter-glacials. The main characteristic of inter-glacials is that ice melts. A status quo does not exist on the real Earth although a condition of climatic equilibrium appears to have become engrained in the minds of those who study and model Earth's climate. Ice sheets and glaciers, in a state of continual flux, must either grow or contract. We should consider ourselves extremely lucky that we are currently experiencing a retreat of ice since ice-sheet advance and renewed glaciation would be totally disastrous for mankind.

That is our first message. There is absolutely nothing unusual about glaciers melting during inter-glacials. But in this article we want to try and

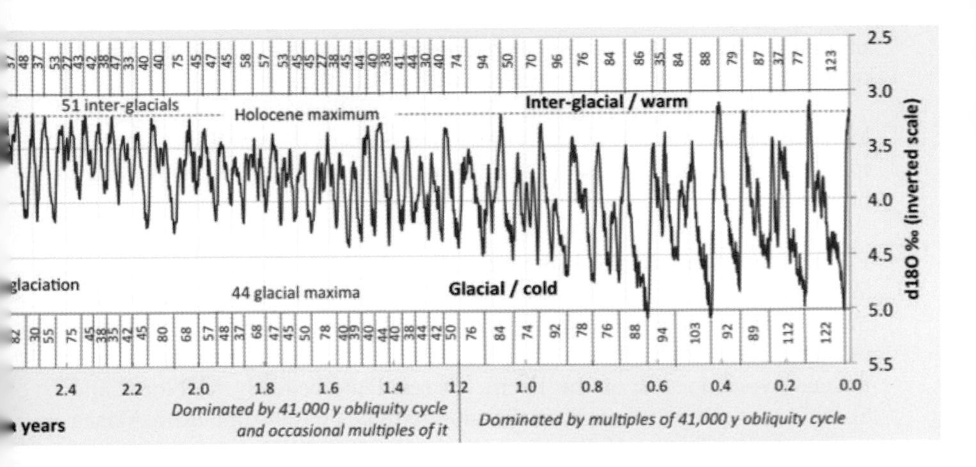

provide some understanding of the geological processes that are responsible for the cyclical advance and retreat of ice sheets that began 2.8 million years ago. This takes us into the world of plate tectonics, Earth's orbital cycles around the sun, cycles in solar activity and the geochemical data that record all this information in ice cores from Antarctica and Greenland and sediment cores drilled in the deep ocean basins.

The temperature story from the ocean basins

Foraminifera are microscopic creatures that forage in water columns of the deep oceans. Their skeletons are made of calcium carbonate ($CaCO_3$) otherwise known as calcite, the same stuff seashells are made of. When they are alive and growing, foraminifera extract calcium, carbon and oxygen from seawater to make their shells. Oxygen has two isotopes of interest: ^{16}O and ^{18}O. The ratio of these isotopes in a shell depends largely but not only upon the water temperature at the time the foraminifera were alive and growing. When the foraminifera die, they sink to the ocean floor and are slowly covered in mud, buried and fossilise. The oxygen isotopes ($\partial^{18}O$) lock in the temperature of the water that prevailed during its life. Measuring $\partial^{18}O$ in a series of foraminifera from boreholes can therefore provide insights to past temperature changes and climate.

The so-called LR04 stack (Figure 1) is one of the classic geochemical data sets compiled in recent decades[1]. It comprises 38,229 individual $\partial^{18}O$ measurements made on foraminifera from 57 boreholes from around the world, but concentrated in the Atlantic Ocean basin. The data cover from 5.3 million years ago to the present day. In Figure 1, time passes from left to right with the present day to the right of the plot. The vertical axis plots $\partial^{18}O$ with the scale inverted so that warm is up and cold is down. There are a number of key observations to be made. The first is that throughout, the $\partial^{18}O$ temperature oscillates with a semi-regular rhythm. From 5.3 to 2.8

1. L E Lisiecki and Maureen E Raymo 'A Pliocene-Pleistocene stack of 57 globally distributed benthic $\partial^{18}O$ records,' *Palaeoceanography*, vol 20, 2005.

million years ago $\partial^{18}O$ was low and temperatures were high and the amplitude of oscillation was low compared with what followed.

After 2.8 million years the amplitude of oscillation increases with the lows progressing steadily towards colder temperatures. 2.8 million years ago marks the onset of the Ice Age and formation of ice sheets in the northern hemisphere.

Plate tectonics and the Gulf Stream

Why did Earth enter an ice age 2.8 million years ago? Two macro-scale plate tectonic events may offer a partial explanation. The first is the formation of the Panama Isthmus about 4.6 million years ago[2]. The isthmus was formed by subduction of the Pacific Ocean Plate beneath the North and South American plates creating the mountain chain that runs from Alaska to Patagonia. Closure of Panama drastically altered the pattern of ocean circulation, creating conditions for the establishment of global 'thermohaline' – temperature and salinity – circulation that would profoundly impact climate in areas like north-west Europe. In the North Atlantic, this global current is known colloquially as the Gulf Stream because it moves warm water from the Gulf of Mexico northwards, creating a climate that is uncommonly warm and wet for the latitudes of the UK and Norway. The global thermohaline circulation goes under a number of names but for simplicity we will call it the Gulf Stream.

As it moves northwards, evaporation makes the water of the Gulf Stream increasingly salty and it cools. These processes combine to increase the density of the water, which eventually sinks in the North Atlantic off the coast of northern Norway. The freezing of the Arctic Ocean every winter also creates cold dense water that sinks. Combined, these processes that cause surface waters to sink, drive thermohaline circulation.

In the last five million years Antarctica has also been drifting southwards, covering the South Pole about one million years ago. This created a large permanent ice sheet with a knock on effect for global atmospheric circulation and climate. The ice sheet cooled the Earth by increasing albedo, or reflectivity. All the sunlight that lands on Antarctica now gets reflected straight back into space.

Combined, these processes are believed to have created conditions for the growth of ice sheets on Greenland, Europe and North America. The LR04 stack indicates the failed beginning of the ice age 3.3 million years ago (Figure 1). We would have to wait another half million years before things would get going properly.

Orbital Milankovitch cycles

There was one final ingredient required to trigger the Ice Age and that was the configuration of Earth's orbit. Russian physicist Milutin Milankovitch was the first to recognise that the patterns of variation seen in ice cores

2. G H Haug & R Tiedemann, 'Effect of the formation of the Isthmus of Panama on Atlantic Ocean thermohaline circulation,', *Nature* 393, 1998, pp673-676.

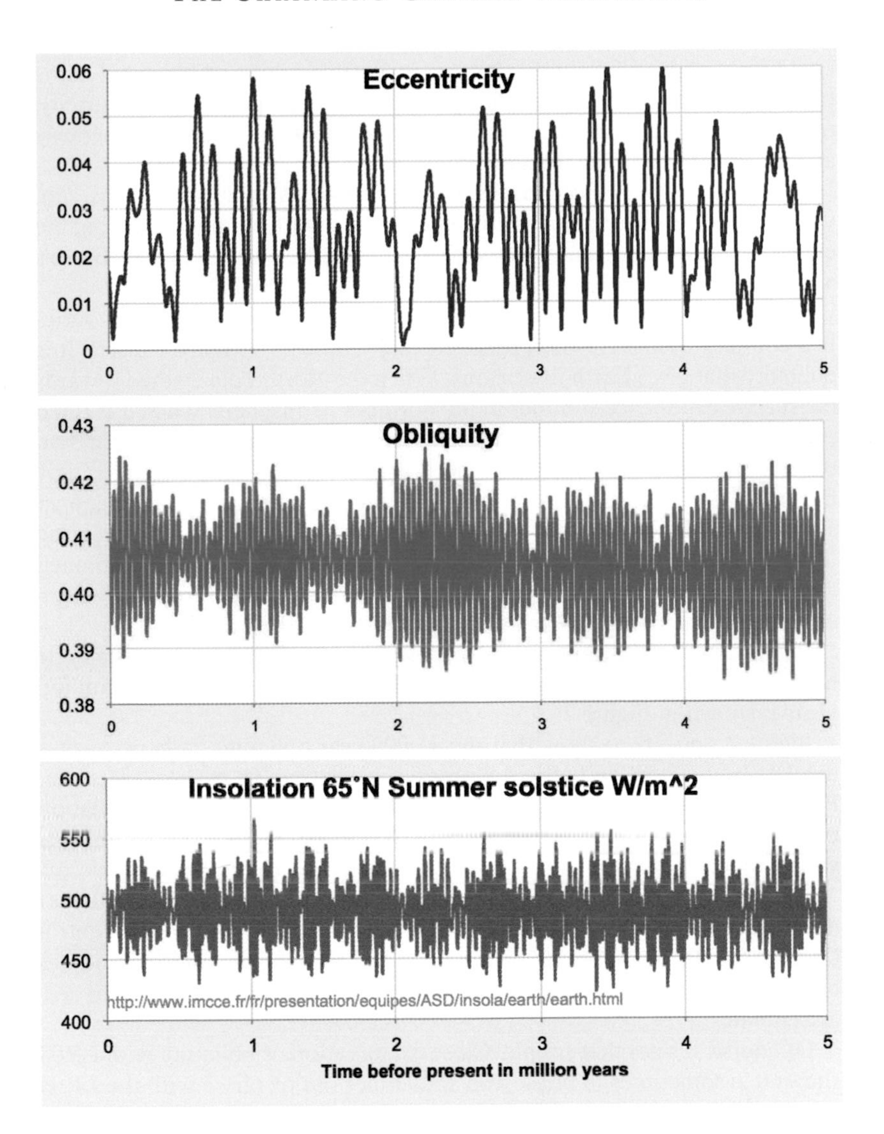

Figure 2 The charts show how eccentricity and obliquity have varied during the last five million years[3]. The total amount of solar energy (insolation) arriving at Earth does not vary much with these cycles, but the distribution of where it arrives does as illustrated in the lower panel. The variations in insolation arriving at 65°N are quite substantial and 2.7 million years ago extremely low values are shown for a short spell. Whether this was enough to trigger the onset of the northern hemisphere glaciation is an interesting question.

3. Data from *www.imcce.fr/fr/presentation/equipes/ASD/insola/earth/earth.html*

could be explained by subtle changes in Earth's orbit and gives his name to these Milankovitch cycles. They have three components: eccentricity, obliquity and precession. These three components all act simultaneously and are illustrated in the inset of Figure 1.

So what are they? Eccentricity describes Earth's orbit around the sun, which varies between being almost circular to slightly elliptical. During the elliptical phase the distance between Earth and Sun varies during Earth's annual orbit. This cycle lasts between 100,000 and 400,000 years.

Obliquity is a measure of the angle of tilt of Earth's axis that varies in a complex cyclical fashion between 22.5° and 24.5° (Figure 1 inset). It is obliquity that gives Earth its seasons. When the North Pole is tilted towards the sun we experience summer in the northern hemisphere, when it is tilted away from the sun, as the Earth makes its annual journey around our star, the northern hemisphere experiences winter. When the obliquity angle increases, Earth experiences greater and more extreme seasonality: longer summers and longer winters. The Arctic Circle moves south with increasing tilt and longer winters may result in more high-latitude snowfall combined with longer summer melt. It is not clear which would win through to begin or end a glacial cycle. The obliquity cycle lasts 41,000 years.

Precession describes rotational wobble around the Earth's axis. Its cycle is 21,000 years. How these components have varied over the last five million years is shown in Figure 2.

Figure 1 appears to show that the 41,000-year obliquity cycle permeates the data both before and after the onset of glaciation 2.8 million years ago. Following the onset of glaciation, the amplitude of temperature oscillation increased; 1.2 million years ago the pattern changes to longer cycles and it is widely reported that the 100,000-year eccentricity cycle took control.

In fact, Figure 1 shows very few of these cycles have 100,000-year duration; our analysis points to multiples of 41,000 years being in control (Figure 3). Glaciation begins with 82,000 and 80,000-year cycles: multiples of 41,000. So maybe it's the 41,000-year obliquity cycle that rules the ice-age climate.

Of course, it's not that simple. Close examination of obliquity with LR04 shows it is sometimes in phase and sometimes out of phase with the LR04 observations (Figures 4 and 5). This puts a joker in the pack; it suggests there are no hard physical rules linking the glacial state to obliquity. Sometimes the ice melts when the angle of tilt is high (Figure 4) and sometimes Earth is in the deepest part of a glacial cycle (Figure 5).

The last turning point of the obliquity cycle occurred 10,000 years ago. That happens to coincide with the end of the last glaciation and the onset of the Holocene. Obliquity is now rising and we are halfway to the next turning point. But if there aren't any rules, are imperfect orbital alignments a red herring when it comes to glaciation?

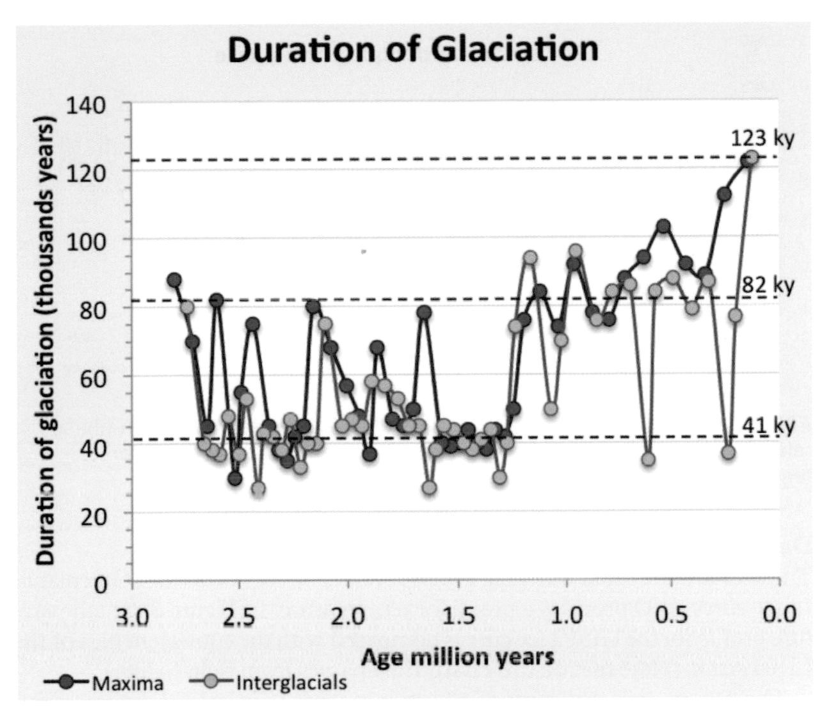

Figure 3 This chart displays the glacial cycle lengths as read from Figure 1. Note that the time between cycle peaks and troughs is not always the same. It has long been claimed that the 100,000 year eccentricity cycle expressed itself 1.2 million years ago. There is little evidence for that in these data that appear to vary according to multiples of the 41,000-year obliquity cycle Lisiecki and Raymo[1] do say that the ages of samples from different boreholes are aligned by tuning to the 41,000-year signal. It may be possible that this statistical adjustment has given rise to this cycle length dominating the profile.

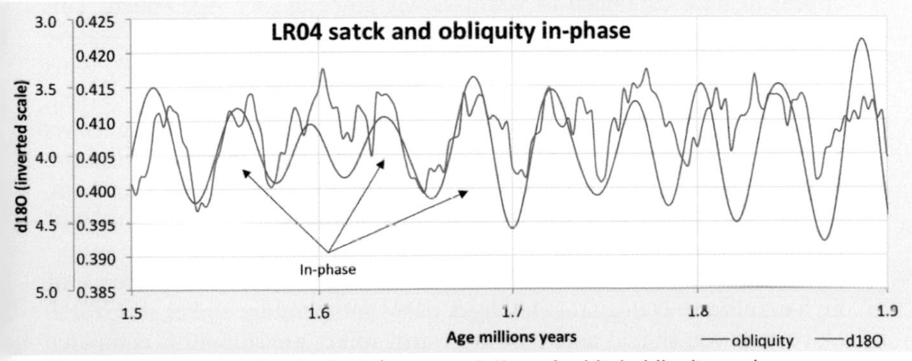

Figure 4 A more detailed look at the co-variation of orbital obliquity and temperature shows that from 1.5 to 1.9 million years ago obliquity and temperature were in phase, temperature rising with high obliquity. LR04 $\partial^{18}O$ data source[1] and obliquity data source[3].

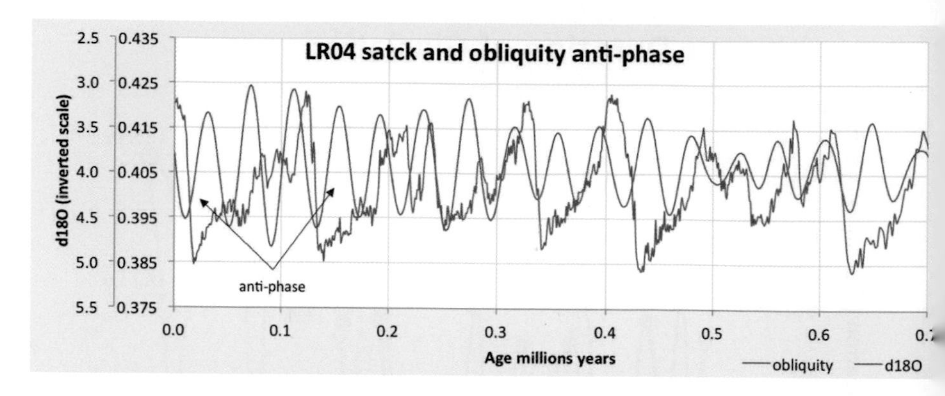

Figure 5 Looking at the interval 0 to 700,000 years we see that the in-phase relationship described in Figure 4 does not hold and there is a greater tendency for intense cold during the high obliquity part of the cycle.

Dansgaard-Oeschger events

These events are rapid warming cycles revealed in ice cores from Greenland. In ice cores, $\partial^{18}O$ provides a proxy for temperature. In Figure 6 the temperature profile for the GISP2 ice core is compared with the equivalent part of the LR04 stack. (Note that on this chart, time passes from right to left.)

The macro-scale structure of the two records is in splendid agreement. Yet in detail there are clearly many differences. One has to bear in mind that the GISP2 ice core is recording the air temperature at the summit of the Greenland ice cap while LR04 is recording temperature change throughout the Earth's oceans. The very large thermal mass of the oceans means that they respond more slowly to change and do not record short-lived local events like those recorded on the top of Greenland.

It's important to pay attention to a fundamental difference between the ice core and oceanic data during the last 10,000 years. In this period, oceans appear to have continued to warm slowly since the Ice Age ended. This alone may account for the recorded global warming and sea level rise we hear so much about. And since the slow warming trend began 10,000 years ago it clearly has nothing to do with humans burning fossil fuels. In contrast, the ice core data shows more constant temperature and if anything shows a recent cooling trend. It is the uniform temperatures seen in ice cores from Greenland and Antarctica that have given rise to the notion of a uniform, unchanging climate on Earth. Note that the temperature on the summit of Greenland is -30°C.

The most obvious difference between the two records is the presence of high-amplitude Dansgaard-Oeschger event temperature spikes in GISP2. (Although you should note that the warm spikes are still -40°C compared with less than -50°C during cold intervals and -30°C during the modern interglacial.) Dansgaard-Oeschger events are periodic – sort of. Sometimes they're regular, sometimes two or three cycles merge into one and sometimes the events are much smaller than the 10°C norm.

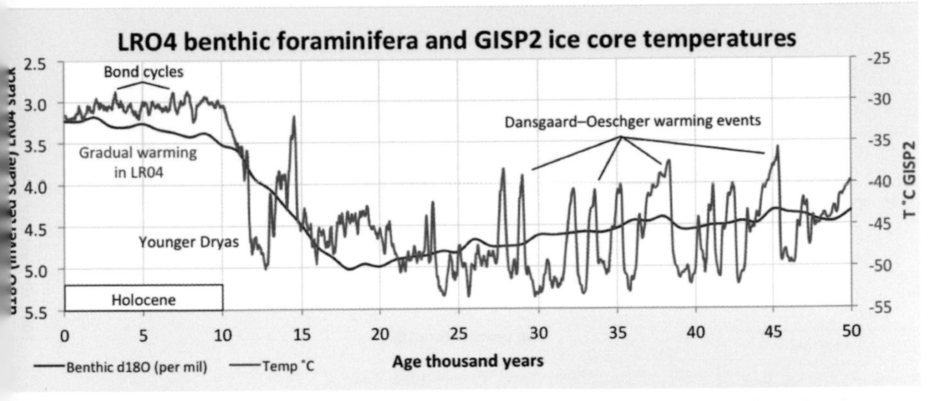

Figure 6 This chart compares temperature from the GISP2 ice core from Greenland with the LR04 stack. The macro-scale agreement is excellent but the details are quite different. GISP2 temperature data source[4] downloaded from[5].

There are around four or five Dansgaard-Oeschger events in 5,000 years, between 1,000 and 1,250 years per event. The origin of these is not understood with certainty but a leading contender is cyclical shifts in the intensity of the Gulf Stream[6]. This is interesting, because we know the creation of the Gulf Stream may be implicated in creating conditions for the Ice Age to begin, and now we see that oscillations in the Gulf Stream may influence the intensity of cold on Greenland. The Dansgaard-Oeschger cycles are all but absent in ice cores from Antarctica suggesting they are local to the North Atlantic. They are not visible in the oceanic LR04 stack.

Fourteen thousand years ago there was what seems to have been a larger than normal Dansgaard-Oeschger event that threatened to bring glaciation to an end. But the ice did not give up its grip; the period known as the Younger Dryas Event 12,000 years ago was the last gasp of the last glaciation. In the Holocene, Dansgaard-Oeschger events appear to have continued – but on a much smaller scale. The forces that caused the Gulf Stream to oscillate appear to still be active but with much reduced effect when the Gulf Stream is in full flow, as it is today.

What physical mechanism lies behind these Dansgaard-Oeschger events and oscillations in the Gulf Stream? Isotopes from ice cores provide a clue. This time we look at the concentration of Beryllium 10 (^{10}Be), called a cosmogenic isotope because it forms in the atmosphere through the action of cosmic rays on oxygen and nitrogen. Beryllium is a solid and so falls out of the atmosphere in rainwater and snow and accumulates in ice.

The main control over the concentration of ^{10}Be in ice is the rate of snowfall. More snowfall means a lower concentration of ^{10}Be. But the rate

4. R B Alley et al, 'History of the Greenland Ice Sheet: paleoclimatic insights', *Quaternary Science Reviews* 29, 2010, pp1728-56.
5. Greenland Ice Sheet Project 2 ice core temperature and accumulation data, ftp://ftp.ncdc.noaa.gov/pub/data/paleo/icecore/greenland/summit/gisp2/isotopes/gisp2_temp_accum_alley2000.txt
6. 'A paleo perspective on abrupt climate change', National Climatic Data Centre, *http://www.ncdc.noaa.gov/paleo/abrupt/data3.html*

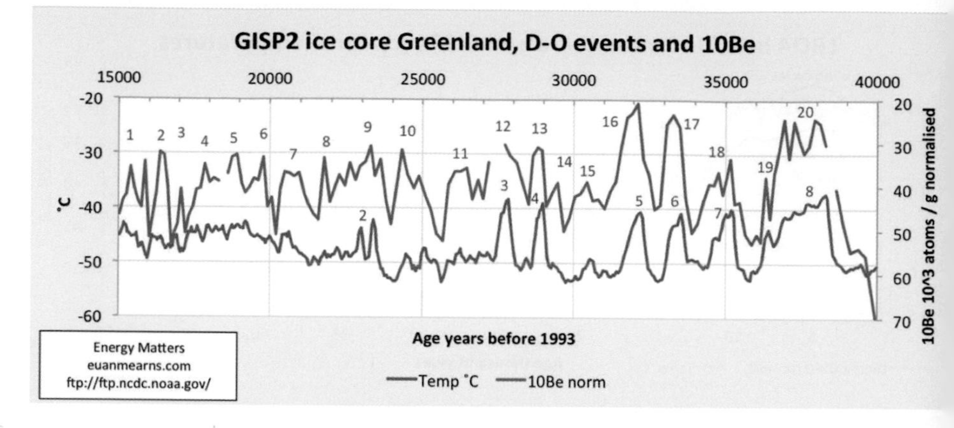

Figure 7 Comparison of temperature and ^{10}Be in the GISP2 ice core[7]. The ^{10}Be concentrations are corrected for ice deposition rate[5] and should therefore reflect the rate of ^{10}Be production in the atmosphere via the action of cosmic rays on oxygen and nitrogen. Note that the ^{10}Be scale is inverted. The main variable controlling cosmic ray penetration on Earth is the sun's magnetic field carried by the solar wind. When the sun is covered in sunspots and active, the magnetic field is strong shielding Earth from cosmic rays and ^{10}Be production falls. Warm ^{10}Be events labelled in red 2 to 8[4] correspond to periods of active sun.

of production of ^{10}Be is not constant. The combined magnetic field strength of the sun and the Earth shields the Earth from galactic cosmic rays. When the field strength is high the rate of ^{10}Be production falls and vice versa.

Figure 7 shows ^{10}Be concentration through part of the GISP2 ice core. (Concentrations have been corrected for levels of snowfall.) These data suggest that cyclical changes in solar activity are linked to Dansgaard-Oeschger events. It also shows that each Dansgaard-Oeschger event is aligned with a ^{10}Be anomaly, although there are many more ^{10}Be anomalies than there are Dansgaard-Oeschger events. We count 20 ^{10}Be events from 15,000 to 38,000 years ago. The numbered Dansgaard-Oeschger events follow Alley[4]. But you can see many more small amplitude Dansgaard-Oeschger events may be present when temperature data are compared to ^{10}Be. (For example: small Dansgaard-Oeschger events may be present at ^{10}Be events 2, 7, 10, 11 and 15.)

All this implies that the sun is creating rhythmical changes to the Gulf Stream. How could that be? We look at this later, but for now suffice to say that changes in solar activity may impact the pattern of atmospheric circulation and winds. Changing wind patterns may affect the Gulf Stream and climate in general.

Bond cycles

The final part of this story, zeroing in on the present day, comes from the mineralogy of sediment core samples from the North Atlantic. Bond

7. Beryllium 10 concentrations in the Greenland Ice Sheet Project 2 ice core, ftp://ftp.ncdc.noaa.gov/pub/data/paleo/icecore/greenland/summit/gisp2/cosmoiso/ber10.txt.

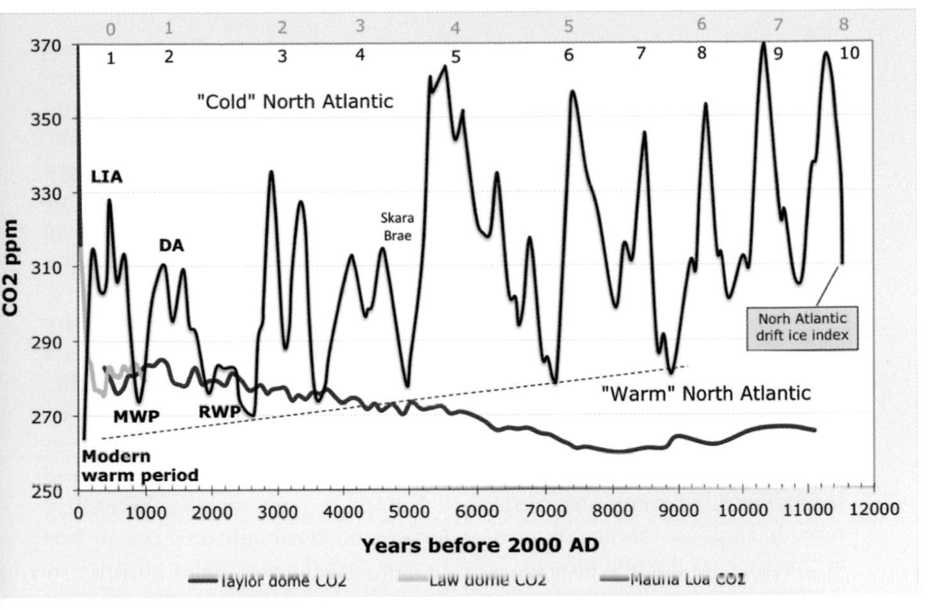

Figure 8 The black trace labelled 'North Atlantic drift ice index' is copied from Bond et al[8]. When the index is high icebergs drifted much further south than today implying cyclically cold North Atlantic waters. The drift ice index shows no correlation with CO_2 apart from during the current Modern Warm Period where the rise in temperature and CO_2 could be viewed as coincidental. The Bond cycles also correlate with ^{10}Be and with historic evidence for cyclical climate change in the North Atlantic. RWP = Roman Warm Period; DA = Dark Ages cold period; MWP = Medieval Warm Period; LIA = Little Ice Age. At the very top in grey are the cycles 0 to 8 as labelled by Bond et al. We have re-labelled these 1 to 10 in black.

et al[8] identified three geological markers: volcanic glass from Iceland, iron-stained grains from east Greenland and Svalbard and carbonate grains from northern Canada. The absolute and relative abundance of these grains in the sediments was observed to vary and Bond postulated this was a reflection of the patterns of drift ice movement in the North Atlantic during the Holocene. Stacking all their data from four boreholes produced the North Atlantic drift ice index (Figure 8). The cyclical variation is quasi-regular with 10 cycles in the last 12,000 years giving a 1,200-year duration that is similar in length to the ^{10}Be cycles.

You can think of Bond cycles simply as alternations between a warm and cold North Atlantic. Bond et al suggest the northern part of the Gulf Stream was periodically truncated as the Labrador Current cut across the North Atlantic, bringing much colder conditions to Europe. Bond cycles also correlate with ^{10}Be anomalies, suggesting that variations in solar and terrestrial magnetic activity were once again the driving force.

8. G Bond et al, 'Persistent solar influence on North Atlantic climate during the Holocene', *Science*, vol 294, 2001, pp2130-36.

Bond data overlaps with written history. For example, the Roman climate was warmer; vines were grown in the north of England and Hannibal crossed ice-free Alps. The Roman Empire came to an end as the climate cooled and northern tribes encroached onto Roman territory. The Roman era has become known as the Roman Warm Period (RWP) and stands out as a prolonged spell of warm North Atlantic waters – see Figure 8. Wood, in the form of pre-fossil trees, from beneath the Mer de Glace in France give dates ranging from 666 to 3,671 years ago, demonstrating that the treeline was much higher in the past, clear evidence that the climate has been warmer than today[9].

By the early medieval period, the climate had warmed again; Vikings were trading around the globe, settling in Greenland and Newfoundland under a climatic regime that was more benign and pleasant than today. The Medieval Warm Period gave way once again to a cooling climate with the onset of the Little Ice Age when long cold winters became common if not the norm. Viking history relates how the sea ice encroached on south Greenland and Iceland making communication with Europe in their wooden long-ships more hazardous. Viking colonies on Greenland eventually died out. It was at this time, as documented by Jean Grove, that the last major advance of Alpine glaciers took place. It is from this cyclical advance 500 years ago that the Alpine glaciers began their cyclical retreat that continues today. The cold conditions of the Little Ice Age that gave way to the Modern Warm Period are written into the sediments of the North Atlantic.

Physical process

We have seen how Earth's climate is restless, changing continuously, and how in the North Atlantic region, changes in the strength and configuration of the Gulf Stream may have caused the Ice Age to begin 2.8 million years ago and how fluctuations in the Gulf Stream, as documented in Atlantic sediments and ice cores, cause quasi-periodic fluctuations in climate on a time-scale of around 1,000 to 1,250 years. We are in the middle of the most recent warming episode, which explains in part why Alpine glaciers are retreating. We have also seen how the Bond and Dansgaard-Oeschger cycles correlate with cosmogenic ^{10}Be without fully understanding why this should be the case.

Danish physicist, Henrik Svensmark has proposed that increased bombardment by cosmic rays at times when the sun sleeps may increase the nucleating rate of clouds. This creation of cloudier conditions may explain cooling and the onset of mini cold spells[10]. But clinching evidence to support this theory has yet to be found.

The winter of 2010-11 brought extreme cold weather and plenty of snow to western Europe. This happened at a time when the sun had grown anomalously quiet compared to the previous 80 years. Scientists and the public could observe the conditions that may have prevailed during the

9. J Grove, *The Little Ice Age*, 1988, Methuen.
10. H Svensmark et al, 'Experimental evidence for the role of ions in particle nucleation under atmospheric conditions', *Proceedings of the Royal Society A* 463, 2007, pp385-96.

Little Ice Age. The jet stream became more meandering with large loops sucking Arctic air off Siberia and blowing it over Europe. Lakes and rivers that hadn't frozen for many decades froze that winter. So much, many people must have thought, for global warming.

Researchers at the UK's Met Office perhaps provide the answer[11]. Satellite measurements of solar output during the last solar minimum in 2010 found a higher than expected decline in mid-ultra violet (UV) radiation. UV radiation is trapped by ozone in the upper atmosphere and less UV would result in cooling at high altitudes. The Met Office team was able to model this effect and showed it could result in the modifications observed in the jet stream resulting in extreme cold winters.

We will only be able to fully understand the causes of natural fluctuations in Earth's climate once we have the opportunity to observe these fluctuations in action using satellites. Change in the spectral emissions from the sun that correlate with the sun's geomagnetic activity is a leading contender. Following a period of hyper-activity from 1933 to 2010 the sun has now become very quiet and will likely remain so for another 30 years. We may be about to find out if this marks the return of cold and snowy winters to Europe.

Glacier retreat in the Modern Warm Period

What are the implications of all this for the modern era? Glaciers grow, mainly through snowfall in winter, and ablate at the snout, mainly in the summer. Current research shows the Mer de Glace is retreating on average nine metres per year[12]. (Nevertheless in years of substantial snow fall there is evidence that the glacier has advanced.) The glacier is estimated to have retreated 1.27km since records began in 1878. Historical data suggests the Mer de Glace has been retreating since the Little Ice Age. The key issue is whether this retreat has accelerated due to the influence of the dramatic increase in CO_2 since the beginning of the industrial age. Currently there is no compelling evidence in the Mer de Glace research for an acceleration in the glacier's retreat. More research is needed to unravel the influence of CO_2 emissions, which will be challenging against a background of natural glacier retreat.

The current glacial retreat observed around the world is the product of a long-ranging climatic warming that began five hundred years ago at the end of the Little Ice Age and onset of the Modern Warm Period. Our belief is that this is part of a glacial cycle that can be tied to the sun's activity. The effect of the recent CO_2 spike in the Earth's atmosphere may be contributing to the recent global temperature increases, but it is unlikely, given the evidence of long-range glacial cycling, to be the controlling factor. The question is, given the choice, would we rather have global warming or the alternative, global cooling, and the extension of glacial systems into alpine valleys, with the devastating outcome this would have on mountain communities?

11. S Ineson et al, 'Solar forcing of winter climate variability in the northern hemisphere', *Nature Geoscience*, 2011.
12. M Le Roy et al, 'Calendar-dated glacier variations in the western European Alps during the Neoglacial: the Mer de Glace record, Mont Blanc massif', *Quaternary Science Reviews* 108, 2015, pp1-22.

The Competitive Spirit

Figure in a Landscape
In the upper reaches of Zero Gully, Ben Nevis.
Rob Fairley, 1982. (Pencil. 130cm x 80cm. Private collection.)

VICTOR SAUNDERS

Seconds Out

Jerry Lovatt and Glyn Hughes square up in Pakistan's Swat valley during the 1968 Innominate Mountaineering Group expedition to Miangul Sar. The expedition made the second and third ascents. The fight was a draw. *(Glyn Hughes)*

This story begins in a tent. Tents are interesting: they insulate you from space and time. From the outside a tent is a small insignificant dot in the landscape. From the inside it is the whole universe. According to Caspar Hauser tents are larger than the outside, because when outside you can see the landscape AND the tent. But from the inside you see only the tent, so they hide the outside world, which means they must be bigger than it.

So in this tent, somewhere in the world, which was hidden from view, Fowler began to talk about London. For all we knew we could have been there: in London, in the tent, camped on the pavement, drinkers staggering past us on the way from the pub to the Indian restaurant. I felt the tent rustle; maybe it was a glacial breeze, maybe a drunk passing too close to our section of pavement. Fowler rolled onto his side and said:

'I know a pub where you can box your friends.'

'You mean a gym?'

'No, I mean a pub. Where you can box your friends. There's a ring and a referee and they have gloves you can borrow.'

'Okay, next weekend.'

There it was: the start of something new. Suddenly I had questions.

'But… fighting? I don't know how to do that.'

'Easy, just like in school.'

I didn't say anything but I didn't think I had been to the same kind of school as Fowler.

'But, what about wearing glasses?'

'Easy, just put in your contact lenses.'

We must have been at the end of the expedition, or else we were already in London. In any case, next weekend came, and so did we, to the Kings in Seven Kings, not a pub but a nightclub in Ilford. I drove over from Islington with Fanshawe, who agreed to be my second. The saloon was long and at the far end was a boxing ring. The atmosphere was boozy, filled with tobacco smoke and a sort of blood lust. A man in a check suit was telling jokes over the PA. He was in the middle of a story about a prostitute and a lorry driver.

Fowler and Fenwick eventually found us. The place was heaving. Judging by the tattoos on display the Kings served as watering hole to the local branch of the National Front, eventually eclipsed by the BNP – the 'British Nasty Party'.

At this point I have to tell you something quite important. I am dark-skinned, and when visiting glaciated mountains I go very dark indeed. Without a shirt on, it is obvious that my un-tanned body is reasonably European. But my face takes on the shades of Asia. We had just returned from Pakistan. Perhaps I should not have mentioned that so often. I was already getting some strange looks from the other customers.

The Kings was in Fenwick's backyard so he explained it all to me when we arrived.

'They have a pub professional here.'

'Eh?'

Lovatt and Hughes shake hands 48 years later. *(Ed Douglas)*

'The boxing ring, you can fight your friend or you can fight the pub professional.'

'Hmm.'

'They had Nigel Benn here once.'

'But this is skinhead territory?'

'Yeah, but it was Nigel Benn. They don't mind blacks if they can box.'

'Oh, I see. A bit like ten-pin bowling, I suppose.' I had a happy image of a huge black ball scattering white skittles.

'Eh?' Fenwick was shaking his head. He couldn't grasp what I was saying against the noise. He shouted: 'It's Asians they don't like.'

'Oh.'

Glasses and the fight game do not go together. I had learned that in the tent. So the day before our bout I found an optician who sold me some contact lenses. I had forgotten to ask how to use them but set off to the loo to try and figure that out.

The face in the mirror grimaced out at me as I tried to poke contact lenses into its eyes. Yet the only contact the lenses seemed to make was with his fingers and cheeks. Like identical poles, the lenses seemed magnetically repulsed from the corneas. After half an hour I gave up and emerged from the loo with red eyes, my vision blurred, having failed quite comprehensively to insert the lenses. I was just going to have to try without. I dropped my spectacles in the sink and returned to the bar. Pushing through the crowd without them would be good training for the fight, I thought. Provided I didn't spill anyone's beer.

The man in the check suit was now telling a story about a Pakistani and a lorry driver. He seemed quite keen on lorry drivers. He had a hoarse, smoke-damaged voice and a loud tie that only emphasised his rolls of neck fat. He was enjoying himself, and his audience chuckled beerily at his coarse jokes.

Without glasses I couldn't see much. It was all a blur, a bit like opening your eyes under water in a pool. At the edge of my vision I could make out the one black man in the room. He was huge, and no one was bothering him. I managed to make my way over without bumping into anyone.

'Hello.'

He turned round slowly. 'Yes?'

'I've never boxed before.'

'And?'

'I am fighting my friend. The one over there? He is bigger than me. I don't know your name, but I wonder if you could possibly help me. Any tips on how to survive, for instance?'

'S'easy. You just hold your mitts up – like this. He jabs at you – you keep your guard up, duck and weave. Kna-wha'-I-mean?'

Ignoring my shake of the head, he put his fists either side of his temples. Peeping through the gap he said: 'You have to move, use your legs.' The professional danced around a bit to illustrate the point. 'And when there's a gap in his guard, you smack him – like this.'

He jabbed his left, stopping an inch from my nose. It was actually rather a beautiful movement. Starting from his right toe you could see the force flowing through his body to culminate in the weapon that was his fist. Then he shook my hand for luck and pushed me in the general direction of the ring.

Our seconds, Fenwick and Fanshawe, helped us lace up the big red boxing mitts. Then we climbed into the ring and touched fists. The ref introduced us to the crowd who began to howl and bay. He said various things, which I couldn't hear. I noticed how much harder it is to hear without spectacles, but this didn't seem like the moment to reflect on that. I expect the referee was explaining the rules he wanted us to fight by. I was still trying to listen, head cocked to one side, boxing mitt to the ear to act as some kind of ear horn, when he stood aside.

The bell rang and I immediately understood the disadvantage of not being able to see. From out of the blur emerged a charging Fowler. There was a sort of aura, a halo around him, which on closer inspection resolved itself into a cloud of whirling arms and fists. I think this might be called the 'windmill technique', but I'm not sure. The crowd of faces round the ring cheered and roared.

I don't remember the pain so much as the noise – noise and a very confused state of mind. I had the recommended guard up to each side of my head. I could more or less squint thorough the gap between my gloves. I was doing everything right and still the blows were raining down all round my head. While it was true that Fowler was not battering my face, now guarded, he was hammering the top of my head, my neck, my shoulders, and even the back of my head. How did he reach there?

The pub professional had not given me any advice about countering windmills so I retreated gracefully. That is to say, I ran away into the ropes of the ring. I had forgotten about them and didn't see them till they emerged from the blur of faces at chest height. The Fowler fists were now drumming on my back. The crowd was going wild. The bout had only just started and already they were howling. I thought I might be in danger from them too.

They were chanting, altogether: 'Kill 'im! Kill 'im! Kill 'im!'

Kill him? Not all of us are swift at taking personal vilification to heart. Sometimes you need to reflect. It takes a while to understand you are the object of universal vilification. Besides which, I was rather pre-occupied. Yet slowly it dawned on me. Apparently, I said to myself, they want to see me dead. They want my opponent to kill me. Me. It all seemed rather personal – and such thoughts are not destined to offer peace of mind to the *ingenu* boxer. I held my gloves up against the onslaught. I weaved. I ducked, most usually straight into an oncoming fist. I still don't fully understand how that works.

The referee remained a white blur with a dark patch marking out his natty bow tie. I am not particularly anti-authoritarian. I don't make a habit of blaming umpires, but in this case I have to say the referee was not much help. Every time I got behind him. He moved out of the way. He just would not stay put. And every time he stepped aside there was Fowler and the crowd cheering him on:

'Go-fer-it! Kill 'im! Kill 'im! KILL 'IM!'

I had been told the bout would last a minute but that was a very long 60 seconds. More like an hour, I would have said. I have often wondered if the ref kept it going to entertain the crowds. As time passed, the Fowler windmill slowed down a little; at times he seemed to be resting his tired hands on me. I understood Fowler had finally exhausted himself when he collapsed onto my shoulders in a kind of tired bear hug. The referee stepped in to separate us.

At this point, I remembered the words of the pub professional and attempted a right jab in the general direction of Fowler's face. But I think I may have caught the referee because immediately he sat down. When he got up again he kicked me in the shin, and to uproar from the disappointed crowds, stopped the fight.

Back in the loo, someone had removed my glasses from the basin. Punch drunk and half blind, I staggered back to the bar, pushing through the crowd, which had now forgotten me. Fenwick and Fowler had lined up several pints for me.

'Great entertainment!' Fenwick said, slapping me on the back and handing over my spectacles. 'I rescued these from the bog.'

I had a headache for days. At work someone asked me who had won.

'I can't say,' I told him and then thought a while. 'But I'm pretty sure it wasn't me.'

ERIC VOLA

Walter Bonatti and *The Ghosts of K2*

K2 from Concordia. When Charlie Houston heard the news of the Italian success he wrote to the *New York Times*: 'Something is gone which has filled my thoughts for 16 years since my first visit to K2, but I salute, with all my heart, the Italians and their success.'

In 2004, on the 50th anniversary of the first ascent of K2, the Italian Alpine Club (CAI) published a statement that supported Walter Bonatti's version of what happened on the mountain at the end of July 1954 as the expedition reached its climax. This version, for which Bonattti had fought so hard, became the new 'official' one, and was accepted by the Italian press and the mountaineering community.

In his new book, *The Ghosts of K2*, Mick Conefrey aims to convince us that this 'new "official history" is more flawed than the old one it was designed to correct,' being typical of the 'Machiavellian' mind of Italians. Far from the CAI's statement closing the matter, Conefrey states that the 'truth' remained to be told and that it is in his new book that you will find it; he claims that Bonatti was wrong, that Achille Compagnoni and Lino Lacedelli were not the liars Bonatti claimed they were, and the plot against

Bonatti was merely the work of his imagination.

In a preamble to all this, Conefrey suggests that such chaotic bickering is not surprising in 'a country where vendettas can run for centuries and legal battles for decades, where conspiracies and cover-ups abound and where, as Machiavelli puts it, many people prefer "to look at things not as they really are, but how they wish them to be."' Bonatti, in Conefrey's judgement, may possibly have been the 'greatest mountaineer ever' but he was also typically Italian and a paranoiac.

The problem is that Conefrey's theory is based more on speculation and opinion than facts. 'The more that I look at documents from the period, the more I am convinced that Compagnoni and Lacedelli were telling the truth,' he wrote on his blog when his book was published. But these are the same documents the CAI had access to when making its assessment. Even his new detail that he offers as damning proof, the colour of one of the oxygen bottles filmed on top of K2, does almost nothing to address the reasons behind Bonatti's 40-year struggle for justice or to contradict the detailed analysis Bonatti made over that long and often lonely period.

'It will be up to the public to make their own minds up,' Conefrey concludes, but British climbers do not have access to Bonatti's thoughts nor those of his friends, despite the excellent translation of *The Mountains of my Life* by the Australian Robert Marshall. Later books, particularly *K2 La Verità: Storia di un casa*, have not been published in English, neither has Reinhold Messner's 2013 *Walter Bonatti: Il fratello che non sapevo di avere*, not to mention Luigi Sanzi's *K2: Una Storia Finite*. This article is written so that British readers can be better prepared 'to make their own minds up.'

Let's review the last key four days of the summit ascent, beginning on 28 July 1954, according to the new official version Conefrey criticises. Erich Abram, Pino Galotti, Achille Compagnoni and Lino Lacedelli put up a tent at camp VIII, the penultimate camp, at an altitude of 7,627m, 100m lower than planned. Galotti and Abram, who is in charge of the oxygen sets, go down to camp VII, leaving Compagnoni and Lacedelli to establish camp IX next day at around 8,100m before coming down to camp VIII. By then more men and material will have arrived.

On 29 July, Abram, Galotti, Ubaldo Rey and Walter Bonatti start from camp VII with equipment and two oxygen sets for the summit assault. Several Hunza porters are expected to come later from lower camps with more equipment and food. Rey and Abram are forced to give up 50m above camp VII. Rey is so exhausted he has to go down to base camp while Abram stays in camp VII to rest, intending to go back up next morning.

Galotti is too tired to add the oxygen set Abram was carrying to his own load. Bonatti decides that carrying only one oxygen set isn't logical so he leaves behind the second set he is carrying, exchanging it for a second tent, vital for camp VIII, food, an air mattress and an additional sleeping bag. They arrive in the late afternoon at camp VIII to find Compagnoni and Lacedelli, who have only managed to go up 100m, stashing their rucksacks before coming down.

The situation looks quite desperate. They discuss at length what to do, deciding that the only hope of reaching the summit is to bring up the two oxygen sets of three cylinders each, left slightly above camp VII, up to Camp IX, yet to be established. Bonatti was the fittest of all the climbers; the effort to go down and bring up the oxygen loads was thought too much for Compagnoni and Lacedelli. Finally they decide Galotti and Bonatti will go down and carry the oxygen sets up to camp VIII and then to camp IX before nightfall. Meanwhile Compagnoni and Lacedelli will establish camp IX and wait for them.[1]

They agree that the proposed site for camp IX in the expedition plan, below a band of red rocks, is too high for the party carrying up the oxygen sets to reach before night. (This fact is omitted in Conefrey's account.) It should instead be established 100m lower down, at around 7,900m or 8,000m. Even so, Bonatti and his companions carrying the oxygen sets will first have to descend almost 300m towards camp VII, then turn around and climb up 500m with 20kg loads. All four expect to stay in the small tent at camp IX. As Bonatti wrote: 'A folly, but considering the situation the success on K2 will result from this folly.' As things turn out, he will have to climb up not 500m but 700m.

On the morning of 30 July, at 8am, Bonatti and Galotti leave camp VIII (7627 m) for camp VII (7345m) to collect the oxygen cylinders. They meet Abram coming up with the two best Hunza high-altitude porters, Mahdi and Isakhan. They share out the loads and go back up to camp VIII. Galotti is exhausted, Isakhan is sick and feverish, but Mahdi is in great shape. Abram and Bonatti promise him a premium to go to camp IX. Mahdi, who was with Hermann Buhl on Nanga Parbat the year before, forms the idea – wrongly – that Bonatti will try to attempt the summit on his own and without oxygen as he saw Buhl do.

Abram now feels slightly better and agrees to continue, taking turns to carry a load. They share some broth and leave camp VIII at 3.30pm. At 4.30pm, they reach the shoulder and now have a full view of the last part of the bottleneck at the vast serac below the summit slopes. They call to Compagnoni and Lacedelli and get some response but do not see their tent. They follow their tracks but these then disappear. They call again and hear Lacedelli shouting: 'Follow our tracks!'

Reaching 7,950m, they pass the site where camp IX should be. Of course, it isn't there. The sun has now disappeared behind K2; the cold is already severe. Abram can no longer feel his feet. Bonatti helps him undo his boots to rub them. At 6.30pm, Abram starts down to camp VIII. Bonatti and Mahdi continue on steeper and steeper slopes for two hours or so until night envelops them. Bonatti has now been working for nine and a half hours and has had nothing to drink since 3.30pm. This follows 23 days of being continuously at high altitude.

1. No climber on K2 in 1954 used oxygen except for Compagnoni and Lacedelli on the summit bit, six cylinders out of 151 brought to base camp, save two cylinders used to try and save the life of Mario Puchoz, who died on 20 July from pulmonary oedema.

"Gli Scala-
tori al Cam
po-base.
Da sinistra
in piedi:
Rey,
Angelino,
Bonatti,
Prof. Desio,
Lacedelli,
Abram,
Soldà,
Compagnoni
Floreanini.
In ginocchio:
Viotto,
Fantin,
Pagani,
Gallotti."

Postcards from the edge: anticlockwise from above. The team at base camp, with Bonatti standing, third from left, next to Desio; Vittorio Sella's stunning image of K2 with the *Abruzzi Spur* in profile; a publicity poster for the expedition film; a postcard of Ardito Desio, *Il Ducetto*, the imperious, non-climbing expedition leader, stands between his lieutenant Achille Compagnoni and Tenzing Norgay.

Lacedelli's Dräger oxygen set.

It is too late now for Bonatti and Mahdi to go down in the dark on such steep slopes. Cold and the prospect of a night out at 8,100m tip Mahdi over the edge. In an interview with French journalist Charlie Buffet in 2001, Bonatti recalled:

'We yelled, insulted them. Beside myself, I finally shouted: when I go down, I will denounce you… After some time, a light flashed not far away and I shouted.

Bonatti: Why did you not get out earlier?

Lacedelli: You don't imagine that we are going to stay out all night to freeze for your sake? Do you have the oxygen?

Bonatti: Yes.

Lacedelli: Leave it and go down.

Bonatti: We cannot. I could manage but Mahdi? No, he has lost control of himself.

'At that point, Mahdi, as if hypnotised by the light, rushes onto the impossible slope that separated us, yelling: "No good, Compagnoni, sahib, no good Lacedelli sahib." The poor chap, this is all he could say… Then the light went off. I thought they would put on their crampons and come to help us: but nothing. We yelled again, we cursed them, with all we had on our tongue, but they didn't reappear. If we are alive, it is only due to ourselves.'

Bonatti told Buffet, 'that night I should have died. I hoped that back at base camp my companions would come to me and apologise with a slap on

Mick Conefrey's book suggests the Italians took smaller capacity red Dalmine bottles to the summit but film footage, from which this image was taken, was colorised. Did the process change the bottles' colours? The stills image on the facing page shows a slightly different angle, with the Dräger bottles a very different shade of blue.

my shoulder saying: "Sorry Walter, we made a fuck-up." I was young and naïve! Not only did those excuses never come, my silence allowed an unjust and erroneous official version to impose itself on essential points.' Bonatti had no choice in keeping his silence. Like all the climbers, he had signed a contract preventing him from publishing anything or being interviewed for two years. Even if he had talked, in the immense patriotic euphoria generated in Italy by the team's success, his voice would not have been heard.

It's daybreak on 31 July and Mahdi wants to go down; Bonatti helps him put on his crampons. It's 6am. Bonatti clears snow that fell during the night off the two oxygen sets to make sure Compagnoni and Lacedelli can find them. Then he puts on his own crampons and starts down. At one point, he hears a shout and responds by waving his ice axe. Before descending a steep section above camp VIII, he turns around and has a good look at his bivouac site. He sees no one. It is now exactly 7am.

Compagnoni and Lacedelli leave camp IX, recover the oxygen sets and climb the bottleneck to reach the summit at or just before 6pm. They are back at camp VIII by 11pm.

The immediate aftermath of this success was protracted, sometimes bitter and quite complex; Italy celebrated while rumours swirled about the identity of the summit pair, information initially withheld by expedition leader, Ardito Desio. There were acrimonious disputes over the expedition budget. Compagnoni, in defiance of his teammates, would unsuccessfully sue the producers of the official K2 film for a share of the profits.

For Amir Mahdi, the consequences of his night out were far more catastrophic. Desio had not issued high-altitude reindeer boots to the Hunzas. (The Italians had the same boots Tenzing Norgay wore on his Everest expeditions in 1952 and 1953. See the article 'Hadow's Sole' on pp243-53.) As a consequence Mahdi's toes were badly frostbitten; he would lose them all. At base camp, he gave his version of what happened to Col Mohammad Ata-Ullah, the Pakistani liaison officer, accusing Compagnoni of having forced him and Bonatti to bivouac in the open and causing his frostbite. He also told Ata-Ullah, erroneously, that Bonatti had wanted to bypass Compagnoni and Lacedelli and dash for the summit. Given his almost non-existent English, that was understandable.

Conefrey goes out of his way to challenge the idea that Compagnoni was not 'a compulsive liar.' What happened next contradicts that notion. Ata-Ullah repeated Mahdi's accusations to Desio, who challenged Compagnoni, who in turn used Mahdi's claims about Bonatti's ambition to lay all the blame at Bonatti's door. Compagnoni also accused Bonatti of having used some of the oxygen to avoid frostbite and then of abandoning Mahdi to save his own life. Compagnoni told Desio that Bonatti and the others were carrying the oxygen masks and regulators as well as the bottles, yet another lie that would make its way into the official account, *The Ascent of K2*.

Ardito Desio, with the agreement of the Italian ambassador and Ata-Ullah, decided to keep the whole affair secret in order not to tarnish their success. For the good of Italian-Pakistan relations, the young Bonatti became a scapegoat. As Reinhold Messner wrote 50 years later: 'Bonatti was thrown to the wolves.'

Neither Desio nor the Italian ambassador questioned Mahdi, at the time or later, and Desio didn't ask Bonatti for his version of the ascent as he did with the other climbers. There is little doubt he believed the accusations about Bonatti to be true. Desio, who had chosen Compagnoni as his climbing leader for the final assault, relied on him. Senior figures in CAI authorities were told, but had no reason to doubt such a distinguished figure. The calumnies against Bonatti would remain hidden both from him and the public, at least for the next 10 years when Nino Giglio wrote his articles based on Compagnoni's mendacious accusations. Faith in Desio and an unwillingness to disturb a patriotic legend would prevent the CAI answering Bonatti's questions for another 40 years.

After K2, while Compagnoni was embroiled in his legal case, Walter Bonatti was well on his way to becoming one of the greatest alpinists of all time. In 1955 he had stunned the climbing world with his solo first ascent of the *Bonatti Pillar* on the Dru; there followed a hard new route on the Grand Pilier d'Angle in 1957 and the first ascent of Gasherbrum IV in 1958 by the difficult south-east ridge. There were several first ascents in Patagonia and the *Red Pillar* of the Brouillard in 1959.

In 1961, Bonatti finally broke his silence about the night of 30 July, describing in his first book *My Mountains* his terrible night at 8,100m on a small platform dug in the snow, on which he can just sit, beside Mahdi, mad from anguish and suffering, enduring temperatures of minus 25°C, scraping a hole in the snow to hide his head. Above all there is incomprehension: why did his companions abandon them? He concluded his K2 Chapter with this sentence: 'This [experience] marks with a red-hot iron the soul of a young man, undermining his character, which had yet to fully form.' Bonatti's story, of Compagnoni and Lacedelli, the two K2 heroes, criminally endangering the lives of Bonatti and Mahdi, was viewed as scandalous. It made Bonatti highly unpopular in Italy.

That same year he came under bitter attack in the Italian press for his role in the Frêney disaster. He was held responsible for the deaths of his com-

Walter Bonatti sits next to Lino Lacedelli at base camp following the first ascent, with no sign of the later antagonism that would divide them, following Compagnoni's accusations in July 1964. Lacedelli would later ask Bonatti for forgiveness – and be denied.

panions, accusations wholly without merit. (Pierre Mazeaud, caught up in the tragedy, said: 'the question that one should ask is not what more should Bonatti have done? But rather: how could he have done so much?' Bonatti was awarded the Légion d'Honneur by a grateful French state.) Such unfounded accusations could not have happened without Bonatti having powerful enemies. The CAI thought they knew all about Bonatti, having been told Compagnoni's lies by Desio, allegations wholly unknown to Bonatti. It's hard to maintain Conefrey's view that what happened on K2 was more cock-up than conspiracy.

The impact of Bonatti's stellar career on the older Compagnoni was toxic. As Reinhold Messner wrote: 'Achille Compagnoni feels crushed by this ubiquitous Bonatti who has now proved himself the master of all trades, pushing into the shadows the self-proclaimed hero of K2.' His response came during celebrations for the tenth anniversary in July and August 1964: publication of two articles from journalist Nino Giglio based on an interview with Compagnoni under the headline 'Ten years after, the truth about K2', and subtitled 'How Bonatti tried to get ahead of Compagnoni and Lacedelli'.

Compagnoni was repeating in public the accusations made against Bonatti in 1954: cowardice and theft. He told Giglio that Bonatti had tried to get ahead of him and Lacedelli, had used some of their oxygen which had caused them, according to the official account, to run out of oxygen

200m from the summit, and to have abandoned Mahdi to save his life and been solely responsible for Mahdi's frostbites. They were lies in 1954 and they were still lies ten years later.

Stunned, Bonatti went to justice and was cleared on all counts three years later. By then he had quit alpinism, depressed at the continuing hostility he faced from the Italian climbing establishment. Two members of the team testified in court, Pino Galotti and Erich Abram, who confirmed Bonatti did not have any oxygen masks and so could not use the oxygen as Compagnoni said, that he did not abandon Mahdi who reached Camp VIII before Bonatti. Mahdi's written testimony cleared Bonatti of the charge that he had abandoned the stricken porter or of trying to go to the summit ahead of Compagnoni and Lacedelli. Nino Giglio and his newspaper were condemned.

Yet the controversy did not end. The CAI and Desio refused for another 40 years to modify the official account of K2's ascent, which was celebrated every decade, just like Everest in the UK. Bonatti was more unpopular than ever in Italy. It was as if the justice system had made a mistake in condemning Giglio and his newspaper rather than Bonatti. He never stopped fretting about the conspiracy against him and what had really happened.

It was inevitable that Bonatti would consider the official account's claim that Compagnoni and Lacedelli had run out of oxygen some 200m from the summit. Compagnoni had accused him of using some of the oxygen in the night, the implication being that they had run out because of Bonatti. This was, as Bonatti termed it, 'the base lie'. It was only one of the lies Compagnoni told about Bonatti, but it is the heart and soul of Conefrey's argument.

In 1985, Bonatti wrote his own account of the controversy, *Proceso al K2*. The book was read by an Australian trekker and mountain literature fan called Robert Marshall, who was so incensed that he taught himself Italian and translated Bonatti's book *The Mountains of my Life*, including his own analysis of what had happened. The two men became friends. In 1994, Marshall came across a published photograph of Compagnoni on the summit with his oxygen mask on and the tube reaching down to an oxygen bottle. The set must have been working on the summit and had not given out after all. With the CAI still rejecting his request for an enquiry, Bonatti published a further account, *K2: La Verità* in 2003, incorporating some further analysis.

In 2004, for the 50th anniversary, a journalist, Giovanni Cenacchi, interviewed Lino Lacedelli, then aged 79, and published the results in a book, *K2: The Price of Conquest*. It was explosive stuff. Lacedelli confessed that the last camp, camp IX, had indeed been deliberately placed higher than agreed and hidden away in rocks far to the left from where Bonatti and Mahdi bivouacked. Lacedelli admitted this was done to prevent Bonatti from joining them for an attempt on the summit the following day. This was conspiracy, not cock-up. Lacedelli put all the blame onto Compagnoni and did not offer an explanation for why he had kept silent for 50 years. He did however maintain that they ran out of oxygen before getting to the top, only admitting that it could have been very near the summit, perhaps only 50m

Amir Mahdi being carried on a stretcher following his severe frostbite injuries. The Italians used the same boots as Tenzing wore on Everest in 1953, but Desio didn't issue them to the high-altitude porters.

below and not the 200m in the official account.

This time, finally, the then CAI president agreed to review the official narrative and appointed *tre saggi*, three 'wise men', who confirmed Bonatti's version on all counts. One of them, Luigi Sanzi, wrote a book, incorporating their report, published in 2007, *K2: Una Storia Finite*. At last, Bonatti was given back his honour and his proper place in the story of K2. And then, after this 50-year struggle to have Bonatti's version recognised as the truth, Conefrey produces a narrative that says Compagnoni and Lacedelli did not lie and that the whole story is a typical Machiavellian Italian mess.

Conefrey's argument is in reality quite narrow; it focuses only on whether or not Compagnoni and Lacedelli ran out of bottled oxygen before the summit and where that happened. His theory rests on two pillars. First, the kind of oxygen bottles Compagnoni and Lacedelli took to the summit, and second, the timings of the summit day.

On the timings of 31 July, when they left camp IX and so forth, Compagnoni and Lacedelli changed their story several times. One of the most ridiculous examples was during an interview by a RAI Uno journalist in 1984 when they said that they started at 4am or 4.30am, and had consequently taken 14 hours to get to the top. Yet a photograph in Compagnoni's own book, *K2: The Price of Conquest*, shows Lacedelli putting on his crampons at camp IX in daylight. Given that first light on 31 July was after 5am, the photo appears to have been taken nearer 7am, in accordance with Bonatti's timings. Why the exaggeration? To provide a sequence of events that explains using up their oxygen well short of the summit.

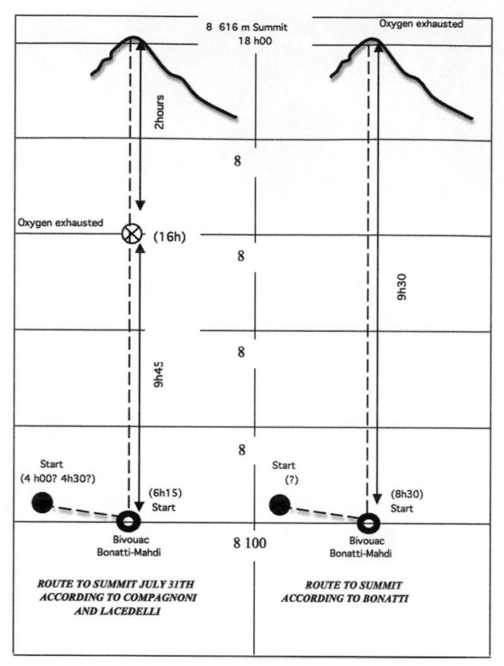

Figure 1 A diagrammatic illustration of the difference in timings between Bonatti and Compagnoni on the Italians' summit day in 1954.

In his book, Compagnoni writes that their cylinders emptied at 4pm and 8,400m, two hours before reaching the summit and after 9h45 of usage, meaning they would have started with the oxygen on their backs at 6.15am: impossible as Bonatti would have seen them. And yet still they were on the summit two hours later? That's a climbing rate of 100m per hour with empty oxygen bottles on their backs. And yet their rate of ascent *with oxygen* had only been 45m per hour.

Such lies are so demonstrably daft they can only be explained by the fact that as Italian heroes they could say anything and be believed – and that Compagnoni wanted to undermine Bonatti. In May 2004, Compagnoni, pressed by a *Corriere delle Alpi* journalist interviewing him after the publication of Bonatti's book *K2: La Verità*, admitted after 50 years: 'Thirty minutes without oxygen, and then the summit.' Conefrey excuses these wild inconsistencies: 'The fact that they were vague and inconsistent and their story unlikely, does not however means that they were liars.' That's a strange way of looking at things. Perhaps Conefrey has some Italian blood of his own? (Perhaps he also doesn't know that Lacedelli had a reputation for exaggeration before K2; his claim to have done the second ascent of Bonatti's route on the east face of the Grand Capucin was widely discounted by, among others, Hermann Buhl, Jean Couzy and Robert Paragot. To put it bluntly, Lacedelli had form.)

Conefrey states first that Bonatti got his timing wrong and that Compagnoni and Lacedelli did start their ascent at 7.30am and not at 8.30am as Bonatti evaluated. So their ascent would have taken 10h30 and not 9h30, providing a schedule for how their oxygen cylinders could be empty before they reached the summit. These timings are based on what Lacedelli told Giovanni Cenacchi in 2004. Since Compagnoni and Lacedelli's original statement of starting at 4.30am from camp IX was obviously untrue, Lacedelli corrected this 'mistake' and claimed they must have started at 6am or 6.30am, reaching Bonatti's bivouac an hour later.

Bonatti had a last look at 7am behind him at the place he bivouacked and saw no one in the area. (All parties agree it would have taken an hour to get there.) Conefrey says this is because Compagnoni and Lacedelli were hidden from view by terrain or because the weather was misty. 'Is K2's topography really so simple and regular that he could have had a completely uninterrupted view of the slopes above him, during the whole time of his whole descent?' The short answer to that question is: yes. Conefrey ignores Bonatti's painstaking analysis and doesn't publish any of the very clear photos that show someone who has not reached the bottleneck that what Conefrey says is fantasy.

The second pillar of Conefrey's argument rests on the kind of oxygen system Compagnoni and Lacedelli used. There were two kinds of bottle available, Dräger and Dalmine. A red Dalmine set with three cylinders would provide 10 hours of oxygen. A blue Dräger three-cylinder set would give 12 hours, as stated in 2004 by Erich Abram, the oxygen specialist. Now the reason for revisiting the timings issue becomes clear. In the still photos of the expedition film *Italia K2* you can clearly see one red cylinder behind a blue one on the summit. This is Conefrey's evidence not just for contradicting Marshall's analysis published in 1993, but also for questioning the entire CAI enquiry of 2004.

Erich Abram told that enquiry that he checked the cylinders selected for the summit assault: because the Dräger were filled at 220 bars and were reliable, he chose those and only those. All the cylinders with a pressure of 200 bars were left at base camp. So Conefrey's 'discovery' clashes with Erich Abram's testimony. In fact, Conefrey's idea is not so new: in 2003 Bonatti published a photo in *K2: La Verità* showing clearly not one but two red cylinders on one of the oxygen sets.

There are two explanations for this. Abram's testimony in 2004 was wrong or the film is. Compagnoni and Lacedelli were provided with black and white film. The K2 expedition film footage made by Mario Fantin on the lower part of the mountain up to camp IV was in colour with a 35 mm camera and the film director Marcello Baldi had the Compagnoni and Lacedelli summit photos colourised before incorporating them into his film. I decided to modify the summit photo used in the expedition film simply by reducing their saturation level. The photos with a higher saturation rate gave a red colour to the oxygen bottle but are much nicer to look at.

The film was shown in every Italian school for decades and brought much money to the CAI coffers to finance future expeditions. Black and white photos in the film or on posters weren't acceptable. The editor of Bonatti's book *K2: La Verità*, Baldini Castoldi Dalai, is available. A journalist from *La Republica*, Leonardo Bizzaro, who also interviewed Conefrey, claimed last year it was obvious that the black and white summit photos had been colourised. The film's rushes sit in the archive of the CAI in Turin, where they have lain untouched for the last 60 years; so it would be possible to check. Or one could check with Erich Abram, the sole survivor of the expedition, the man who selected the six cylinders for the summit party, not someone known for doing botched jobs. Conefrey seems to have done neither.

Conefrey offers a lot of evidence about the unreliability of oxygen sets in the 1950s, some of it demonstrably wrong, and there is evidence he misses about the types of mask that Compagnoni and Lacedelli used. But let's for a moment assume he's right, and that Abram, an otherwise wholly reliable man, made a mistake and sent the wrong bottles, and that one of the two summit climbers had Dalmine cylinders and a maximum of 10 hours of oxygen (or less due to loss in pressure) and the other one 12 hours. With Bonatti's timing of 9h30 to the summit from the bivouac, both would have had enough oxygen up to the summit. With Lacedelli's timing of 10h30, the one with Dalmine cylinders would have run out roughly 20 minutes before the top, given Lacedelli's statement that they reached the summit at 5.50pm. Let's even forget for a moment that Lacedelli's timings are wholly undermined by Bonatti's testimony. Even then, the story amounts to little more than that one of them ran out of oxygen just before the summit.

Why else would Compagnoni and Lacedelli have continued to carry their oxygen sets up to the summit when their cylinders were empty? Because as Lacedelli conceded in *K2: The Price of Conquest*, they were on the summit ridge, at possibly 8,550m or above on easy ground. If the man using the Dalmine bottles ran out of oxygen it could only have been just short of the summit. Their average climbing rate was 45m or 50m per hour, so that would fit better with their initial report to Desio of their oxygen failing one hour before summiting, but for just one of them. In fact, it is far more credible that they did not discard their second empty cylinder because they still had one cylinder going, so making the extra weight of the second empty cylinder still bearable.

Whatever happened with the oxygen near the summit, it is, ultimately, a minor point compared to the reckless decision taken by Compagnoni to move camp IX higher, putting at risk the lives of Bonatti and Mahdi in order to prevent Bonatti participating in the summit bid, not to mention his accusation of being a traitor to the summit team and a coward in abandoning Mahdi. Bonatti used the argument of the oxygen to reinforce his arguments of these crimes but even if he and Marshall were wrong on this account, the crime remains.

Conefrey took much of the argument in favour of the oxygen running out before the summit from Lacedelli's replies to Giovanni Cenacchi in his book *K2: The Price of Conquest*. So why did he avoid analysing in detail the most important point of the book, Lacedelli's confession about camp IX and his

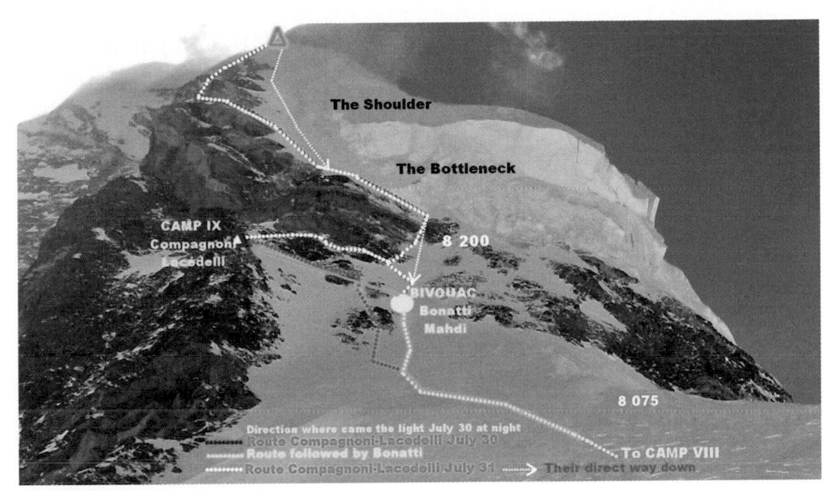

Bonatti and Lacedelli's illustration of events put on one photo in *K2: La Verità* and *K2: The Price of Conquest* illustrating the position of Bonatti and Mahdi's bivouac to the right of Camp IX. Large blue triangles line going left: line followed by Compagnoni and Lacedelli to camp IX. The green line shows Compagnoni and Lacedelli's line of ascent, the white dotted line their descent to Bonatti's bivouac and subsequent line of ascent to the summit.

desire that Bonatti forgive him? That seems extraordinarily prejudicial on Conefrey's part. (Bonatti, who said that his experience on K2 and its bitter aftermath changed him forever, couldn't do as Lacedelli asked.)

Conefrey finishes his book without making any analysis of Desio's conduct after returning to Italy. Instead he says that Bonatti's 'elaborate conspiracy theories are just an attempt to bring order to the chaos of life.' The implication being that Bonatti was paranoid and invented the conspiracy, a conspiracy that Lacedelli admitted he shared in. Conefrey ignores Desio's determination not to allow anything to tarnish the success of his expedition. But he drew a veil of silence over the injustices and suffering Bonatti endured for 50 years. He would not allow the account of the expedition to be changed.

Giovanni Cenacchi asked Lacedelli: 'You say Bonatti was the victim of an injustice. Was that more because of the events at camp IX, or because of what happened afterwards back in Italy with the press?' Lacedelli's reply demolishes the idea Bonatti was paranoid. 'I would say afterwards… I think he suffered the real injustice later, and I think that had more an effect on him. I cannot but agree with him.'

Desio had links with leaders of the Italian state and establishment, including the then prime minister, Alcide De Gasperi, who had involved himself significantly to secure permission from the Pakistani government for the K2 expedition. It may be that ignoring Bonatti was not just a decision taken by the autocratic Desio but was backed up by the Italian government. Conefrey would have done better to look for evidence in those areas instead of trying to prove that Bonatti was a paranoiac.

After directing his documentary on K2 in July 2014 and publishing an article in *Geographical*, Conefrey was interviewed by an Italian journalist, Leonardo Bizzaro, from *La Republica*. Conefrey said at the end of the interview that he had limited himself to stating that Compagnoni and Lacedelli had not lied about the oxygen, which is far from the case in his book. Bizzaro wasn't fooled, ending his article: 'And then, this man who lives in Oxford but knows Italy well, smiled and did not say what he wanted to say: "If it had been British alpinists, such chaos would never have happened."'

When Luigi Sanzi, one of the 'three wise men', was asked, three days after Conefrey's interview, to comment on Conefrey's revelation, he laughed wryly. Pointing out that a cylinder was red on one photo, he said, did not demonstrate their assessment was wrong. He reminded the interviewer that Abram had told him he had selected six of the best cylinders, all Dräger. Perhaps Sanzi rejected Conefrey's finding too quickly; he could have checked if the colour came from processing the film or it was in fact red, although Conefrey didn't do that either. Whatever the truth, every other detail of the Bonatti issue stands.

In his book, Conefrey doesn't really capture the human qualities of those strong Italian mountaineers who finally made a success of their expedition despite an inadequate and autocratic leader and their own strong and potentially conflicting personalities: the great Gino Solda who had fought with the resistance, for example, or Erich Abram and Mario Puchoz, who had been on the other side with the Germans. Conefrey forgot that the essence of climbing lies within the individual, not the nation he lives in. When Doug Scott climbed with my friend Jean Afanassieff or when I climbed with my friends Chris Bonington, Nick Estcourt, Martin Boysen, Armando da Roit or Marcello Bonafede, we were climbers, citizens of the world, not British, Italian or French. We shared the same passion, the same fundamental need for adventure, and the same ethics.

Conefrey could have discussed his theory directly with Luigi Sanzi, who has since unfortunately died, or the other two CAI 'wise men'. He could have contacted some of the competent mountaineers who went a long way to have Bonatti's version recognised as the truth, like Reinhold Messner. He could have approached Erich Abram, who selected the oxygen equipment. But Conefrey discarded them all. He has no lesson to offer climbers on the subject of Machiavellianism – be they Italians or any other nationality.

Acknowledements
A number of climbers and authors, friends of Walter Bonatti have contributed to this article in checking some of it, particularly Mihai Tanase, Ruggero Montesano, Luca Signorelli, Sandro Filippini and Roberto Mantovani.

History

Quin Ego Hoc Rogem: the Girl from Swayambhu (third version)
Rob Fairley, 1999. (Egg tempera. 30cm x 25cm. Private collection.)

KIM SOMMERSCHIELD

The Priest Who Disappeared

The Mystery of Don Giuseppe Buzzetti

Don Gino Buzzetti.

The wind screams louder, driving hail and sleet into the tall man's eyes; an ominous rumble of thunder makes him glance instinctively skywards. Blackness. He peers down, but can see no trace of the glacier he knows to be 500ft beneath him. Hesitating briefly before abandoning his exposed perch, he lowers himself gingerly a few feet into an icy couloir. Using his good leg, he wedges himself into a tiny crevice and takes off his small knapsack.

Crouching lower against the strengthening wind, the man scribbles a few lines in a notebook with numbed fingers, then tears out the leaf and grips it in his teeth. Next he extracts a small tin from the canvas bag, slips the note carefully inside and then secretes it deep in a cavity between wet rocks behind him. It will be safe there. The routine is a well-practised one, but never before has he left a message in such precarious circumstances.

The violent clamour of the storm increases in pitch; the thunder swells as the interval between flashes of blue-green lightning narrows. It is time to move. The climber shoulders his knapsack, tightens a broad leather belt around his flapping soutane and inches upwards. Once more on the treacherous crest, he eases a leg over and sits astride it. A few phrases muttered under his breath are torn from his lips by the wind. But he is calm now. Edging steadily southwards, bent double against the tempest, a charge of lightning illuminates his dark outline one last time before he vanishes into the maelstrom. Don Buzzetti is heading home to Uschione from the Bocchetta Torelli. He will be late for mass.

Born in Chiavenna in 1886, Giuseppe Buzzetti, known locally as '*al prévet Buzèt*', was ordained in 1910 and took up pastoral posts at several communities in the neighbourhood as well as teaching in local schools. When the *reverendo* wasn't ministering to his flock he was usually to be found seeking communion with his Maker on the lofty peaks that crowd in on the valley.

Though generally respected by his parishioners, there was a mischievous streak in Buzzetti's character perceived to be at variance with his vocation. Yet it endeared him mightily to children. They warmed to his boyish innocence, revelling in his pranks and the complicit attitude concealed behind earnest features. His trusty walking stick carved with the Passion of Christ in hand, he would trek for hours along solitary pathways to preach in isolated communities. Or, roads permitting, he would piously mount his beloved MAS motorcycle and roar from village to village on this improper means of transportation.

Buzzetti might well have continued to preach in diligent anonymity had not his hidden vice frequently got the better of him: though deeply committed to his faith – he was awarded a gold medal at the seminary *pro virtuti praemium* – Buzzetti's loyalties were perennially and fatally divided between mass and the mountains.

Exactly how he came to be infected with the mountaineering bacillus remains a mystery. His was the generation which set about reappraising the awkward legacy of the agnostic Italian pioneers of the *Club Alpino Italiano*, transforming the peaks from patrician playgrounds into potent symbols of national – meaning Catholic – unity. Acknowledging that some degree of political involvement was inevitable if the church were to maintain its influence in the newly minted Italian state, in 1895 the Vatican found it expedient to lift the prohibition on Catholics' participation in elections in return for a commitment to moderation.

Encouraged by Pope Leo XIII and his clerics, as the twentieth century was ushered in, the rural faithful took to the uplands in earnest, constructing twenty commemorative sanctuaries on as many summits across the land, permanently scarring them in the process. Mass was celebrated on Mont Blanc in 1892; the Matterhorn became the first Alpine peak to be formally claimed for Christ when a three metre-high cross was erected atop its craggy pyramid on 24 September 1902; two years later a statue of the Virgin found its way to the Dent du Géant. One by one, peaks high and low the length and breadth of the Alps and Apennines were similarly consecrated as conspicuous symbols of the church's unflagging commitment to social causes, civil liberties and its own survival.

Buzzetti however was not one to proselytize. His attraction to the mountains was far deeper and more instinctive than ecclesiastical iconography; he climbed from the heart, not the head. Despite having suffered a foot infection, which left him with a pronounced limp, he was clearly a fearless and resourceful mountaineer well before ordination. He made pioneering ascents in 1905 and 1906 of the awesome south-east wall of the 9,000ft fortress of Sasso Manduino and of the treacherous north face of Pizzo Prata. On a single day he traversed the saw-tooth crest from the Bocchetta Alta di Schiesone to the Bocchetta di Prata, scaling two hitherto virgin peaks in the process, one of which bears his name to this day.

He climbed alone, a stranger to pitons and crampons, scaling sheer granite cliffs with nothing but an ice axe, a coil of hemp rope and hob-nailed boots. An intuitive feel for rock and genuine love of high places engendered a complete disregard for technical problems. His climbing enterprises were suffused with a sense of spiritual levitation, of unfettered joy, common to so many pioneering climbers of the rugged pre-technological era, for whom the mountains were not just windows on nature but metaphors of the human condition. Typically, Buzzetti was equally renowned for his spectacular descents; almost challenging the Lord to abandon him, he was often sighted sprinting down screes at breakneck speed. To those who accused him of being reckless he replied: '*Non importa, a me piace andare e se muoio in montagna è la sorte più bella, sono il più vicino al Signore.* It doesn't concern me, for I like my outings and if I should die in the mountains it is the sweetest destiny, for I am closer to God.' It was a destiny ultimately to be fulfilled.

Like all mountaineers, time was of the essence for the unorthodox Don Giuseppe. One suspects that he subordinated religious duties to his climbing itineraries, timing *officium divinum* in such a way that he could celebrate matins or lauds before absenting himself, making it back in time for sweat-soaked vespers or compline. In the words of Jerzy Kukuczka, better by far to be in the mountains thinking of God than in church thinking of the mountains.

It was inevitable that this clambering clergyman would gain a reputation for being more hell-raiser than heaven-sent, and his infectious ability to stimulate enthusiasm for climbing in his pupils concerned many families. Shoes and socks were often confiscated to discourage unruly youngsters from joining their teacher on his expeditions. He taught his nephews how not to fear heights – 'Overcome your vertigo and you will know no danger.' – by making them balance on beams raised increasingly high over the ground, then putting the petrified lads to the test by hounding them up some rocky outcrop under the appalled gaze of their parents.

Despite this flamboyance, which some thought made him unsuited to the priesthood, he was otherwise modest and reserved, never boasting about

his achievements. The joy he felt in traversing inaccessible places was expressed with a simple excitement provocatively at odds with the stuffy sanctimony of many of his priestly colleagues. He succumbed only to the temptation of occasionally leaving teasing 'Buzzetti was here' messages in bottles and tins concealed deep within cairns and crevices on summits and passes. They are still being found today.

On 12 July 1934 Don Buzzetti celebrated mass before departing Chiavenna, walking up the Val Codera and reaching the Gianetti hut in the Val Porcellizzo where he spent the night. Described thus prosaically it sounds like a stroll, and Buzzetti probably considered it such. Yet this 'routine' outing meant a vertical difference well in excess of 8,000ft. The next day he set off for a bracing constitutional up the 11,000ft Piz Badile, returning to the Gianetti for the night. In the morning the weather was bad and deteriorating. Ignoring warnings by local guides, the priest made a brisk detour over the Punta Torelli, a tricky little peak of just under 10,000ft, leaving word that he was heading home for Valchiavenna where he would hold Sunday Mass in Uschione the following morning. He never kept that appointment. A peasant who saw him as he headed north that stormy morning shouted half in jest that they would have to send out search parties for him if he continued. But Buzzetti's pact with God held good and around lunchtime he was sighted again, now on the summit of the Torelli, after which the thunderclouds closed in. No one saw in which direction he was headed.

It was the silent bells in Uschione next morning that heralded something to be amiss. Search parties were despatched from Novate and Masino to look for the priest, but with the alarm having been raised over twenty-four hours after the last sighting, no one could have been in the area before Monday morning. By then all trace of Don Buzzetti had been lost. The Italian Alpine Club (CAI) sent in its own rescue team, the military participated,

The Pizzo Prata, including the Punta Buzzetti, named in his honour, from a watercolour by the author.

as did the priest's brothers and nephews, and such was the victim's fame that volunteers came from far and wide to seek out some trace of his passing. Gullies, crevasses, snowfields and screes were combed, but to no avail. He seemed to have vanished from the face of the earth. Not even flocking birds, normally a sure indicator of a corpse, were spotted, though a rumour got round that an eagle had been seen clutching a boot in its talons.

Then, a month later, on 15 August, two climbers on the Bocchetta Torelli stumbled on a clue. Hastily scribbled on a scrap of paper inserted in an

The south face of Piz Badile from another watercolour by Kim Sommerschield. Buzzetti had climbed the peak the day before his disappearance in another mammoth day's effort typical of the priest.

empty tin and concealed in a cairn was one of Don Giuseppe's messages: '*Don Giuseppe Buzzetti CAI sez. di Chiavenna, da Bresciàdiga, passo Sceroia, capanna Gianetti, pizzo Torelli, bocchetta Torelli per Brescàdiga 14-VII-34.*' It was his entire itinerary. It was now clear that he had made it safely off the Torelli summit and was heading south, almost certainly for the Val Codera via the Porcellizzo pass, several hundred metres along the treacherous crest. Even in the misty gloom he would have known that this familiar terrain would be on his right. Somewhere along the razor-sharp edge he must have been struck by lightning or simply lost his footing in the snow and wind. The drop on both sides is sheer. But whilst a fall to the east would have deposited the body on rocky screes, easily identifiable and accessible to animals and birds of prey, to the west in Val Codera lay the Porcellizzo snowfields where the corpse could have been wedged in the gap between rock and ice, then quickly covered by new snowfall. No trace of his body was ever found.

As Guido Scaramellini observes in his book about Buzzetti, there is something arcane and epic about the vision of this lone, limping man in black sitting astride that bleak, tempestuous crest. We will never know what was going through Buzzetti's ordered mind as he dutifully noted down his position and destination then secreted it beneath the rocks. Was he acting out of habit? Or because he was concerned some accident might befall him? Given his vast experience and faith he was probably quite lucid; the note holds no trace of fear. Was he worried at keeping the tiny congregation in Uschione waiting next morning, or pondering whether there was time to chalk up another summit on the way back? We'll never know. Locals believe this unlikely mountaineer was summoned on high by his creator and, to paraphrase Yeats, paces still upon the mountains overhead. Despite no formal recognition from ecclesiastical authorities, he remains something of a patron saint in the Chiavenna-Codera range. Several climbers report having seen his earnest countenance smiling encouragement at them during moments of peril, or recognizing his dark billowing form halting past them through the mist.

Romilda del Prà was a teenager when Buzzetti embarked on his final trek. He was a familiar figure to her, for the del Prà family owned large swathes of pastureland in the upper Val Codera, which still bear their name today. Sitting in the cosy kitchen of the Brasca mountain hut, this elfin lady, now curved and crumpled to a question mark as she approached her 90th birthday, related to me how her father admonished the priest prophetically that if he persisted in climbing in such conditions they'd find no bones to bury. That summer of 1934 Romilda came across some solitary leaves of grey paper fluttering across the Porcelizzo glacier. They were pages from Aldo Bonacossa's famous mountain guidebook, a precious breviary Buzzetti was known to possess. She has no doubt that the priest plummeted to his death on the ice and remains entombed there.

The spry little woman told her well-honed tale with the grisly relish of frequent repetition. Then, casting me a twinkling glance, she leaned her diminutive frame impressively across the bleached oak table and declaimed a touching poem in a hesitant monotone before stooping out into the deepening gloom where 30 Sicilian boy scouts and girl guides awaited her round their campfire. They had travelled 2,000km from the country's southernmost tip to an isolated Alpine valley at its northern extreme to listen in reverential silence as the ancient self-anointed bard of the Val Codera narrated affectionately a now vanished culture and the mysterious disappearance of Don Giuseppe Buzzetti.

Buzzetti was a simple man and his is a simple, albeit emblematic, tale. The photograph taken of him on the summit of Pizzo Tambò the year before his disappearance shows a slim, tanned face, one hand resting resolutely on an ice axe, his wry gaze surveying the surrounding peaks. Like many mountain people even today, he had an enviable ability to view our copiously shaded world in penetrating blacks and whites. Certainly the mystery that shrouds his disappearance has had a tendency to inflate the man and his achievements out of all proportion – a process of deification he would no doubt have abhorred. Yet the disappearance of a lame, cassocked priest on a rocky mountaintop retains an irresistible allure for the collective imagination. It is the stuff of romance, an adventure story, hagiography and mystery rolled into one.

In an age when we have forfeited much of our spiritual innocence, one marvels at the nature of the calling the mountains exerted on Buzzetti when he had already answered a higher calling by taking holy orders. What answers did he seek in the aerial solitude that his own faith could not supply? I suspect that he conceived of the mountains and God as one inseparable unity, and saw himself as a pilgrim or disciple whose arduous climb to the summit was a metaphor for the road that led to Christ. Beyond the need to test himself both physically and mentally, climbing was a tangible way of communing intimately with God.

The duality of godhead and mountains, the hint of eternity and pantheist mysticism in the void that surrounds the highest peaks, has exerted a profound influence on mountaineers at all times. But the pragmatic Buzzetti penetrated beyond this commonplace by recognising the fact that true confidence in these hostile environments – as indeed in all walks of life – comes not from improved safety equipment or physical preparation, but from self-awareness and the ability to confront our own mortality with equanimity. This does not imply fatalism or sanction imprudence, but simply acknowledges that factors of safety cannot be generalised. Individuals possess their own unique set of cognitive values, which ultimately determine that person's vulnerability. Achieving a precise awareness of those values is the challenge that confronts us all in life, but is one from which most of us shy away.

Buzzetti had already dinned into his young nephews a golden rule of mountaineering: fear nothing, except fear itself. His faith dictated that he take this maxim a step further, out of the physical dimension, aspiring to a state of grace that can only be attained when the individual is able to contemplate and gauge his own spiritual serenity. Buzzetti summed it up thus: '*L'alpinista, il vero e genuino, l'atleta dell'alto, scalatore di canaloni e strapiombi, vincitore di abissi e di vertigini, non solo accompagna il suo inflessibile volere contro il ghiaccio e la rupe, contro la tormenta e la valanga, ma egli ha vinto e vince qualcosa di più grande e forte delle montagne – ha vinto e dominato se stesso.* The true and genuine alpinist, athlete of the heights, he who scales couloirs and sheer cliffs, overcomes the abyss and fear of heights, not only imposes his inflexible will upon ice and cliff, upon tempest and avalanche, but has overcome something bigger and stronger than the mountain – he has prevailed over and dominated himself.'

Postscript: 'During an excursion at Predarossa on Wednesday, Aristide Gaggini and his wife came across an old boot containing the mummified foot of the owner, plus a femur and the remains of a forearm and skull. The objects have now been taken by the *carabinieri* to Ardenno, perhaps with a view to subsequent DNA analysis. Speculation is already rife as to whether they might belong to Don Buzzetti, the climber-priest who vanished without trace in the summer of 1934. The style of hobnailed footwear is certainly appropriate for the period and no other mountaineers were reported missing at the time. However the location where the macabre find was made does not correspond to the itinerary drawn up by Don Buzzetti, who was last seen heading southwest from the Punta Torelli towards the Porcelizzo pass. On the other hand, the clergyman was notorious for his stamina on wide-ranging climbs…' *La Provincia di Sondrio*, 12 August 2012

MARC KÖNIG

Hadow's Sole

Mountaineering boots between the first ascents of the Matterhorn and Everest

Hadow's shoe worn on the Matterhorn in 1865. *(Matterhorn Museum/Villars Grafic)*

Alongside the snapped cord and other relics gathered in Zermatt's museum to tell the story of the Matterhorn's first ascent and its subsequent tragedy are the boots of Douglas Robert Hadow. Born in 1846 in London, Hadow was just 19 when he undertook his first Alpine season. On the recommendation of his mentor, Rev Charles Hudson, he was included in Edward Whymper's party for the Matterhorn, but during the ascent Hadow needed constant help and it was Hadow who fell as the team descended, dragging three men off the mountain after him.

A number of reasons are usually offered for the cause of his slip: first, he was an inexperienced and clumsy rock climber; he was exhausted from the fast ascent of Mont Blanc he'd made with Hudson a few days before; his footwear was hopelessly inadequate for such a climb. Looking at his boots in Zermatt, you can't help feeling that while they would be fine for climbing a flight of stairs, they were nowhere near sufficient for the Matterhorn, a simple leather shoe with a nailed sole for what was the equivalent in 1865 of Everest in 1953 as the measure of all things in mountaineering.

As early as 1770 the Dutch physician and comparative anatomist Petrus Camper acknowledged the problems associated with manufacturing mountaineering boots. He saw that our feet are as important as the feet of horses, donkeys, oxen and other animals but that little effort or expense was invested for human feet. The design and manufacture of specialized boots to this point had been neglected and left to uninformed craftsmen.

Around 1850 the anatomist Hermann Meyer from Zürich addressed this point in his book *Procrustes ante portas: why the shoe pinches*. He focussed on detailed anatomical investigations of the feet. This article attracted little attention in Germany. Yet after translation into English in 1861 the practical English appreciated the suggestions and shoemakers began to construct shoes according to his new ideas. Most of the climbing boots worn by English climbers in the Alps were manufactured according to Meyer's pattern, including those of Douglas Hadow.

In 1876 Andreas Madlehner suggested in the *Mitteilungen des Deutschen und Österreichischen Alpenvereins* that one should, if possible, do without a heel. The trend was for a lace-up shoe without too high an ankle. In addition the sole was nailed all round with *Kappennägel*, literally 'capping nails'. In 1884 Pfeiffer described lace-up boots with a double sole consisting of four or five rows of nails, so called *Durchzugsflügelnägel* or 'wing nails'. Leather laces did not yet exist, but were instead of hemp or linen.

A large proportion of research on mountaineering boots was conducted by the military. Their big dilemma was that every single foot needs its own last. For reasons of cost, the military developed production of standard shoe lasts in different dimensions. They also developed hooks and eyelets for lacing.

In 1887 a medical review of the demands and requirements for climbing boots was published in the magazine of the German Alpine Club. It stated that the most necessary piece of equipment for climbing is a healthy foot and mountaineering boots should support this in every way. The optimum boot should give enough space for vulnerable toes, the heel of the boot should embrace the heel of the foot and the upper should hold and push the dorsum of the foot in such a way to prevent the foot sliding. Leather at the heel of the shoe should not move against the Achilles' tendon and irritate it, distortion of the foot should be prevented, and the heel of the boot should be low but not completely absent. It was generally accepted mountaineering boots should serve universally on ice, rock and mixed ground, saving the need for additional climbing shoes or crampons.

By the beginning of the 20th century mountaineering boots were being produced and sold in German sports shops. The 1900s catalogue of the sport shop of Schwaiger in Munich gives a good overview of the mountain boots and shoe nails available at that time. The Munich sport shop Schuster equipped, for example, the Kangchenjunga expedition of G O Dyhrenfurth in 1930 and the American K2 expedition in 1938 led by Fritz Wiessner.

Ideally mountain boots were made to measure; a worn shoe was frequently presented as a template. Delivery time was only six to eight days; the cost was 27 marks, equivalent to £70 today. Hand-forged shoe nails could be individually crafted on request. A hundred nails cost £3. For nailing, the shoe needed a protruding double or triple sole.

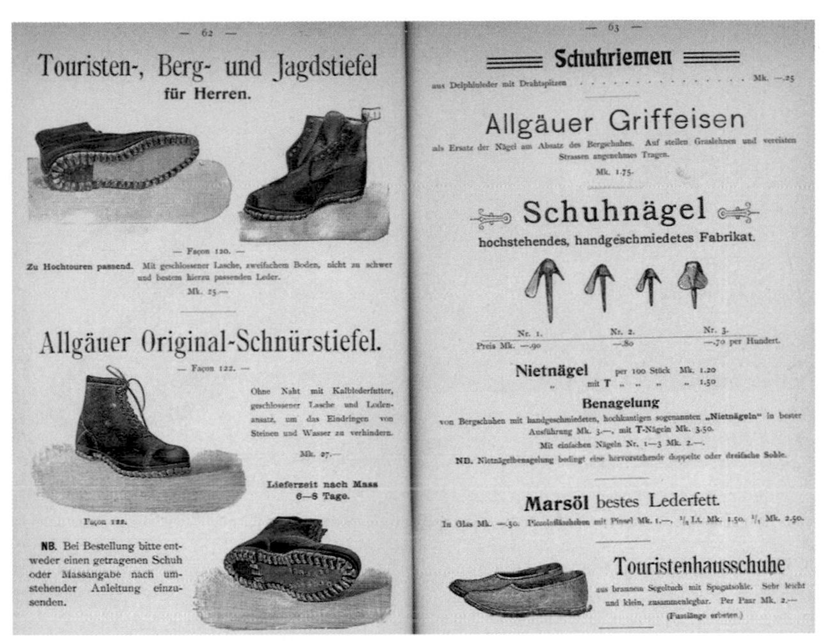

Early advertisement for mountaineering boots and nails from the Sport Schwaiger catalogue for 1900.

Advertisement for Tricouni. *(Alpine Journal)*

Above: The nails on Mallory's boots. *(Rick Reanier/Archiv Jochen Hemmleb)*

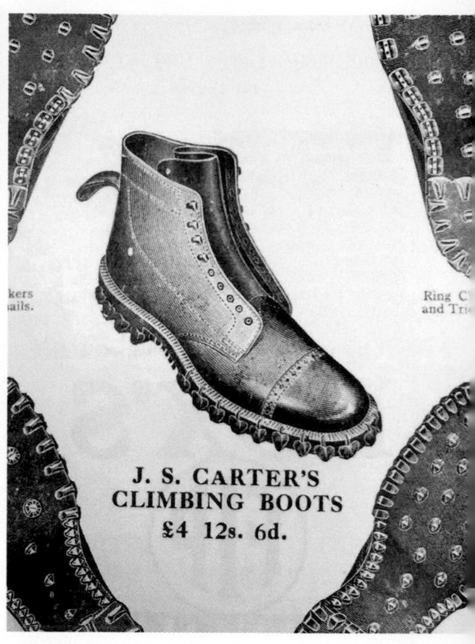

Right: Advertisement for Carter. *(Alpine Journal)*

Until about 1910 mountain-boot nails were as a single leaf wrapped externally around the sole and by then these bent nails were produced in different sizes. In 1912 the Swiss jeweller Félix-Valentin Genecand designed a new type of boot nail and a new nailing system. He was able to produce nails made from two pieces, one hard gripping part brazed to a softer malleable part, which was attached to the boot by two nails. He gave the nails his own nickname: 'Tricouni'. These nailed boots were very effective on ice-covered rocks. This slowed down the development and use of crampons.

After the First World War, in Germany mountaineering boots were produced double or triple stitched fashion. Manufacturers started avoiding a heel seam, to better protect the Achilles. Because of the lack of metal for nails and fittings, nails from the 1890s were still used. In England, there were two leading boot-makers and suppliers of equipment for climbers, James Carter and Robert Lawrie. In Carter's advertisement from 1924 you can see a climbing boot with ring clinkers, hobnails and tricounis.

Edward Norton, the British Everester, wrote in 1924: 'These boots are the result of years of experience. Their essential feature is the leather sole, which should be nailed (with the points of the nails turned down) before being attached to felt soles. Mr Carter supplied two members of last year's party with these particularly good boots of Lampar pattern, the boots were of a size to take stockings and two pairs of socks: the soles should be treated similarly to the above to avoid conductivity of nails and with a felt sole between the welt and the nailed sole if possible.'

This description illustrates clearly the boots George Mallory used. These were found in 1999 during the research expedition to Mount Everest supported by the historian Jochen Hemmleb. Mike Parsons and Mary B

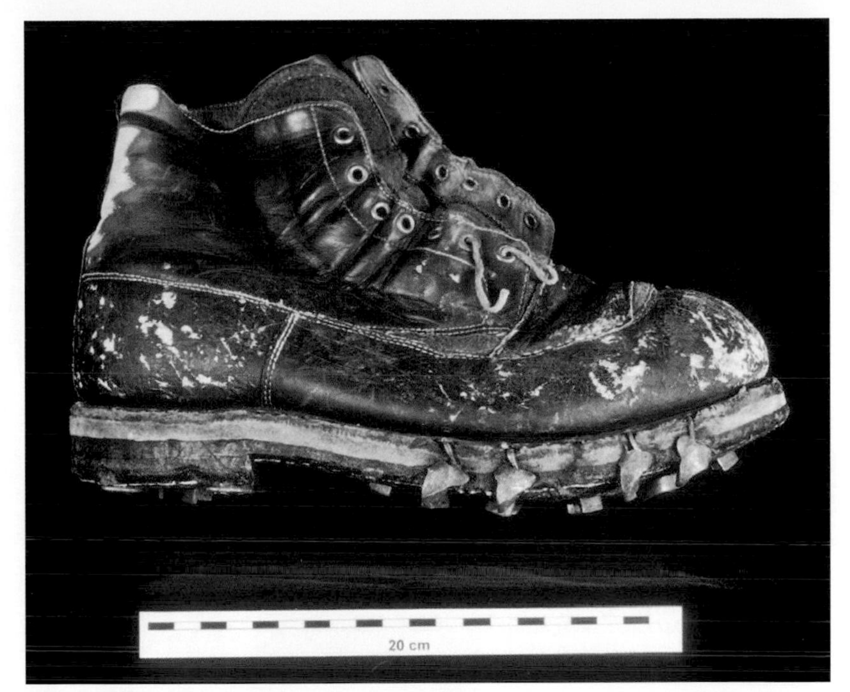

George Mallory's boot from 1924. *(Rick Reanier/Archiv Jochen Hemmleb)*

Rose at Lancaster University evaluated the boots, which are today in the Royal Geographical Society in London.

Mallory's boots had novel hobnails attached through a 3mm calfskin leather sole but insulated from the feet by a 10mm felt. (See illustration above.) The weight of each boot was calculated to be 800g. He wore three layers of socks, worked in with three layers of long johns and military-style puttees. Altogether these weighed only 500g, for a total weight of 2.1kg. This pioneering equipment can be seen as the beginning of the current lightweight trend in outdoor gear.

At just 800g, these boots are likely to be the lightest ever worn on Everest. Early on the English had recognized that weight savings on the boots provides a huge performance advantage at heights. For this reason, compromising the stability of the shoes was accepted. Some of the boots fell apart during the expedition, according to Mallory's climbing partner Sandy Irvine.

After the British Expedition of 1922 to Everest, George Finch described in the *Alpine Journal* the equipment for high-altitude mountaineering with special reference to climbing Everest. He proposed that leather is too good a heat-conductor and it should not be relied on for warmth. The uppers of the boots should be of felt, strengthened where necessary to prevent stretching by sewn on leather stripes. The felt should be covered by Duraprene canvas. Toe and heel caps must be hard and strong; the former should be high. The sole should consist of thin leather, a layer of three-ply wood hinged in two sections at the instep, and a thin layer of felt. The boot should be large enough to accommodate in comfort two pairs of thick socks. Ten tricouni nails per boot should be sufficient. These should be fastened by screws,

Above: *(Wayfarers' Journal 1935)*

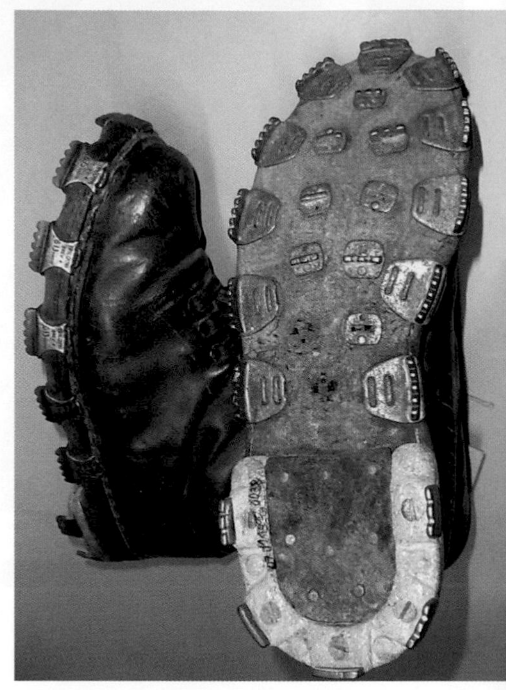

Right: Mountaineering boot c1930. *(German Alpine Club Archives, Munich)*

passing through the leather sole and entering into, but not penetrating, the three-ply wood. Short-length ankle putties would prevent ingress of snow into the boots. Crampons were unnecessary. This is a good description of the 1924 boots, apart for the wooden sole, which was never used.

In the 1930s, Robert Lawrie brought out a new high-altitude design with several novel elements including interior felting and a lambskin inner sole. He would be the only supplier of boots to Everest climbers from the 1930s until 1953.

Similar models were also used in Germany and Austria. In this picture from around 1930, above right, iron fittings on the sole are easy to see, resulting in a nearly flat bottom surface without heels.

A critical issue with this type of boot sole was insulation; nails were the perfect conductor for drawing heat away from the feet. So the next revolution was in the development of a new shoe sole, not from three-ply wood as Finch suggested, but from rubber. This development came from the development of ski boots and was described in 1931 in the *Mitteilungen des Deutschen Alpenvereins*. In 1936 the Italian Vitale Bramani further enhanced this sole, in the aftermath of an accident blamed on inadequate footwear that killed several of his friends. His 'Carrarmato' sole went into production with financial support from Pirelli. He used a combination of his first name and surname to create his company name: Vibram, still the outstand-

Thermal Conductivities of Various Insulating Materials

Material	Description	Temp (°F)	Density (lb./cu.ft)	Thermal conductivity in gm. cals per sq. cm for a temp. gradient of 1°C per inch (x 10^4)	Source of data
Rubber.	Light sponge.	90-95	12 - 31	1.2 - 2.5	BRMRA.
	Cellular.	90-95	2.6-9	0.9 - 1.2	
Eider down	-	300	6.8	0.46	H.C.P (Peclet 1878)
			0.1	1.5.	
Cotton wool.	Firmly packed	-	-	1.0	S.P.T.
	-	-	-	0.43	H.C.P. (G. Forbes)
	Felted	-	-	0.33	" "
	-	-	-	0.40	P.H.R
Felt.	-	-	-	0.87	H.C.P.
	† -	68	-	0.90	N.P.L
		15	-	0.78	
	Hair felt.	-	11	0.58	H.C.P (Nat Bur Stds)
			13	0.58	
	Haircloth, felt.	-	-	0.42	H.C.P.
Kapok	-	68	1	0.54	N.P.L.
			6	0.45	
		15	1	0.45	
Kapok between burlap or paper	"Dry Zero"	*	1	0.54	H.C.P. (Nat Bur Stds)
			2	0.56	

would be required to give an equiv...
Since it was not practical to use more than 3/8" of cellular rubber a 3/8" of felt extra insulation was introduced in the form of a single layer of Tropal and a woven vinylidene insock.
Details of these are given later.

Research results on thermal insulation of different materials.
(SATRA Technology Centre)

ing brand in the outdoor footwear world.

After the Second World War, the political scene changed. Nepal opened up and the French mounted an expedition to Dhaulagiri and Annapurna in 1950. Their success in putting Maurice Herzog and Louis Lachenal on the summit of Annapurna was extraordinary, but came at a high price: both men suffered frostbite to their feet from inadequate boots. The British had made seven expeditions to Everest from the Tibetan side before the war. Now, with Tibet closed following China's occupation, they also turned their attention to Nepal. Eric Shipton led a reconnaissance to the Khumbu in 1951 but the Nepali government chose to award the permit for a full attempt in 1952 to Switzerland. Raymond Lambert and Tenzing Norgay fell short of the summit by only 150m. The Swiss, and Tenzing, wore reindeer skin boots made by Bally. The British physiologist Griffith Pugh tested these boots, found them excellent and wanted them for Everest but they were too expensive.

So in October 1952, Harry Bradley, director of research at the British Boot, Shoe and Allied Trades Research Association (SATRA), was asked to submit trial samples of boots suitable for use in the final stages of the assault on the mountain at heights above 7,000m. The specification for the boots seemed straightforward: lightweight, with very high thermal insulation, while at the same time sufficiently strong and well fitting for climbing. They also had to take a lightweight crampon. Durability was not important since the boots would only be required to last a few days. Scientists developed several concepts to solve these challenges; 30 companies of the SATRA association were involved in improving materials.

Little information was available on how to maintain a satisfactory temperature for the feet under conditions at high altitude. The image above shows studies to estimate the amount of thermal insulation required. In the early stages of development it was postulated that with expected temperatures waterproofness was unimportant since water was unlikely to be encountered. After the first tests in the Swiss Alps in November, it became obvious to the designers that during the day wet snow would be an issue and the boots needed to be waterproof to some degree.

Climbing boots had traditionally been made from deerskin cocoons, which were bulky and rather cumbersome to move in. SATRA used leather with a lightweight rubberized fabric backing selected for the insoles. The linings were also made from rubberized fabric, all seams being sealed with latex. A light and flexible leather with reasonable water repellence was used for the uppers, which were made larger than the linings to allow ample amounts of kapok fibre insulation. The boots were designed to have room for two pairs of wool 'duffle' socks. A vapour barrier allowed sweat to disperse from the socks, preventing feet and boots becoming soaked and freezing, and an integrated rubber outer gaiter prevented melting snow soaking into the boot itself. Since the toecaps of the boots might often be used for kicking steps in frozen snow they were reinforced to withstand the wear.

The outer sole was not the Italian Vibram, but was made by Dunlop from micro-cellular rubber to further improve insulation and decrease weight: one boot was 1.01kg or 1.09kg with the disposable waterproof cover. It was still a significant difference compared to the 800g of Mallory's boot.

In only 14 days SATRA had presented their first prototype. There were ultimately four different models, which were tested in early December in the Alps. Cold weather tests at minus 40°C were performed at the Royal Aircraft Establishment at Farnborough. The boot proved so successful that on 11 December 35 pairs were ordered. All were handmade to fit the

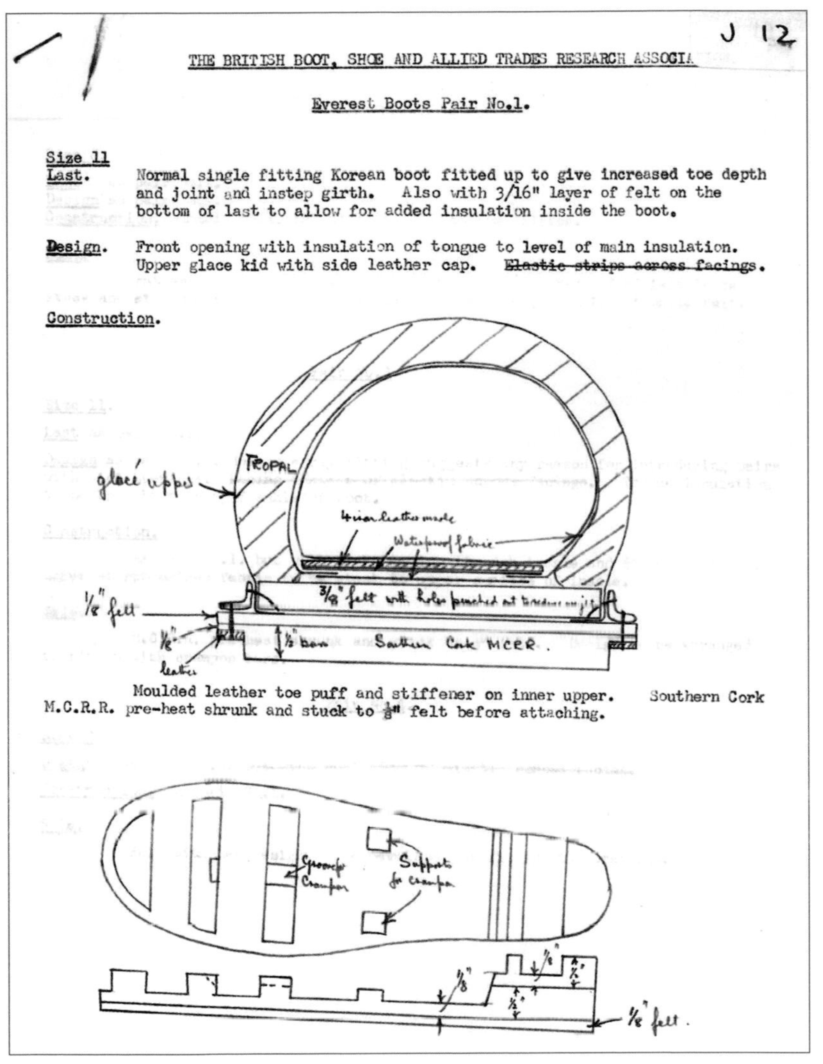

J 12

THE BRITISH BOOT, SHOE AND ALLIED TRADES RESEARCH ASSOCIA

Everest Boots Pair No.1.

Size 11

Last. Normal single fitting Korean boot fitted up to give increased toe depth and joint and instep girth. Also with 3/16" layer of felt on the bottom of last to allow for added insulation inside the boot.

Design. Front opening with insulation of tongue to level of main insulation. Upper glace kid with side leather cap. ~~Elastic strips across facings~~.

Construction.

Moulded leather toe puff and stiffener on inner upper. Southern Cork M.C.R.R. pre-heat shrunk and stuck to ⅛" felt before attaching.

Cross-section and sole of SATRA boot for Everest expedition in 1953 *(SATRA Technology Centre)*

individual foot sizes and exact measurements of each member of the expedition. Sizes varied from UK 6 for some of the Sherpas to UK 12 for Hillary's feet. Special lasts had to be made for the Sherpas from diagrams and foot measurements sent by the Himalayan Club in Darjeeling.

The boots were delivered on 16 January 1953, just five weeks later. After the successful ascent, John Hunt wrote to Harry Bradley to tell him that the boots had been a great success and had been worn by all members of the party at altitudes above 6,100m. Unlike any previous Everest expeditions, no member of the British team had suffered from frostbite of their feet.

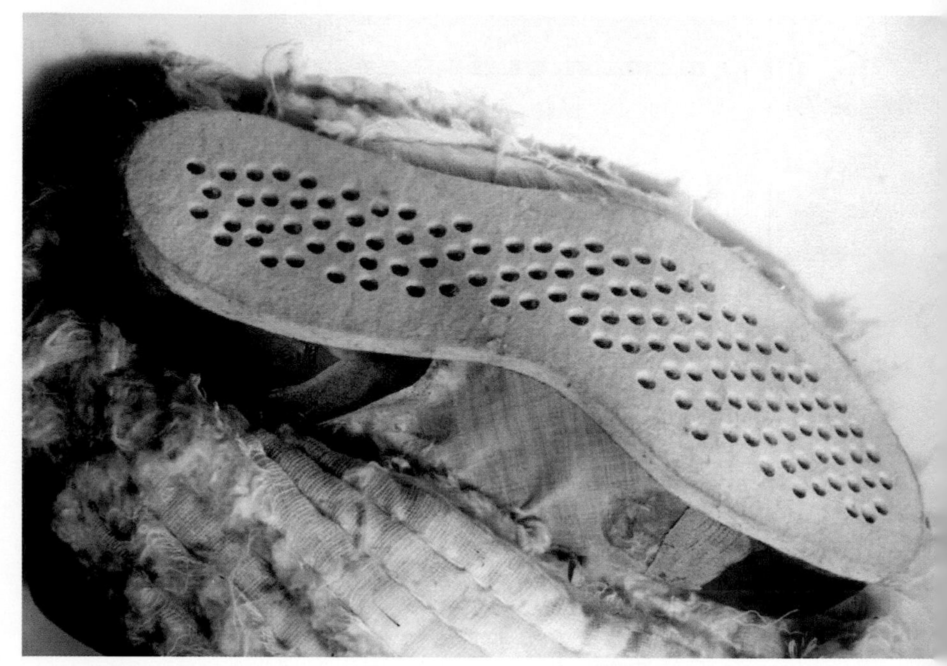

Manufacturing the inner sole and insulation material. *(SATRA Technology Centre)*

In fact, no one on Everest had suffered cold feet let alone frostbite. It was a far cry from Hadow's street shoes.

It had been a long way from Hadow's street shoes to Hillary's SATRA mountain boots. A great deal of experience had had to be collected in the Himalaya and implemented at home by scientists, technicians and shoemakers to end up with the successful result.

Bibliography

Zeitschrift des Deutschen und Österreichischen Alpenvereins, 1887.

Mitteilungen des Deutschen und Österreichischen Alpenvereins, editions for 1877, 1884, 1889, 1893, 1923, 1931, 1938.

Bernhard Pestel, E Diener ,'Der Menschliche Fuß und seine naturgemäße Bekleidung', 1885.

'Botschaft des Bundesrates an die Bundesversammlung, betreffend die militärische Fußbekleidung', *Schweizerisches Bundesblatt* 22, 27 May 1908.

Mike Parsons and Mary B Rose, *Invisible on Everest: Innovation and the Gear Makers*, Old City Publishing, 2003.

Charles S Houston and Robert H Bates, *K2 The Savage Mountain,* Collins, 1955.

Georg Hermann Meyer. *Procrustes ante portas: why the shoe pinches*, trans John Stirling Craig, 1861.

Jochen Hemmleb, Larry A Johnson, Eric R Simonson. *Die Geister des Mount*

Hillary's boots for the summit of Everest. *(SATRA Technology Centre)*

Everest 1924, Hoffmann und Campe, Hamburg, 1999.
John Hunt, *The Ascent of Mount Everest*, Hodder & Stoughton, London, 1953.
E F Norton, 'Bis zur Spitze des Mount Everest 1924', *Die Besteigung* 1924, 1926.
C G Bruce, 'Mount Everest Der Angriff 1922', Benno Schwabe Verlag, Basel, 1924.
George I Finch, *The Making of a Mountaineer*, Arrowsmith, London, 1924.

Thanks to:
Edy Schmidt, president of the Zermatt museum, Jochen Hemmleb, Jake Locke, SATRA head of communications, Tadeusz Hudowski, Glyn Hughes, Martina Sepp, German Alpine Club, Mike Parsons and Mary B Rose.

TED NORRISH

Chitral 1958

Nigel Rogers holding polo balls, a gift from the Oxford Chitral Expedition to the Mehtar of Chitral. *(All images courtesy of Ted Norrish)*

When I was aged 10 my grandfather gave me the *Times Atlas* of the world for Christmas. I spent hours studying every map on every page, especially those of the great mountain ranges. From as early as five I remember that I loved beautiful country and hills, and had decided one day I would be a mountaineer. In my atlas I noticed the small independent states of Chitral and Swat, both now parts of Pakistan. In Chitral I traced my finger over the Hindu Kush peaks of Tirich Mir, Noshaq, Istor-o-Nal and one labelled 'Sad Istragh'. For some reason I decided that, if it was still unclimbed, one day I would organise an expedition to Sad Istragh.

My first ambition was Everest. However, on 2 June 1953, as I stood in The Mall with my father watching the coronation, I saw the news the mountain had been climbed on a newspaper hoarding. I was delighted that after all those years it was a British success, but secretly disappointed for myself – foolish, because I was not a good enough mountaineer to have had a chance, even when older, of selection for an Everest team. I comforted myself that one day I would organise my own expedition to a major peak. I was also delighted that two members of the successful team, Tom Bourdillon, who reached the south summit, and Mike Westmacott were Oxford University Mountaineering Club climbers who had graduated a few years

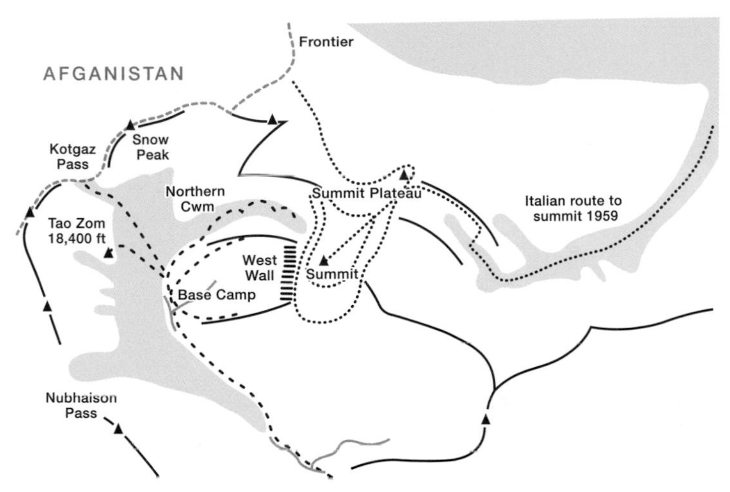

The approach to Saraghrar

previously; I had met them both at lectures and dinners.

At Oxford I began to plan my expedition from 1956. I became a member of the Royal Geographical Society, and enjoyed visiting their map room and library. I discovered the correct name of our mountain was, in fact, Saraghrar (7349m) and not Sad Istragh, that it was the fourth highest peak in the Hindu Kush, and, most important, that no attempt had yet been made on it, although the other three, Tirich Mir, Noshaq and Istor-o-Nal, had all been climbed. I read all I could find about Chitral, its history, local conditions and mountaineering there up to that time. I intended our expedition should be small scale, following the sound advice of Eric Shipton, but have equipment and supplies to make a serious attempt. We did not have the experience to climb alpine style.

The first requirement was to form a team. I invited Peter Nelson, a graduate of St John's College and a fine climber with good Alpine and other experience, to be our climbing leader. He readily agreed: a great compliment, because he had been invited to join an expedition to a higher and better-known peak, Ama Dablam in Nepal. I asked three other Oxford friends and good climbers: Eric Plumpton, studying medicine at Christ Church where he was college goalkeeper; Bill Roberts of Exeter College, studying English and a college rugby player; and Nigel Rogers, who took a first in chemistry at my own college, Brasenose. Eric agreed to be our doctor, and Bill took charge of equipment and food supplies.

I asked David Cox, a don and senior member of the OUMC, for advice on funding; with his help I applied to the Mount Everest Foundation and the Royal Geographical Society. It is good they trusted us, although, with the exception of Peter, we were young and inexperienced. This was the Oxford tradition, and long may it continue. We were awarded a grant of a thousand pounds from the Mount Everest Foundation, and a good grant from the RGS, and we each paid just £100.

Bill saved us a small fortune by writing to companies and firms for equipment and supplies at reduced or even no cost; we acquired huge brown fibre boxes, recommended by previous expeditions, strong enough to survive being dropped into the raging rivers we would have to cross. Despite studying for my DipEd, I spent much of my time in expedition organisation, visiting the Foreign Office and the Pakistan embassy. Since the Afghan wars, Chitral had been dangerous for the British; permission to enter was only granted after much correspondence and many interviews. As expected, we would be provided for our safety with a Pakistani liaison officer and I had to promise not to cross the mountain border into Afghanistan.

I was due to pack our supplies at Tilbury after taking my DipEd, but the shipping company called to say our slot had been brought forward. I now had to be at the docks on the very day of my exam. I arrived that morning in the exam hall, put my details on the first sheet, signed my name and after five minutes handed it in and left – to everyone's surprise. (I still qualified as a teacher, thanks to good reports from my teaching practice and my Brasenose tutors – but sadly no diploma in education.) I rushed to Tilbury and checked all our boxes were put on board. Given our plan to be a lightweight expedition, I was a little alarmed at the number and weight of our heavy boxes.

Our plan was that I should travel by ship from Liverpool to Karachi. I would find our baggage at Karachi and check it from the docks to the airport and fly to Peshawar. My four friends would have a more unusual journey: by boat from Harwich to St Petersburg and then by rail to Moscow,

Above: The expedition with its local Chitrali porters at Saraghrar base camp. The team-members, left to right, are: Eric Plumpton, Ted Norrish, Peter Nelson, climbing leader, in the white hat, Bill Roberts and Nigel Rogers; the photo was taken by expedition cook Ali Murad Khan.

Left: On the road to the Lowari pass (3118m), also known as Lowari Top, gateway to Chitral, in 1958.

where academic friends of my uncle had generously offered to host them. From Moscow they would fly to Kabul before continuing to our planned rendezvous on the Khyber Pass.

My father drove me to Liverpool and I embarked the Anchor Line ship RMS Cilicia. Every day I ran ten miles round the top deck working up a good thirst and appetite for the memorable dinners; on the last night I dined with the captain. After a week of such luxury we reached Karachi. I found all our baggage safely at the dock, found the necessary porters, quite a difficult task but completed cheaply, and was soon airborne, catching my first sight of the Hindu Kush – this really stirred my blood.

The streets of Peshawar were crowded, packed with rickshaws and small bicycle-carts, and I spent two days exploring a city that has become so infamous in today's troubled times. I had arranged to stay at Edwardes College, situated in the green and pleasant military cantonment; the principal and the pupils were hugely welcoming and helpful. After two days I travelled to the Khyber Pass and right on time met my four friends beside the old fort. Back at the college we spent four days checking our equipment and repacking everything into loads suitable for porters, mules and donkeys.

With the help of the principal we hired a huge painted wooden lorry, which set off from Peshawar's caravansarai. Our route lay over the Malakand pass, where Winston Churchill had served as young officer, then, passing the villages of Dir and Drosh, we reached the summit of the Lowari pass (3118m): gateway to Chitral. We sat on top of the lorry with 20 other

The northern cwm, as the expedition dubbed it, leading to the heart of the north-west face of Saraghrar (7340m); the expedition placed two camps on the glacier leading to camp III below the couloir to the upper plateau of the mountain.

passengers and two guards with rifles to protect us from bandits, looking at the distant mountains.

A colonel and a detachment of the Chitrali Scouts met us at the pass; their captain presented me with a ceremonial dagger and in Chitrali tradition they fired their rifles in the air by way of greeting. It was clear they were pleased to welcome us; the few who spoke English told us how much they respected the old British traditions and remembered them with pleasure. The descent to Chitral and the Mastuj valley was then only open to jeeps, so after a delicious lunch, we changed vehicles to begin a seemingly endless sequence of hairpin bends, passing camels, mules and men hauling huge quantities of timber. This area was well forested, but further into Chitral there were few trees.

The headquarters of the Chitrali Scouts was 12 miles short of the small town of Chitral. Here Colonel Ibrahim Khan from Peshawar welcomed us warmly and we sat down to a fine dinner served in regimental style by Chitrali Scouts in uniform. There were photos and mementos of the past, and books and maps in a special room. We found an old British map showing the way almost to our intended base camp in the Rosh Gol, but the mountain was unsurveyed – no map could help us there. After breakfast on the beautiful terrace 200ft above the Mastuj river, we walked to Chitral, a town distinguished by its situation and the astonishing palace of Chitral's hereditary prince, the Mehtar, few of whom had died in their beds. The Mehtar was then a boy, having inherited the title aged four in 1954, but his uncle welcomed us, with two well-armed bodyguards in attendance. They invited us to a specially arranged polo match the next afternoon. As a gift for the young Mehtar, we had brought a box of eight polo balls from a shop in Bond Street. Although polo is Persian in origin, it was played in Chitral from early times, perfect for their tough little horses.

We sat for the match, as guests of honour, at the front of a small wooden pavilion, next to the Mehtar, with two bodyguards behind him. He was dressed in a smart cowboy-suit that the American ambassador had recently presented to him. Riders came to compete from villages as far as a hundred miles from Chitral – a journey on their horses of several days. The game was played at a furious pace and looked dangerous, with riders falling from their horses at speed, and thick clouds of dust kicked up by the horses' hoofs. The playing area didn't seem to have any bounds. After the match we were served with tea, cake and fruit; then a wind band struck up and there was dancing and singing, and an atmosphere of great celebration. The young boy, Muhammad Saif-ul-Mulk Nasir, lost his kingdom when Chitral was formally absorbed into Pakistan in 1971. He became a diplomat and died in 2011.

Next day we met Mulai Jan, the only Chitrali we met who was not by nature kind and generous, being both arrogant and dishonest, but he was of great influence and consequently indispensable. Only through him could we obtain mules, donkeys and porters. He lined up about 400 men, and left us to select 80 of the strongest and fittest. We paid them in cash and highly valued cigarettes.

Camp III at 5,460m, below the critical snow and ice couloir, leading to Saraghrar's summit plateau.

They did not become rich from our expedition, but longed for the adventure. None of them had been anywhere near our mountain, nor had Mulai Jan. It is to be admitted he was handsome with an aristocratic bearing, and he accompanied us on a fine white horse. While making our preparations we met a skilled and intelligent man, who asked if he could be our cook. His name was Ali Murad Khan, and he owned a small tailor's shop in Chitral. We immediately agreed; he was a first class cook and on our long walk at base camp purchased and cooked chickens and vegetables for us, made naan and all manner of delicacies, and in particular his speciality, apricot omelettes.

On our walk he chose our campsites for us, always a grassy patch by a side stream of the Mastuj shaded usually by apricot trees. He was so attentive and so willing that we became a little lazy, but he was more than happy to do everything for us. He arranged facilities for us with discretion, and even cut our hair. He saw that villagers brought baskets of apricots regularly to our base camp, and runners collected our cards and letters, which somehow by long stages reached Peshawar and home.

We left Chitral with 80 porters, 20 mules and some donkeys. After the polo match, the Mehtar's uncle had shown us his orchard full of apricot, mulberry, peach and pear trees, so they carried plenty of fresh fruit. We followed the Mastuj for about 80 miles, each stage being 12 miles. This suited us,

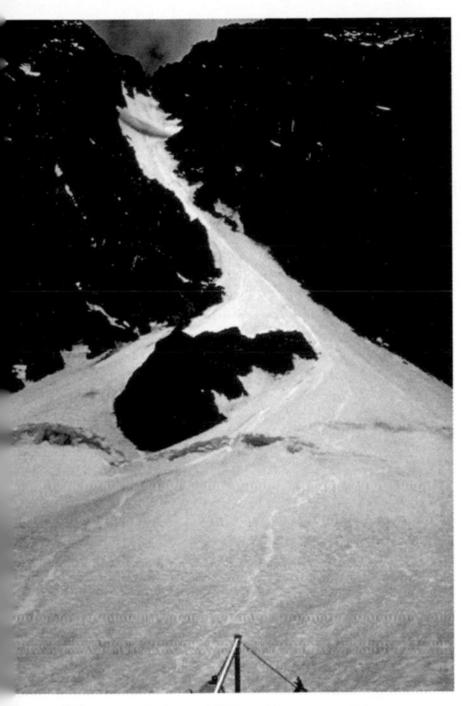

The couloir splitting the west face. Camp IV was placed about halfway up this from where climbing leader Peter Nelson and Eric Plumpton attempted to reach the summit. Nelson died in a fall on the way back to Camp IV having missed the top.

giving time to take photographs or talk to villagers. Peter, who was to be the first on our climb, was more mature and often last on our walk. The several villages we passed had small mosques and the houses, usually of one room with a hole in the roof for smoke to escape, were well constructed of blocks of stone and surrounded by beautiful gardens with roses and many other flowers. The villagers, although poor, seemed to us happy and well content with life. All the Pakistanis with us were as interested to see this new world as we were.

The trail often lay hundreds of feet above the raging river; it was a spectacular walk and I began to feel very fit. I great enjoyed the hot weather. The Hindu Kush is a rough, boulder-strewn range, with vast amounts of bare rock and scree. Because it is not forested like the lower slopes of the Himalaya, it is perhaps a little less beautiful, but I was thrilled and well satisfied. In Chitral, wherever small streams flowed down to join the Mastuj small alluvial deltas of fertile land formed, which the villagers irrigated with great skill, often cutting into the steep cliffs above. In these green deltas they built their houses and cultivated the land, usually covered with wild flowers.

After 10 good days, we began the ascent of the Sarth-An pass. I remember the most beautiful blue irises on the lowest slopes. Feeling very fit by this time I almost raced to the summit and arrived there first, eager to see our mountain and there it was, at the head of the 20-mile-long Rosh Gol valley: steep and formidable, as we expected.

We descended steeply to the small village of Zundrangam, at a height of about 10,000ft, the last village below our planned base camp, at the confluence of the Rosh Gol and a larger river. Here Murad arranged for our mail-runners and our welcome supply of apricots. From Zundrangam, following the Rosh Gol uphill, the going was completely pathless and very rough at times, with wide areas of boulders to cross. Our mules and donkeys could go no further than Zundrangam, and our porters now carried heavy loads of about 60lb without complaint. A few of them developed huge painful blisters on their backs, which Eric did his best to treat. After a few miles we passed a huge waterfall on our right. Another day brought us to a small green oasis called Duru, and here we enjoyed our last sight of trees and wild flowers.

After three days of hard going we reached the snout of a great glacier, below the precipitous 10,000ft wall of our mountain. At the glacier snout, on a small area of green grass, we pitched our tents for our base at a height of about 13,800ft. All around us were huge mountains, none of them as yet climbed; at night there was the roar of avalanches. Murad organised everything and made us feel at home in this wild place, which we were probably the first to see.

Our next task was to select four porters to help us to carry our loads to the higher camps, although the Chitralis, while courageous and cheerful, had no previous experience of high mountaineering. Finally we chose Khalid, Abdul Karim, Neap and Sher, to the disappointment of the others who returned home; before they left we took a large group photograph. We gave our four porters extra warm clothing, strong boots and sleeping bags, with which they were delighted. The colonel, a charming man quite unsuited to mountaineering, returned to the comforts of Peshawar. Mulai Jan stayed with us for a time. Returning to base camp, Bill and I were amazed to see him making off with one of our good tents and a sleeping bag. We caught him in the nick of time. He left on his white horse without a word or an apology.

I had enjoyed being organiser, and so far the leader, and all had gone well to this point. From now on, Peter was in charge, and it was in his hands to plan the reconnaissance, and eventually to make an assault plan and choose the team.

There followed four weeks of reconnaissance. I remember especially two wonderful expeditions shared with our cheerful porters. On the first we climbed and walked about 12 miles up a small side glacier and an icy ridge to a narrow pass looking into Afghanistan, from where we had a wonderful view of range upon range of mostly unknown mountains in Afghanistan and in the further Pamirs. On the second we enjoyed a climb up another crevassed glacier and along a narrow rocky ridge from where we looked down vertically about 2,000ft to the most amazing glacier I have ever seen: brilliantly blue and green, and riddled with a thousand crevasses. We immediately knew this was no route to the summit. We finally decided to try by what we called the northern cwm, climbing a huge glacier at least 10 miles in length, before finding a route up the steep west face.

We began the slow process of establishing three camps, all carrying heavy loads. It was exhausting in the hot conditions, but enjoyable as we started to make progress. There were many wide crevasses to cross and we had brought with us a 12ft aluminium ladder, which proved invaluable on several occasions. Finally, our camp three was established, and eventually fully stocked, at about 18,500ft or 5,650m. The weather on Saraghrar was perfect throughout our time; the monsoon did not affect us here.

It was wonderful to be there but very cold at night although excellent

Peter Nelson shortly before his death. A graduate of St John's College, Oxford, he had been working as a civil servant in the ministry of power. J H Emlyn Jones, in his obituary for the *Climbers' Club Journal*, wrote: 'his last letters were full of the joys of mountain travel and appreciation for the beauty of the unknown mountain area which he and his party were exploring for the first time.'

sleeping bags and thick duvet clothing served us well and we were not too uncomfortable. Murad was not with us here, but Bill made a fine job as chief cook. At night there was always the roar of avalanches, and on one occasion heaps of rocks and ice and snow reached within 400m of our tents. Above the tents an ice and snow couloir rose steeply for about 1,000ft, leading directly to what we thought was the summit plateau. Peter made the final decision this would be our chosen route, and he asked Eric to join him on our first attempt. We were a happy small group and I think there was no jealousy between us; Nigel must have been disappointed, but he never showed it. Our plan was that Nigel, Bill and I would follow later as a three-men team; my dream was now at last within reach.

As Virgil wrote: *expectata dies aderat*. The long-expected day arrived. We shook hands and wished Peter and Eric good luck. They spent a day carefully cutting steps and climbing up the steep couloir, and established camp four on a narrow ledge at about the halfway point, resting there for the rest of the day. Early next morning we saw them leave, climb slowly and safely up the rest of the couloir, and disappear from our sight to the right. We waited nervously and in hope for about six hours. Eric told me later that they nearly reached the summit on the high plateau, but the climbing continued steep and difficult. Finally, they made the decision to return to camp four, hopeful that they would succeed the following day.

We were glad to see them again at last re-entering the couloir and climbing slowly down. Then, after about half an hour, we saw a figure fall the full remaining height of the couloir – a thousand feet. Eric explained to us later how Peter had decided to climb unroped here because secure belays were impossible. As he was passing his ice axe from his right hand to his left, he slipped. Eric now faced the severe task of climbing down on his own, which he achieved without mishap. He stopped briefly at camp four, which sadly we had to abandon. Our four porters were as dismayed at the accident as we were. They carried Peter down to base camp, and then to Zundrangam, and we cleared base. They built a grave outside the village and made a small cross out of apricot wood, and we buried our friend beneath an apricot tree. I recited the Lord's Prayer and then said: 'God rest his soul in peace.' It was a sad occasion but we did not regret our expedition. Peter had accepted the risks and we were proud to have him as our leader.

There followed the long walk back in the same hot weather. On the second day I fell and sprained my knee. Murad obtained a black horse from a village and for a day I rode. The horse insisted on trotting on the very outside of the narrow track, hundreds of feet sheer above the river, and with no previous experience I was happy that next day I was able to walk again. Back in Peshawar we stayed again with the kind principal at Edwardes College. He was most sympathetic, and through him I was able to phone our Oxford friend Miles Rucklidge; he had the sad task of contacting Peter's parents and brother in the Isle of Man, and the Alpine Club. The principal also contacted the *Peshawar News*, and at their office I gave a short interview.

We decided Bill and Eric would return home by plane, and that Nigel and I would travel by train from Peshawar to Karachi, change trains there, and south to Bombay, where we had managed to book two passages to Marseille. Our trains were crowded, and had no restaurant cars, but I always enjoy long journeys seeing new country from the train window. To while the time away we tried to remember and write down all the 92 teams that then made up the Football League. By the time we reached Bombay we'd reached 91, tantalisingly one short. Arriving home, having hitchhiked through France, I bought a newspaper and found the 92nd team: Coventry City. I had never visited the city, and little knew that I would spend so much of my life there.

In 1959 an Italian team, led by Fosco Maraini, succeeded in climbing the mountain by a different route from the north-east. Fosco wrote a superb book on their successful expedition, *Where Four Worlds Meet*. In the inside cover of his book he wrote: 'To the memory of Peter Nelson from his Italian colleagues'. In his book he gives an account first of our expedition, and wrote appreciatively of the information we provided. Fosco considered himself too old for the ascent but on 24 August two pairs reached the summit, first Franco Alletto and Paulo Consiglio, and half an hour later, Giancarlo Castelli and Carlo Pinelli. I feel in a way that I partly shared their exaltation, and from my atlas at the age of 10 I had led the way.

C A RUSSELL

One Hundred Years Ago

With many Alpine resorts severely affected by the First World War and bitter fighting continuing in the Dolomites and other regions the opportunities for mountaineering in the Alps in 1916 were, in the main, restricted to climbers based in neutral Switzerland.

During the early months of the year several notable expeditions were undertaken in the Bernese Alps. Hans Morgenthaler and G Chiardóla, both members of the Akademischer Alpen-Club Zürich, made the first winter ascent of the Bietschhorn and parties led by Hans Lauper completed the first ski ascents of the Balmhorn, Altels and Grünegghorn. Other peaks ascended for the first time with the aid of ski included the Aiguille d' Argentière, climbed by G de Choudens with the guide Théophile Theytaz.

Early in the summer a skier who would later achieve international recognition arrived in Switzerland. Arnold Lunn, who was unable to enlist for military service due to a severe leg injury, had been appointed to manage two hotels owned by his father's companies. Some weeks later, accompanied by Boris de Croustchoff, he made the first ski ascent of the Gletscherhorn.

The weather during the climbing season was unsettled with prolonged periods of rain affecting the principal regions. New routes completed by parties confined to the lower peaks included the steep north-east ridge of the Vorder Tierberg above the Susten Pass climbed by Bernhard Lauterburg and Hans Morgenthaler and, in the Bernina Alps, the north-north-west, Eisnase ridge of Piz Cambrena by Hans Frick with Christian Zippert and Hans Kaspar.

In May Alpine Club members were informed that a generous offer of hospitality in Switzerland had been received from a friend of the Club.

> *Dr Alexander Seiler, the well-known head of the Seiler interests in the Zermatt Valley, and between whose family and English travellers there exists a very deep-rooted and old-time friendship, has written to express his desire to receive as his personal guests at Zermatt any wounded officers who are members or connexions of members of the Alpine Club. The invitation is also extended to Red Cross nurses who are friends of members, nominated by the AC.*

As in the previous year some climbing was possible in other mountain regions not directly affected by the conflict. In South Africa, where several members of the Mountain Club had enlisted in the armed forces, W T Cobern continued his exploration of Table Mountain (1087m). Climbing with C W Campbell he opened *Kleinkop Buttress* and *Grootkop Buttress*, both severe routes for the period.

Bugaboo Spire, Purcell range, British Columbia. The left skyline is the south ridge. *(Basil Goodfellow, Alpine Club Photo Library)*

In New Zealand Conrad Kain commenced his third season in the Southern Alps, this time as a private guide. As in the two previous seasons he completed many fine climbs including a traverse of the Middle and High Peaks of Mount Cook (3764m) with Mrs Jane Thomson. Some weeks later this feat was repeated by Samuel Turner with the guides Frank Milne and Jack Lippe; this party also ascended the Low Peak to complete the second traverse of all three peaks.

After returning to Canada Kain joined Albert and Elizabeth MacCarthy's party to establish a number of outstanding new routes. After scaling Mount Louis (2682m), an imposing rock tower in the Rockies near Banff, he led the first ascents of several major peaks in the Purcell range including the north, highest, tower (3399m) of Howser Spire, Mount Karnak (3399m) and Monument Peak (3094m). As his final achievement of the season Kain led the first ascent, by way of the south ridge, of the spectacular Bugaboo Spire (3185m), a route he considered to have been his most difficult climb in Canada.

Further north in the Rockies A J Gilmour, E W D Holway and Howard Palmer made the first ascent of Mount Longstaff (3180m), one of the high peaks to the north-west of the Robson group.

At home in Wales, two of three notable routes were established on the Idwal Slabs in Cwm Idwal. A party led by I A Richards, who in the previous summer had taken part in the first ascent of *Hope*, added *Faith* and *Charity* in April.

In September the death occurred of Lucy Walker, the first lady to ascend the Matterhorn. A member of the famous Walker family and in later life president of the Ladies' Alpine Club, she made numerous ascents in many parts of the Alps during a long and successful climbing career.

In January Siegfried Herford, remembered for the first ascent of *Central Buttress* on Scafell and other outstanding climbs, was killed in action. Writing in the *Alpine Journal* Geoffrey Winthrop Young recalled that 'During the last few years there has been no climber of the younger generation in Great Britain whose leading position has been accepted so unanimously, I will venture to say even affectionately, by climbers of every age and school.'

During the year several members of the Alpine Club lost their lives on active service including Morris Slingsby, who had reached a height of some 7100m on Kamet (7756m) before being defeated by bad weather. In December the president, Lord Justice Pickford, concluded his valedictory address by expressing the hope that his successor 'may soon be able to celebrate the conclusion of peace and a return to our ordinary life, freed from the cloud of sorrow and anxiety caused by the war.'

Area Notes

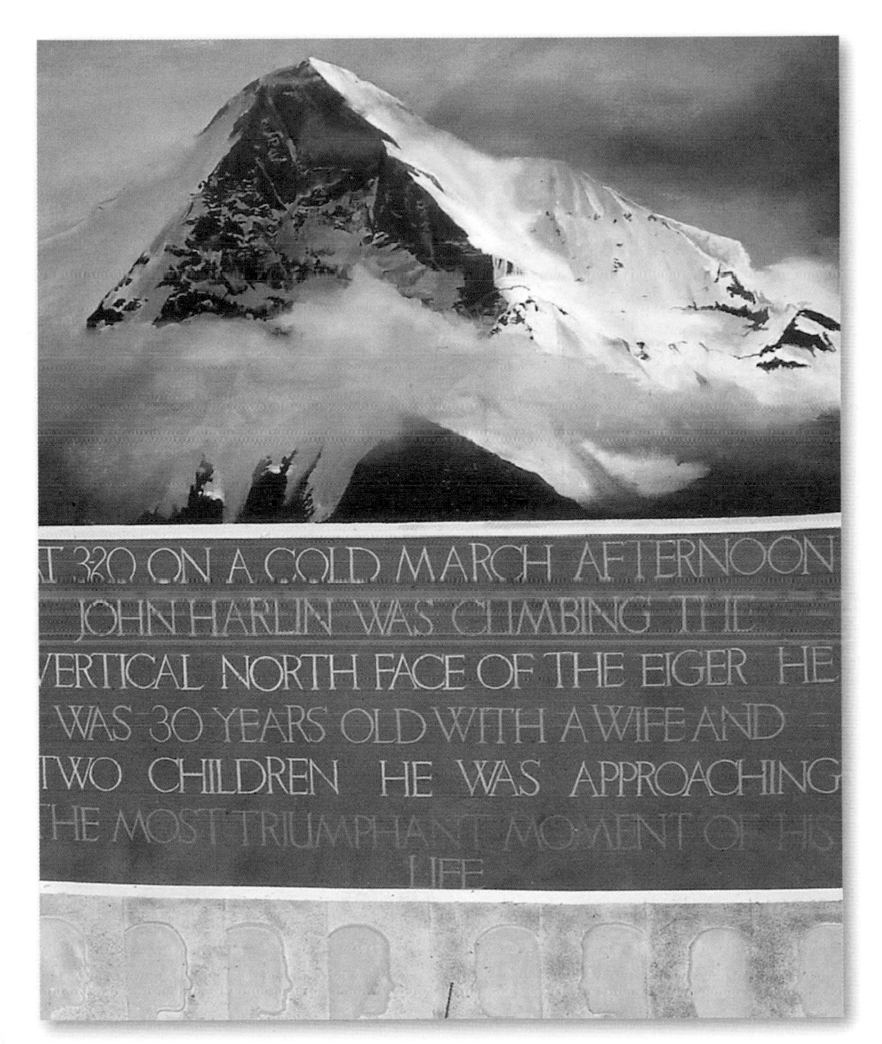

John Harlin

Rob Fairley, 1969. (Acrylic on board. 150cm x 120cm. Destroyed.)

LINDSAY GRIFFIN

Alps & Dolomites 2015

For a variety of reasons – weather, politics and, in the case of Nepal, earthquakes – significantly fewer major new lines than normal were completed in the world's mountains during 2015. This was also true in the Alps, where dry conditions and, during the summer, incredibly warm temperatures, confined most to objectively safe rock. Although there were a number of new additions to the Mont Blanc range, there appear to have been no leading first ascents.

On 18 August 1983, three of the top alpinists of that time, Eric Bellin, Jean-Marc Boivin and Martial Moioli started up the compact granite face to the right of the initial corner system of the *American Route* on the south face of the Fou, emerging at the summit the following night under a full moon. Their route, *Balade au Clair de Lune*, is mixed free and aid, and has seen few repeats. There are several fine but often poorly protected pitches of free climbing up to 6c, and at least one demanding aid pitch of A3/A4 (hooks and copperheads) above the point where the line crosses the famous Diagonal Crack.

Ascents of the south face have declined in recent years due to the danger of access during the summer months. Climbers now either choose spring to approach on ski or the more lengthy option of traversing the main ridge of the Aiguilles from the Aiguille du Midi and abseiling to the base of the route. Fabien Dugit and Cedric Lachat made several attempts in the spring to climb *Balade*, before deciding to try a free ascent, in one day, from the Requin hut. Leaving at 3.30am they moved remarkably fast, negotiating the second pitch at 7b+ (with poor peg protection), the third at 6b+ (but very, very run-out) and the crux fifth pitch at 8b. They then found the upper wall more straightforward, with former A2 pitches well protected by Friends. The last section was a fine, widening crack, which required Friends 4 and 5 and was felt to be around 7c+. They reached the top at 8.30pm, coincidentally in full moonlight.

On 8 January AC members put up the first of three short technical mixed routes above the Vallée Blanche. Earlier in the winter Nick Bullock had attempted a line on the west face of the Tour Ronde, very close to an unnamed rock route climbed in 1975 by René Corompt and Pierre de Galbert (TD, V+) but known to have been done (by an unknown party) at least a couple of years previously. Bullock climbed three pitches before retreating and then teamed up with Matt Helliker around a week later for a complete ascent. The line is an obvious winter dry tooling objective, which follows a groove with very loose rock that needs to be well frozen to make the climb safe. The seven-pitch line was named *Night Fever* (250m, M8),

Matt Helliker on the M8 third pitch of *Night Fever*, on the west face of Tour Ronde. *(Nick Bullock)*

Helliker, right, and Nick Bullock after the demanding descent. Patrick Gabarrou had been so concerned for their safety in a gathering storm he alerted mountain rescue: an unnecessary but much appreciated gesture. *(Nick Bullock)*

the pair finishing in the dark, strong winds and whiteout conditions. Patrick Gabarrou spotted their headtorches high on the climb, and given the conditions, chose to alert the rescue service. It was not needed, and Bullock later commented it was good find that one of his heroes was 'caring'.

On 18 February Helliker teamed up with regular partner Jon Bracey for a new winter line on the north-east face of the Pyramid du Tacul. After an easy ski to the base, the pair followed a line based around the grooves and corners of the 1984 Domenech-Remy-Remy rock route, *Le Ronfleur Paradoxal* (D+, V). Thin ice and hard, steep mixed gave excellent sustained but well-protected climbing, and the 250m, six-pitch route M7 was named *Mastabas*. Future ascensionists will need to be patient to allow the ice to form well enough in the grooves; the pair had studied the line for a few years, waiting for the right conditions to materialise.

Jon Bracey on the first piece of Mastabas, on the Pyramide du Tacul. *(Matt Helliker)*

The final mixed route for Helliker came on 13 March, again with Bracey but this time on the third pillar of the east face of Mont Maudit. Here, Helliker had identified a winter line between *Filo di Arianna* (Faré-Grassi-Longhi, 1984) and the *East Pillar Grassi-Meneghin* (350m, TD+, VI+). The line involved four pitches up a lower angled buttress to a snowfield (also crossed by *Filo di Arianna*), followed by another four up the steep headwall forming the left flank of the east pillar. As the lower section appeared to be broken, the pair waited for reasonable snow cover. This worked, as the lower buttress gave good mixed climbing in icy cracks and corners up to M5+, and the upper dry buttress fine steep climbing in rock shoes up to 6b. At the start, and in the sun, the two were able to climb the top section in bare hands, but when the sun disappeared there was a lot of gloves-on, gloves-off, and violent body shaking before they reached the top. The route has been named *Zephyr* (400m, M5+ 6b).

'The Lonely Pillar' in *AJ* 2015 details Simon Richardson's 20-year love affair with the Greuvettaz Cirque above the Comino bivouac hut. In the summer of 2015 he was back, this time with Roger Webb, and on 25 September completed a new route on the south-west face of Punta 2825m on Mont Vert du Greuvettaz. This lies roughly midway between the routes climbed on Puntas 2810m and 2873m, climbed in 2012 with Tom Prentice. The line was 11 pitches with an overall grade of D and a first pitch crux of about 5+. From the summit they traversed the connecting ridge to Punta 2810m and abseiled the bolted line of the 2010 *Carletto Route* (TD, 6b).

On 15 July Vincent Fournier and Jeff Mercier climbed *Efareb* on the south face of the Aiguille d'Argentière. This climbs the Tour Jaune, right of the Couloir en Y. The total height of the route from bergschrund to summit is 1,200m but it is hard to say how much of it is new, maybe only seven pitches that reach and climb the hanging corner between the 1968 *Bellin-Ravanel Route* and *Elévation*.

Further west, in the Écrins massif, two new routes are worthy of mention. In mid October a local guide, climbing the *Goulotte Grassi* on the Ailefroide, noticed that the long *dièdre* in the lower part of the north face of the Pic Sans Nom (3913m), right of the *Raie des Fesses*, was chocked with ice. The rock immediately to the left of this *dièdre* is taken by the classic 1950 *George-Russenberger Route* (ED2), which high on the face finishes up the north-west arête. The observation prompted local activists Benjemin Brochard, Fred Degoulet and Jonathan Joly to set off on 19 October from Pré de Madame Carlé for the three-hour approach to the face.

The initial climbing proved hard and difficult to protect and after five pitches they had to bivouac. They had planned for one night on the face, but next day climbed 10 hours and 11 difficult mixed pitches before having to stop again. On the third day they completed another 13 pitches to join the *brêche*, and given the lateness of the day and the long descent ahead, chose to forego the summit and descend directly to the south. They named their 1,000m climb *Le Prestige des Écrins* (M6+ AI5 6a). However, their ascent proved somewhat controversial, as only the first 500m are new and they lie very close to the *George-Russenberger*.

Motivated by the ascent reported above, Pierre Sauget enlisted Alexandre Michel and Stefano Morino to try a line on the north face of Ailefroide Orientale (3847m) that he had spotted the previous year. The route climbs the left flank of the north-west spur, left of the drainage falling from the Brêche du Glacier Noir. The climbing turned out to be very varied, sustained but never desperate, and with all the qualities to make the route a future classic. The team left Pré de Madame Carlé at 2am on 26 October and were back in the village of Ailefroide 20 hours later, naming their line *Winter is Coming* (700m, of which 550m is new, F5, M5+, 80°).

In 2002 Patrick Gabarrou climbed a hard new rock route on the south face of the Matterhorn, which reached the crest of the Furggen Ridge just left of the summit of Picco Muzio, the c4190m tower below the shoulder. *Padrepio, prega per Tutti* (ED3, 7a 6c obl) was completed with

Jon Bracey on the east face of Mont Maudit, during the first ascent of *Zephyr* (400m, M5+, 6b). *(Matt Helliker)*

Cesare Ravaschietto after three previous forays with different partners. In the intervening 13 years, with seven different partners, Gabarrou worked on forcing an independent finish, left of the Furggen nose, exiting directly onto the summit. This was finally completed on 6 August, 10 days after his 65th birthday, with his old friend Pierre Gourdin. However, this upper section was climbed in stages, either traversing in from the Furggen Ridge, or abseiling from above. The complete line has been christened *Padre Pio, Echelle vers le Ciel* (1300m, 7a) but still needs an integral ascent.

Still proving that there are new lines left to climb on the north face of the Eiger, the all-star team of Simon Gietl, Robert Jasper and Roger Schäli (Italian-German-Swiss) completed a hard line that Jasper and Schäli had been attempting since 2009. The new route climbs through the Rote Fluh and up the *Czechoslovakian Pillar*, left of the *Ghilini-Piola Direttissima*. Protected by a mix of bolts and traditional gear (including pegs), it crosses *La Vida es Silbar* and *Paciencia* to exit onto the west flank at c3700m. On 11 August, the team finally redpointed all 33 pitches to create the most technically difficult rock route on the Eiger: *Odyssee* (1400m, 8a+).

The Arnold-Steck speed ascents, on the high-profile walls of the Alps, continue. On 22 April Swiss Dani Arnold climbed the *Schmid Route* on the north face of the Matterhorn in just 1h 46m, 10 minutes faster than the previous record established in 2009 by Ueli Steck. However, Steck was to 'retaliate'. On 16 November he climbed the *1938 Route* on the north face of the Eiger

Smile for the camera. Matt Helliker on *Zephyr*, east face of Mont Maudit. *(Jon Bracey)*

Already reported in *AJ* 2014, this is the amazing 55m crux pitch of *Chancer*, on the north-west face of Tour Ronde, which Matt Helliker climbed at M6. *(Jon Bracey)*

in 2h 22m, six minutes faster than Arnold's 2011 time, which was the fastest on record. Steck's time was 25 minutes faster than his own 2008 record, but he used different tactics. That year there were no tracks on the face and Steck climbed the route free. At the time of his 2015 ascent the track was in place (in fact Steck had climbed the route one week previously with a partner in 3h 46m, possibly the fastest time for a roped pair), and he elected to use any means available for increasing his speed, such as pulling on pegs and using in situ fixed rope.

Arguably, Steck's most notable Alpine event of the year was a continuous self-propelled traverse of all the 82 4,000m peaks of the Alps, as designated in the UIAA list. He climbed the majority with various partners, including his wife, but around 30 were solos. Speed is always paramount in Steck's mind: during a cycle link between two venues, Steck was overjoyed to hit 90kph while descending the Grimsel Pass road with his brother (and fortunately very little traffic). Steck completed the traverse in 62 days from 11 June to 11 August, but this is not a record; Diego Giovannini and Franco Nicolini covered the same ground in 60 days during 2008.

British national and Italian resident Tom Ballard became the first person to solo all six classic north faces of the Alps during a single winter season. He used the *Colton-MacIntyre* to make the ascent of the Grandes Jorasses north face, and climbed each of four of the six faces comfortably in one day.

On Piz Badile's *Cassin Route*, always notoriously difficult to climb in winter, he found difficulties up to M7 and spent a night in a snowhole at the second Cassin bivouac. He also made one bivouac while climbing the *Comici Route* on the north face of the Cima Grande, the first of the six completed during the winter season. Although he had climbed the north face of the Eiger before, including solos and new lines, he had never previously attempted the *1938 Route*. However, it could be argued that he had passed that way before: as a foetus in his mother's womb when she climbed the route, almost six months pregnant, in 1988. Ballard, the son of the late Alison Hargreaves and who is based in the Dolomites, put up several hard new routes in the Catinaccio region during the summer, up to IX-, VIII obl.

In the Bregaglia-Masino, on the big granite walls above the Val di Mello where there is a strong no-bolts ethic, two new routes were established on the famous Scoglio delle Matamorfosi. In 2014 Daniele Bianchi, Pietro Biasini and Mirko Masè spotted a series of grassy cracks and then proceeded to clean them, ground up, to create a seven-pitch line with a wildly overhanging crux sixth pitch. By November 2015, when the lower cracks were dry after a long, hot autumn, Biasini was gone, killed the previous February in Norway during the annual Rjukan festival when an icefall collapsed. The two remaining climbers returned and freed all seven pitches to create *Here Today, Gone Tomorrow* (215m, X- or 8a+). In the April prior to this successful climb Simone Pedeferri had completed the first ascent of *Io non ho Paura* (225m, 8b+, 7b obl) with Alberto Marazzi, a line immediately to the right of the celebrated, wonderful classic *Luna Nascente*.

On the great east face of Monte Qualido (2707m) Paolo Marazzi, Luca Schiera and Matteo de Zaiacomo opened the 18-pitch route, *King of the Bongo* (c800m, 7c+). They began working on the route in 2014 and finished with a continuous two-day ascent in July 2015. No bolts were placed and the crux, ninth pitch, which was a traverse below a roof, required skyhook protection.

A notable event for female rock climbers was the third (and fourth) overall and first female ascent of *Die Unendliche Geschichte* on the seventh Kirchlispitze on the Rätikon. This technical 420m 8b+ put up at the start of the 1990s by Beat Kammerlander, was for some years considered one of the three hardest alpine sport climbs in the world and had to wait until 1995 for a second ascent. Unlike Kammerlander's nearby masterpiece *Silbergeier*, also one of the three, *Die Unendliche Geschichte* has remained neglected. Nina Caprez and Barbara Zangerl, climbing as a team, both redpointed the entire route.

There were interesting winter ascents and big new routes in the Dolomites, where traditional ethics can still prevail. On 10 January, Alessandro Rudatis and Ruggero Zardini made the first winter ascent of the 1993 Igor Koller route, *40 Anni per il Falier* (380m, FFA 2010, 7c+) on the south face of the Marmolada. They were able to travel light, as this nine-pitch route finishes on a halfway ledge from where the route is normally abseiled. It is not clear whether the Italian pair completed the route free.

Two days before Christmas, Nicolas Tondini and Emanuele Pellizzari made the first winter ascent of the Kurt Astner-Christoph Heinz route, *Rondo Veneziano* (470m, IX or 7c) on the south face of the Torre Venezia, Civetta group. The route requires some commitment, as above the long traverse at mid-height it becomes impossible to abseil the climb. On the day in question the alarm went at around 2.30am for Tondini and 3am for Pellizzari (the latter told his wife he was going out with the dog and would be back for dinner). The pair started walking around 5am and began the climb at 8am. They reached the summit at 4pm, having made an on-sight ascent, and were down in a pizzeria at 6.30pm when Pellizzari's wife phoned him, a trifle upset that he was late.

In August a significant new route was added to the big, north-west face of the Civetta (3220m), when Italians Martin Dejori, Marta Mozzati, Titus Prinoth, Giorgio Travaglia and Alex Walpoth completed *Via Degli Studenti* (1000m, VIII- A0). The route first climbs the 500m pillar right of the 1967 Messner route *Friends*, then crosses the Messner route to tackle the most overhanging section of the face. This required a few simple aid moves and rests before reaching an exposed bivouac. Next day the team joined the classic *Solleder* route for two pitches, then continued direct to the top where the *Solleder* moves right. No bolts were placed, although a few were carried, and sections that required the leader to use aid or rests were freed by the seconds. However, a free ascent remains for a future party, and the authors have no plans to return.

On 27 August, Much Mayr eventually made the first free ascent of the *Carillo-Gallego-Gomez-Lozano* route on the north face of the Cima Grande. This 1977 aid extravaganza from a well-known team of Spanish climbers had been pretty much ignored until it caught the eye of Italian Mauro 'Bubu' Bole in 2003. At that period Bubu was making free ascents of some of the great aid routes on the walls of the Lavaredo, and after making the second ascent of the *Spanish Route*, solo, he eventually climbed it at 8a+ with three points of aid through the gigantic roof on pitch three. Climbing with Guido Unterwurzacher, Mayr freed this section at a declared 8b+, though Unterwurzacher thought it might easily be 8c.

For historical reasons a notable ascent was that of Hansjörg Auer, who made the first free solo of the famous *Mephisto*, left of the Livanos Pillar on the west face of the Sass dla Crusc (or Heiligkreuzkofel). This route was put up in 1979 by two of the best Austrian rock climbers of the time, Luggi Rieser, who now goes under the name of Swami Prem Darshano after his religious conversion, and Reinhard Schiestl. The latter's lead of the crux pitch, without bolts, is now considered the first confirmed 'alpine' VIII-/VIII in Europe. In 1968, while making the first ascent of the central pillar some way to the right, a certain Reinhold Messner climbed an off-vertical wall above an ankle-snapping ledge on slightly friable rock to bring in undoubtedly the first 'alpine' VII in Europe. This pitch had only been repeated on a top rope until the mid 1990s, and even today opinions vary on the grade: from VII through to VIII-.

Auer had climbed *Mephisto* with a partner shortly before his lone ascent and despite feeling the crux was not simple, suddenly became highly motivated for the solo. He was full of praise for the authors: 'What they did back then with the gear of that era was quite simply incredible, visionary, and a masterpiece of hard free climbing in the mountains.'

The perennial Italian activist Rolando Lacher and partners (including his son) climbed *50 Anni son Volati, 25 Regalati* on the east face of Monte Fabbion (2672m) in the Brenta Dolomites. The 215m route, while only six pitches long, is demanding throughout and the top pitch overhangs by 10m. Characteristically, Lacher climbed ground-up using a mix of spaced bolts and trad gear to provide his normal run-out climbing. The last (and crux) pitch is 8a+ and the route has obligatory 7b moves. The route name needs some explanation: Lacher celebrated his 50th birthday in 2015, 25 years after he miraculously survived a 50m ground fall.

Finally, in the Far Eastern Alps, one of the most notable ascents was that of *Optimist*, a winter route on the west face of the Schneefernerkopf (2875m) in Austria's Wetterstein region. The protagonists were Germans Joachim Feger and Michael Wohileben, who opted to place no bolts on their new line, though the last four pitches are common with a bolted summer climb. Protection was difficult throughout due to the typically poor rock of this massif. The 1,300m route, rated M6, was completed over two days in February with a bivouac at around half height.

SIMON RICHARDSON

Scottish Winter 2015-16

Adrian Crofton about to be 'bamboozled' on the first ascent of *Bamboozle Buttress* (V,6) in Corrie Bonhard. The route eventually went up and left. *(Simon Richardson)*

The 2016 winter started late and finished early, and is unlikely to go down as one of the great Scottish seasons. Snow came late to the mountains, and even through December, winter climbing was a start-stop affair with frequent thaws. The mountains were then hit by an almost unprecedented series of storms over the Christmas-New Year period, which made climbing almost impossible; the trend continued through January and February with ferocious winds. As the weather cooled down in February, the gales transported and redistributed the snow causing dangerous avalanche conditions and making mountain travel difficult. Despite the challenges, there was a high level of activity, mainly centred on calmer periods in the middle of January and February and a glorious weekend at the end of February. A major thaw in early March brought most climbing activity to an abrupt halt, although cool weather later in April brought the classic ice routes on Ben Nevis back into condition.

The most significant event was the first repeat of *Anubis* on Ben Nevis by Swiss climber Dani Arnold. The first winter ascent of this overhanging summer E8 on The Comb was made by Dave MacLeod in February 2010. It is widely regarded as the most difficult winter route on Ben Nevis, and along with *Banana Wall* in the Northern Corries, it is the only route in Scotland that merits a Grade XII rating. Arnold is perhaps best known for setting speed records on the north faces of the Eiger and the Matterhorn, but he also made an early repeat of *The Hurting* in the Northern Corries in 2012 so is no stranger to top end Scottish mixed. He succeeded on *Anubis* on his second visit: conditions were too warm in January, but the cliff was well frozen and well rimed up in March. Continental climbers have visited Ben Nevis in winter for many years, however most have focused on the classic snow and ice routes. Dani Arnold's repeat of *Anubis* is undoubtedly the most difficult Scottish ascent ever achieved by an overseas visitor.

Gates of Paradise

The finest new route of the season took place in February when Iain Small and Murdoch Jamieson climbed *Gates of Paradise* (VIII,8) on Church Door Buttress in Glen Coe. This spectacular route starts further right than the existing summer routes and climbs overhanging mixed ground to gain a hanging icicle. Small had noticed the icicle start to form when he made the second ascent of *Crusade* (VII,8) with Uisdean Hawthorn earlier in the season. 'The line had formed up into some ice-coated lower walls and slabs from the dripping icicle fringe, then a steep mixed section to roofs and through them to gain the icicles,' Iain explained. 'The main pitch started up a rather run-out icy arête leading to a strenuous roof with a knee-bar rest on an icy tufa-like feature. A hard pull then gained the ice and some short screws after which it was all over. With it being short, but intense, we thought VIII, 8 might cover it." The grade should be treated with respect, as Small is reluctant to give relatively short routes a grade IX rating.

Earlier in the season in Glen Coe, Small and Uisdean Hawthorn made the first winter ascent of *Shadhava* (VIII,9) a summer E3 on the right wall

Iain Small just reaching the hanging icicle on the crux pitch of *Gates of Paradise* (VIII,8) during the first ascent. This very steep route lies high up on the right side of Church Door Buttress in Glen Coe. *(Murdoch Jamieson)*

of *Unicorn* in Stob Coire nan Lochan, and Mark Chadwick and Simon Tietjen added *Moonshine* (V,7) to Lost Valley Buttress. Further south, Dave MacLeod had a good day with Helen Rennard making the first winter ascent of *Southern Freeze* (IX,9), an E2 on The Cobbler's South Peak.

The Cairngorms

The wild weather and difficult snow conditions limited exploratory activity in the Cairngorms, although Andy Nisbet used the west-facing aspect of Lurcher's Crag to his advantage and added nine new routes. The finest additions of *Have an Ice Day* (V,5), *The Force Awakens* (VI,6) and *Snowbird* (VI,7) were climbed with Steve Perry and took advantage of early season ice. Glen Clova proved to be a sheltered venue away from the westerly gales and saw activity from Henning Wackerhage, Adrian Crofton, Sophie Grace Chappell and Simon Richardson. The finest routes were *The Age of Enlightenment* (VI,7) in Corrie Farchal, *Bamboozle Buttress* (V,6) in Corrie Bonhard and *King Herod* (VI,7), an unusual pinnacle-like feature on Cairn Broadlands.

Early in the season, the Northern Corries saw third ascents of *Pfugga-lule* (VIII,9) by Andy Inglis and Neil Adams, *Swallowtail Pillar* (VII,8) by Dave Almond and Ian Parnell, and *Babes in the Wood* (VIII,8) by Almond and Helen Rennard. Uisdean Hawthorn and Tom Livingstone also made the second ascent of *The Vapouriser* (VIII,8) on Creag an Dubh Loch. Big news in the Cairngorms however, was two ascents of *The Needle* (VIII,8) on the Shelter Stone the same weekend by Inglis and Adams, and Parnell and

Nick Bullock leading the thin ice smear on *Capricorn* (VIII,7) on Ben Nevis. This outstanding two-pitch addition climbs the thin snaking ice line directly above the twin grooves of *Gemini* on the north face of Carn Dearg. *(Tim Neill)*

Kenton Cool. Although *The Needle* was first climbed in winter as long ago as February 1985 by Andy Nisbet and Colin MacLean, it is still regarded as one of Scotland's big grade VIIIs, so ascents on consecutive days was something of a landmark event.

Central Highlands

New route activity on Ben Nevis was unusually quiet although a couple of good pitches were added in January. John Crook and Pete Graham climbed the bold *Gothic Edge* (VII,7) up the arête left of the *Gargoyle Cracks* on Number Three Gully Buttress, and Ramon Marin and Douglas Russell found *Tangerine Dream* (VII,8) the prominent chimney-crack to the left of *The Rattler* on South Trident Buttress. Later in the season Nick Bullock and Tim Neill tip-toed up *Capricorn* (VIII,7), the ice smear that often forms to the left of the twin grooves of *Gemini* on Carn Dearg Buttress, and Dave MacLeod added a serious mixed route on the east face of Tower Ridge. The two-pitch *Night Fury* (IX,9) had seen a couple of prior attempts and lies just left of *The Urchin*.

On Creag Meagaidh, Simon Richardson teamed up with Henning Wackerhage, Pat Ingram and Roger Everett to explore an attractive unclimbed, mixed buttress in Coire Choille-rais. *Birthday Route* (IV,4) and *Cat Burglar* (V,5) took the obvious lines of weakness on the left side of the cliff, and the full challenge of the buttress was met with *The Day After Tomorrow* (VII,8) that climbs the front face.

Northern Highlands

The cold weather in January resulted in a number of significant repeats in the Northern Highlands. On Beinn Eighe, the spectacular *Shoot the Breeze* (IX,8) saw its second ascent courtesy of Andy Inglis, Iain Small and Murdoch Jamieson, and Jamieson also repeated *Bruised Violet* (VIII,8) with Guy Steven and *Immortal Memory* (IX,8) with Ian Parnell and Uisdean Hawthorn. Other notable second ascents include *Reach for the Sky* (VII,6) on Mainreachan Buttress by Inglis and Small, and *Fishmonger* (VI,6) on Foinaven by Erick Baillot and Dave Kerr.

The most significant addition to the Northern Highlands took place in mid February on Beinn Bhan when Malcolm Bass, Neil Silver and Simon Yearsley climbed the eight-pitch *Nam Famhairean* (VII,7) in Coire nam Fhamair. This major expedition takes a mirror image line to *Der Riesenwand* on the Giant's Wall and shares a pitch at half-height. Later in the month, Beinn Bhan proved a popular location as its proximity to the sea meant it avoided most of the heavy snowfall inland, and multiple ascents were made of *The Godfather*, *Gully of the Gods* and *Great Overhanging Gully*. Also on Beinn Bhan, Andy Nisbet, Dave McGimpsey and Steve Perry climbed an excellent, three pitch *Direct Start* (V,5) to *Wall of the Early Morning Light* resulting in one of the longest ice routes in the country. Further south in Knoydart, Roger Webb and Simon Richardson added the long and serious *Tir na h-aoise* (VI,6) to the 400m-high Spider Buttress on Ladhar Beinn.

Cul Mor in Coigach saw a couple of good thin ice additions with the first winter ascent of *Buffalo Ballet* (VII,7) on the south face by Rennard and Richardson and the first ascent of *The Wrecking Light* (VIII,7) in Coire Gorm by Nick Bullock, Andy Inglis and Guy Robertson. The latter team also made the long-awaited second ascent of Mick Fowler and Dave Wilkinson's *Ice Bomb* in Beinn Dearg's Coire Ghranda adding a spectacular *Direct Finish* in the process.

Skye

The Cuillin on Skye provided several of the season's finest exploratory routes spearheaded by local guide and guidebook author, Mike Lates. The Skye Winter Festival in mid January saw some excellent additions, notably the first winter ascent of *Crack of Dawn* (VIII,8) on Sgurr Mhic Choinnich by James and Doug Sutton. Mark Francis and Dave Bowdler climbed the excellent *North Rib* (IV,5) of Banachdaich Gully, and Lates made the first winter ascent of *Owl Chimney* (IV,5), but it was Michael Barnard who proved most prolific with several difficult new routes including *The Bogeyman* (VI,7) and *Mr Charlie* (VI,7) on the Stone Shoot face of Sgurr Thearlaich.

Spurred on by Mike Lates' informative reports, several parties made traverses of the Cuillin Ridge in February. Conditions were excellent which led to a six-hour record time by Finlay Wild and Sam Gomersall, and an eight-hour solo traverse by Uisdean Hawthorn. Attention then swung to the ice routes when Lates made the second ascent of *White Wedding* (IV,4) with Mark Francis. This route was first climbed by Mick Fowler, Victor

Uisdean Hawthorn on the third pitch of *Immortal Memory* (IX,9) during the second ascent. This demanding winter-only line on the Far East Wall of Beinn Eighe was first climbed by Guy Robertson and Jason Currie in January 2013. *(Murdoch Jamieson)*

Saunders and Chris Watts almost exactly 30 years ago. News of their ascent focused attention on the other great Fowler-Saunders route, *Icicle Factory* (VI,6) on Sgurr a'Mhadaidh. James Sutton, Ben Wear and John Smith just beat Uisdean Hawthorn, Adam Russell and Dougie Russell to the coveted second ascent, who instead, added *Spectacula* (VI,6), the prominent line of ice to the left, before abseiling down to make the third ascent of *Icicle Factory*. The following day Hawthorn and Lea MacLeod made the first ascent of *Spirulina* (V,5), the line of ice between these two routes.

Across on the Coruisg side of the Cuillin, Andy Nisbet, Steve Perry, Dave McGimpsey and Sandy Allan had a good run of new ice routes including *The Inaccessible Icefall* (IV,4), *Griffin* (III,4) and *Skyefall* (IV,5). In a winter of difficult and testing conditions it was ironic that the most fickle venue of all, namely the Cuillin on Skye, should provide some of the finest routes of the season, but then that's Scottish winter climbing for you.

IAN WALL

Nepal

Sadly for all involved, Nepal suffered two major disasters over the autumn 2014 and spring 2015 seasons. Cyclone Hudhud hit Nepal in October 2014, at the height of the mountaineering season; as described in the Nepal area notes of *AJ* 2015, the massive snowfall led one of the worst disasters in Nepal's history, and certainly the worst trekking disaster. Then, in April 2015 Nepal suffered the worst earthquake in generations at the beginning of the spring season, with its epicentre north-west of Kathmandu. Close to 9,000 people were killed, including 19 who were overwhelmed by the earthquake-triggered avalanche on Everest. Hundreds of thousands of Nepalis were left homeless, with those who still had homes standing afraid to return to them because of the continuing aftershocks. It is surprising that any mountaineering was achieved during these two seasons but several teams and expeditions managed to work around both disasters and succeeded on their objectives.

Autumn 2014

Ama Dablam was summited by 35 teams from all over the world via the normal route, the south-west ridge. New Zealander Russell Brice attempted the technical north ridge. However, just as in 2013, the team had to abandon the expedition at about 6,500m due to difficult snow conditions. **Baruntse** saw four teams from the US, the Netherlands, Poland and Switzerland summit on 4 and 5 November. However, four other teams who were on the mountain earlier in October found the snow conditions too dangerous to summit and abandoned their efforts. **Cho Oyu** was summited by 26 teams from the northern side.

Chugimago (6259m), also referred to as Chukyima Go, in Rolwaling received the first ascent of its west face by Domen Kastelic (Slovenia) and Samuel Hennessey (US) on 12 November 2014. The expedition set out carrying light loads to reach previously stashed equipment halfway up the approach route. They continued to the west face at which point they bivied under a large boulder. Bad weather created by Cyclone Hudhud kept them grounded for the remainder of the day.

By early next morning the weather had settled a little and the team climbed the face, pitching camp when they reached the ridge. Leaving with light sacks the pair set off the following morning to complete the final 150m to the summit. However, due to technical difficulties, progress was slow and it took the climbers three hours to reach the summit. The pair descended via the route of ascent to base camp the same day. They gave the route an overall rating of 900m, 90° and M4.

Chugimago showing the *Kastelic-Hennessey*. An earlier recorded ascent by a Scottish expedition in 1952 had been discounted. *(Hennessey-Kastelic archive)*

While dealing with formalities at the ministry in Kathmandu, Kastelic and Hennessey were told the mountain was unclimbed. However, they had already discovered the peak had been climbed in 1952, an ascent that impressed them when viewing possible lines from the summit.

In 1952 a Scottish party led by Tom Mackinnon and including W H Murray, Tom Weir and Douglas Scott climbed three peaks in the area, which have historically been identified as Chugimago, Ramdung (c5925m) and Yalung Ri. The Scottish party gave no names. Study of their rather vague articles, sketch maps but more usefully photos from that period reveal that their third summit was not Chugimago but Peak 5794m and Yalung Ri more likely to be Yalung Ri North.

Several attempts on Chugimago were reported in the 1970s, and on one a German team retreated 200m from the top of the north ridge. While Chugimago's location makes it likely to have received one or more unauthorised ascents, none appear to have been reported, giving Kastelic and Hennessey the first official, if not the first absolute, ascent.

Chhochenphu Himal (6260m) was climbed on 30 October by Philip James De-Beger (UK), Ross Lesslie (US) and Ang Phurba Sherpa (Nepal). **Himlung** had three teams summit successfully; however, four other teams had to abandon their attempts due to Cyclone Hudhud. **Lhotse South Face**

Above: Narphu Peak with the *British-Nepali* route marked. *(Brian Jackson)*

Right: The line and bivouac sites for the first ascent of Gave Ding, via its north face, in a seven-day round trip in October 2015. *(Mick Fowler)*

was attempted by a South Korean expedition but they had to abandon their attempt at 7,900m due to bad weather and a lack of time. Three teams attempted **Makalu** but they abandoned their expedition due to deep snow and dangerous conditions on the mountain. Makalu seems to be receiving a lot of autumn snow, which makes it more of a spring climbing peak.

Manaslu has received a lot of attention over the last two seasons, mainly because of the problems on Everest and the difficulties in getting to the north side of Cho Oyu; 22 teams summited in autumn 2014. **Mustang Himal** (6195m) received its first ascent by American female climber Melissa Arnot together with Ben Jones and Jonathan Mancuso on 2 November 2014.

Nangamari 1 (6547m) saw a first ascent via its south ridge by Swiss climbers David Berther and Reno Decurtins, with Hira Lal Gurung and Tul Singh Gurung from Nepal. Nangamari 1 is north-west of Kangchengjunga and east of Makalu on the border of Nepal and Tibet. The expedition summited on 17 November 2014.

Narphu Peak (5921m) also saw its first official ascent on 22 November 2014 by a British-Nepali team lead by Brian Jackson. Six people reached the summit. The peak lies to the east of the Chulu group of peaks north of the Kang La. The expedition approached the peak from the Kang La. The team estimated the route to be PD+. That included ascending a short ice wall 45°-70°. A steeper ice wall and a large crevasse higher up near the summit was breached by a snow bridge. The summit bid was made from

Jabou Ri via the north-east ridge. *(Ryan Waters)*

the high camp at 5,230m, setting out at 3am. The team returned to camp by 4.40pm the same day. (GPS, 28° 43' 00.71"N, 84° 07' 20.19"E)

Putha Hiunchuli was summited by four teams while Cyclone Hudhud prevented others from even reaching base camp.

Spring 2015

Annapurna I was summited early spring 2015, before the earthquake, by 13 climbers from Iran, Macedonia, China, Turkey, Finland and Nepal all reaching the top on 23 March. Sadly, strong Finnish climber Samuli Mansikka and his climbing partner Pema Sherpa, also known as 'Technical Pema', slipped and fell to their deaths on the descent. After the earthquake most teams abandoned their expeditions. **Manaslu**, however was summited by a Czech Republic climber, Pavel Bim and a Frenchman, Daniel de Gabai, who waited it out for about a fortnight after the first earthquake. They succeeded on 8 May 2015, a couple of days before the second earthquake. All other teams on expeditions to Ama Dablam, Everest (north and south sides), Lhotse, Makalu and some other smaller peaks abandoned their attempts due to the earthquake.

Autumn 2015

Jabou Ri (6166m) in Rolwaling received its first ascent by Ryan Waters and polar explorer Eric Larson from the US, via the north-east side. **Manaslu**

(8163m) was successfully summited by a 14-member team led by Daniel Lee Mazur on 30 September. Sadly, Austrian climber Zoltan Benedek died while descending from camp 4. Benedek's partner was rescued from camp 4 and was flown by helicopter from 6,800m. Both climbers were climbing without any support above base camp. Thirty-eight foreign climbers along with 20 Sherpas reached the top of Manaslu on 1 October, while 15 climbers including six foreigners summited on 30 September. A further 38 climbers abandoned their summit attempts citing bad climbing conditions followed by a week-long deteriorating weather pattern. Boyan Petrov became the first Bulgarian to ascend Manaslu.

At least 73 climbers including 44 foreigners successfully summited **Makalu** in the period 1-3 October 2015. The ministry of tourism issued permits to 106 climbers, representing 11 different expedition teams for the 2015 autumn season.

Everest was quiet during the autumn 2015 season with only the 33-year-old solo Japanese climber Nobukazu Kuriki on the mountain making his fifth attempt to reach the summit. Kuriki lost nine fingers to frostbite during a 2012 Everest attempt. Having failed in late September 2015 Kuriki restocked and on Friday 2 October headed back up to camp 2 for a second attempt. He eventually retreated from the mountain due to bad conditions. Elizabeth Hawley said that allowing and promoting a 'crazy' man to convince the world it was safe showed how desperate the Nepali government was to revive the industry it was promoting.

ANTONIO 'SEVI' GÓMEZ BOHÓRQUEZ

Peru 2013-14

CORDILLERA BLANCA 2013

On Nevado Ishinca (5530m), *Carlito's Way* (D+, M5, 60°–80°, 480m) is a possible new direct variation on the north-west face climbed on 5 June. Carlos Esteban Pineda Beyer and Carlos Eduardo Solé Perozo arrived in Huaraz at the end of May 2013. On 3 June, the Venezuelan Andeans crossed the Quebrada Ishinca and slept in the refuge at c4350m. They arrived the next day at the Mariscal Castilla refuge (4950m), which has been renamed Bivouac Longoni (Vivacco Longoni) after its restoration. At 5.45am on 5 June, Beyer and Perozo headed up moraine intending to climb the north-west face by a direct route from the refuge to the snowy peak. The ascent began properly at about 5,050m, with an icefall of 30°–40° for the first 190m, followed by two pitches (30m and 60m) of mixed climbing, another three 60m pitches at 60° and 80°, and a short (20m) pitch of some 50°–60° to the summit at 11.15am. They descended by icefalls to the north-north-east, arriving at the Vivacco at 11.55pm. This is a direct variation on the *Cosley-Houston* 2003 route.

References. Carlos Esteban Pineda Beyer and Carlos Comesaña; Morales Arnao, C, *Andinismo en la Cordillera Blanca*, Lima, Turismo Andino, 1968; *Slovenski alpinizem* 2009–10; *American Alpine Journal* (*AAJ*) 1965, 2014; www.cosleyhouston.com/recent/03-06-ishinca.htm.

When Carlos E Pineda and Carlos E Solé were on the Nevado Ishinca, they had the opportunity to contemplate the central couloir of the north face of **Nevado Ranraplca** (6062m), including the north face central couloir and made this their next target to give *Learning of our Weaknesses* (ED, M6, 5.10+, 70°–90°, 960m) on 9 July 2013. They left the Mariscal refuge at 12.30am on Saturday 8 June, and from the glacial moraine traversed below the enormous snow apron at the base of the couloir. The pair moved together for the first part to get as high as possible before the first rays of the sun. They passed the first crux, a section of thin ice and snow mixed with rocks over a near-vertical slab. They suffered a few small powder avalanches and reached their first decent piece of gear just before 6am. After this they climbed to avoid the danger of the main couloir, which was throwing down great quantities of ice and rock. The pair climbed a central pillar that was largely loose and decomposing rock. A little after sunset they arrived at the upper section of the couloir, where they took the leftmost of three gullies; this took the shape of a series of vertical ice cascades that resembled a giant staircase.

The temperature plummeted at nightfall, to around -20°C at 5,700m. They tried to fend off the cold by rubbing their knees, taking short rests and carrying on climbing to keep body heat up and to keep from falling asleep. Just as the night ended they reached the last icefall, climbed that and finished up the last pitch through an unstable cornice to the ramp and up to the glacial plateau. At 11.30am on 9 July, whipped by strong winds, with frozen faces and in very poor visibility they reached the summit. They descended by the normal route on the north-east face, wandering around for a while before they found the abseil point, still set up with stoppers and carabiners by a Chilean team that had come up the north face the day before. That took them to the bottom of the glacier, and at 7.30pm they arrived, exhausted, at the refuge, 43 hours after leaving.

References: Carlos Esteban Pineda Beyer; *Revista Peruana de Andinismo y Glaciología*, 1958-9; *AAJ* 1969 and following.

After climbing *Karma de los Cóndores* (300m, 5.11+; *AJ* 2006 pp320-321) on the rocky prow of **Hatun Ulloc** near the Quebrada Ishinca, the Swiss team of David Hefti, Marcel Probst, Mathias Schick and Florian Zwahlen travelled to the south of the Cordillera and installed themselves in a base camp at c4,500m at the foot of the west face of **Nevado Shacsha (Shaqsha) South** (5697m), for an attempt on the west face. (The mountain is called Nevada Huanchan (5632m) on sheet 20-i of the Peruvian Instituto Geográfico Nacional (IGN).) They climbed the route *Würmligrüber* (7a+, 60°, 240m) on 23 July 2013, without visiting the summit.

After a day of reconnaissance they spotted a promising system of cracks in the rock face west of the south peak of Shacsha, which is 5,697m on the German *Alpenvereinskarte* (DAV) of 1939. The four Swiss left camp on 23 July at 4am, skirted a small lake and crossed the bergschrund. The difficult climbing started here, at c5,350m, with two pitches of 5c (35m) and 6c+ (65m), before gaining a large dihedral. The route went up the corner (30m) at 6b, before an easy ramp took them to the two hardest pitches, 7a+ (40m) and 7a (35m), which led to a chimney. Six pitches finished the rock face and they then climbed 60m of 60° snow and ice to a point at c5,600m on the south-south-east arête of the lower summit to the south-west of Shacsha South. Four abseils took them down the route, they down-climbed over the bergschrund and returned to base camp at 8pm. Much of the route consists of clean finger and hand-sized cracks.

Nevado Shacsha is called Shaqsha in the book *Yuraq Janka* by John F Ricker, who gives the summit height at 5,703m, and 5,697m to the south top. Shacsha is given an erroneous name of 'Huantsán Chico' in the 1939 map published by the German Alpine Club (DAV); the 2005 edition kept that name, but added 'Nev Shacsha' in brackets and 5,632m as per the Peruvian map. Shacsha South is given the name 'Nevado Huanchán' and given 5,632m on sheet 21-h of the Peruvian IGN.

References: *Alpine Journal* (*AJ*) 2006; *AAJ* 2014; Sheet 20-i *Recuay* IGN (Peru); *Cordillera Blanca (Perú)*, 1:100,000, DAV 1939; Sheet 21-h *Huayllapampa* IGN (Peru); Ricker, J, *Yuraq Janka*, Map 3, 1977; *AAJ* 2000, 2011, 2015; *Planetmountain.com* 12 June 2010; *Alpinist.com* 28 June 2010.

CORDILLERA HUAYHUASH 2013

On 15 June Yasushi Yamanoi and Masuru Noda started climbing steep, excellent rock on the lower section of the south-east face of **Nevado Puscanturpa Este** (5410m). Arriving at the middle of the route the lightweight-style team were then faced with large patches of snow, and it took some effort to overcome the steep slopes of sugar snow and loose rock, including a very cold sitting bivouac at c5300m. The next day they finished off the route up the easy, higher icefalls and the headwall, arriving at the summit in mid-morning. This was probably the fourth ascent of this peak. Their route name, *Qiumplirgun Swerminganta* (ED+, VII M5+, A1, 700m) means 'dreams come true' in the local Quechua language. Yamanoi lost five fingers and all the toes on his right foot in 2002 after an alpine-style repeat of the 1999 *Slovenian Route* on the north face of Gyachung Kang (7952m) in the Mahalangur Himal.

References: Yasushi Yamanoi; *AJ* 2008, pp338-9; 2013, p308.

After Puscanturpa East, Yamanoi and Noda camped by a lake (c4750m) at the foot of the south-east face of **Nevado Trapecio** (5653m). On 24 June the team repeated the *Fernandez-Pita* route. The pair overcame slopes of ice and snow at 50°–70° in the lower section, with a section of steep ice and loose mixed terrain (M5+) in the upper part of the face. They arrived at the summit in 14 hours and bivouacked at c5,200m on the descent, concerned that abseiling in the dark could send them off route. They finished their descent in the warmth of the next morning's sun.

References: Miguel Ángel Pita Galego and Yasushi Yamanoi (p.c.); *Desnivel* 251 June 2007; *AJ* 2008, p340; *AAJ* 2014.

CORDILLERA URUBAMBA 2013

On 30 November, the Peruvian Andeans Jorge 'Coqui' Gálvez Aramburu, Manuel Urquizo Cereceda and Dominique Riva Roveda ascended the river called Joñayhuaiyo (according to the official Peruvian map) in the direction of the southern slope of **Nevado Capacsaya (Qhapaqsaya, Ccapacsaya, Huayurioq, Media Luna)** (5060m or 5044m) in the Cordillera Urubamba. They passed the village of Sutoc (c3750m) then Laguna Manallocsec (4050m); then, with heavy rucksacks, they made their way up a steep moraine. On top of the moraine they switched to big boots and crampons and some 10 hours after starting carved out a snow hole in a shelf at the base of the east wall of the western summit. At first light the next day they observed this wall sheds a lot of rock far too frequently; they traversed east to situate themselves under the south-west face of the eastern summit. The first part of the ascent on 1 December was on deep soft snow, followed by 100m on mixed ground (60°) that was lovely but loose, with some airy and exposed sections. At a system of shelves they traversed to the right, heading for an outstanding corner (25m, 70m; 6c+ A1) with a good crack that occasionally made it hard to protect. Four further pitches (250m) of climbing at IV brought them to the summit. They descended by the line of ascent. This new route contains some 450m of difficulty at about 6c+ A1, and is probably the first route with hard climbing on the walls of Capacsaya.

The first recorded route on Nevado Capacsaya is that of Malcolm Moore (USA) and John F Ricker (Canada), by the west glacier and north-west ridge, on 29 April 1970. Ricker wrote afterwards (*AAJ* 1970 p410) that the published height of 16,600ft (5060m) seemed too low. The Canadian alpinist, who was a student of the Quechua language, spelt the mountain's name as Ccapacsaya, also known as Huayurioq, and never came across anyone who called it Media Luna as had been annotated on the sketch maps of the Italian alpinist Mario Fantin. Note: it remains to be verified whether the Peruvian team climbed the same peak as Ricker; in the opinion of Gálvez it doesn't seem to be the case.

References: Jorge Gálvez and Manuel Urquizo; Sheet 27-r, *Urubamba*, IGN (Peru); Fantin, M, *Pioneri e Epigoni Italiani sulle vette di Ogni Continente*, Italia, Commissione delle Publicazzioni del Club Alpino Italiano (CPCAI), 1975; Fantin, Mario. *Le Ande*. Italia: CPCAI, 1979; *Montañas Peruanas* 59; *AAJ* 1970; 1973; 2014.

CORDILLERA VILCANOTA 2013

Nathan Glenn Heald, Thomas Ryan (USA) and Luis Crispín Quispe (Peru) left the village of Pacchante on 31 May 2013. They camped before and below the pass of Jampa (or Campa), in the valley that forms **Nevado Caracol** (5625m), **Concha de Caracol** (5640m), **Pucapunta** or **Puca Punta** or **Pachanta** (5740m), at the tail end of the mountains that join the Nevado Caracol with the Pachanta (also called the Pucapunta). (Heights are from Heald's GPS.) At 1am next morning the trio left for the Caracol. To gain entry to the south face of the Caracol, they started via a rocky spur on the east side, then had to get past some 15m of bullet-hard, 80° ice, followed by knee-deep soft snow at 45°–55°. Once they made it to the west ridge of Caracol, they found an easy bergschrund. After another 30m of 80° ice and in four hours they reached the summit of Caracol by the north-west arête following this to the Concha del Caracol where, at 6am, they rested for 10 minutes.

At this point that Ryan decided to stop, waiting for his companions. Heald and Crispín carried on with the traverse to the col between the Concha del

Caracol and Puca Punta, with snow at 45°–55° and exposed, but with little technical difficulty. The final section was at 70°–80° but on good névé, with small cornices and hard snow-ice. On the ridge they stayed on the north (left) side, as the cornices hung over space on the south. Heald touched the summit (5740m by his GPS) at 10am, describing in the *AAJ* 2014 (p201): 'Several sections were vertical, and we barely spoke while delicately passing the cornices that hung over the west face. As we arrived at the top, I saw that the actual summit was just a large flake of ice, about the size of a car, balanced on top. It was too dangerous to stand on it, so I just touched the top with my hand.' The north-west ridge of Puca Punta/Pachanta was TD, AI3, 200m.

Puca Punta/Pucapunta (5740m) is the Pachanta Peak whose first ascent by William W Hooker and Craig Merrihue was recorded in the article 'The Harvard Andean Expedition 1957' (*AAJ* 1958). The name Pachanta also appears in the map in Günter Hauser's book *Ihr Herren Berge*. The map indicates from north-west to south-east the peaks of Caracol (5619m), Concha de Caracol (not named, but given a height of 5630m), Pachanta (5727m) and further to the north-east is Ccapana Peak (5725m). The Harvard expedition stayed in the haçienda named after this last. Pachanta (Pacchanta) is called Nevado Puca Punta in the Peruvian IGN sheet 28-t *Ocongate*, located to the north-north-east of the pass of Nevado Campa, but is not given a height. The same is to be found in the Tinqui-Auzangate trekkers' sketch map, drawn by Healy and printed by the South American Explorer Club in 1985. The sketch-map of Wilkinson and Rubens (*AJ* 2005, p48) has the summit of Pachanta/Puca Punta coinciding with the third summit to the south-south-east after Cayangate IV.

References: Nathan Heald; *American Alpine Journal* 1967; 1981; 2014; Hauser, G, *Ihr Herren Berge*, 1957; Piero Ghiglione, *Nelle Ande del Sud Perù*, 1953; Cronk and Wortis (sketch), *AJ* 1959; Mario Fantin, *Le Ande*, 1979; Sheet 28-t *Ocongate*, Instituto Geográfico Nacional (IGN); Wilkinson and Rubens, *AJ* 2005; *Revista Peruana de Andinismo y Glaciología* 15.

CORDILLERA VILCABAMBA 2013

After attempts in 2011 and 2012, Nathan Heald, Thomas Ryan and Luis Crispín climbed the north-east ridge of **Salcantay** (6279m) on 16-17 June 2013, 27 years after the only previous ascent by Mark Lowe and Pete Leeming (UK). Heald records the height at 6729m, and checked it when he ascended the route again on 31 July with James Lissy (USA) and Edwin Espinoza (Peru). The route is given D with sections of AI2 or AI3 on ice. Salcantay received its name and a height of 6,271m on the map by Piero Ghiglione, in his book *Nelle Ande del Sud Perù* (1953). The orographic map of south Peru, published by the Swiss Foundation for Alpine Exploration (SSAF) is based on Ghiglione and indicates two peaks, and only one height given at 6,160m next to the eastern summit.

References: Nathan Heald; *AAJ* 2013; *Desnivel.com*; Ghiglione, P, *Nelle Ande del Sud Perù*, Officine Grafiche Aldo Garzanti Editore, 1953; *Sud Peru* (SSAF) is a sketch of ridges and rivers based on five expeditions by Ghiglione between 1939 and 1955.

CORDILLERA BLANCA 2014

Quilluhirka (5047m), also **Quillujirca**, might mean 'orange hill' in Quechua, as the locals call it, and it is accessible from Olleros. The peak is approximately 1.1km to the south-south-west of Schacsha Sur (5697m) and a few kilometres to the south of the summit of Nevado Shacsha/Shaqsha (5703m). On 15 July, Ecuadorians Rafael Cáceres, Esteban Mena Yañez, Nicolás Navarrete and Carla Pérez climbed five pitches on the south-east face (5.11d, 5.7, 5.11a, 5.10, 5.10), to the right of *El sueño de los Excluidos* (*Dream of the Excluded*) that was put up by Iannilli, Scappatura and Di Donato in 2010. The team arrived at the wooded shelf at the beginning of the south face and continued up the *Italian Route* on the south-east ridge, then 500m of possibly unclimbed terrain on the upper south-east face to the summit. The Ecuadorians estimate 850m for the route, with a difficulty of 5.11d. The team then opened a new route from the same wooded shelf up the south face (5,11 +/5.12-, 300m), but didn't continue up to the summit.

Quilluhirka has another local name: Yuraqmuru-muruhirka, which might mean 'hill of the white spots'. The first recorded ascent to the summit was by North Americans Cameron Tague and Kent McClannan, who climbed the right side of the south-east face (*Mission Control*, 5.11+ A2+) on 27-28 June, 1999. The south-east face was climbed in August 2003 by the Spaniards Enrique Barberá Llansol, Vicente Casquel Lopez and Antonio Gómez Bohórquez (6b, A2, 320m), but they didn't summit. From 11-17 May 2010, Roberto Iannilli, Ivo Scappatura and Andrea Di Donato climbed the left of the south-east face, calling their route *El Sueño de los Excluidos* (VII/VII+, A2, 1400m). They climbed the most logical line and found no sign of previous ascents on the wall nor on the summit, the lowest and to the left of that reached by the North Americans; they gave the peak the name Punta Giampiero Capoccia; this name doesn't follow the nomenclature of the Geographical Society of Peru, nor of the Peruvian Institute of Geography (IGN).

Later in May 2010 Luca D'Andrea and Massimo Massimiano shared the first 300m of the *Sueño*, then continued on the left side of the south face, possibly without reaching the summit (*La Teoría de la Gota de Agua*, VII, A2, 800m).

References: Kent McClannan; local people in Olleros and Canray; Sheet 21-h *Huayllapampa* of the IGN of Peru. *AAJ* 2000; 2011; 2015; *Planetmountain.com* 12 June 2010; *Alpinist.com* 28 June 2010.

On 7 June 2014, Peruvians Marco Jurado Ames, Jack Sierralta Infante and Rodrigo Mendoza entered the Cátac by the Sector Carpa (the point of access by Pastoruri), crossed the pass of Acococha (4600m) and spent the night in the Quebrada Queshque. Next day they reached a base camp (c4600m) at the foot of a laguna called Pamparaju in the 2005 edition of the German map of the area. (The name Laguna Pamparajo on the Peruvian map shouldn't be confused with the Lagunas Pamparaju Ricker drew on the Quebrada Pamparaju, below the north-west slope of the Nevado Qeshqe.) On 9 June at 3am the three climbed the moraine of **Mururaju** (5711m), (also Morroraju or Pongos Sur), then crossed avalanche debris from the north-west face, to reach the glacier and north-west ridge. The route started with loose rock, then mixed, steep ground with 70°soft snow up the north-north-west flank of the mountain. The ascent took 12 hours camp to camp, and four days after arriving at the laguna, and they then walked 8 hours back to Cátac. This was probably the first repeat of the route since 1971. The north-north-west ridge was first climbed on 3 June 1971 by the Germans D Fritz, H Güner, W Hummel, R Röcker, P Schmil, D Schwenkglenks, W Weber and F Wibmer from a high camp (c4500m), at the head of the Quebrada Queshque, called Tranca Ruri by the official Peruvian map and the 2005 German edition.

References: Marco Jurado; *Alpenvereinskarte Cordillera Blanca Süd Peru* 0/3b, 1:100,000, Österreichischer Alpenverein, 1939 and 2005; Hoja 20-1 *Recuay*, 1:100,000, IGN (Peru), 1986 reprint; *AAJ* 1972, pp162-163; Map 4 of Ricker, J, *Yuraq Janka: A Guide to the Peruvian Andes Part I: Cordilleras Blanca and Rosko*, Banff, Canadian Alpine Club, 1977.

CORDILLERA DE HUAYHUASH 2014

On 7 July 2014, Beto Pinto and William Alva from Peru and Daniel Araiza Chávez from Mexico camped on Cuargelhuain at c4300m. Next day a three-hour walk took them to Carhuacocha, a lake at 4,138m, and then they carried all their gear to a moraine camp by Nevado Yerupajá, where they met with Austrian alpinist Florian Burger. On 10 July, they gained the glacier between the peaks Yerupajá (6617m) and Siulá (6344m) and set up a base camp at 5,300m, at the foot of their primary objective: the south-east face of **Yerupajá Grande**.

The team left early to study the route from c5,600m on the plateau. From this vantage point they could see conditions were dangerous, with big avalanches, as was the glacial slope of Siulá Grande. They knew **Jurau B** (5727m), the north peak of Peak 5740, was unclimbed but the whole of the west face looked unstable except for the possibility of one couloir. They decided on the couloir and returned to camp. At midnight on 13 July they left for their new objective, reaching the col (c5500m) between Yerupajá and Peak 5578m to the north-east of Siulá Grande. They descended, negotiating crevasses, and at 3am were at the base of the west face of Jurau B.

The gullies held mushroom cornices for as far as they could see with their headlamps; the team climbed sections of 60°, 70° and 90° in the first pitches, until they reached an ice mushroom that effectively formed a roof over the only possible route. They climbed that, which was easily 100°, then continued over ice cascades of 60°, 70°, 80° and 90°, until just below the summit ridge. The last two pitches were icicles over snow slabs; this rare glacial formation did help the climbing, but the leader had to put huge effort in to avoid knocking his second unconscious with the falling ice. That often involved horizontal movement before going directly up, and at times breaking up the ice in order to advance. They reached the north summit at sunrise then carried on for the main summit by the north ridge, a narrow arête that after 30m took them to the base of a wall of ice some 20m high. The wall looked very dangerous, as it was covered in ice chandeliers. Here, at 6.30am, they ended their ascent. The route took eight ice screws and six snow stakes. This was probably the first ascent of the north peak of Jurau B. They called their route *El Inca, el Cachaco y el Azteca* (TD, 60°–100°, 300m).

They returned to the base of the wall at 10am. After some 20 minutes of coiling the ropes, when they were starting to downclimb, the ice they were standing on broke off and sent Araiza into a crevasse. Pinto slid down the snow on the downhill side of the crevasse, holding his companion on the rope; fortunately Araiza wasn't seriously injured, just bruised. Burger and Pinto pulled him out, as one ice axe had fallen into the crevasse, and the team returned directly to base camp. On 14 July, they crossed the crevassed glacier to Carhuacocha, and the following day made it to Huaraz after a three-hour walk and four-hour car journey.

References: Beto Pinto Toledo.

Still in the Cordillera de Huayhuash, the French team of Frédéric Degoulet, Benjamin Guigonnet, Helias Millerioux and Robin Revest climbed *Looking for the Void* (M7, WI6, R, 900m) in alpine style, on the west face of **Siulá Chico** (6265m). The route appears to coincide to a large extent with the intended route of the Catalans Jordi Corominas and Jordi Tosas, in 2003. The French team found no friends or pegs that the Catalans abandoned on the abseil, and they abseiled off abalakovs. Except for the third and last bivouac on the Catalan route, the French team covered unclimbed ground, spent four nights on the wall between 16 and 20 May 2014 and reached the summit.

The first day the French team climbed about 400m, with the greatest difficulties in one of the last pitches (6a). They bivouacked for two hours on a carved-out shelf at 5,800m. At 2am next morning they braved the crux of the day (M6 +), a 45m corner with little ice, which Ben Guigonnet overcame in two and a half hours of climbing. Four pitches of vertical ice (WI5 +, WI6, WI5 +, WI5) took them to 5,980m, where they had their second bivouac, somewhat less protected than the first, and stone fall put a hole in their tent. At 3am of the third day Degoulet overcame a

The line of the attempt on the south-east face of Tsacra Grande (5774m) by Italians Saro Costa, Tito Arosio and Luca Vallata. *(Tito Arosio)*

'very psychological' pitch (M6, WI5 +, R) with a complicated step about 8 metres above the last piece of gear, took five minutes to catch his breath and then climbed 20m to the next belay. At the end of the day another hard pitch (M5, WI5) led them to third bivouac (6170m), where they took a couple of hours to carve a terrace. On the fourth day of ascent they started climbing at 5am, followed a small ridge of snow, then a precarious pitch (45m, M6, WI6), very demanding because of the altitude, now c6,200m, and only Guigonnet could lead it. Two pitches later Revest reached the summit ridge and after the last stretch of deep snow, the four reached the summit. They quickly descended to the last bivouac, and next day abseiled 800m in three hours to reach advanced base camp.

References: Benjamin Guigonnet, Jordi Corominas, Mick Fowler, Robin Revest; *Desnivel.com*

On 26 May 2014, Italians Carlo Cossi and Davide Cassol arrived in Huaraz (3090m). They bought food for a month, and travelled the six hours to Llamac (3250m) in the Huayhuash. With cook Pio Polo, local herdsmen Omar Abner and nearly 300kg of supplies, they loaded onto nine mules and two horses for the three-day approach. They crossed the Macrash Punta (4272m), camped near Jahuacocha, a lake at 4,050m, climbed the Quebrada Huacrish to the pass of Llaucha Punta (4850m), then that of Tapush Punta (4770m), dropped down to Incahuahin to camp on the plain of Huatiaqpampa at c4300m, continued to Auquimarca, Calinca (4175m) and Cutatambo (4265m) and on 1 July set up base camp (c4300m) between the lakes of Jurau (4343m) and Sarapo (4482m) in the Quebrada Ruri Relle, also known as Quebrada Sarapococha. They were 26 days at base camp, shared with compatriots Tito Arosio, Saro Costa and Luca Vallata.

Cossi and Cassol acclimatised on **'Cerro Gran Vista'** (5152m), a summit that isn't named on official maps, west of the north side of the Sarapo. On 5 June they climbed the north face of **Jurauraju** (5335m), comprising high-quality grey limestone, just to the right of a prominent ridge and a distinctive gully. This they called *Laurapaq* (V+). The Italians then intended to climb **Jurau** and **Yerupajá South** (described later), and in their final days in the area, in later June, returned to Jurauraju, where they opened another magnificent rock route named *La Zuppa di Pio* (IV+) in homage to Pio's soup.

The Jurauraju is Cerro Jurau, but with no height given, on the official Peruvian map; its main summit is to the east of the Ogo mine, east-north-east of the old Vaquería Cutatambo and east-south-east of the laguna Jurau. The 1939 *Alpenvereinskarte* gives the main peak of Jurauraju as 5,340m, the 2008 edition puts it at 5,335m. The first ascent of the main summit was on 27 June 1963 by Walter Schnyder, Heinz and Edwin Gebauer Schelling, members of a Swiss expedition that reached the south summit (5271m) from a base camp in Juraucocha.

References: *Cordillera Huayhuash (Perú)*, *Alpenvereinskarte* 0/3c 1939 and new edition 2008; Sheet 21-j *Yanahuanca* IGN (Peru); *Planetmountain.com* 28 July 2014; *AAJ* 1964; 2015.

Cossi and Cassol left base camp for the east and climbed, by the Jurau glacier, **Jurau D** (5674m) the south-east summit of Nevado Butcher (5960m) and slightly north-west of Huaraca (5537m) or Jurau E. The climb began on the snow and ice of the west face of Jurau, just to the left of the line of the summit pyramid, until they reached the top of the wall and the north ridge, calling the route *La Siesta del Bodacious* (WI4+, M4+, 600m). The two Italians continued on the eastern side of the peak to the east ridge but, as they said in *AAJ* 2015: 'We stopped 80m below the true summit due to huge, dangerous-looking cornices. This proved to be a wise move, as the following day we saw a cornice collapse on the ridge, causing a large avalanche 200m left of our new route. To descend, we rappelled our route using V-threads and a couple pieces of rock protection.' The north ridge of Jurau (5674m)

Having missed out on Tsacra Grande Arosio, Costa and Vallata set their sights on the west face of Quesillo (5600m), or Jurau F. In two days they climbed *El Malefico Sefkow* (ED2, AI5, M5+, A1, 800m). *(Tito Arosio)*

was climbed in 1961 and the east ridge in 1966, both by German expeditions. British climbers Brian Barker and Jonathan Preston opened a 15-pitch route on the west side of Jurau D in 1988 (TD-, 60°–90°).

References: In addition to the above map references, see *AAJ* 1962; 1967; 1989.

Italians Saro Costa, Tito Arosio and Luca Vallata shared base camp with their compatriots. From 9 to 10 June 2014 Arosio and Costa climbed 800m 'with mixed sections (up to M6) and ice (AI4+)' on the south-east face of **Tsacra Grande** (5774m) that faces the Quebrada Seria, mistakenly called Segya. They reached the south-west ridge, but because of the soft and dangerous snow retreated 150m from the summit. Arosio, Costa and Vallata then set their sights on the west face of **Quesillo** (5600m), or Jurau F. For two days they climbed what may be new terrain, on ramps of snow, ice and rock. They called the route *El Malefico Sefkow* (ED2, AI5, M5+, A1, 800m). Cornices prevented them from summitting. They also attempted the Siulá Grande and the Huaraca or Jurau E. Nevado Tsacra Grande is given 5774m in *Alpenvereinskarte* 0/3c 1939, but the 2008 edition erroneously gives 5610m. Nevado Quesillo is further south of Jurau D (5674m) and Huaraca (Jurau E 5537m), which were climbed by the German expedition of 1961.

References: In addition to the map references, see *Planetmountain.com* 8 July 2014; *AAJ* 2015.

During the first ascent of *El Malefico Sefkow*. Cornices prevented them from reaching the summit. *(Tito Arosio)*

After climbing the Jurau, Cossi Carlo and Davide Cassol had four and a half days of bad weather. They then tried to open a route on the south face of **Yerupaja Sur** (6515m), but were stopped by powder snow that had built up on slopes of 90°, as a result of which Cassol had three falls.

Yerupaja Grande (6634m), west face, combination of routes
12 September 2014
The American Nathan Heald, resident in Cuzco, his compatriot Duncan McDaniel and the Peruvian Crispin Luis travelled from Huaraz to Llamac on 5 September. The next day they set up a base camp between Jahuacocha (4050m) and Solteracocha (4120m), lagoons on the west side of the Jirishanca and Rondoy snowfields. On 7 June they carried their equipment, following a path along Solteracocha, then along the edge of the glacial moraine, with an ABC (c5300m) near Jirishanca where the Yerupajá glacier meets the east face of Nevado Rasac. They left their tent at 1.30am next morning, and climbed the Rasac via a col to Yerupajá. On 9 June they descended to rest at base camp. The next day Heald and Crispin returned again to their higher camp. On 11 June they climbed the glacier to Jirishanca, but with dangerous glacial conditions decided to change objectives, camping on the western edge of Yerupajá glacier. At 11.30pm that night they travelled under a clear sky to the west side of the Nevado. They climbed along the north-west ridge, reaching the point where Roger Bates and Lloyd Gallagher came to the

The highpoint reached by the three Italians on Huaraca. *(Tilo Arosio)*

Arosio and his friends also attempted the 2001 Slovenian route on the west face of Siulá Grande *Noches de 'Juerga'* (ED, 65°-90°, mixed VI, 1,000m). *(Tito Arosio)*

lower north summit on 30 June 1968. However, the first ascent of the full north-west ridge of **Yerupajá Grande** (6634m) is attributed to Dick Renshaw and Dave Wilkinson, climbing from the lower summit; they followed the north ridge and reached the main peak on 13 August 1979.

Heald and Crispin alternated pitches of 60°–70° ice through the first 400m, to névé on the north-west ridge. With an ascending traverse of the west face under large blocks of ice, they were diverted to the route followed by Thomas (Tom) Pulaski and Geoff Conley (USA) on 11 July 1979. They moved together on good snow to a long pitch of ice (70°–80°) then snow (65°) then crossed the bergschrund to the final slope, which gave two long and well-protected couloirs (70°–80° ice and snow). Crossing hanging ice through a gap, they moved onto the east face for good snow (60°–70°), and moved together up to the summit snow mushrooms. At 11.56am on 12 September and in a whiteout, they were careful not to break through the cornice at the summit ridge. This was the first ascent of the summit in 11 years. They descended the ridge to the mouth of the couloir, then straight down the west face in 13 rappels from pickets and abalakovs to spend the night at their ABC.

References: Nathan Heald; *Cordillera Huayhuash (Perú)*, *Alpenvereinskarte* 0/3c 1939 and new edition 2008; *AAJ* from 1969 to 2014.

Alberto Hung from Peru and Steve Meder of France travelled from Lima to the city of San Mateo in Huarochiri province and on to Dam Yuracmayo. On 22 March 2014 they climbed the north-west ridge of **Tatajaico** (5342m), descending via the west ridge. They called their route *A Puro Huevo* (D, V, M3, 60°). The Nevado Tatajaico is halfway along the Quebrada Quillacocha, the part of the Central Cordillera mountain range known locally as Pariacacca and Cordillera Huarochirí (see *AJ* 2011 p83), about 100km north of Lima. William F Jenks included Tatajaico and Jija (5513m) in the group of Nevado Tunshu (*AAJ* 1941 pp174-175), and wrote, 'to the best of my knowledge neither has been climbed.' On 22 July 1958, Hugh Simpson, William Wallace and Miss Myrtle L Emslie recorded the first ascent of Tatajaico, giving it a height of 18,058ft; in *AAJ* 1972 (p176), Evelio Echevarría corrected the height to 18,343ft or 5594m. In 1967 it was climbed by a German expedition led by Ekke Rubel, and on 5 September 1972 the Swiss Christian Brückner, Ruedi Merker and Magdalena Hohl climbed Tatajaico to 16,634ft. In 2002 the Peruvian Bruno Castro, Guillermo Portocarrero, José Usquiano, Carlos Verdeguer, Marisol Carbajal and Alberto Hung made an attempt, but near the top had to give up due to a severe thunderstorm. The following year, Castro, Juan Narvaja and Nice Trujillo got the first Peruvian ascent via the easy western face.

References: Emslie, M, 'Conquering Peru's Virgin Peaks', *The Scotsman*, 4-5 November, 1958; *AJ* 1967; 2001; *AAJ* 1941; 1959; 1969; 1973; 2014, 2015; *Montañas Peruanas* 57.

Tunshu Sur (Tunsho Sur 5420m), first ascent
7 June 2014
The IFMGA Peruvian guide Beto Pinto Toledo, Guy Fonck (Belgium) and their cook Habram Morales left Huaraz on the night of 3 June 2014 for Lima and La Oroya for the first ascent of the virgin summit of **Tunshu Sur** (5420m), to the south-west of Tunshu Central and one of the four Tunshu *nevados*. Geographically this is in the Junín department, specifically in the North Yauyos Cochas, in the valley of Cochas-Junín. The next day they toured the valley Pachacayo and a three-hour march took them to the end of the lake Azulcocha where they set up base camp (4520m). On day five they explored the way that the shepherds of Alaca call Suicicocha, which they cross to go to the town of Suicicanchas. Sheet 24-l of the IGN (Peru) does not show this pass. The same day they climbed the north ridge on a mountain south of the pass with easy sections of V to a rocky summit at 5,200m. From this, they observed Tunshu and the route they would take.

On 7 June, Pinto and Fonck left at 1am for the south face of Tunshu Sur. They took two and a half hours to the start of the glacier, crossed several crevasses and dangerous snow slabs, and reached the south face at 6am. The compact glacier snow changed little before reaching the five-metre-wide bergschrund, which took them some 40 minutes of work. They sank into soft, 50° snow on the first part of the south face. Climbing for 200m at an average gradient of 70° to 80°, they arrived at 9.36 am on the previously unclimbed south summit of Nevado Tunshu or Tunsho, where a GPS marked 5520m instead of the 5420m on the German map. They called their route *Mel & Lies* (70° to 80°, 200m), the names of their girlfriends.

References: Beto Pinto Toledo; Alberto Carlos Hung Pitman (*Montañas Peruanas*); Diego Fernández Chávez; Hans Huber; John Harlin (*AAJ*); Peter Brill; Ricardo Rivadeneira Samaniego; Toño Rodríguez Verdugo; Akademischen Sektion München des DAV. *Cordillera Central Yarumario-Gruppe*, 1:60,000; IGN (Peru) sheets 24-k *Matucana* and 24-l *La Oroya*, 1:100,000; *AAJ* 1941-2006; Echevarría, E, 'The Cordillera Huarochirí, Peru' *AJ* 2001; Volgel, Jochen, et al *Münchner Anden-Kundfahrt*, 1967. 'Verlauf, wissenschaftliche und bergsteigerische Ergebnisse', Minich, Akademischen Sektion München des Deutschen Alpenverein, 1969.

CORDILLERA URUBAMBA 2014

Germans Phillip Moser and Chris Romeike left Munaychay, a village at about 3,300m in the Chicón (Ch'iqun) valley in the Cuzco province of Urubamba. They carried two loads to advanced base camp (c4900m) on moraine beneath the central glacier on the western side of the Chicón massif. After a day in camp, they climbed 400m to the central summit of Nevado Chicón (5490m) via the steep south-west couloir up to a ridge of loose rock and snow; they reached the central summit about 7.30pm and bivouacked (c5486m) slightly north of the top. At dawn they followed the ridge to the north by dangerously loose rock and reached the main summit (5526m) around 10.30am. Descent was from the north of the peak, and they 'traversed around the massif by crossing the northern glacier.' (*AAJ* 2015, p202). Their route was called *Vía del Corazón* (TD+, WI4, M5, 550m).

Records of the first ascent of Chicón seem confused if we compare data from the 1958 expedition, in which Italians gave names to at least nine peaks in the Yucay area, with various subsequent publications of lists and notes on tops climbed and the 1958 note of the 'Nevado Alessandro Volta 5572m' marked on the sketch map published by Mario Fantin in 1975. This does not match the description of Michael G Andrews in *AAJ* 1974, p188: 'Chicon III lies in the group also known as the Yucay. This particular peak was climbed once before by a different route by Mario Fantin and others in 1958 and named by them Nevado Alessandro Volta. The three peaks of this group are known locally as Chicon.'

References: *AAJ* 1959; 1961; 1962; 1974; 1975; 2015; Sheet 27-r, *Urubamba*, IGN (Peru); Fantin, *M, Pioneri ed Epìgoni Italiani sulle vette di Ogni Continente*, Italy, Commissione delle Publicazzioni del Club Alpino Italiano, 1975.

Nevado Sahuasiray (Saguasiray, 5721m, 5777m or 5818m), south-west face

10 April 2014

On 8 April 2014 Nathan Heald and Eduardo Baca from Peru travelled from Cusco to meet Erich Nordt in Calca before the three continued to Huarán, a village at 2,900m. The local porter Alejandro brought their luggage on donkeys to the rural community of Cancha Cancha (4000m) after three hours. The president of the community prevented the porter continuing because two years before a Chilean hiker died while trekking.

Heald, Baca and Nordt, with heavy loads on their backs, took two hours to the pampa (4600m) where they camped on the right (south) side of the moraine down from the south-west face of **Nevado Sahuasiray** (Saguasiray 5721m, 5777m or 5818m). Next day they continued along rocky spurs to reach a secondary west ridge of the south-west ridge. Easy but exposed traverses took them to a couloir of about 35m, third grade, although with heavy packs it was not that easy. They found greater difficulty (V/V+) on a rocky passage of 4m. They arrived at the snow above the ridge, followed this for half an hour on ice of 45° and camped on it at about 5,300m. Before going to bed they had to locate the exit from the spur to the glacier requiring a 30m rappel.

At midnight, Baca felt anxious about continuing. Nordt left two hours later with Heald, but was also anxious and decided to accompany Heald as far as the glacier plateau to protect him over the concealed crevasses of early season. They left the rope fixed at the 30m abseil for the return journey. Heald led the way in the knee-deep snow. After dodging several small crevasses in steep terrain, they arrived about 5.30pm at 5,500m, under the north and south peaks. The rest of the climb was more technical, and Nordt waited on the glacier, with the rope and snow stakes. Heald came to the hanging blocks on the ridge and crossed to the left before returning to the north side of the ridge, where the snow offered better conditions. He climbed the ridge in two long sections of 70° snow, and after several rocky steps reached the summit: 'A rock platform nearly four square metres between two fingers like a snow cone of ice cream.' This is probably a new route and the second ascent of the summit of Sahuasiray. It was 7.24am; in the spectacular scenery without a GPS, Heald couldn't verify the correct height of the three given to this summit. Nevado Verónica (5682m), whose summit had long ago been measured by GPS at 5911m, seemed higher than Sahuasiray. Heald returned to Nordt by the same route, climbed the fixed rope and reached the camp where Baca waited. Descent from the summit took one and a half hours. They arrived tired at Huarán at 7pm.

Nevado Verónica is also called Huacrahuilki, according to John F Ricker the local name of the peak, also spelt Wakaywillque. Sahuasiray Nevado is also called Saguasiray. The south (5670m) and north peaks (5720m, or 5800m) were climbed on 21 June 1963, by Italians Fulvio Ratto, Franco Riva, Antonio Zappa and Carlo Pivano. The latter died from stone fall while descending from the north summit.

References: Nathan Heald; *AAJ* 1964; 1970; *Revista Mensile del Club Alpino Italiano* 1964.

On 7 January, Nathan Heald, with Peruvians Eduardo Baca, Sequel Camasa and Jorge 'Coqui' Galvez climbed the north-west face (AD, 70°) of **Nevado Sirijuani** (5400m). The crux of the route included a 150m ice wall (60°–70°) under a large but stable serac. Nevado Sirijuani, 'a fine isolated ice and rock peak' (*AAJ* 1965, p446), was first climbed on 9 July 1964 during a quick run from camp at c15,000ft by members of the Scottish expedition (see *AJ* 1964, pp240-245) that approached via Calca to Quebrada Cancha Cancha. 'Kenneth Bryan and Robin Brooks made a route up the west flank, following three ice fields linked by buttresses, while Norman Tennent and Robin Chalmers approached by the more continuous rock of the south ridge.' (*AAJ* 1965, p446). Italians Giuseppe Agnolotti and Giorgio Pettigiani climbed the east face, reaching the summit on 6 May 1976 at 2.30am.

References: Nathan Heald; *AJ* 1964; *AAJ* 1964; 1965; 1977.

CORDILLERA VILCANOTA 2014

In April, Nathan Heald and Crispin Luis explored the south face of **Nevado Colque Cruz** (Alcamarinayoc, 6102m) in the extreme north of the Cordillera Vilcanota. They made it to c5,900m but had to abandon due to avalanche. They returned in July and could not get past the previous high-point; consolation prize was **Chumpe** (6110m) by its north-west ridge to get a better view of the original target. At the end of September, Heald and Crispin returned with Edwin Espinoza (Peru) to try again. They climbed a large unstable moraine – they called it 'the gravel pit' – to set up the first camp. From here, on 24 September at 11.30pm, the three crossed crevasses to reach the base of the south face of Colque Cruz; they found more snow than expected because the rainy season had started a week before, pouring powder snow on the mountain.

Heald wrote: 'When we reached the crux ice wall, Luis turned back due to an ankle injury he had sustained on Yerupajá. As he made his way down alone, we watched an avalanche almost hit him far below us; however, he was okay and we continued. Edwin and I climbed up and left across the ice wall toward its apex. Most of this wall is 60°-70° until the final, steep five metres. Above the icefall, we simul-climbed for 300m on good snow (60°) until reaching a bergschrund below the final summit block. From here we traversed right (east) across the south face to gain a lower-angle ramp. We arrived at the summit at 10.25am just as the clouds began to blow in from the jungle to the north. From the top, we down-climbed and rappelled from V-threads on the icy south face. We reached the tent around 4pm and hiked out the next day. Nevado Colque Cruz is known to have been climbed seven times, first by Germans in 1953, by the Japanese in 1965, a Canadian–New Zealand–Australian team in 1974, by Germans in 1984, by Italians in 1987, and most recently by a British team up the mountain's technical south-west face (*AAJ* 2007). In 2005, Dave Wilkinson explored the south face but judged it out of condition and made an ascent of nearby Nevado Ichu Ananta instead (*AAJ* 2005).'

References: Nathan Heald; *AAJ* 2015 p.204

CORDILLERA VILCABAMBA 2014

In early July 2014 Nathan Heald, Michael Church, Michael Hauss (USA) and Brazilian Waldemar Niclevicz travelled from Mollepata to Soraypampa. They walked under the north-west slopes of Nevado Salcantay to see if it was possible to climb the west face. They camped at about 5,000m, under the north-west buttress; Church contracted altitude sickness and Niclevicz had no faith in a route hidden by clouds. They then tried to climb the north ridge but stopped because of the mixed climbing and broken rock. From this camp they saw that the Humantay chain and its north summit seemed accessible. Heald had previously studied this possibility, and he believed the north-west ridge or north face offered the best opportunity to reach the summit of **Humantay Norte** (5403m). Niclevicz was skeptical, decided not to go and lent his ice axes to the porter Macario Crispin (Peru) so that he could climb. On 8 July they approached the peak, found a good camp on the north-east arete just below the glacier; they saw that the rest of this ridge had sections of steep rock and opted for a ledge system on the north face that connected with the ridge.

They left the tent at 1am and reached the north face by a mostly easy glacier. At about 5,150m the slope got very steep and they climbed the right side of a rock wall 'via two pitches of unprotected climbing in a chute-like feature (5.7)'. Above this wall they climbed good snow at about 70°, 'until reaching a steep, sheer rock wall.' Two long traverse pitches to the right and they reached the summit ridge. With another long pitch (AD) they reached the summit at 8.30pm, when the clouds began to rise from the valley. They down-climbed from the summit to the top of the rock wall, where they abseiled to the lowest angle of the glacier. They arrived at the high camp about 12pm, and walked up to the Ahobamba valley the same day, arriving at 5pm.

The 'Nevado Huamantay' on the IGN Peruvian map has three peaks: north-west (5217m), north (5473m) and south (5459m). The top edge of the latter extends south-east towards the Nevado Salcantay. It is therefore likely that when the Japanese expedition of 1968 added the sub-name Humantay in brackets to the name Soray, this may have led to the mistaken belief that the summit was climbed by Terray and his companions in 1956. The height given for Humantay is from Heald's GPS and doesn't correspond to the IGN map.

In October 2014, Nathan Heald, Luis Crispin, Edwin Espinoza and Alexis Trudel (Canada), climbed the south-west ridge (PD, 350m) of **Cerro Jatunjasa** (5350m), locally called 'Incachiriasca' (*AAJ* 2014, p293), according to Conny Amelunxen. Cerro Jatunjasa is given 5338m in the IGN (Peru), and was climbed in June 1970 (possibly by the north face) for the Jubilee Expedition of the Sektion Bayerland of the German Alpine Club, and by Canadians Conny Amelunxen and Karen Perry, probably in 2003.

References: Nathan Heald; *AAJ* 1971; 2004; also see *AAJ* 1963 for the New Zealand ascents in the Pumasillo area.

Translated by Susan Jensen

MARCELO SCANU

Argentina & Chile

In 2015 South America suffered from the El Niño phenomenon with rain, snow, wind and low temperatures. It eased off, however, promising better weather for the New Year. A new government has taken office following the elections of October 2015, while the Argentine *peso* lost much value relative to hard currencies.

Charly Contartese, Juancho Torres and Esteban Degregori put *Jumanji* (6c) in March 2015, the second route on the Torre Blanca de Ectelion in the Agujas del Sosneado. *(Esteban Degregori)*

Jujuy

Granada is a volcano in the Puna region, a high desert near the point where Chile, Bolivia and Argentina meet, and was climbed by Incas for ceremonial purposes. During the southern hemisphere winter, on 21 June, Argentines Agustín Piccolo, Diego Simari and Carlos Torino opened a new route on its south wall. After a five-hour trek through moraines the group reached the base; the wall has many potential new routes of some 400m, all of them with mixed terrain and ice falls. They reached a lower summit (5670m) after a four-hour push, and named their route *Tata Raymi* (PD, WI4, 400m). They descended by Granada's west ridge and camped at 4,500m in a local hut.

La Rioja and Catamarca

Mount Parofes (5845m, S 27° 53.282', W 68° 40.767') is a volcano that lies between mighty **Pissis** and **Bonete**, in La Rioja province. It had the claim of being the highest unclimbed American mountain until a party ascended it on 11 November 2015. Argentine born but Brazilian resident Máximo Kausch, with Brazilians Pedro Hauck and Jovany Blume, made a difficult

Above: Cerro Tito (4905m) in the Cordón de los Clonquis had its first ascent in 2016 by the Argentines Lisandro Arelovich and Glauco Muratti. *(Glauco Muratti)*

Right: Last camp on Cerro Tito. Behind to the right is Cerro Colorado (4621m). *(Glauco Muratti)*

approach, breaking trail east of Pissis and ascending two passes to reach base camp. The temperatures were so low that one of the jeeps froze even with antifreeze in the engine. They climbed the cone by its north-east face in a 22km round-trip, returning to base camp late at night.

During October the same group was active in the area due north of the Paso de San Francisco, ascending some Chilean volcanoes, some of them first ascents, ranging in height from 5,200 to 5,300m. On 27 October they ascended **Sierra Nevada** (6137m), an isolated volcano in the Argentine-Chilean border. The group entered Argentina (Catamarca Province) leaving the vehicles at the base and camping at 5,300m. The next day the group climbed to the summit by its west face. It must be noted that this western summit is the highest of the massif, being 10m higher than the border summit.

Mendoza

On 14 November, an Argentine party departed from Punta de Vacas, trekking the Quebrada Tupungato and camping on Quebrada Potrero Escondido. The next day they reached the foot of the unclimbed **Cerro Colorado** (4621m). On 16 November they attempted the east face, beginning the climb

at 4am. Their high point was 4,500m, after climbing easy 45° slopes and a 20m rock band. They retreated due to high temperatures and avalanche risk, and the next day saw an avalanche had swept their tracks.

Part of the group left the expedition and Adrían Petrocelli and Ramiro Casas continued on 17 November, camping at 3,900m near the Portezuelo (pass) Cerro Colorado. In the afternoon they suffered from the high winds and some snowfall; the poor conditions continued on 18 November but they managed to ascend a little needle they christened 'La Yeserita' because of its summit formations, *yeseria* being a type of plaster carving. The weather turned very good next day so they began the ascent of the west face at 7am; the route started up scree followed by snow gullies (30°-40°), with some steps up to 60° and reached the ridge after a four-metre rock step (V). Following the ridge they reached the summit at 11.30am, returning to their tent on the same day.

On 20 November the good weather continued so they left at 4.30am for another summit. Climbing to a pass (4230m), they descended to a snowfield (3900m) to avoid a tricky traverse and then climbed up an easy snow slope, which steepened at a rock band. They avoided the rock band via a 15m icefall with a 90° finish, then traversed to the north face by 40°-50° slopes, to avoid snow cornices and avalanche risk. On the summit ridge they saw three unclimbed rock summits with vertical walls, the highest being on the left, which they climbed using only three cams on the grade V route. The summit (4970m) was very small, and they abseiled down off a block of rock, triggering an avalanche on the way. They reached their tent at 2.30pm, after 10 hours and 1,220 vertical metres of climbing.

Cerro Tito (4905m) in the Cordón de los Clonquis had its first ascent on 10 January 2016 by the Argentines Lisandro Arelovich and Glauco Muratti. They departed on 7 January from Punta de Vacas camping at 2,800m, 3,400m and 4,100m. The last part of the trip took place in a high, unnamed valley on the mountain's west side. On the climb they had a 150m section of 50° snow with plenty of rock fall, and grade III rock between the second and third camps, which they abseiled on the way down. The rock on the summit block was also III, exposed and of very bad quality. They called the mountain Tito in homage to the nickname of Alfredo Magnani, the excellent climber from Mendoza.

Argentines Roberto Piriz and Gabriel Fava ascended a new route in a satellite summit of **Cerro Tolosa** (5432m), although the official height seems to be a hundred metres lower) near **Aconcagua**. From base camp at 3,950m, they climbed *Dioses del Ocaso* (6c, 900m) in a single-day push, reaching the lower summit that they christened **Pico de los Zondinos** (4850m). They had an incredible bivouac at c5,000m and next day reached the highest summit. The descent route was via the normal route, taking the north ridge to the Cerro México col. The expedition took place during 20 to 22 March.

Argentines Charly Contartese, Juancho Torres and Esteban Degregori opened a new route in the Agujas del Sosneado on 23 March; *Jumanji* (6c) is the second to be opened on the **Torre Blanca de Ectelion**. They soloed the initial easy ramp of 200m of third and fourth grade, then took the evident central groove by its right in five rope lengths to the summit: 6a+, 6a+, 6b, 6b+, 6c. Part of the route has rotten rock making it unstable. Before this, the group had climbed the **Torre Principal** via *Nalgas de Loncho* (450m, 7b+) on perfect granite.

Chile

In Northern Chile (Copiapó, Atacama), a Brazilian team led by Hauck and Kausch ascended the previously unclimbed **Sierra del Aliste** (5167m) on 13 October. They left from a camp at 4,600m, climbing the east face and north-east ridge, suffering in the high winds and very low temperatures.

During November and December well-known Spanish climber Baró Oriol opened new routes in the Chilean central Andes with a variety of different partners. On 6 November, Baró and Chilean Andrés Zegers climbed a route they called *Yeguas Salvajes* (VI, M5, 1110m) on the west face of **Cerro Yeguas Heladas** (4771m). They returned to their 3050m base camp via the south ridge and couloir, taking 20 hours in total. A week later, the same pair climbed **Cerro Gemelo Este** (5117m) by its west face. The middle of the route *Turbera* (HVS, WI4+, M4+, 1100m) had a crux consisting of a 90m

WI4+ icefall and two M4+ pitches of poor rock. They climbed from a base camp at 3,550m.

On 22 November, the pair teamed up with another Chilean, Aike Parvex, and climbed **Cerro Morado**'s south summit (4490m) by a variation of the *Tangol-Vasquez* 1961 south face route. They ascended 400m of the Tangol-Vasquez then traversed to the right, continuing up the Cascada Central for another 350m up to snow slopes and the summit (*Fina y Sucia*; ED, 6a, WI5, M4+,750m). All this was in 11 hours round-trip from camp.

On 30 November, Baró, Zegers, Seba Rojas and Xavi Farré climbed a couloir in the central-right side of the south face of **Cerro Yeguas Muertas** (4912m). The route was largely snow with some mixed terrain and waterfall ice (*Wenatti*; V+, 1150m). On 3 December, Baró and Farré ascended the south-east face of **Cerro San Francisco** (4307m) starting from Laguna El Morado (2400m). The covers snow slopes (which they climbed unroped), up a couloir then wound their way through the upper headwall, finally gaining the summit ridge. (*Antiparkes*; 1000m, D+).

Brazil

Pedra Riscada is a granite dome in the Brazilian state of Minas Gerais, in the south-east of the country. In 2009, Germans Stefan Glowacz and Holger Heubert, Brazilian Edmilson Padilha and Argentine Horacio Gratton ascended a line that they called *Place of Happiness* (7c/+, 850m). Gratton spotted a line on the north-east wall that was distinctive for its conspicuous yellow overhang, and returned to inspect it in 2015. Gratton was joined by Argentines María José Moisés, Cintia Percivati and Ignacio Elorza with Noel Martinez de Aguirre taking photos and filming. They left the village of Sao Jose do Divino some 20km from the rock. They had some problems with Africanised bees; the bees had killed one climber and injured another badly in a previous incident. In this expedition, the climbers also encountered bees and were very frightened, but kept very still and the bees went away. The group opened a new route in 12 days, with some pitches overlapping *Place of Happiness*. The 7c+/8a crux took two days to negotiate. The route starts up the easy pitches of *Place of Happiness* and then continues direct in new terrain. They camped 500m high on the wall on a portaledge in strong winds and rainy nights, with the rain ending in mid morning each day. After the yellow overhang they had 200m of excellent rock that finished in the easy pitches of *Place of Happiness*, summiting on 23 July. The new route was called *Viaje de Cristal* (8a, 900m).

Mount Everest Foundation Expedition Reports

SUMMARISED BY GLYN HUGHES

The Mount Everest Foundation (*www.mef.org.uk*) was established as a registered charity following the successful ascent of Everest in 1953, and was initially financed using surplus funds and royalties from that expedition. It is a continuing initiative administered jointly by the Alpine Club and the Royal Geographical Society.

Surprisingly the word 'mountaineering' does not appear anywhere in its memorandum and articles of association, the prime object being the promotion of 'exploration' in mountain areas; this is mainly geographic, but can also include other exploratory disciplines in these areas, such as geology, botany and zoology.

The MEF has now distributed well over £1m to more than 1,600 British and New Zealand expeditions undertaking such exploration. Most of the grants have been awarded to ambitious young climbers who help to maintain Britain's reputation as one of the world's leading exploratory nations. In return for supporting an expedition, all that the MEF requires is a comprehensive report. Copies of these reports are lodged with the AC and the RGS, who make them available to all interested parties. All MEF reports will be accessible online on the AC website by the end of 2016.

Donations to the MEF are always welcome and help us meet the continuing demand for support. If you have benefited from MEF support please consider including a bequest to the foundation in your will.

The following notes summarise reports from the expeditions supported during 2015, and are divided into geographical areas.

NORTH AMERICA

Cathedral Spires Alaska 2015 – Tim Blakemore and Mike 'Twid' Turner (May 2015).
A trip to the Cathedral Spires with several possible objectives of new hard routes on North Triple Peak and/or Mount Nevermore. Commercial flights to Anchorage and Talkeetna were followed by a thrilling trip to the Tatina glacier by Talkeetna Air Taxi. A reconnaissance on skis showed that conditions were best on North Triple Peak, so that became their target. After several days of heavy snow the weather cleared, and they set off for a single push on a route following ice smears to the left of the NW Couloir. After several pitches of AI 4+/5 things became more serious, with a crux of AI 6, and they summited in a white-out at about midnight. They managed to make a call by satellite phone to book their flight out before an abseil descent. They named the route *No Country for Old Men*. MEF ref 15-06

Two expeditions visited the Hayes Range in Alaska:

British Hayes Range Expedition – Will Sim and Jonathan Griffith (April/May 2015).
A two-man expedition with the objective of the unclimbed NW face of Mount Deborah. (See Alaska section in this year's volume.) They had been led to believe that they could fly into the Upper Gillam glacier from Talkeetna, but this turned out to be a misunderstanding, and they had to fly in by helicopter from Anchorage. During their first night on the glacier a violent storm destroyed their tent, and they resorted to building a snow cave. After 1,000m of insecure mixed ground they exited the face onto the NW ridge because of avalanche risk on the central line. After a bivouac they continued up the ridge for another 1,000m to the summit of Deborah. They descended the S face to the Yanert glacier, re-ascended to the bivouac on the NW ridge for a second night, and returned to their base the next day. The quality of rock was very poor, and the best climbing is on ice routes in the spring. MEF ref 15-11

British Hayes Expedition 2015 – David Chapman and Guy Wilson (April 2015).
The principal objective was Peak 10910, SW of Mount Hayes. They flew in from Fairbanks to an unnamed glacier to the W of Mount Hayes. They spent nine nights in this camp, and it snowed most of these days, resulting in a very unstable snow pack and deep snow. The objective changed from climbing to exploration on skis. They did make an attempt on a technical mixed climb on a peak to the NE of the base camp, but were forced to retreat after only three pitches of unstable snow and loose rock.
MEF ref 15-12

Silvestre/Graham Revelation Mountains 2015 – Ben Silvestre and Peter Graham (March/April 2015).
The original objective for Ben Silvestre and Peter Graham was the central couloir on Pyramid Peak, but they discovered that they would not be able to land on the Revelation glacier, so transferred their attentions to the E Face and E Summit of Jezebel. (See Alaska section in this year's volume.) Their first attempt was aborted in bad weather, and the second due to insufficient ice screws for the first hard pitch. They returned with more gear, and completed the pitch, which turned out to be the crux. Further hard pitches led to a good bivouac site. The next day included a 50m pitch of steep good ice, followed by easier ground to a rock tower. From here they abseiled into an easy couloir which they followed to the summit. They bivouacked a few pitches below the summit, and descended the next day. They hoped to attempt another route after a few days rest, but the weather intervened with another big snow dump. MEF ref 15-16

SOUTH AMERICA

Avellano Towers 2014 – David Brown, John Crook, Will Harris and Andy Reeve (December 2014/January 2015).
A party of four, with the principal objective the NE face of the southernmost Avellano Tower. The approach was by air to Balcamada, crossing the Lago General Carrera, and then using packhorses to a base camp. From an advanced base they spent three days climbing 250m up the face in worsening weather conditions. They were then confined to base during a storm, after which they found the face plastered with snow. A rockfall had removed a section of fixed rope, and when they resumed climbing they had to use an alternative route. Continued poor weather forecasts led to them abandoning the climb. They reported that the face seemed to be of solid high-quality granite. MEF ref 15-02

Sheffield Patagonia Expedition – Tom Ripley, Matt Burdekin and Polly Harmer (December 2015/January 2016).
A party of three led by Tom Ripley attempted routes on Aguja CAT and Aguja Bifida. After unsuccessful attempts on the *California Route* and the *Afanassieff Ridge* on Fitzroy, they repeated the *Comesana-Fonrouge* route on Aguja Guillaumet, and the *Austrian Route* on Aguja de la S. Ripley and Matt Burdekin then addressed a new line on the E Face of Aguja Bifida. The line was between two existing routes, the Bonapace-Dunser and Cogan. The route follows a huge slab, mostly climbed at S/VS, and leading in 13 pitches to a junction with Cogan, where they bivouacked. The next day, in good weather, they continued upwards to join the S ridge, and followed this to the summit of Aguja Bifida Sur. The descent was by abseil down the ascent route. MEF ref 15-23

Nameless Peaks of the Andes – Suzie Imber and Máximo Kausch (August/September 2015).
This expedition made use of a digital elevation model of the Andes developed by the Earth Observation Science Department of the University of Leicester. This enabled them to identify all mountains in the Andes over a specified height, and they found a total of 110 independent peaks over 6,000m, and 1,129 over 5,000m. They selected 20 peaks, believed to be unclimbed in the modern era, so not including possible Inca ascents, mainly in the Puna region, which encompasses northern Argentina, the adjacent Chilean Andes, and extends into southern and western Bolivia. In spite of extreme weather they reached the summits of 12 mountains, six of which they believe to be unclimbed. Inca ruins were found on several of the summits. They plan to return in 2016 to continue their explorations.
MEF ref 15-28

GREENLAND

North-east Greenland Caves Project – Gina Mosely, Robbie Shone, Chris Blakeley and Mark Wright (July 2015).
The aim of this project was to collect samples of deposits from caves in Kronprins Christian Land in order to study past climate change. The team flew to Mestersvig, where equipment was sorted and packed, and then on to a landing strip at the SW end of Centrum So. They crossed Centrum So by boat, and hiked up Grottedalen to set up a camp at the caves. They were able to investigate far more caves than anticipated, many of which had never been entered before, and with far more calcite deposits than expected, and collected a wide cross section of samples. These will be analysed to provide information on temperature and moisture change, vegetation processes, and dating. MEF ref 15-04

Bio-glaciology in Western Greenland – Joseph Cook, Arwyn Edwards, Michael Sweet, Ottavia Cavalli and Sophie Cook (July 2015).
An expedition to study the role of glacier microbes in shaping ice surfaces by monitoring the changing shapes of ice surface landforms and biogeochemical fluxes. The team included four young researchers from UK universities, led by Dr Joseph Cook (University of Derby). They examined microbial habitats, fungal ecology, carbon and nutrient cycling, metabolomics, and ice physics. The trip was successful, and the science objectives met. Analysis of the data collected is on-going. MEF ref 15-08

INDIA HIMALAYA

Unexplored Karakoram 2015 – Ed Poulter, Andrew Basford, Katie Farrel, Mathew Fuller, Steve Hutton, Katie McKay and Dan Slome (June/July 2015).
The objectives were to explore the Upper SE Shukpa Kunchang and Sagtogpa glaciers in the Rongdo valley, and climb at least one unclimbed remote 6,000m+ peak. After five days acclimatising around Leh, the team ascended the Rongdo valley and established a base camp at 4800m, followed by an advanced base at 5,450m just below the SE Shukpa Kunchang glacier. After a rest day at base camp (several members were suffering from altitude sickness) five team members set off at midnight to climb Peak X3 (6100m) from the ABC. They followed the Sagtogpa glacier to the col below the SE ridge, which was corniced and looked steep. Good progress was made up to 6,050m, but with the weather closing in, and fears that cornices would weaken in the sun, they retreated to ABC and base camp to recover, and prepare for another attempt. Unfortunately the weather then deteriorated and delayed this. They went back to ABC when it improved, it deteriorated again, and they ran out of time. The climbing as far as it went was alpine PD. MEF ref 15-03

UK/US Himachal Pradesh Expedition – Andrew Nisbet, Robert Adams, Tom Adams, Steve Kennedy, Bill McConachie, and Paul Swienton (May/June 2015).
Exploration of a side valley branching from the Darcha-Mayar valley in Himachal Pradesh, and ascent of a peak of 6,010m. A camp was established at the foot of the mountain, and a higher camp on the S ridge at 5,730m. After a windy and snowy night the weather improved, and Bill McConachie followed the S ridge to the summit. At the summit he found bamboo wands, probably from an unofficial ascent from the Shingo La side. The team descended to ABC. Steve Kennedy and Paul Swienton later climbed a smaller peak of about 5,300m. An attempt on a peak of 5970m failed because of dangerous snow. MEF ref 15-07

2015 Tamasa Nala Expedition – Derek Buckle, Drew Cook, Gus Morton, Knut Tønsberg and Stewart Worsfold (August/September 2015).
Exploration of the upper reaches of the Korlomshe Tokpo, a valley to the west of the Tamasa *nala* which flows south of Padam in Zanskar, and first ascents of one or more peaks. From Padam they first established a base camp at 4,153m, and then an advanced base at 5,130m. From here they explored the lower reaches of the Korlomshe glacier and climbed Peak 5916 via its glacial SE ridge at Alpine grade AD. After exploring the upper glacier they set up a further camp at 5,500m, from which they attempted a 'Matterhorn-like' peak at the head of the valley, but retreated after running out of time. Two members of the expedition climbed Peak 5947 via the ENE Face and SE ridge at Alpine AD. They enjoyed good weather conditions throughout the expedition. MEF ref 15-09

2015 Nanda Devi East Expedition – Martin Moran, Mark Thomas, Thomas Coney, Kenton Cool and David Morton (September/October 2015).
A very experienced team with the objective the first ascent of NE ridge of Nanda Devi East (7434m). A base camp was established at a height of 4,275m at Bhital Gwar in the Lwan valley, and an advanced base at 5,300m close to the starting col. Two of the party made progress along the ridge via a series of four camps, with the uppermost one at 6,640m. From here they made a dash for the summit with bivouac gear, and made good progress until they faced a 500m horizontal section of the ridge with steep snow flutings on one side and overhanging mushrooms on the other. They decided to retreat from the high point of 6,865m. They felt that with more stable snow conditions, an alternative line bypassing the fluted ridge could be feasible. MEF ref 15-20

Katkar Nala Expedition India 2015 – Calum Nicoll, Struan Chisholm, Sam Newmark, and Calum McLellan (July/August 2015).
Objective to make first ascents of peaks at around 5,900m in the Zanskar/Ladakh region of northern India. They travelled to Leh and then by road to Kargil and Padam. On arrival at Reru they found that the bridges and main

road connecting the Tsarap river villages had been washed away by floods two months earlier. This meant a longer than expected walk in. From a high base camp they made a first ascent of peak L5 (5897m). The climbing was PD+, with ice to 50° and extensive loose rock. An attempt was made on another peak (L4), but they were forced to retreat to avoid the approaching bad weather. MEF ref 15-31

NEPAL HIMALAYA

British Gorakh 2015 – Julian Freeman-Attwood, Ed Douglas, Phil Bartlett Nick Colton, Skip Novak and Crag Jones (April/May 2015).
The objective was to climb one of the 6,000m peaks of the Gorakh Himal. After an eight-day approach march they got to within 12km of the mountain Gorakh Kang. Very heavy snowfall prevented them getting closer with pack mules and no porters were available, so they decided to try an ascent from this remote base. They then got news of the Kathmandu earthquake, and as two members of their Nepali staff were from the epicentre area near Manaslu, they had to get them home to their families. The expedition was ended for humanitarian reasons with no climbing accomplished.
MEF ref 15-01

British Far West Nepal Expedition – Mick Fowler, Paul Ramsden, Steve Burns and Ian Cartwright (October 2015).
To make the first ascent of Gave Ding (6571m) via the north face, followed if practical, by a ridge traverse to Lachama Chuli (6721m). Fowler and Ramsden reached the summit of Gave Ding via the north face in six days from base camp. (See the Nepal section in this year's Journal.) From the summit they felt that the proposed traverse to Lachama Chuli was not a worthwhile extension of their climb, and would not have added significantly to the success of the trip. Steve Burns and Ian Cartwright reached 5,600m on Pt 6045, but retreated in the face of continuous hard ice. The weather was generally clear but cold, though there was snowfall of two feet on the summit day. MEF ref 15-10

Investigating Mass Loss Processes on Khumbu Glacier – Ann Rowan, Duncan Quincey, Scott Watson and Owen King (October/November 2015).
Expedition objectives were to study how the Khumbu glacier is responding to climate change. There was concern about the impact of the earthquakes in the area earlier in the year but trails had been mostly repaired, and lodges open, though there were very few tourists around. All the measuring equipment was installed as planned before the glacier surface froze in late October, and measurements collected. Results will be reported in published scientific papers. MEF ref 15-21

PAKISTAN

Ogre North Face Expedition 2015 – Bruce Normand, Marcos Costa, Jesse Mease and Billy Pearson (June/July 2015).
The team started with acclimatisation climbs on peaks of 6,100m and 6,400m. The first attempt by the full team was abandoned at 5,900m because of heavy daytime rockfall. A second attempt was made by Normand and Pearson, climbing at night and sheltering in snow caves by day. The terrain up to 6,600m involved snow and ice up to 60°, and with one steeper step. From 6,600m to 7,100m the ground was of friable unprotected slabs, completely unlike the excellent rock on the S aspect of the peak. The attempt was abandoned at 7,100m due to lack of anchors and unsafe climbing. MEF ref 15-13

Virjerab Expedition 2015 – Pete Thompson, Phil De Berger, and Aiden Laffey (June/July 2015).
The first ascents of one or more peaks of around 6,000m above the Virjerab glacier in the Pakistan Karakoram. The team trekked to base camp from Shimshal village. Thompson and De Berger attempted a route on the N face of Peak 6140 in the Spregh Yaz valley, but were forced to retreat at 5,100m due to snow conditions and avalanche danger. The full team then attempted a route on the W face of Peak 6020 in the Chot Pert *nala*. At 5,900m Thompson was climbing a snow ridge when he triggered two big avalanches. He fell but managed to stop himself using an ice axe brake, so they retreated. The full team made the first ascent of Peak 6104 (Harjoldur Sar) by the S couloir and W ridge at Alpine PD. MEF ref 15-15

The Karakoram Anomaly Project – Sergiu Jiduc, Forster Oliver James, and Taylor Timothy (June/September 2015).
Glaciers in most regions of the world are in retreat, but in the Karakoram they seem to be stagnating or even growing, a phenomenon termed the Karakoram Anomaly. The KA is increasing the region's exposure to hazards such as glacial lake outburst floods (GLOFs). The project is a multifaceted research programme to study the state of health of the Karakoram glaciers in the Hispar-Muztagh and Panmah-Muztagh regions, and assess water availability and glacial hazard risk. The work involved GPS realtime kinematic survey, geomorphic mapping and repeat photography to investigate how glaciers are changing in Shimshal valley, and how this might be impacting the GLOF risk. Preliminary observations found no immediate major risk of GLOFs in Shimshal, though Khurdopin glacier is likely to surge in the next five years. Historic flooding of Shimshal valley has occurred roughly every 25 years, in synch with the surging of the Khurdopin glacier. MEF ref 15-27

Tangra Tower Expedition – James Monypenny and Max Fisher (September/October 2015).
An attempt on the unclimbed Tangra Tower (5620m) in the Khane valley, Pakistan Karakoram. They travelled by road from Delhi to Skardu, where they purchased supplies, and set up their base camp in the Khane valley, where they spent nine days while it snowed. For acclimatisation they tried an alpine-style objective 'Twin Peak 2'. Their attempt involved an approach through deep snow, and some great ice climbing, until lack of acclimatisation led to deep fatigue, and they retreated from a point about 150m below the summit. After a day of rest at base camp they started on Tangra Tower itself. There were five days of rounded cracks, friction climbing, aid climbing and pendulums, until they had to retreat after running out of water and gas.
MEF ref 15-29

K6 Central 2015 – Graham Zimmerman, Scott Bennett and Steven Swenson (July/August 2015).
An attempt on the S face of K6 in the Pakistan Karakoram: the early part of the expedition had bad weather but they used the time to establish an advanced base on the far side of 'Hidden Col' at 5,400m. From here they spent two days finding a route to the cirque below the unclimbed Changi Tower (6500m) and to the 'Polish Col'. A marginal weather window was used to make the first ascent of Changi Tower via its N ridge. Climbing was 600m on high quality granite and graded M6, 5.10, A2. They now intended to attempt the central pillar on the S face of K6 but found that the route was threatened by huge seracs, so moved the ABC to find an alternative target, settling on the SW ridge of K6 West (7040m). The route was very sustained with a wonderful variety of climbing over 1,800m, climbed with two bivouacs, grade M6. They descended the same route, largely by rappels, and reached base camp just before a storm came in. MEF ref 15-33

CENTRAL ASIA

British Southern Fergana Expedition – Paul Josse, John Venier, Peter Nugent, Gabriel Oliver, and Peter Duguid (August/September 2015).
The original objective was exploration of the eastern end of the Southern Fergana Range in Kyrgyzstan, with first ascents of peaks in the range 4,400m–4,700m approached via the Kokbel valley. However they were prevented from entering this valley by a hunting party already established there and had to come up with an alternative plan. This involved setting up a base camp at the base of the Karakol valley at 3,000m and an advanced base up the valley using locals with mules to ferry equipment. From a further ABC Josse and Duguid went off to attempt Peak 445, but Duguid had to descend, suffering the effects of altitude. Josse continued to the summit up an easy snow ridge. It being still early in the day he continued along the Pinnacle (Vershina) ridge to the south to Peak 4557 with mixed ground grade II/III. He then tried to extend the traverse to Peak 4701,

but deteriorating weather forced him to retreat. From the original ABC Oliver and Josse completed another traverse, the Horseshoe (Pokova) ridge, which included Peaks 4361 and 4330. An attempt on the N ridge of Peak 4485 by Venier and Nugent finished about 50m from the summit in rapidly deteriorating weather. MEF ref 15-05

British Universities Unclimbed Peaks – Seth Ford, Tim Miller, Will Kernick and Cameron Holloway (July/August 2015).
First ascents of around 5,000m+ above the North Inylchek glacier in Kyrgyzstan. In an interesting approach to acclimatisation Miller and Kernick climbed Khan Tengri (7010m) before joining Ford and Holloway for the main objectives. Their first choice was Peak 5023, on the opposite side of the glacier, and the approach involved first crossing the glacier, then an unattractive scree slope to the snowline, and an icy traverse up to 65° to hit the ridgeline where they pitched tent. The final 700m ascent was largely ice Scottish II/III, with a short vertical section before the summit. All four members reached the summit. MEF ref 15-19

New Zealand Western Kokshaal-Too – Paul Knott and Vaughan Snowdon (July/August 2015).
The objectives were first ascents at the head of the Pagov glacier in Kyrgyzstan, including Peak 5602. Base camp was established at the confluence of the Palgov and Grigoriev rivers at 3,474m, 18km from the roadhead. From a 4,200m camp in the hanging valley west of the summit they climbed Peak 5190 via snow on the western slopes to the N ridge, and hence to the summit. On the descent they continued north over the previously unclimbed summit of 4973. Their first attempt on Peak 5602, from a 4,600m camp on the upper Pavlov glacier, was curtailed by a storm that put down 20cm of snow. Fortunately conditions cleared quickly, and they set off via a snow/ice couloir on the W face, which led to the N ridge. This ridge was followed on good snow to the summit, which was reached in less than three and a half hours from camp. MEF ref 15-22

Kosmos 2015 Expedition – Emily Ward, Mikael Abrahamsson, Harry McGie and Heather Swift (September/October 2015).
Pik Kosmos is the second highest mountain in the Western Kok-shaal Too in Kyrgyzstan. The objective was a new route on the N face. After an eventful and extended journey from Bishkek, interrupted by several vehicle breakdowns, they reached the drop-off point near the Kotur basin. From here there was a long walk-in, which took more time than planned because of the illnesses of two of the party. During the walk-in two acclimatisation ascents were made: Pk Alpini (4578m) by Ward and McGie, and Pk 4326 by Ward, both in the Kotur Basin. A base camp was eventually established where the two arms of the Grigor'ev glacier meet, and where there was running water. From here they were able to reconnoitre the N face of Kosmos, and witnessed several substantial serac falls and avalanches, decided

that it was too dangerous for them, and looked for alternatives. Ward, McGie and Abrahamsson chose Pk 5190 above the Grigo'ev basin. A glaciated couloir led to a series of ice and mixed pitches, before the final snow slopes to the summit. The couloir had a height gain of 700m at 45–55 degrees, followed by a series of ice falls with mixed pitches (AI 3 or 3+, M3), leading to ice/snow slopes and the summit. Other peaks attempted included Pk 5013 (Ward) and Pk 5007 (Swift); both retreated in poor conditions. They then made the long trek back to the road, during which Ward climbed Pik Oleg (c 4600m). MEF ref 15-24.

Muzkol 2015 Tajikistan – George Cave, Clay Conlon, Emily Ward, Alistair Docherty and James Monypenny (August 2015).
An exploratory expedition to the Ak Baikal valley in the Muzkol range in the Gorno-Badakhshan Autonomous region of eastern Tajikistan: the team flew variously to Bishkek in Kyrgyzstan, or Osh in Tajikistan, met up in Osh, and drove to the Ak Baikal valley where a base camp was set up at the foot of the glacier. This was done with the help of a family living in yurts low down in the valley, and who were able to provide transport to the base. The original plan was to attempt a traverse of the unclimbed ridge at the back of the basin. Unfortunately this turned out to be a long and committing route on very unpleasant ground, so they changed their objectives. Four ascents were completed, three of which were on new routes on the previously climbed Peak 5560: one route on the N face (Monypenny, 500m PD+), later repeated by Cave and Conlon, and another on the W face and SSW ridge (Ward, 500m F). The first ascent of Peak 5792 by Monypenny was made via the NW face and NE ridge, and the name Mt Emily was proposed for this peak. MEF ref 15-26

NEW ZEALAND

There and Back Again, New Zealand 2015 – Rhys Tyers, Jack Hare, Tanguy Racine, James O'Hanlon, Oliver Myerscough, Cecilia Kan, Chris McDonnell and Alex Seaton (April 2015).
Eight members of the Imperial College Caving Club went to the South Island of New Zealand for a three-week expedition to find new caves. Due to high winds and early snowfall the original plan to base themselves on Mt Owen had to be abandoned, and the expedition relocated to the Takaka Hills, a lower series of mountains in the same Marble region as Mt Owen. With now only two weeks in the field, the expedition found a new passage deep in an already discovered cave (Ed's Cellar) as well as finding several new caves (Weta than Ever, Black Helix and Red Dog/Dead Rogue) in the Canaan Downs region. These caves were surveyed to BCRA Grade 5.
MEF ref 15-25

Reviews

A Line of Fox Bones
Looking to Castle Tirrim from Roisbheinn.
Rob Fairley, 1998. (Watercolour. 71cm x 40cm. Private collection.)

Reviews

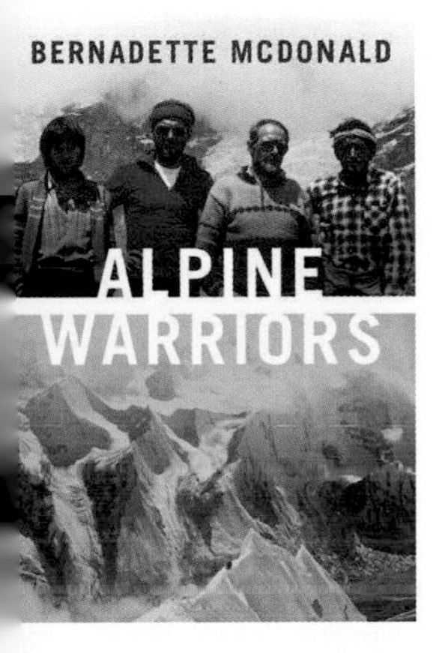

Alpine Warriors
Bernadette McDonald
Rocky Mountain Books, 2015, pp352, £24

Alpine Warriors was a worthy winner of the prize for mountain history at the Banff mountain book festival in 2015 and speculation naturally followed that it could be a winner of the Boardman Tasker. So it came as a surprise that this important contribution to our understanding of extreme mountaineering was not even short-listed. At the award ceremony, Robin Campbell, chair of the judges, offered the following explanation: 'Regarding [*Alpine Warriors*] and also her prizewinning *Freedom Climbers* from a few years ago… I find it an odd thing for a Canadian to write histories of Polish and Slovenian climbing. How would Canadian climbers like it if some Polish or Slovenian writer rolled up and wrote their history for them? Not a lot I fancy!'

This was such an odd comment; I half expected him to ask what Mary Beard thinks she's doing writing about the classical art of Greece and Rome? That she should stick to something nearer to Cambridge? His joke provoked laughter, but a lot of it was nervous laughter. It was a typical piece of pantomime from the jester Campbell, the sort of myopia that gets individuals and even nations into trouble, combining the ignorance, prejudice and arrogance on display in the recent Yugoslavian civil wars that *Alpine Warriors* tries to explain.

Campbell's comments did provoke me to ask some questions of my own. What do we ever truly understand about other cultures or motivations so different from our own? Was Williams Carlos Williams right, that 'the local is the only universal', that we should study only our native stones? That was the implication of Campbell's comments. It's a comforting but limited position. It doesn't prepare us for the unique tribalism of each culture; it makes no attempt to understand the other.

The story of Slovenian alpinism cannot be separated from centuries of violence in the Balkans culminating just a couple of decades ago with the break-up of Yugoslavia. It was only then that Slovenia emerged as a nation for the first time, miraculously almost unscathed compared to Croatia and Bosnia but not without deep psychological scarring.

If you're looking for Slovenia's native stones, then you have to start with the highest: the three-headed summit of Triglav, the cornerstone of the Slovenian nation and their national symbol. Slovenia is the world's only nation conceived around a mountain summit. Most Slovenians believe it is their sacred duty to climb Triglav at least once in their lives. And McDonald purposefully starts her story of this remarkable nation of climbers with interviews of people on the summit of Triglav making this pilgrimage.

Reading *Alpine Warriors*, I had to change my own perceptions formed over a number of years visiting and climbing in Slovenia and Croatia. The title was chosen cleverly. If you feel the burden of centuries of both invasion and internecine warfare, leading to corrupt power politics, the reasons to climb become more of a struggle to escape to a new reality than just a part of an adventurous lifestyle. That is perhaps the key to what has made this extraordinary climbing community so successful in all aspects of high-altitude mountaineering, but also very different in nature and far removed from Anglo-Saxon climbing traditions.

Slovenian mountaineers can be fanatically possessive about their own sacred mountains, as McDonald explains early in the book in a gripping account of the first winter ascent of *Cop's Pillar* on the north face of Triglav by Tone Sazanov, Ales Kunaver and Stane Belak in 1966, beating the Germans and Austrians to the prize. Kunaver and Belak went on to provide the other side of the 'local' versus the 'universal' argument. They were involved in visionary first ascents of the south face of Makalu, the *West Ridge Direct* on Everest, the south face of Manaslu, the south face of Lhotse and the south face of Dhauligiri. The list goes on. And the list of major ascents is accompanied by a list of remarkable climbers: the Stremfeljs, Groselj, the Croat Stipe Bozic and then onto the more recent era with Prezelj, Karo, Knez, Jeglic, Cesen, Sveticic and Humar with their own list of increasingly extreme routes on Kangchenjunga, Dhaulagiri, Manaslu, Annapurna and many more in South America, the Garhwal and North America.

Although Slovenians may be firmly rooted locally, their ambitions seem truly universal. But there is another driver, something that Slovenian climbers cannot find at home that goes way beyond national pride, military teamwork and personal ambitions. McDonald I believe comes close to providing the explanation. To get there, she has totally immersed herself in the Slovenian climbing community with great sensitivity. What she uncovers is a religious, almost mystical, spirituality shared by most Slovenians so alien to secular Britain. All Slovenian climbers appear to possess their own tattered copy of a book called Pot (meaning 'The Way' or 'Path') by Nejc Zaplotnik. His writing and philosophy is used throughout to illustrate both individual emotions and uncertainties, and the shared philosophical heart and soul of Slovenian climbers. Zaplotnik himself was a superb climber, a character to the Slovenians as important as Whillans or Haston are to British mountaineering but someone who also wrote a book of psalms that perhaps all climbers should read. Here's an example: 'He who is in pursuit of a goal will remain / empty once he has attained it. / But he who has found the way / Will always carry the goal within him.'

The nation was devastated when Zaplotnik was buried with Ante Bucan in 1983 by a serac collapse on the unclimbed south ridge of Manaslu.

The following year, Stipe Bozic and Vicki Groselj with Ales Kunaver in support, returned to make an alpine-style ascent of the ridge in Nejc's honour.

McDonald does not attempt a linear interpretation of Slovenian climbing. As new individuals arrive on the scene, there are at first subtle and then fractious transitions from the old to the new, from the heavyweight, multi-month expeditions of Kunaver to smaller, faster ascents and finally, the pursuit of the perfect solo ascent. Overall, the helping hand – or is it the menacing shadow of Big Brother shadow?) – of the Slovenian Mountaineering Association is forever present, handing out financial support to those who play the right game. But the old order was changing in the early 1990s as the new nation emerged from Yugoslavia. Commercialism and sponsorship first introduced by Cesen and later exploited by Tomas Humar created wounds that have never properly healed. In 1990 a massive controversy exposed the growing divisions in Slovenian mountaineering. As McDonald puts it: 'Tomo Cesen's contested south face of Lhotse route and the changing ideology of Slovenian climbers morphed into one convoluted mess.'

Today the echoes of that hostility still resonate, and to some extent the Slovenians have returned to the insularity that was a feature of their early great ascents on Makalu and Everest's west ridge. These were equal in stature to anything being done in the Himalaya in the 1970s and 1980s but without the fanfare. If the outside world didn't know much about Slovenian climbing, that was their problem. (Regarding Cesen, Marko Prezelj comments: 'I am not saying it is true. I am saying I believe. I believe in the fundamentals of alpinism, which is trust. From this perspective, it is not my problem. He has to live with whatever is true.')

Edward Thomas wrote in the preface to *The Icknield Way*, 'Today I know there is nothing beyond the farthest of far ridges except a signpost to unknown places. The end is in the means.' This book takes us to some of those unknown places, and proves that even though we may think we know the motives of others, different cultures bring surprising and distinctly different responses to the mountains and their own native stones. It seems for Slovenian climbers, finding themselves as individuals, as groups of friends and as a nation are all part and parcel of one quest. As Nejc Zaplotnik put it: '...long days on my fingertips / teach me how to live with my feet on the ground. / When I become a true master of dancing on vertical walls / I will also know / How to walk on firm ground.'

Alpine Warriors combines well-researched and interpreted historical detail with dramatic storytelling that makes the book both thought provoking and, at times, hair-raising. It provides a welcome addition to our knowledge of eastern European climbing, bearing similarities to *Freedom Climbers* but highlighting how different in character the Slovenians are. I look forward to Bernadette McDonald's upcoming biography of the Pole Wojciech Kurtyka, who, like Zaplotnik, connects a nation spiritually with the mysterious attraction of very high mountains.

John Porter

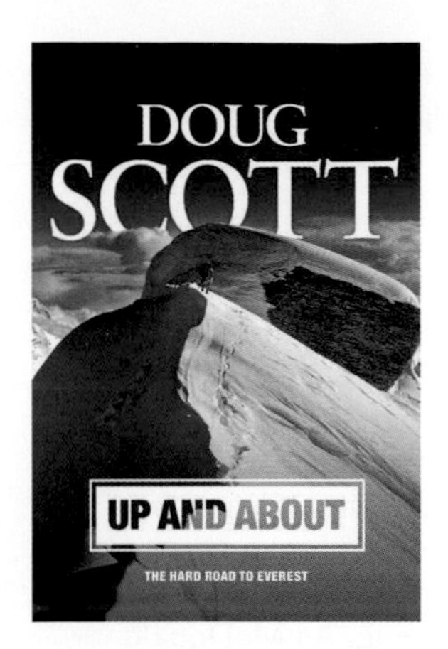

Up and About
The Hard Road to Everest
Doug Scott
Vertebrate Publishing, 2015, pp404, £24

'As a teenager my mother Joyce visited a fortune teller…' Thus our foremost mountaineer opens his autobiography. But this is no fairy tale: it's an enthralling, factual read, warts and all. More than that, it effectively records much of the climbing history of our times, at least the times of those of us of mature age. Luckily Doug has a good memory, for he records it all in considerable detail and in a fluent style, as climb follows climb and expedition succeeds expedition, so that on completing a chapter the reader is left wondering what craggy adventure the next will reveal – and where. Were this but an annotated list of his climbs, it would be most impressive, but every trip, every location, every exploit is qualified by personal comment, intriguing asides and context, the latter enabling readers to place the occasion in their own historical time scale.

The story proper starts in 1941 when Douglas Keith Scott was born to Joyce and her policeman husband George. His childhood in a hardly-affluent suburb of Nottingham during the war and the straitened, fiercely-rationed years that followed, is one with which many of us older readers can identify, whatever our own personal circumstances; scrumping apples, fighting at school, learning to ride a bike, falling in the canal and receiving a clip round the ear from an avuncular copper, these were all part of 1940s boyhood. It seems natural that simple, local adventures, often with the Scouts, should lead in due course to the Peak District, and so to rock climbing and the Nottingham Climbers Club. It would spoil the story to go into further detail, but like this reviewer, many readers will find the book packed with familiar names – Dez Hadlum, Bob Pettigrew, Dennis Gray, Geoff Sutton and others – for the climbing world of the 1950s and 1960s was a small one and Doug and his chums were familiar figures on the crags and in the pages of the primitive climbing periodicals of the time.

It soon becomes obvious that from early on Doug's life was climbing and still more climbing, driven by a determination to succeed at the game. Not that he was able to ignore normal life, for fifty years ago there was no way to support oneself without a proper job, let alone support the wife and son who materialised fairly soon. Doug went to Loughborough and became a teacher, specialising in PE and Geography, and was quite soon exploiting the 'educational' rambling and climbing trips encouraged by the supportive Nottingham education authorities. I recall Doug in those days as a be-spectacled, tweed-jacketed, leather-elbowed, pens-in-pocket schoolmaster, though more powerful, more tanned and more enterprising than the typical 'schooly' – adept at wangling time off for his expeditions, initially overland to the Tibesti in army surplus trucks, and subsequently to the Cilo Dag and then the Hindu Kush. But respectable though he appeared, teaching was too cloying and when in 1971 leave was reluctantly refused for a first expedition to Baffin Island, Doug became a self-employed jobbing builder, earning much better money, climbing when he wanted to, and keeping really fit into the bargain. He freely admits to being a selfish and eventually unfaithful husband, sacrificing his marriage in order to climb, and one is forced to feel desperately sorry for Jan, his wife, and young Michael. At least Doug is honest; throughout the book he indulges in regular introspection, examining his motives, admitting his mistakes and even washing his dirty linen in print. This is very refreshing and reflects well on the man he has become.

These were great years in the development of British climbing. In the early 1960s climbing and mountaineering were minority games that few people played; the only 'professionals' were instructors at the new 'outdoor education' establishments such as Plas y Brenin. Leading climbers were still amateurs, frequently hard-driving and hard-drinking weekenders; gear manufacturing was a cottage industry, advertising was primitive, while sponsorship was non-existent. But standards were rising steeply with the use of such things as PAs, curved axes and the deployment of nuts. Aid climbing had already come to Britain, especially to the limestone walls of the Peak, and Doug soon hammered out a not-entirely complimentary reputation as a 'dangle & whack' man, confirmed by his ascent of the huge overhangs on the Cima Ovest north face, and more visibly, his ascent with Henry Palmer, over 22 hours with 40 peg placements, of the *Big Overhang* in the huge Parliament House Cave at Gogarth North Stack. Indeed, in certain Llanberis pubs it was even whispered that Scotty only perfected aid climbing because he couldn't climb free, an unfounded jibe because he was climbing many of the hardest routes in Snowdonia at the time, though unlike some, he usually contrived to keep himself out of the mainstream. But the expanding media, both print and broadcast, was slowly realising that crazy people climbed steep rock and icy mountains and might provide good stories. They discovered Doug in 1969 on Sron Ulladale, the intimidating, overhanging crag on Harris. Nevertheless he never sought fame; there were no agents, no lucrative deals.

Baffin Island became a Scott stamping ground. It sounded attractive; the mountains were only semi-explored but bristling with soaring granite walls and virgin summits, ripe for the plucking. Doug and his chums organised several expeditions and achieved much in typically awful weather, experience which obviously did much to harden even more his resolve, while confirming what was physically possible in the worst conditions of cold and wet. It is interesting to note that on these and other of Doug's trips there was no leader, *per se*. Everyone did their bit and decisions were democratic; this became the Scott style. By now it is obvious that Doug is a driven man, driven to succeed on every climb he attempts, though not at the expense of aesthetics.

Doug's eventual Damascene conversion came in Yosemite and against considerable scepticism he proved a strong advocate of the British clean climbing ethic. He helped convert Royal Robbins and other leading Valley climbers to the use of the nut and the chock. Not long afterwards I remember lunching in Seattle with Larry Penberthy who insisted that Robbins was crazy to advocate and import such things, how could a jammed nut, however well placed, ever hold a serious fall? (It was an excellent lunch.) Doug's style fitted in with the laid-back ethos of the American climbers; he made many good friends and it is fascinating to read of the antics of the Yosemite denizens of the day and the goings-on in the Valley. He even confesses to an unintentional LSD trip, which forced the postponement for a couple of days of his ascent of *Salathé Wall* with Peter Habeler.

But of course the book is a 30-year prelude to the crescendo of Everest. Surprisingly Doug had not already been to the Himalaya when invited by Whillans to join him and MacInnes as the token British contingent of Herrligkoffer's 'European' south-west face attempt in the spring of 1972. In those days Doug affected the then fashionable John Lennon look, with long hair, droopy moustache and round spectacles, and Herrligkoffer was rather taken aback. The organisation proved something of a shambles and the expedition failed to reach the high point reached by Whillans and Dougal Haston on our own international effort of the previous year, but crucially much of Whillans' high mountain savvy rubbed off on Doug. Meanwhile Bonington, who had opted out of both the 1971 and the European attempt, had obtained an Everest permit for that autumn, and Doug was an obvious candidate for the team, which included Haston, who of course had partnered Whillans on both Annapurna in 1970 and on Everest in 1971. But to everyone's dismay Whillans was not included, and both off and on the mountain there was muttering about autocratic leadership. Nevertheless Doug, climbing with Haston, reached 8,300m before the expedition retreated in mid-November.

In a single year Doug had twice been high on Everest, and was now busy lecturing when not climbing. For the next two years his climbs and expeditions run virtually back-to-back. They include a reconnaissance to the Ogre, an ascent of Pik Lenin during the disastrous Soviet international climbing meet in the Pamirs, and the ascent of Changabang, climbed with a small Anglo-Indian team which included Haston, by now a trusted partner. Despite a daunting reputation, the climb proved straightforward but there was no comment on W W Graham's claimed ascent of 1883, which Haston once told me he considered to have been quite possible.

Somehow Bonington obtained the 1975 post-monsoon Everest slot that the Canadians had relinquished, and the rest is history. As a magazine editor at the time and myself an Everest veteran, I well recall the reams of reports, the massive publicity and the book that the expedition generated, so far be it for me to précis Doug's own recounting of his part in the final ascent of the south-west face; of how he and Dougal Haston became the first native Britons to stand on the summit of Everest. Having read this book, I realise that Doug had spent some 20 years training for just this climb. I now understand how he and Dougal were able to survive the subsequent fearful bivouac unscathed. The politics of the expedition are intriguing; Doug's retrospective insight is illuminating and answers many long-standing questions, for despite its success, the enterprise was not his style. In Bonington's own words, Doug is 'undisciplined, warm-hearted and emotional, full of a vast, restless energy.' It fits.

As a reviewer however, I would be negligent to ignore failings in the book: the typeface is unusually small, a size that as an elderly reader I found a trifle uncomfortable, while I felt the text could sometimes have been more tightly edited. But more serious to my mind is the poor reproduction of the frequent black and white pictures. Doug is an excellent photographer, one of the very best camera-wielding climbers, and although the several folios of glossy colour plates are well reproduced, the frequent monochrome images scattered throughout the text are a travesty. Good illustrations used in context can make even the best text sing, and with modern printing methods, black and white images should be really telling.

There is no doubt that this is an important book. It is not just 40 years in the life of a remarkable mountaineer: it is history. It contains an excellent bibliography and an exhaustive index so it's likely to prove a valuable reference to happenings, both on stage and behind the scenes, over a period when our game was changing like never before. But there's another 40 years to come and Doug is already sharpening his pencil!

John Cleare

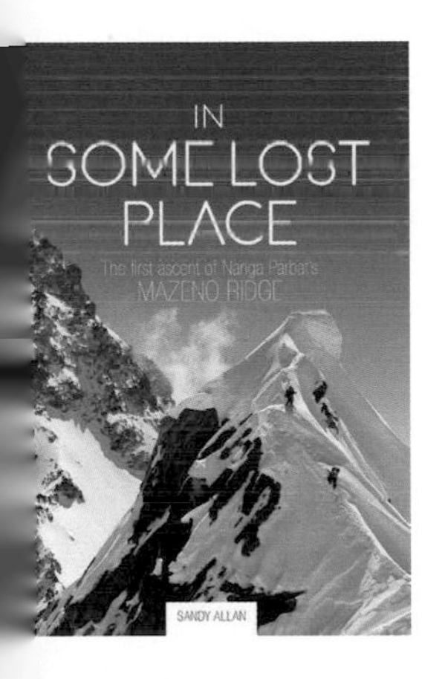

In Some Lost Place
The First Ascent of Nanga Parbat's Mazeno Ridge
Sandy Allan
Vertebrate Publishing, 2015, pp224, £24

When George Foreman regained the world heavyweight championship in November 1994 it was, for me, a choice moment, a comfort of sorts, though I'm no particular fan of boxing. Foreman had seized back the title at the age of 45. I too was 45 years old at the time. To me, and a good many others in their forties and over, Big George's comeback was a reassuring sign – and he's preacher after all – that maybe I wasn't over the hill just yet.

Eighteen years later, the news that Sandy Allan and Rick Allen had completed the first ascent of Nanga Parbat's Mazeno Ridge was a similar 'Foreman moment'. Both were in their late fifties. Age was clearly no barrier to high achievement in the mountains. Indeed it may have been a key to their success – and survival. Decades of climbing in remote places, often together, seemed to have given the pair a stoic resilience, a quiet confidence that, whatever the difficulties, somehow they'd cope.

Yet looked at in a contrary way, these same qualities so nearly proved fatal. Sandy and Rick arrived at the Diamir base camp emaciated and totally spent after 11 days on the ridge to the summit and three more descending the *Kinshofer* route. The Mazeno is the longest route to any 8,000m summit: 10km of towers, cornices and deep snow at mind-numbing altitude. In such a place, strung out physically and mentally, small things can have big consequences, maybe a stumble, a few dropped matches, or the fortuitous meeting of a Czech climber with a cigarette lighter.

What was that Dylan song from *Blood on the Tracks*? 'A simple twist of fate.' Well, there are twists of fate a-plenty in Sandy Allan's story, his road to Nanga Parbat and the slow motion drama of attrition that unfolds there. *In Some Lost Place* takes an increasingly tight grip on the reader, Sandy's self-questioning mounts, along with his prayers and hallucinations, as he and Rick struggle down the mountain.

If they'd perished, the verdict may well have echoed the opinion attributed by Sandy to Cathy O'Dowd when she and Sherpas Lhakpa Rangdu, Lhakpa Zarok and Lhakpa Nuru bailed at the Mazeno Gap. That Sandy and Rick were 'crazy old men, pushing too hard'. As it was, fortune and fortitude were with them, the long coveted Mazeno route was completed and in recognition the pair were awarded a 2013 Piolet d'Or. Twists of fate?

Sandy seems a bit sensitive about the age thing and says he doesn't really understand why it was so often remarked upon after their climb. 'In my head I still feel as enthusiastic and excited as ever,' he says. Well good: if I've harped on about your age Sandy it's only because I drew such encouragement from it.

I thought twice about whether to read *In Some Lost Place*. During my tenure as editor of *AJ* I'd published Sandy's account of his and Rick's 2009 ascent of Nanga Parbat by the Diamir Face[1], and then Rick's account of the Mazeno climb took centre stage in the 150th anniversary *AJ* in 2013[2]. I thought I knew their story pretty well. In addition, a surfeit of mountaineering books to read during my *AJ* decade had left my taste for the genre somewhat jaded. I'm glad I thought twice. Sandy pours out so much of himself – youthful rebellion, divorce, his religious nature – that the book tells a personal journey as well as an account of an extraordinary climb.

Sandy emerges a freewheeling character, happy to stand apart from mountaineering's celebrity clique, and for whom his eventual life as an IFMGA guide was perhaps the most appropriate calling. In his youth he was scornful even of this elite body, thinking guides 'slow and pedantic'. Independence is clearly important to him; as he reflects during one of several bone-chilling bivies, he was on the mountain because he chose to be. 'I wasn't here for any other reason – like fame or to please a sponsor.'

My one criticism concerns the arrangement of the narrative, and it is really a criticism of an arrangement common to several books I've read recently (not only 'mountain' books) of which *In Some Lost Place* is just a further example. It's the practice of lifting a passage from a dramatic part of the story and plonking it at the front of the book to create a cliffhanger,

1. 'To Get Closer', Sandy Allan, *AJ* 115, 2010/11, pp11-17.
2. 'The Long Ridge', Rick Allen, *AJ* 117, 2013), pp3-14.

literally so in the case of Sandy's prologue. When the last sentence reads, 'All Rick and I could do was watch in horror', in my head I hear the *di-di-di-DAH* of Beethoven's 5th, 'fate knocking on the door' as the motif has been described.

But we already know that the expedition ended in success, not tragedy. Furthermore the need to create such tension exposes the literary abilities of the author too soon. Not all climber-writers are Shakespeare. Prologue over, Sandy tells his story with the natural pace of an expedition coming together, after a gestation of almost 20 years, and builds through nine hard days on the ridge to arrive at the Mazeno Gap, from where the dramatic opening has been snatched. By this point I was comfortable with Sandy's style and totally absorbed in his story. This is where I would have preferred to read of Zarok and Rangdu's slide towards the ice cliffs.

Publishers, who after all care deeply about sales, should remember that the world's runaway bestseller begins quite literally, 'In the beginning…'. Modern fashion would open Genesis with Abraham's knife poised over young Isaac and then oblige the reader to race through 22 chapters before learning that an angel of the Lord intervenes and bids Abraham spare the lad. Such breathlessness is unnecessary.

The Bible reference may not be so out place here. Few climbers today are as open about their strong Christian faith, at least in writing, as Sandy Allan. He writes of himself, prior to the summit bid, of feeling 'full of a spiritual grace' and wondering if he was being guided. Yet engagingly he punctures this reverie with the realisation that their one lighter is in Cathy's pocket, and she is already way down the mountain. Not so providential after all. Rick and Sandy will be sorely tested, and Sandy's prayers gain added fervency as, on the long descent, their predicament becomes critical.

Stephen Goodwin

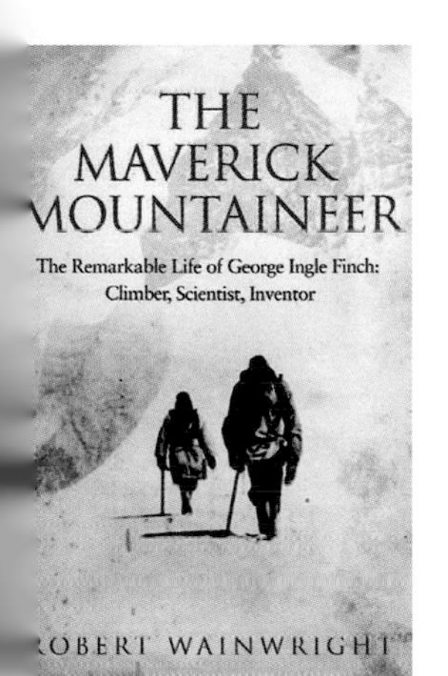

The Maverick Mountaineer
The Remarkable Life of George Ingle Finch:
Climber, Scientist, Inventor
Robert Wainwright
Allen & Unwin, 2016, pp416, £18

George Ingle Finch became an unsung hero in the early history of Everest who fell victim to the elitism of the English establishment and the shadow cast over the mountain's history by the disappearance of Mallory and Irvine in 1924. There was also his refusal to suffer fools in the least bit gladly. This excellent and closely researched biography of a truly maverick mountaineer makes clear the contribution Finch made to mountaineering and to a much wider scientific field. Although he did ultimately become president of the Alpine Club and chairman of the Mount Everest Foundation, such possibilities would have seemed inconceivable to the organisers of the early attempts, critical of any suggestion that bottled oxygen, or 'English air' as it became known, should be used to reach the world's highest summit or that an outspoken Australian with robust opinions should be included in the team, even though his mountaineering ability outclassed most of the early pioneers.

More than half this biography is devoted to Finch's long wrangle with Everest. Robert Wainwright had full access to family records and correspondence to bring together the jigsaw of experience that led George Finch, born into a wealthy but dysfunctional family, to his own adventurous but equally dysfunctional life. Edward Whymper's classic *Scrambles Amongst the Alps* inspired Finch and his younger brother Max towards an interest in mountaineering. A 'grand tour' of Europe by the family allowed the brothers to begin their own exploration of the Alps, largely ignoring their mother's insistence that they should employ a guide and indulging their own independent zest for mountains, ticking off an impressive number of summits and high level traverses. In Paris, only the timely intervention of a priest stopped them from attempting an outside wall of Notre Dame.

As a student, Finch rejected medicine as unsuited to his academic curiosity. Concert pianist was a possibility; he was a zealous performer, but when he demanded to know from the Austrian pianist Arthur Schnabel: 'How good am I?' Schnabel replied: 'You are first rate second rate.' 'I thought so,' said George, immediately abandoning both the idea and, almost entirely, the piano. Instead, he turned to chemistry which in the early 1900s was making impressive strides and Finch found himself at the cutting edge of new scientific methods as the untapped mysteries of science were meeting the industrial demands of a new century. By 1913, with world war threatening, Finch joined the staff of Imperial College in London, running a course on explosives.

The biography ploughs deeply into Finch's troubled personal life. His first impulsive marriage was to a pretty but flirty ash-blonde called Betty whom he met shortly after enlisting as a second lieutenant assigned to the Royal Field Artillery. Posted to Macedonia he supervised the salvaging of 62,000 artillery shells that had become dangerously unstable through damp. This success declared him a war hero by dint of chemistry and he returned to the UK nine months later to discover that his wife was having an affair and had given birth to a son, leaving in doubt the father's identity.

Back in the Balkans, Finch used his expertise to deal with a German fighter pilot who specialised in attacking British observation balloons with tracer bullets, causing them to explode. The 'Richthofen of the Balkans' had menaced the British effort for a year until Finch equipped a balloon with a dummy observer and 550lbs of explosive detonated by a trigger switch from the ground. The balloon was duly attacked by the twin-gunned Albatros fighter, but as it moved in for the kill George pressed the switch and blew the balloon and the Albatros from the sky.

Shortly after this success Finch became one of the 160,000 men in the Balkans who fell ill with malaria. His second marriage was to Gladys May, the Red Cross nurse who had cared for him. Even before their wedding he had misgivings and three weeks later he moved out, abandoning her even though she was pregnant. Two days after their son was born the marriage officially ended and, as Wainwright observes: 'In the space of six years George Finch had been married twice, divorced twice and been named on birth certificates as the father of three young boys.' Gladys' petition through the courts demanded that a judge order Finch to return to the marital home and 'issue a decree of restitution of conjugal rights.'

In 1920 Everest had become the joint focus of the Royal Geographical Society and the Alpine Club as an object for national prestige with Finch a natural candidate on his mountaineering record but not on his social standing. The Alpine Club, it was explained, was a club for gentlemen who climb whilst the RGS was represented on the Everest organisation by Arthur Hinks, a brilliant Cambridge astronomer credited with determining the mass of the moon and the distance of the earth from the sun. Described by one writer as a 'fleshy, humourless and bitter man who had never climbed higher than his chair,' Hinks took a powerful dislike to Finch and in a chapter entitled 'the Bastardy of Arthur Hinks' set about his exclusion.

As organisation for a reconnaissance expedition went ahead, Finch was once more smitten, this time by a secretary at Imperial College. Agnes Johnston was a disarming Scottish beauty with a head of wild curls, for which he called her 'Bubbles'. But although Finch had powerful supporters he was excluded from the first expedition on medical grounds. Two doctors deemed him to be unfit, but as the Everesters were failing to reconnoitre beyond 23,622ft, Finch promptly and successfully climbed the southern flank of Mont Blanc, the biggest climb in the Alps that summer. Not even Hinks could argue against his inclusion the following year when Finch, the pragmatic scientist, not only produced a padded outfit that kept him warm while others shivered, but oxygen equipment that allowed him and Geoffrey Bruce to reach 27,320ft, higher than man had ever reached.

Finch was famously excluded from the 1924 attempt after being accused of breaking a gentleman's agreement over use of confidential material, infuriating Hinks. Andrew Irvine, his replacement and a 'genius mechanic', was given charge of the oxygen equipment, which was redesigned, but without help from Finch. Due to neglectful haste the cylinders arrived in India, broken, half empty and leaking. Wainwright does not disagree with the prevailing view that Mallory and Irvine died on the ascent or with Finch's belief that defective oxygen equipment was the cause. This biography presents fascinating detail about the mores of mountaineering in the early 20th century and the aftermath of the early attempts on Everest, affirming the respected position George Finch holds in British mountaineering.

Ronald Faux

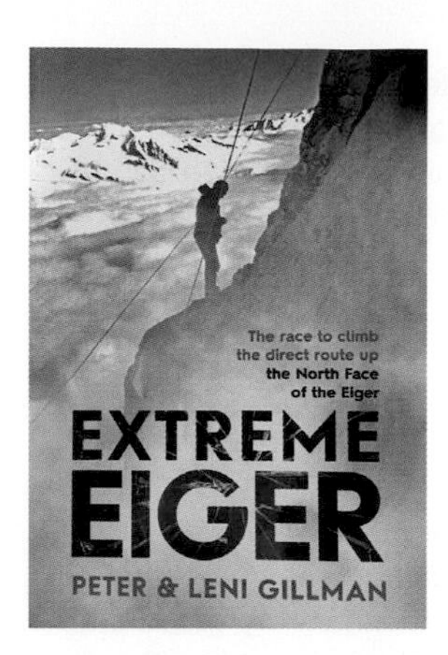

Extreme Eiger
The Race to Climb the Direct Route up the North Face of the Eiger
Peter and Leni Gillman
Simon & Schuster, 2015, pp394, £20

Halfway through *Extreme Eiger* I started wondering what Martin Heidegger or Jean-Paul Sartre would make of it. The events it describes, the famous first ascent of the dangerous Eiger Direct in 1966, the rivalry between German and Anglo-American teams, their decision to come together after the death of John Harlin, the presence of the enigmatic Dougal Haston with his fondness for Friedrich Nietzsche, beg questions that are profoundly philosophical: why do we do what we do? If we do the same thing for different reasons is it still the same thing? In fact, given the media frenzy that frothed around the foot of the Eiger during the weeks of this epic climb, like spume on the ocean, it might be useful to hear from Jacques Derrida as well. Would this 'thing', whatever it was, have existed in the same way if the media had ignored it? Was it changed by being observed?

In the closing pages of this remarkable book, Peter Gillman writes: 'five people had previously ascended the rope that broke, four of them that same day. So did Harlin die because he had prevaricated that morning? Or was his death pure chance, the outcome of a lethal game of existential roulette, just as it was pure chance that I happened to be watching at the moment he lost the game? Was the flaw in his character? Or in the rope?'

Gillman was watching through the telescope when Harlin fell, a young man on virtually his first big assignment as a journalist, a new father who knew Harlin's own young family; how could it not have had a profound impact? He filed his pieces and then wrote a book with Haston about it, moved on to other stories, worked for the great Harold Evans at the *Sunday Times*, wrote books with his wife Leni, as he did this one, watched his kids grow up and move out, grew old himself and, after half a century, returned to that image of that figure in red turning through the sky. Such immense themes, coupled with the passage of time and new perspectives, make for powerful reading.

In the first adrenaline rush of youth, it's hardly surprising that Gillman didn't get everything right and he is modestly open about his misunderstandings – without taking it too far. Instead, he uses his opportunity to reassess, most notably in tracking down the surviving members of the German team, a low-key, blue-collar lot for the most part, a team of friends, not stars, who came up with a workable plan of how to climb this great challenge and stuck to it. This is where much of the book's new ground lies. The Gillmans fill in their backgrounds, try to understand their motivation and then, most poignantly, trace the passing years and how the climb seemed to them after the passage of time.

Harlin, Gillman now more fully understands, was a different kind of animal, self-absorbed, ambitious, creative with his own life story and at times indecisive, even moody. Whillans took one look and offered his verdict: 'bull-shitter'. While the Germans plodded upwards doggedly, the Anglo-American climbers lurched forward and then ground to a halt, like a sports car in first gear, never quite getting going. The irony is that Harlin was on his way to what most likely would have been a resolution of the competition that had so fascinated the media – and perhaps the anxieties within himself – when the rope he was jumaring snapped.

The paradoxes of the climb reach out to you across the years, most obviously in the ambivalence of one of its key players, Chris Bonington, who withdrew from the team and then ended up leading one of the hardest pitches of the route – and of his life. He could sense the enterprise was somehow misshapen, mostly because of Harlin's leadership, but could not help being drawn – moth-like – towards something so bright.

The presence of competing teams made each of them behave differently, the irony being, given how savage criticism was in the Alpine press at the tactics employed, that the climbers ended up enduring far more discomfort, being stuck to the face to take advantage of breaks in the weather and keep their noses in front, than if they'd been on their own. Layton Kor had the right idea, abseiling down whenever he could to chat up the postmistress at Kleine Scheidegg. Kor, in fact, proved Harlin's secret weapon, his aid skills unlocking key sections of the climb in rapid order.

The Gillmans capture the protracted agony of the route, which took over a month thanks to the hostile weather, with plenty of atmosphere, the squalor of the snow caves, the dogged courage, the sudden bursts of panic, the final, rather desperate lunge for the summit that so nearly ended in further tragedy. They catalogue the inadequacies of both teams' equipment, which had far more in common with the decade or two before than those that followed. Most powerfully of all, they delve into the psychology of men born into the chaos of war and its aftermath. The book is meticulously researched.

If this account lacks anything, it's in how public recognition stretched and warped the enterprise itself. Gillman does quote Robbins that Harlin 'would have risked his life ten times over if he could have done it in a grand and heroic way.' But there were more prosaic considerations too: the money that Gillman's newspaper had advanced. The uneasy, often unwelcome relationship the media has with alpinism is on full display here. What did Bonington learn? How to sup with the devil? I wondered too how it impacted on the generation then coming of age. *Mountain* magazine launched in the *Eiger Direct*'s aftermath; its dogged preservation of the authentic must have been in part a response to the circus that unfolded 50 years ago.

Always compassionate, almost never indulgent, the Gillmans have crafted a rich and layered story, one that captures a particular time, enough to make me feel nostalgic for a place I didn't know, one that explores the vagaries of memory, our weakness for rationalisation and the darker recesses of human motivation – without ever losing sight of the better human qualities.

Ed Douglas

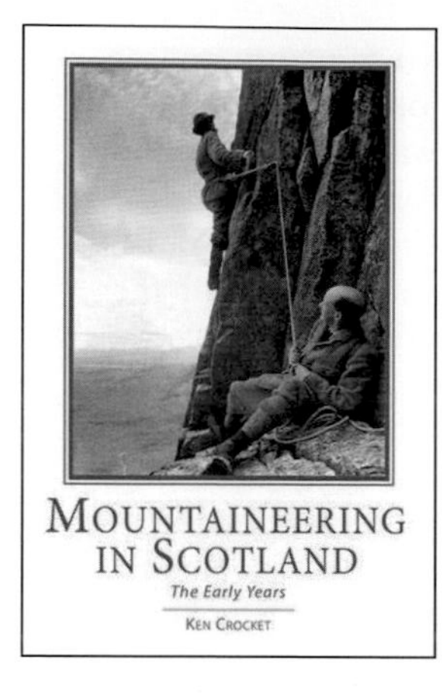

Mountaineering in Scotland: The Early Years
Ken Crocket
Scottish Mountaineering Trust, 2015, pp360, £24

Whymper's 1865 ascent of the Matterhorn, the last of the major Alpine summits to be climbed, closed the curtain on the Golden Age of mountaineering in the Alps. But in 1865, as that curtain closed, the curtain on the Golden Age of Scottish Mountaineering – the era of Naismith and Collie, Glover and Goodeve, Raeburn and Ling – had barely begun to twitch. Oddly enough, the Swiss Alps were much more accessible, and hence better known to British mountaineers, than the Highlands of Scotland. Although some of the mountains on the western seaboard could be reached by boat, travel around much of the Highlands was, until the coming of the railways towards the end of the 19th century, fraught with difficulties.

A few peaks became must-go-to destinations for tourists. For example in 1818 the poet Keats attained the summit of Ben Nevis in 'sullen mist', accompanied by his friend Brown, a local guide, and copious libations of whisky, which may explain why he found himself negotiating much of the summit plateau on all fours. The only other non-locals to venture into the hills were geologists, botanists and cartographers. There were of course cragsmen about, such as the bare-footed fowlers of St Kilda, who scaled the massive sea cliffs of those remote islands to catch birds for food. But these men were motivated by sustenance not sport, and so cannot be regarded as mountaineers in the currently accepted meaning of the word.

The Alps long dominated British perceptions of what mountains should look like. The nearest equivalent in Britain were the jagged Black Cuillin of Skye. The Cuillin were also relatively easy to get to. Gradually, some of the more intrepid visitors to the island ventured onto the main ridge, and in 1836 Professor Forbes of Edinburgh University made the first ascent of Sgurr nan Gillean. As this required some scrambling, involving the use of hands as well as feet, Crocket awards him the accolade of 'Scotland's first known mountaineer'. In 1859 Charles Richard Weld of the Alpine Club visited the Cuillin, and saw what was later to become known as the Inaccessible Pinnacle. 'Surely some bold member of the club,' he wrote, 'will scale this Skye peak ere long, and tell us that it is but a stroll before breakfast.'

The gauntlet had been thrown down, but it was to be many years before systematic exploration of the Cuillin – and the other ranges of Scotland – was to get under way. The Inaccessible Pinnacle itself had to wait until 1880 for its first ascent (by the Pilkington brothers, both AC members). The Alpine Club had been formed in 1857, but in Scotland the early clubs were more interested in fine dining than heroics on the hills. The first major club, formed in 1889, was the Cairngorm Club, followed two months later by the Scottish Mountaineering Club. The latter was to prove the main driving force in Scottish mountaineering, at least up to the outbreak of the First World War, and inevitably much of the remainder of Crocket's narrative involves the SMC and its members.

Transport limitations continued to restrict the areas favoured by Scottish mountaineers. This partly explains why they spent so much time exploring hideous dank fissures such as the Black Shoot of Beinn Eunaich. This was described by one pioneer, with some restraint, as 'disagreeable' but it had the merit that it could be reached from the railway line to Oban. Another favourite playground was the huge but notoriously 'loose, slimy and appalling', as a later guidebook writer put it, north-east face of Cir Mhor on Arran, an island easily accessed from Glasgow by train and steamer.

By the last decade of the 19th century, however, the expanding railway network allowed climbers to explore more widely, notably on Ben Nevis, where all four main ridges received ascents before the First World War, and where Harold Raeburn pointed the way to the future when in 1906 he climbed the unprecedentedly steep ice of *Green Gully* (IV, 4; a grade still attached to several other Scottish winter climbs of the time, such as the Ben's *North-east Buttress*, which received what was probably its second winter ascent a few days earlier that year by a party including a 20-year-old George Mallory). A summit photo taken after Raeburn's ascent of *Green Gully* is just one of many fascinating archive photographs included in the book.

Glen Coe was still only reachable via the old military road, built in the mid 18th century, largely keeping it the preserve of those wealthy enough to own a motorcar; mountaineering in Scotland in these early years was almost exclusively the preserve of the moneyed – and reasonably leisured – middle classes. Nevertheless, before 1914 Glen Coe saw first ascents of such classics as the strikingly bold *Crowberry Ridge Direct* at the hands of the Abraham brothers from the Lakes. Explorations were carried out even further afield, in the far north-west; Crocket's account of an audacious new route by Raeburn and others on Quinag's Barrel Buttress is just one of many thrilling retellings of new-routing in this era.

The mountaineers of the day did not just depend on the railways, or on new-fangled motorcars. Muscle power and stamina underlay many new routes, which were not uncommonly bracketed by punishingly long walks or bike rides at the beginning and end of the day. These were men – and women – of mettle: the Ladies Scottish Climbing Club was founded in 1908, and still thrives. Not only that, the early pioneers possessed extraordinary levels of skill, given the primitive nature of the equipment at their disposal – not to mention their willingness to climb in all weathers, summer or winter. The latter, being outside the shooting season, was often preferred, given the attitude of the proprietors of Scotland's 'sporting' estates.

Most remarkably, as Crocket points out at the end of the book, 'not one fatality was recorded in Scotland to any mountaineer during these early years'. The same could not be said of the four years that followed the outbreak of the First World War. A dark curtain suddenly descended on the Golden Age of Scottish Mountaineering. It was to take some decades before the standards attained before 1914 were to be reached again.

Mountaineering in Scotland: The Early Years is the first volume of a planned trilogy on the history of Scottish mountaineering. Its author, Ken Crocket, is a former editor of the *Scottish Mountaineering Club Journal*, and wrote the SMC's official history of climbing on Ben Nevis. This first volume demonstrates beyond doubt that Crocket is the man for the job. His scope is vast, his copious sources skilfully deployed, and his command of his narrative both meticulous and masterly. Above all, he allows his cast of characters, with all their strengths, foibles and passions for high places, to glimmer through the sullen mists of the years.

Ian Crofton

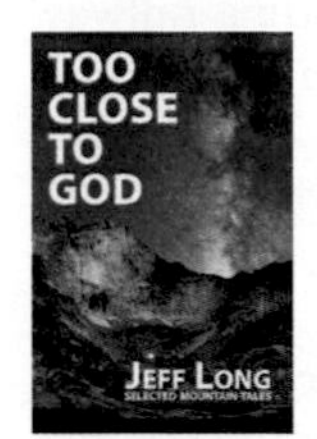

Too Close to God
Selected Mountain Tales
Jeff Long
Imaginary Mountain Surveyors, 2015, pp296, $19.95

Jeff Long is 'indisputably one of the best storytellers of the mountain world,' according to the cover blurb on this collection of short stories. To my loss then, I have to admit I have never read any of Long's novels and therefore it would be unfair to judge his publisher's fulsome claim on this single book.

Collections of short stories are frequently a curate's egg. This isn't necessarily the author's fault. Some settings and characters will inevitably be more appealing than others to an individual reader. *Too Close to God* (the title comes from the final story) is an egg of a good deal more variable quality than even the curate might appreciate; yet paradoxically I was left wanting to read more of Jeff Long's writing.

The most unsatisfying aspect of the collection is that several of the stories are versions of chapters from previously published novels. How much adaptation has been done, the first-time reader cannot tell, but in the case of two of the stories 'Abe', from *The Ascent* (1992) and 'Ike' from *The Descent* (1999) the narrative lacked the tight, yet fully rounded preciseness that distinguishes the best short stories. Abe, a naïve lad caught in an emotional dilemma on a rescue mission, and Ike, a trek leader trapped, with his clients, in a cave of grisly horrors in Nepal, remain only partially formed characters whose paths clearly have some way to run. But that's another story; the novels you've still to read, or so I guess.

Mountain tales lend themselves to short stories, just as expedition accounts lend themselves to 3,000-word journal articles (much longer and they become tedious) and a good many writer-climbers have tried their hand. In the 1980s and 1990s, Anne Sauvy and Dermot Somers both enjoyed success with collections redolent of their particular backgrounds: Sauvy's tales often set around Chamonix and Somers drawing on a rich Irish heritage. More recently Jim Perrin joined the dance with *A Snow Goose and other utopian fictions* (2013), a break, he said, from the 'tyranny of facts'. All well worth your time.

Like Somers and Sauvy, Long draws deeply on the scene he knows best: Yosemite; it is his rock-climbing stories that, for me, are the most satisfying. The closer he is to stone, the more his imagination seems to bubble with possibilities for mesmerising narrative. Included here is 'The Soloist's Diary', the piece that launched Long as a writer. The tale defies description. Three climbers on an infinite wall as seasons roll on endlessly, in no way captures its hallucinogenic quality. Long recalls in a note the 1970s milieu from which it sprang: 'we were writers and poets full of wild nonsense that sounded pure and right to our ears. We climbed, drank jugs of ice melt from local glaciers, and read copiously, from *Finnegan's Wake* (over my head, and probably the others', though no one admitted it) to Calvino and obscurities like *Palm Wine Drunkard*.'

The collection is made up of 10 stories each of which is preceded by an 'author note' reflecting on the composition (and more widely) while also providing a window on the writing life for young writers, a kind of long range mentoring. I enjoyed these insightful introductions as much, if not more, than one or two of the stories that followed. Similarly the depth of the book is enhanced by a thoughtful 10-page foreword by Katie Ives, editor-in-chief of *Alpinist* magazine.

Much of Ives' foreword could be read as a stand-alone essay, dealing with the resistance writers encounter in getting fiction accepted as a valid genre for mountain stories. 'If mountain fiction appears oddly threatening to many climbing readers, it may be because it is inherently subversive,' she writes. 'The best works question precisely what numerous mountaineers consider to be "sacred", daring to tear down the immense architecture that underpins much of our history.'

Long's riposte to the non-fiction realists is equally forceful and comes in his note to the opening story 'When God Throws Angels Down.' (This piece comes from chapter one of his novel *The Wall* (2006) and to my mind is the pick of whole collection. I read it with a shudder: this is how it could be. No-one ever tells of course.)

Long points out that no matter how well written, non-fiction, with its real life epics is born chained to reality. 'That straps it to a fundamental contradiction. Because the thing is, defying reality – breaking chains, transcending borders, trespassing without visas, imagining the unknown, inventing maps, ascending into hearts of darkness, and, even if only for a instant, regaining Eden – is exactly why we climb. And that is fiction's province.'

I agree wholeheartedly; but note also Long's use of the words 'hearts of darkness' and the nod to Joseph Conrad. In his introduction to the whole collection, Long says that once upon a time he had hoped, 'in vain', to be the Melville or Conrad who would elevate mountain literature to prominence. It's a wish that opens up a bigger question. To be sure, Jon Krakauer and Joe Simpson hit the bestseller lists, but is it actually possible to rival Melville or Conrad while remaining within the straitjacket of what might be termed a 'mountaineering novel'?

The devil lies in the dual identity as both climber and writer. While Melville and Conrad both spent a few youthful years at sea (I'm happy to say I attended the same rude 'university') they did not go on to write novels about sailing per se. In the words of Harold Beaver, whose dizzying commentary to the 1986 Penguin Classics edition of *Moby Dick* is almost as long as the novel itself, Melville's theme is the mythopoeic imagination, 'the neurosis of man in usurping the ritual role of Gods; the trauma that converts the pretensions of an Ahab to a suicidal re-enactment of myth.' No mere salty tale.

Climbing may hold the key to the meaning of life to some *AJ* readers, but to the world beyond it is, as Lionel Terray and others have reminded us, a fairly useless recreation. If it touches on the big themes of life, it is more by accident (and regrettably in the course of accidents) than by design. Several of the best works of fiction in which climbing has figured in the plots, have not actually been written by authors who think of themselves as climbers, though some have had a taste of it: for example *The Condition of Ice* by Christopher Burns (1990), *Electric Brae* by Andrew Greig (1992), *The Fall* by Simon Mawer (2003) and *An Afterclap of Fate* (2006) by Charles Lind. If there's a lesson from this maybe it is that the non-climbers have not let the climbing get in the way of the bigger themes of human drama.

However, rivalling Melville or Conrad in producing the great novel was not Jeff Long's business with *Too Close to God*, and perhaps too it would be unkind to draw any comparison with short-story masters such as Chekhov or Kipling. Think of it simply as in the words on the cover: 'selected mountain tales'. Climbers will recognise Long's locations, identify with his characters and on occasion with their pain, but hopefully share none of their nightmares.

Stephen Goodwin

Souvenirs Pittoresques des Glaciers de Chamouny
Gabriel Charton
Foreword for 2015 facsimile by Jaques Perret
Translated by Linda Dubosson
Les Alpes Livres, 1821, pp128, £35

Do you ever wonder, as you travel the countryside or admire a mountain view, how different the scene would have been years ago – a century perhaps, five hundred years maybe, or before the Romans came? I certainly do, and it's not always fruitless speculation, for since the birth of photography some hundred and fifty years ago, there has existed an accurate visual record, sparse at first and then increasingly comprehensive, of how the country appeared – of what we would have seen then, had we been there. Before the birth of photography we must rely on art, descriptive perhaps but inevitably stylised and by definition never exactly accurate. Nevertheless we can learn much, surmise more and even enjoy a whiff

'Le Montanvert... a plateau on a slight incline, covered in beautiful pasture, and serves as a base to the peaks of the Charmos, the Crepan, the Bletlère, the Plan and the Midi.' From *Souvenirs Pittoresques des Glaciers de Chamouny*, first published in 1821 and now beautifully republished by Tony Astill.

of the atmosphere from the best paintings, engravings and drawings from the past.

Most of us have travelled by train, by road or by the *Autoroute du Mont Blanc* from the balmy shores of Lake Geneva, from where Mont Blanc hangs on the horizon, up the wide strath of the Arve, past small towns, through villages and meadows, before the valley narrows, the cliffs loom over and the mountains crowd in. It's about fifty miles to Chamonix where now Mont Blanc and its glinting glaciers rise immediately above the bustling town. It's a classic entry to the realm of the high mountains.

Souvenirs Pittoresques, first published in 1821 in Geneva, is a record of that same journey from Geneva to Chamonix – and then around the Chamonix area – as it was two centuries ago, when Haute Savoie belonged to the kingdom of Sardinia rather than to France. The original volume is considered to be the world's rarest book of the mountain genre and only two copies are known to exist, thus the volume actually under review is a modern, superbly produced facsimile of the original.

It contains 18 plates rendered as hand-tinted lithographs, each backed by the author's succinct text. As an accurate record it obviously suffers from the interpretation of the artist whose technique is perhaps a trifle naive, though doubtless as truthful as he was able to make it within the constraints of his technique. Beautifully reproduced at full page, these charming colour illustrations are atmospheric, recognisable, and will be especially intriguing for those familiar with the Mont Blanc massif. Each plate is accompanied by the appropriate text and the book is bound as a valuable presentation volume.

The illustrations start with views of Geneva and across the Lake towards Mont Blanc, and continue via Bonneville and St Gervais to the Col de Voza in plate eight, a most impressive viewpoint, the picture spanning the northern flanks of the range from the Aiguille du Midi to the Col de Balme, with Les Bossons, Mer de Glace and Argentière glaciers flowing right into the valley bottom. A telling image indeed. Plate 10 is of Chamonix, merely a collection of cottages clustered around the priory, the background dominated by the three ice streams birthed on Mont Blanc itself. The following plate, depicting a view we all know, shows '*Le Montanvert*' and the Mer de Glace, but of course there is no railway and no hotel, only the strange, still standing, little octagonal 'Pavilion'. Plate 15 rather echoes Plate 8, though seen in the opposite direction, this time from the Col de Balme, another excellent viewpoint. Every subject is so familiar yet the detail is different – this is what it looked like in the pre-dawn of Alpinism.

The final three plates show action rather than topography, two illustrating de Saussure's scientific expedition to, and traverse of, the Col du Géant in 1788, the year after he had made the second ascent of Mont Blanc, while the third depicts the tragic accident actually happening to Dr Hamel's party on the Petit Plateau in 1820. Action indeed.

Two text pages accompany each plate, one a facsimile of the original in French, the other a duplicate English translation. Gabriel Charton was an accomplished travel writer, his descriptions are informative and his anecdotes fascinating. He describes the route – the old road often follows a different line to the modern highway – but also captions the plates, naming and commenting on the important peaks and landmarks. I found the spelling of certain names rather interesting, Chamouny for instance, le Crepan and le Bletière. His comment on 'Chamouny' is still appropriate: 'There are excellent inns: one finds there all that one can desire, gourmet meals… and the luxury of the big cities.' Initially mystifying were several references to 'l'Allée', until I discovered that the upper reach of the Val Veni is known as the Vallon de la Lée Blanche, thus the name appears to refer to the several peaks of the Tré la Tête group, which fits the text.

Privately published by our member Tony Astill, this is a magnificent book, of which he and any collector or connoisseur of alpine books, can be very proud.

John Cleare

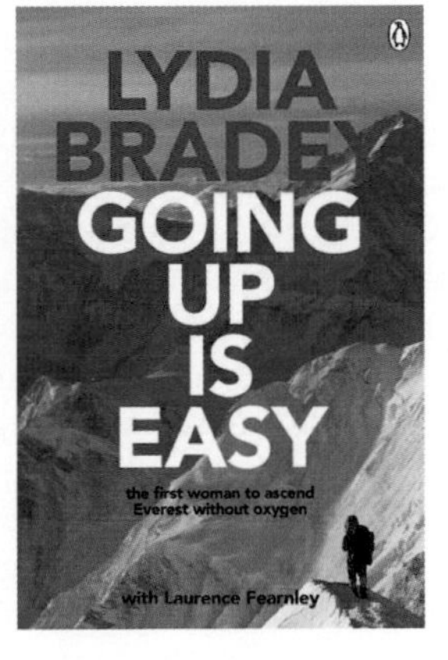

Rock Queen
Catherine Destivelle
Translated by
Marguerite Wright
Hayloft, 2015, pp228, £12

Going Up Is Easy
Lydia Bradey with
Laurence Fearnley
Penguin, 2015, pp272, £12

These absorbing and informative autobiographies come to the reader by means of a process of filtration. In *Going Up Is Easy*, Lydia Bradey had the assistance of Laurence Fearnley, an established author and close friend; Catherine Destivelle's *Rock Queen* has been translated into English by Marguerite Wright. In each case, the collaboration has proved highly successful, but Fearnley has done much more than process the narrative, working through boxes of letters and using hours of interviews and conversations to recreate the significant events in Bradey's mountaineering and personal life. The immediacy of both books is undeniable, drawing the reader into what feels like a conversation with the climbers, both books opening with particularly vivid and startling chapters.

Both climbers rebelled against convention from an early age. Bradey's was the more unusual childhood, brought up by a mother who was fiercely protective of her personal space and who encouraged her daughter to be independent of her from the outset, ready to make her own way in the world. As a result, conventional schools did not satisfy her educational needs and she attended a high school, which fostered her love of the arts and of the outdoors, leading to her first forays into the mountains of her native New Zealand. Soon, she realised, 'Being a mountaineer was the most exciting person I could be in the world.'

Destivelle, too, kicked over the traces both at home and at school. Her parents, great lovers of outdoor life, suggested she join the French Alpine Club and divert her abundant energy into climbing, rather than drifting onto the fringes of anti-social behaviour. Mentored initially by an instructor who spotted her promise she was able to develop her precocious talent, discovering that, when climbing, 'I was complete.'

A foray into the hectic world of climbing competitions brought recognition, then fame, reluctantly embraced, and she was invited by Jeff Lowe on her first mountaineering expedition to the Trango Towers. David Breashers was filming the expedition and a famous and prodigiously talented woman climber would help to attract the funding he needed. There were very similar parallels here with Bradey's route to the high mountains. The opportunity to join an expedition to Cho Oyu presented itself as a political and commercial expedient: the sponsors welcomed a woman whose proven ability on rock and ice and familiarity with mountain environments might well equip her to be the first female to summit the peak.

These introductions to the Greater Ranges serve to illustrate more insistently a theme that weaves subtly into both narratives: the impact of women on the world of high-altitude mountaineering and their position in what is a largely male-dominated enclave. Bradey cites the early female pioneers and their links with the British and American suffrage movements and recognises that, as her own introduction to climbing took place during the feminist movement of the 1970s and 1980s, those climbers she most admired were those who had 'sought equality and recognition in the Himalaya.' Ironically, it was when she achieved her greatest feat, the first female oxygen-less ascent of Everest in 1988, that she came up against 'damning and chauvinistic statements' from Rob Hall whose expedition she had been 'invited' to join, who had failed to reach the summit on this occasion and refuted Lydia's assertion that she had succeeded.

When Destivelle considers what motivates her to climb, one of the factors she considers is the need to 'prove something to myself, certainly as a mountaineer, or as a woman.' In her early climbing years she took huge pleasure in watching 'the idiots charging off to follow a mere girl', assuming, quite wrongly, that the routes she was climbing with such aplomb must be easy. Press reaction to such notable achievements as her solo climb of the Eiger in winter embarrass her because they focus on her sex and unnecessarily exaggerate the difficulties of the climb rather than the purity of the achievement.

Both Bradey and Destivelle have forged memorable careers on rock and in the high peaks and both freely admit an unchanging love of the mountains and dreams of new projects, which allow them to continue to develop and grow. There is a shared desire to pass on their enthusiasm and expertise to others, Bradey as a mountain and ski guide, Destivelle as a technical advisor and lecturer, and, of course, as a mother to her son. Through this process, both feel that they can inspire others to realise their dreams, to set themselves free from convention, to follow a passion, which sets their lives ablaze.

Val Johnson

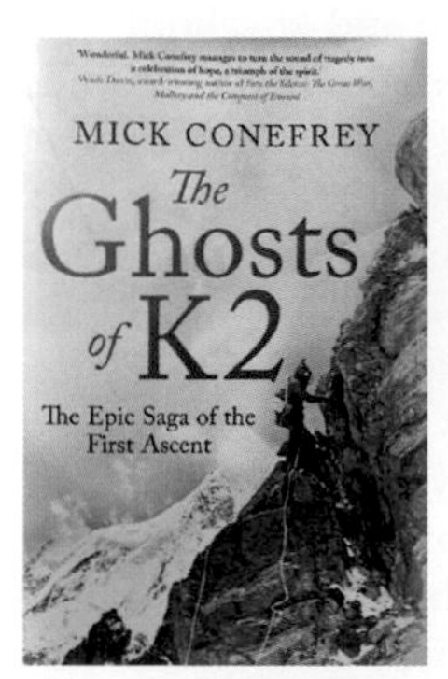

The Ghosts of K2
The Epic Saga of the First Ascent
Mick Conefrey
Oneworld, 2015, pp317, £20

The Ghosts of K2 charts the history of all attempts to climb the world's second-highest mountain from 1902 until its first ascent in 1954. Most of this has already been written about before, first in Jim Curran's *K2, The Story of the Savage Mountain* (Hodder & Stoughton, 1995), *K2: Challenging the Sky*

(Swan Hill, 1995) by Roberto Mantovani and Kurt Diemberger, and Richard Sale's comprehensive *The Challenge of K2* (Pen & Sword, 2011). What I particularly like about Conefrey's version is that he brings to life the characters involved in the early attempts in a way that other books fail to do. His very readable style gives a vivid impression of characters like Oscar Eckenstein, Aleister Crowley, the Duke of Abruzzi, Vittorio Sella, Fritz Wiessner, Dudley Wolfe and Charlie Houston.

Conefrey's justification for yet another book is new archival material that gives a fresh perspective on disagreements regarding the first ascent by Achille Compagnoni and Lino Lacedelli in 1954. The successful Italian expedition led by Ardito Desio has been embroiled in decades of controversy and legal battles, and has consumed the lives of those involved. The fact it took the Italian Alpine Club (CAI) 53 years to publish a detailed enquiry shows how the issues were complicated by contradictory evidence, nationalism, politics, and big egos.

After so many years, and detailed consideration by the CAI, it takes a brave man to challenge this new official version. Yet in *The Ghosts of K2* this is exactly what Mick Conefrey does, asserting that the findings of the esteemed judicial committee representing the CAI to investigate the first ascent controversies are wrong. Just as significantly, Conefrey also states that the mountaineering 'god' Walter Bonatti was wrong in his assessment of events that he was part of in 1954. Not surprisingly this has rather angered the mountaineering establishment in Italy. Imagine the British indignation if an Italian filmmaker and author categorically stated that Captain Robert Falcon Scott was an incompetent buffoon who indirectly killed his men, rather than being an inspiring and courageous leader of a heroic expedition to the South Pole.

Certainly there is a faint whiff of journalistic sensationalism and I for one have lost the appetite for delving through yet more confusing evidence about oxygen mask usage and flow rates, what was said or not said on the mountain, re-interpreting the summit photographs and diary entries, etc. What is clear is that there are some entrenched positions and that everyone has their own story or truth that no one else will ever be able to change.

If you have not read much about K2 history then I can recommend this book for the early attempts but do not be naïve about Conefrey's claims about the first ascent. Of course, make your own mind up, but in some ways I prefer the short story: Achille Compagnoni and Lino Lacedelli successfully reached the summit of K2 with crucial and unselfish support from Walter Bonatti and Amir Mahdi. Bonatti is still rightly regarded as one of the 20th century's greatest mountaineers and the Italians rightly remain proud of a brilliant first ascent.

Chris Harle

Yosemite in the Fifties: The Iron Age
Edited by Dean Fidelman and John Long
Patagonia, 2015, pp176, $60

Rock Climbers in Action in Snowdonia
The 2016 Edition of the 1966 Classic
John Cleare and Tony Smythe
Francis Frith, 2016, pp200, £25/£20

These books are time capsules. *Yosemite in the Fifties* features curated archive photos and first-person accounts of groundbreaking ascents in the Valley during the 1950s; *Rock Climbers in Action in Snowdonia* is a collection of commissioned photos from the mid-1960s by John Cleare, with text by Tony Smythe. They share a strong use of photography, evoking a powerful sense of what it meant to be a climber in that time and place.

Some climbers will already be familiar with *Rock Climbers in Action in Snowdonia*, first published in 1966, although it is unlikely to have registered on the radar of climbers introduced to the sport through modern-day climbing walls. A first edition is highly sought after and comes with a hefty price tag. Fifty years on, Cleare has chosen to publish a new edition, adding the photos 'that got away' to the original iconic 39 black-and-white shots. Aside from these additional photos and a few explanatory words the book essentially remains unchanged in feel and lay-out.

By contrast, the cleaner design of *Yosemite in the Fifties* reflects the fact it is a contemporary publication. Designed by Tom Adler the photos and words are given space to breathe, made possible by its larger format. Published by Patagonia, it is, as you might expect, worthy of the coffee table.

Never feeling weighed down by history, it builds to a remarkable climax with the first ascent of the Nose in 1958. Wayne Merry's account of their eleven days on the 3,000ft wall in 'The Longest Climb', originally published in *Mariah* magazine, was the most gripping and compelling piece of writing in the book. It's quality is summed up perfectly in the essay's introduction: 'And for a few enchanted paragraphs we all become granite astronauts.'

The 'primitive' nature of the equipment available really struck home when Merry describes abseiling with over-the-shoulder friction and a pad to stop it cutting into your flesh. More than the 2014 historical film of Yosemite climbing *Valley Uprising*, Merry's words made me appreciate the herculean effort involved in the 1958 ascent of The Nose.

Co-authored by the writer John Long and photographer Dean Fidelman, the timeline of significant Yosemite first ascents traced by the book during the 1950s is punctuated with short biographical pieces, shining a spotlight on the leading protagonists from this era. These broader brushstrokes give a valuable and fascinating insight to the characters beyond their climbing

These images are taken from Yosemite in the Fifties: The Iron Age, edited by Dean Fidelman and John Long, with the permission of Patagonia. Individual photographers are credited after their image caption. For more details, see www.Patagonia.com/Books.

Above right: Mark Powell, Bill 'Dolt' Feverer and Warren Harding, c1957, hitting the cheap jug after a rainy exploratory climb on El Capitan. *(Beverly Powell Woolsey)*

Left: Overhanging Rock, Glacier Point, a favourite locale for 'I was there' photographs. *(Jerry Gallwas Collection)*

Middle right: Hardware rack from 1957. Pitons beyond two inches were lacking, so on wider cracks Iron Age climbers built them. *(Bill Feuerer Collection, Don Lauria)*

Bottom right: The sorcerer's apprentice. John Salathé stands at the shoulder of Yvon Chouinard, Camp 4, circa 1961. *(Tom Frost)* achievements: the likes of John Salathé, a man who heard voices, and Mark Powell, America's first rock jock.

As you might expect, it is Warren Harding's stubborn and roguish character that steals the show. A memorable caption accompanying the 1956 photo of him, Powell and Bea Vogle in his Jaguar convertible, reads: 'Harding went through three essentials at speed: tyres, wine and girls.' On the cover of the book he is the James Dean of climbing as he cuts a heroic figure prusiking on the west face of Leaning Tower.

Photo captions are often undervalued and nowadays added almost as an afterthought, but when I first read *Rock Climbers in Action* it was the synergy of some of the captions and photos that stayed with me. Gems such as: 'I has this dream, see, and I was falling upwards in a shaft of light,' describing *Pellagra* at Tremadog; Baillie 'bombing' up the *Gates* in the Pass; and 'You go, you commit yourself and it's the big effort that counts,' on *The Plum*.

If I have a criticism of this new edition it is the reproduction of some of the photos, particularly the new ones. I have a sense it is down to the scanning of the negatives, rather than a scan of a print, and some over-sharpening in Photoshop, as opposed to the printing itself. That aside, the book is still a unique insight to what Cleare describes as 'an especially interesting era in British climbing history – the final period when the leading activists were still disorganised 'weekenders' who trained on beer, smoked 20-a-day, drove like furies and thought it was all a big laugh.' The journey for the weekenders racing up to Wales from London was often as dangerous as the routes themselves, 'because the faster the car the sooner the climber gets to bed.'

In *Yosemite in the Fifties*, John Long writes: 'Every period has a footprint unique to its time and place,' and that is exactly what these two books reveal. While one highlights pushing into the unknown on Yosemite's big walls, and the other the gritty romance of poorly protected cragging, they are both inspiring reads.

Ray Wood

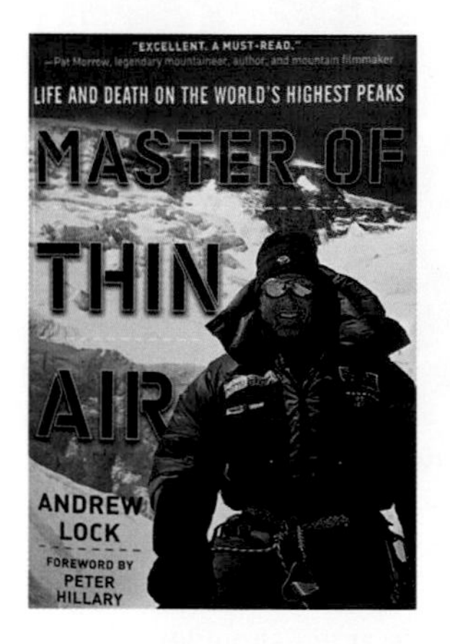

Master of Thin Air
Life and Death on the World's Highest Peaks
Andrew Lock
Arcade, 2015, pp332, $26

Andrew Lock was the first Australian to climb all 14 8,000m peaks and, if you don't accept Alan Hinkes' ascent of Cho Oyu, which remains disputed, the first from a Commonwealth country too. The feat took him 16 years and 23 expeditions. Although there are no startling new routes, and for the most part Lock sticks to regular routes, those 23 expeditions include attempts on significant challenges, like the Mazeno Ridge on Nanga Parbat with Rick Allen and Voytek Kurtyka, and he is a self-reliant man, carrying his own stuff and, like Tilman's herring, hanging by his own tail.

If you have any interest in the steroidal – literally and metaphorically speaking – world of high-altitude peak-bagging, this is the book for you. Lock is a driven man, not overly prone to introspection, straight-talking, opinionated but with a good sense of humour, which is from time to time directed at himself. He had an equally driven father, whose interests – money and prestige – were more conventional, understandably perhaps for someone who grew up in poverty. Lock himself prefers the great outdoors and as he enters adulthood experiments with ways of spending as much time outside as possible, setting off on a career in farming before swerving into a long stint as a Sydney cop, working undercover, and spending his holidays in the Greater Ranges. Later he took a degree in disaster management (your disaster, his management, not managing to have disasters) and worked in Antarctica.

His early high-altitude career wasn't propitious, out of his first six expeditions scoring just one success, K2, and witnessing half the climbers with whom he shared the summit dying on descent. This long and traumatic apprenticeship does seem to have served him well though, because his success rate shot up and he learned how to survive in a world that has a much higher tolerance of risk and death than around most of the climbing population, let alone the general one. In the course of his 8,000er career, he says that 20 friends lost their lives in the mountains, and catalogues them at the end of each chapter.

He was lucky to meet Anatoly Boukreev early on, learning a great deal from the Kazakh climber. Hearing Boukreev, an ethnic Russian, singing a folk song, Lock asks him what it means: 'I sing that the winter is cold, the snow is deep, the cattle is dead, the crops is failed, my wife is leave me and my children is in the war, but… life is okay.' Apart from the farming setbacks, that seems a pretty accurate description of the life Lock has chosen.

His antipathy for Hinkes is clear; they climbed Nanga Parbat together but, as Lock writes, 'I soon learned that Alan wouldn't break trail – he preferred to follow… I knew I was taking the risks and sacrificing my own fitness while Alan preserved his.' I've no doubt as the years passed Lock became adept at preserving his own fitness, but finding the right climbing partners in this rather strange world proved difficult. He seems to have been most happy on his 2006 expedition to Kangchenjunga with the popular Finn Veikka Gustafsson and Gerlinde Kaltenbrunner, also well liked among high-altitude climbers. Some things in alpinism don't change, it seems. Trust is everything.

His failure to climb Everest without oxygen clearly rankles but he is uncharacteristically coy about it. I suspect he's a man who doesn't like being thwarted. He has some pertinent things to say about the crummier end of commercial climbing in the Himalaya and how to fix it, although he's not alone in such opinions, which apparently count for little with the Nepali government in particular.

Ed Douglas

Runner
A Short Story about a Long Run
Lizzy Hawker
Aurum Press, 2015, pp288, £13

In Hawker's memoir, running returns to its most simplistic state. Breath, steps, freedom and pain. We pace her neat rhythm, as she races from a naïve student on the starting line of her first Ultra-Trail du Mont-Blanc (UTMB) to a world-record-breaking high-altitude runner on The North Face roster. In *Runner* Hawker collects her years between journeys of 'discovery', 'exploration' and 'rediscovery and realisation' as racing shows her, to her surprise, her lack of perceivable limits. It is a gentle meditation on the risk and beauty of ambition, though Hawker's ambition is so inherent it can only be heard reverberating in her footfall as she runs past.

She runs because she must, and you believe her when she reiterates that everything that has happened since that first naive UTMB is an accident of faith rather than strategic sportsmanship. She describes an intuitively monastic life, one of perpetual motion, rootless, though without any gypsy romance. Throughout her book Hawker is free from the usual trappings, or even pleasures the rest of us rely on: car, house, a meal more exciting than a cheese sandwich. There are few friends or lovers in her prose. She works and runs, and processes softly, and without arrogance, the wins and lessons running offers her.

Hawker's running takes her from road to the hills, to the fell and eventually to high altitude, and her time in Nepal provides a warm cultural balance to her background as a scientist. Both come together in her quest for simplicity. Working for the British Antarctic Survey provided Hawker with a stark, but safe wilderness to lean into. She thrives on minimalism, and though Nepal is chaotic, she is more comfortable in these environments where everything must be worked for and nothing in the distant future can be taken for granted. Like an extremely long run.

'There is a saying here in Nepal that says it how it is. *Ke garne?*

'What to do? – because sometimes you just don't know. And when you don't know what to do; then what do you do? You just go on doing what you do. You go on trying, you go on failing, you go on trusting, you go on loving, you go on living.'

In a *Guardian* interview, Hawker says her training tip is 'staying in the moment' and later 'and trusting in that'. This book is her eulogy to the moment and her developing faith that living temporally is a release from fear, and so gives her permission to risk failure and dream of where next to run. Before each chapter she passes our hand over a prayer, intention or aphorism, leaving it to spin behind the words as we continue on, following her journey past medals and injuries into pure running. In this way we review her experiences with the same revolving questions: how do we cope with injury, how do we stay in the moment, how do we trust, how do we win, how do we stay humble? To do this Hawker has to accept her identity as someone who spends the majority of her time running.

She makes two contrasting statements: 'Why do we run? It is an expression of who I am. That is why I run. Simply that.' But also: 'Running is a luxury.'

She swings between fearing preoccupation with a luxury, and trusting in this sport that is pulling her through her life and teaching her so much. The book is fractured; the lessons she describes are still in the process of being learnt. Hawker's fear of losing humility surfaces instead as fear of being seen. For example, the book begins with the dedication 'This is for you,' a powerful opening that a reader can fall into without hesitation. But then midway through, without explanation, Hawker stops speaking to the reader and the 'you' she is addressing becomes a partner, though we are never allowed to know how or why the reader has been replaced by a real figure in her life. How did she fall in love? Surely this process is important as a new third wheel in her life, spinning alongside her running and her work.

Despite this frustrating – if unsurprising – shyness, Hawker has written a trustworthy and thoughtful book. Held in her quiet, lyric cadence, her extreme experiences mirror our own rare moments of running flow, and fly us over the boundaries of footsteps and into that moment of space before we land.

Claire Carter

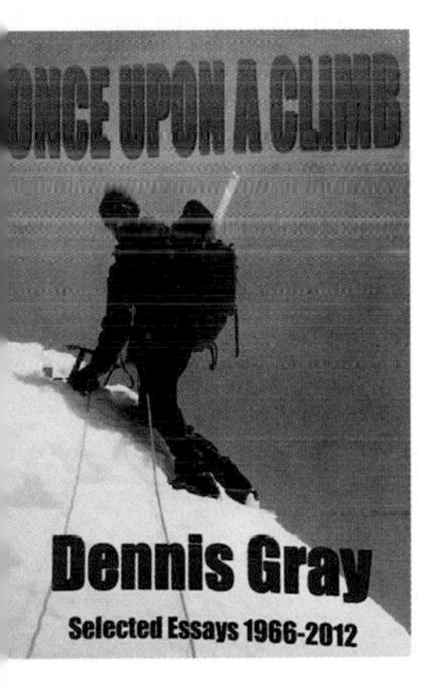

Once Upon A Climb
Selected Essays 1966-2012
Dennis Gray
Flux Gallery Press, 2015, 263pp, £11

Dennis Gray holds an almost unique place in British climbing, a good climber with experience stretching from the gritstone of his native Yorkshire to mountains like Gauri Sankar, a networker, with friends across time and space, having been close to Rock and Ice climbers like Joe Brown and Don Whillans, and pretty much every generation of climbers since, both at home and abroad, and a political operator, running the BMC as general secretary and being enmeshed in all sorts of controversies and causes that introduced him to yet more interesting people. In retirement he has travelled and studied in China, learned the language, and set off in new and unexpected directions. All through his life, however, he has remained an entertainer, something that shines through this book. Only Dennis Gray could give us sketches of Arthur Dolphin in his 'Red Flash' pumps and the reaction of rock god Patrick Edlinger at seeing a stripper take the stage in a northern club, catching Pete Livesey sneaking fibreglass into rock shoes or living in Edinburgh across the street from T Graham Brown.

Joe Brown getting ready for the fray, from Dennis Gray's *Selected Essays*, perhaps for the winner of the bout between Lovatt and Hughes on page 211. *(Doug Verity)*

The stories are largely set in the age of the classic British motorbike: Nortons, Ariels, Royal Enfields, BSAs and Triumphs roar past, with the apparently concomitant crashes which were mostly survived. The car driving was not much better. The dangers of the road blend into climbing. Trevor Peck in his Rolls Royce picking up the hitch-hiking Pete Biven, who was to become his climbing partner; Ned Kelly ice climbing the vertical turf of Slieve League in Donegal after endless alcoholic ceilidhs; Eric Beard and his record runs on the Cuillin and Lakeland – and many more. Naturally Brown, Whillans and Tom Patey make re-appearances, often with the same story fragment, but as in life, repetition does little harm. In Dennis Gray's hands, names in the back of guidebooks spring back to life, fleshing out characters and quirks, adding richness to our understanding of the sport.

I enjoyed his use of language, especially contemporary jargon. For example the Western Gully of Ysgolion Duon is 'a tigerish outing in the snow and I am not a tiger…' I didn't know people were still using 1940s climbing terms in 1972. There is more in the same vein, 'running-belays', 'hands, knees and daisies-a-bum' (still trying to work that one out) and so on. In the same way accents place language in space, this argot places the stories firmly in their time. And then he will quote the Chinese proverb *Wang tian men shan*. 'Look to the mountains and see a heaven.'

I have a couple of very minor gripes about the structure of the book. First, there is no index to cross-reference names. This is a pity in view of the historical value of the book; it would be good in future to be able to easily relate 'this' story with 'that' person, rather than the future inevitable: 'Oh yes, I remember reading it somewhere in Gray, but where?' Second, the contents list is inadequate; it consists only of a list of chapter titles and page numbers. I wanted to know the year of publication, since the range spans 48 years. But these are minor complaints. It's wonderful to think of him turning 60, flying to the States, buying a Buick for $800 and hitting the road for four months of cragging.

Victor Saunders

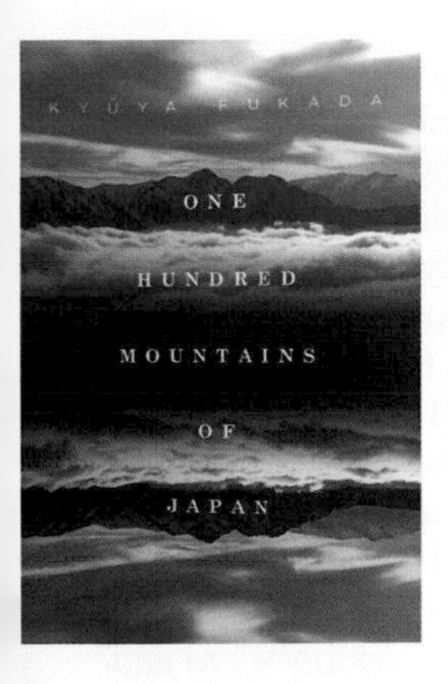

One Hundred Mountains of Japan
Kyuya Fukada
Translated by Martin Hood
University of Hawaii Press, 2015, pp240, £23.50

East of the Himalaya
Alps of Tibet & Beyond: Mountain Peak Maps
Tamotsu Nakamura
Japanese Alpine Club, 2016, pp334, £60

In 1910, an Austrian army officer and military attaché, Theodor von Lerch, was seconded to the 58th infantry regiment of the Japanese Imperial Army based in Takada. He had brought his skis with him with their, for the time, modern bindings. Japanese engineers at the Imperial Armoury in Tokyo had never seen such equipment before and yet within a month they managed to produce copies so good that even von Lerch couldn't tell the difference. He taught 30 officers how to ski, moved to Hokkaido and did something similar and in 1912 went home. Although Japan's ageing population has seen a fall in numbers from its peak, there are still eight million skiers there today.

Taken with the more familiar story of how the missionary Rev Walter Weston introduced alpinism to Japan, this story feeds into the trope of how Japan is great at copying the west – think motorbikes and tape recorders as well as skis – but not so innovative on her own. These two books should dispel that notion. First is a very welcome and very capable translation of Kyuya Fukada's *Nihon Hyakumeizan*, or *100 Mountains of Japan*. Fukada's translator, Martin Hood, (see also Hood's article in *AJ* 2015), describes this classic of Japanese mountain literature as 'a veteran mountaineer writing for a readership of fellow mountaineers.' Which begs the question: what, in Japan, is a mountaineer? Certainly more than Weston's muscular Christian; his parting shot, when he finally left the 'Japanese Alps' he had made famous, was that they had become too popular, having been taken over by artistic types. By then, Japanese mountaineers were dreaming of the same summits their western counterparts had made famous.

Fukada's great achievement was to produce a list of peaks, so appealing to many climbers, that was not simply comprised of the highest summits, or the most famous, but drawn from deep within Japanese culture and experienced over a lifetime, a list chosen, if you like, by a highly evolved aesthetic sense. Weston wouldn't approve, but Sir Hugh Munro, eat your heart out. The appeal of Fukada's list, as Hood explains in his excellent introduction, 'lies in the rich tradition of mountain literature that its author drew on.' Fukada was as much writer as climber, one with highly refined taste, reading Stendhal in his billet in Nanjing when he was passed news of the Japanese surrender in 1945. There are few alpinists who can draw comparisons between H W Tilman and the eighth-century monk Shodo. A peak's inclusion in his list relied as much on its religious traditions as its scenic grandeur. But Hood also points out that plenty of Japanese were climbing mountains just for fun long before Weston arrived. This minor literary masterpiece has been overlooked for too long in the west. If we had something similar for Scotland or the Alps, we would all be wiser.

Another happy synthesis of western inspiration with Japanese depth is revealed in a new book from the Club's honorary member Tamotsu Nakamura. For the last quarter of a century, Nakamura has made a detailed exploration of the eastern Himalayan region inspired, he explains in this new book, by the pundit Kishen Singh and the British explorers Frank Kingdon-Ward and F M Bailey. His methodical record of sketch maps and photographs has been inspiring alpinists ever since and this work brings together in one mammoth volume the fruits of that labour. This fully illustrated, large-format work, full of clear and useful map diagrams, is already a hit, and will remain a source of inspiration for years to come, a fitting climax to the work of Nakamura, who recently turned 82. The information on first ascents is incomplete, it seems to me; so if you're using it to plan one, do some digging elsewhere as well. But as a starting point for climbing and exploring all points east of Lhasa, this is a highly valuable resource. Highly recommended. (Copies of *East of the Himalaya* can be ordered from ibd@kinokuiya.co.jp)

Ed Douglas

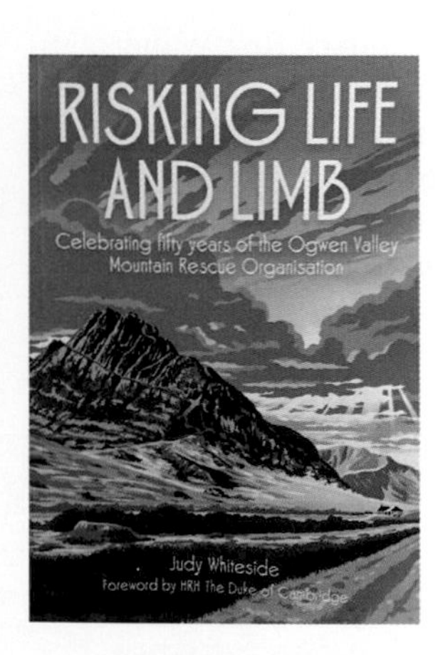

Risking Life and Limb
Celebrating Fifty Years of the Ogwen Valley Mountain Rescue Organisation
Judy Whiteside
OGVMRO, 2015, pp300, £18.50

The Ogwen Valley Mountain Rescue Organisation celebrated its 50th anniversary in 2015 and celebrated with this engagingly written, well-designed and beautifully illustrated history. Mountain rescue continues to be one of the great success stories of the voluntary sector in the UK, its original ethos of climbers looking after their own still intact, but the pressure of so many rescues – 140 at its peak in 2010 – is unrecognisable from the team's inception. There's some background history on rescue leading into the formation of the Ogwen team and a treasure trove of archive images that illustrate the rapid evolution of rescue equipment. Rich with anecdotes and notable rescues, an index would have been useful, given how useful a resource this book will be. (See also: obituary of Dr A S G Jones MBE, pp400-03)

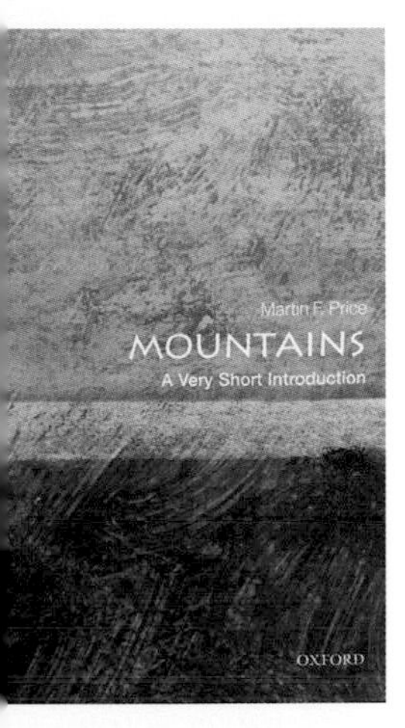

Mountains
A Very Short Introduction
Martin F Price
OUP, 2015, pp134, £8

The well-established format from OUP of 'very short introductions' turns its attention to mountains, in the very capable hands of Martin Price, director of the Centre for Mountain Studies at Perth College, University of the Highlands and Islands and UNESCO chair in sustainable mountain development. Price describes the origins of mountains and explains how, on geological timescales, they come and go. The combination of climate change, so high on the environmental agenda, alpinists' own experience of melting glaciers and population growth, it's demonstrably the case that the natural entropy we know so well in the mountains is going to be a critical issue for policy-makers around the world. A useful book for scientists, geographers and curious general readers alike.

Pembroke Rock
1000 Selected Rock Climbs
Emma Alsford and Paul Donnithorne
Wired Guides, 2016, pp416, £30

It's rare that you find yourself paying close attention to a publisher, but in this case there's a story. Few would disagree that the UK is in the happy position of producing many of the best rock-climbing guides in the world, but the arrival of independent publishers caused panic among the clubs which had fulfilled that task, with little reward, hitherto. For a while they got mad, now they have got even, with five major publishers – the Climbers' Club, the Fell & Rock Climbing Club, the BMC, the Scottish Mountaineering Club and the Yorkshire Mountaineering Club – joining together in a co-operative to share expertise, knowledge and enthusiasm and publish guidebooks. Pembroke Rock is the second they've produced in this new venture, joining a selected guidebook to the Lake District, and it's beautifully done. Culling the best routes from the Climbers' Club four-volume opus, this is the perfect solution for those who are less devoted to what for many is the best rock-climbing venue in England and Wales. The authors are steeped in knowledge and are ably assisted with stunning photo-diagrams prepared by Mark Davies. The ageing alpinist, looking for pleasurable cragging by the sea, should pay careful note to the crags around Lydstep. More power to Wired's co-operative elbows.

Obituaries

Tsering, Street trader, Kathmandu.
Rob Fairley, 2000. (Watercolour. 28cm x 20cm. Sketchbook drawing.)

In Memoriam

The Alpine Club Obituary	**Year of Election** (including to ACG)
Mike Binnie	1978
Robert Caukwell	1960
Lord Chorley	1951
Jim Curran	1985
John Disley	1999
Colin Drew	1972
David Duffield	ACG 1964, AC 1968
Chuck Evans	1988
Alan Fisher	1966
Robin Garton	2008
Terence Goodfellow	1962
Denis Greenald	ACG 1953, AC 1977
Dr Tony Jones	1976
Helge Kolrud	Asp 2011, 2015
Donald Lee	Assoc 2007
Ralph Villiger	2015
Prof Edward S Williams	1959

As usual, the editor will be pleased to receive obituaries for any of those above not included in the following pages.

Mike Binnie
1936 - 2016

Mike Binnie

Mike was born in Mumbai. He lived there for nine years until he went to prep school in Scotland. From there, he went on to Uppingham School, and then to Keble College, Oxford, to read law. While at Keble, Mike joined its climbing club and was also an active member of the OUMC, becoming its president. After going down in 1960, he joined the Oxford Andean expedition to Peru, led by Kim Meldrum. The team completed seven first ascents in the remote Allincapac (now more usually Allin Qhapaq) region, including the highest mountain in the area (5780m). After this, Mike took a job as an instructor at Ullswater Outward Bound, where he lived with his wife, Carol, and their young family for two and a half years.

In 1962, he returned to India to take up a post as a teacher at the Yadavindra public school in Patiala, 90 miles north-west of Delhi, and remained there for two years. This period included one mountaineering trip to Kashmir. He then returned to Oxford in 1964 to complete a diploma in education. Thereafter, Mike taught in a variety of schools in Lincolnshire, London and Surrey. In 1992, he took early retirement, so that he and Carol could join VSO in north-west Pakistan, where they established and ran a village school in the Hindu Kush. During his time there, Mike explored the many valleys and mountains leading up to the Afghan border. He completed these adventures with a solo trek across the Baroghil Pass into Afghanistan's Wakhan Corridor.

In 1996, Carol and Mike returned to the UK, to settle into a more comfortable retirement in their delightful cottage at Ockham, in woods close to the Surrey Hills. During his retirement, Mike became head of a trust running a children's orphanage in central India, Gwalior Children's Hospital. He and Carol visited it on several occasions.

Among other retirement projects in Surrey, Mike carved a 23ft cedar tree, which had fallen near his house during the great storm of 1987, into a Polynesian canoe. Decorated with carvings by his son Alex, and complete with an outrigger and sail, Mike and family sailed the canoe briefly and flamboyantly in the Solent after a launch party on West Wittering beach.

Because of his intense interest in and love for India and its traditions and spiritual life, Mike decided to circumnavigate the sacred Narmada river, the fifth-longest on the sub-continent. He undertook this 800-mile journey alone and on foot, starting at the river's outflow into the Indian Ocean. A long, hard, nine-week walk to the river's source then followed, during which Mike was entirely dependent on the goodwill and hospitality of the people who put him up at village houses and temples, in the tradition of the holy pilgrimage. Having completed half of his trip, Mike returned three years later to the river's source at the temple village of . He then followed the river's south bank, to reach its estuary nine weeks later. There, in a small open boat with about 30 other pilgrims, he crossed from the south bank to the north, a distance of about 20 miles, to arrive with much rejoicing at the village from where he had set out three years before.

Apart from collecting wood to heat his cottage, Mike was a dedicated writer. He published articles in various climbing journals, as well as the *Times Educational Supplement* and the *Guardian Weekly*. He also found time to write poetry throughout his adult life and in 2013 published a collection of his verse, entitled *Grieg's Piano Concerto in Calcutta* – a reference to his childhood experiences in India. He was also a longstanding member of Amnesty International.

In 2014, Mike and Carol moved back to Oxford, where they had met some 60 years before. Mike was a dedicated family man. He is survived by Carol, their four children and eight grandchildren.

Mike Binnie, submitted on his behalf by Kim Meldrum

Bernie Ingrams writes: I first met Mike on either an AC or CC UK meet in 1976. We started talking; very soon after, five of us – Robin Quine, George Backshall and Eddie Hicks from the Croydon MC, plus Mike and I – began planning a trip to East Africa for the following year. We had thought of climbing both Mount Kenya and Kilimanjaro but, unfortunately, the governments of Kenya and Tanzania were not at that time on speaking terms and the only way to travel between them was via an intermediate third country, Uganda being the obvious choice, although then under the control of 'Big Daddy' Idi Amin. So we ended up travelling to Kenya only. During our planning sessions, Mike was always full of enthusiasm.

After several days of acclimatisation on Mount Kenya, based at Kami hut, from where we walked up Point Lenana and climbed a rock ridge on Point Dutton, we went on to make an abortive summit attempt up the *Firmin-Hicks* route on Batian. As there were five of us, we had intentionally bivied part way up the route, but the following day, some way above the Tower, we experienced a very worrying electrical storm when our hair stood on end and our ice-axes and ironmongery started buzzing; we descended as fast as we could.

Mike, however, was still very determined to summit the mountain, so we split into two teams to try different routes. We only learnt after we had left the mountain that George and Robin did not get very far up theirs – Batian's *West Ridge* – before Robin began suffering from pulmonary oedema. Luckily, with help from a couple of UK trainee doctors and the national park staff, they made it off the mountain and Robin made a complete recovery. In the meantime, Mike, Ed and I attempted the *Southern Slabs* route, which was then under winter conditions. Mike tried for a long time to force the ice route, but to no avail, so we found a way to circumvent the iced slabs and eventually made our way up to the summit of Nelion, where the three of us spent a cosy night in the Howell bivy hut. The following day, we climbed across the Gate of the Mists to Batian, and then descended by the *Firmin-Hicks*.

After the mountain, the rest of us travelled by train to Mombasa for a few days' rest – but not Mike: he left immediately to travel round the Kenyan countryside, to explore and visit local villages. Mike was great company on the trip and always a thoroughly interesting person to talk to. He will be missed by many friends from all his walks of life.

Robert Arthur Caukwell
1928 - 2015

Robert hailed from Bognor Regis and was educated at Kingham Hill School in the Cotswolds. This was followed by national service in Palestine and Libya. In 1948, he joined his brother John as a teacher at a prep school in Nairobi. He had, however, started climbing well before this time.

With his ironic sense of humour, Bob, as he was usually known, savoured his 'progression' from the Greater Ranges to the Alps. While serving in the Kenya Regiment as a surveyor – he had joined its mapping unit in 1949 – during the Mau Mau uprising in 1953, he spent weeks in the Aberdares. The magnificent view of Mount Kenya inspired and distracted him, to the consternation of his fellow surveyor and soldier passengers, who preferred him to focus his attention on the frequent hairpins and greasy surface of the clay tracks on which he was driving.

Not that he needed further inspiration. His focus was Mount Kenya's awesome west face. At that time, it was still snow-plastered, the equatorial equivalent of an Alpine north face. In shadow in the clear early mornings and normally cloud-covered in the afternoon, the combination of snowfall and rime nurtured a great steep sweep of névé and two menacing hanging glaciers. It had never been attempted.

Bob had taken a close look in 1952 from Point Pigott. He had picked out a line and, conscious of his negligible experience on ice, had waited. A year later, the Kenya Emergency closed the mountain to the public.

A trip to the Ruwenzori supplied the ice experience but with Mount Kenya still officially closed, the wait continued until January 1955. Rumour reached him of a rival overseas team's interest in the west face. Officialdom was ignored. He recruited a visiting South African, Gerald Rose, who had even less ice experience and gave it a go.

They got lucky: the bergschrund was choked; there was mostly névé in which steps could be kicked; the weather was clear and cold. Boldness was rewarded: the ice-axe brake worked when a step gave way and the belay was not tested by Bob's 30ft slide. Crafty route finding took them through the steep, intimidating headwall, which gave the hardest climbing of the day. Nightfall saw them over the summit and onto the Diamond glacier. Its notoriously hard ice had a good snow cover and they soon reached the *Normal Route* where it crosses the south-east ridge.

Abbing in the dark was a double nightmare. After one rope length, they shared a ledge and the search for a belay. Half their ledge gave way, taking Rose with it. He stopped, fatally injured, after tumbling over 200ft. Bob waited with him for an hour but he never regained consciousness. To quote the letter supporting Bob's AC application: 'He did extraordinarily well after the accident… [he] climbed down to the foot of the peak and ran 20 miles down the mountain at night to summon help.' Inevitably, this event came to the attention of the authorities; they had no alternative but to put a formal reprimand on his civil service record. This was softened by the informal and well-earned compliments he received on his performance.

That year, however, got worse. Arthur Firmin, the doyen of Kenya climbing, had asked to be considered for the 1953 Mount Everest Expedition. His lack of Himalayan experience was probably a sufficient reason for his rejection. He proposed a Himalayan trip to compensate for this and chose the formidable Himalchuli (7893m) as his objective. Bob joined the expedition as probably the best young climber in Kenya. While long on enthusiasm and optimism, the party of six had only two or three committed climbers.

From the start, being short of time and funds, they were out of luck. A strike in Mombasa delayed them, their ship sailed unladen and everyone was seasick. Customs bureaucracy in Bombay (now Mumbai) took days. The only certainty on the rail journey was of further delay. The continuing monsoon made the trek a forgettable experience, only rarely relieved by brief views of the mountains. 'Trying' was Bob's understated verdict.

It got worse. They reached snow, five miles and 4,500ft below their proposed base camp. Their 70 barefoot porters voted with (and for!) their feet. The climbers exhausted their time and energy in a futile effort to reach the foot of the mountain, which, now they could see it, was a hopeless prospect. A couple of brief sorties onto the lowest slopes confirmed this. Real disaster then hit them: a boulder fell on Firmin and broke his thigh. The party needed ten days to reach the hospital at Pokhara, but Firmin died on the ninth.

Bob then went on leave to Britain. He revelled in the rock climbing. He was a natural, being compact and strong (he had been a champion gymnast), bold yet canny. He progressed from the VS classics to the new XS grades. On *Kaisergebirge Wall* he made an inadvertent but significant contribution to safety: he fell off. The ex-Army karabiner literally unfolded under a modest load. A photo of it was widely circulated in 1956 by the BMC and convinced everyone that, while this kit was cheap, it was not cheerful! Bob was fielded by a holly tree and completed the route: a hard man!

His luck had changed. He enjoyed a couple of good Alpine seasons with traverses of half a dozen major peaks, including the Matterhorn via the

Zmutt Ridge. He gave up serious climbing after marriage: he knew how hard it is for those who lose spouses.

Bob had resigned from the Survey of Kenya in 1968, taking up a post as lecturer in land surveying at Nairobi University. On his return there, his last big contribution came in 1970. A 'worst case' accident involved a victim with a badly broken leg in Shipton's Notch, a few metres lower than the 5000m summit and some distance along the west ridge. The local resources, especially of able, acclimatised manpower, were organised effectively by Bob. Although it took a week, the rescue route on the mountain was rigged and the casualty brought down to where the Austrian rescue team could take over and complete the job in hours.

After returning to England with his wife, Margarette, to make their home in Brockenhurst, the last decade of Bob's life was stolen from him by Parkinson's Disease. He bore this condition with characteristic dignity and courage.

John Temple

Bill Jackson writes: 'Kenya needs 16 keen and fit young men who are fond of an open-air life. They are wanted for jobs that will take them all over the Colony, and will give them chances to see the mountains, lakes, deserts and bush country of East Africa and see the big game that lives in these areas.'

This notice in the *East African Standard* in February 1949 was a turning point in Robert's career. Following 'demob' from national service, he had joined his elder brother John as a teacher at a prep school in Nairobi, and struggled to impart the elements of Latin grammar to his class. He made his escape after reading the *East African Standard* and becoming one of the lucky 16 keen and fit young men. They joined the government Survey of Kenya with the job title 'survey cadet'. After preliminary training in the basics of land surveying they spent their early years on safari in the Northern Frontier District.

When a state of emergency was declared in 1952, security forces were handicapped by a lack of up-to-date maps, so in April 1953 a mapping unit was formed in the Kenya Regiment. Their task was to provide information to be added to outline maps compiled from RAF aerial photography. In short, they were required to travel over every road and track, locate every village, and obtain place names, and in the case of European farms, record the owner's name.

Robert was one of the Survey of Kenya's staff to join the unit – as was I. Supplied with a Sten gun, two hand grenades, aerial photographs and outline maps, our first operational area was Isiolo, which had not seen any Mau Mau activity, then Nyeri Station and the less peaceful areas of Chehe and Ragati forests. As a keen climber, Robert was delighted to get so close to Mount Kenya, but had a disconcerting habit of looking at the mountain peak while driving round hairpin bends.

We were both released from the regiment on completion of the mapping task in 1954, and after overseas leave returned to our posts with Survey of Kenya. Robert was a very active member of the Mountain Club of Kenya, and in January 1955 made the first ascent of the west face of Mount Kenya. Later that year he was a member of the MCK expedition to Nepal attempting to climb Himalchuli, which saw the tragic death of Arthur Firmin.

A friend for 65 years, Robert lived up to the definition: 'half the joy of a friend is that he is a person to whom you can, from time to time, boast about trivial things.' His boast to me was his name on the honours board at Kingham Hill School as best individual gymnast 1944 aged 16. Perhaps that's how he became a mountaineer.

The last 10 years of his life were spent in a nursing home at Milford on Sea, suffering from that cruel disease Parkinson's. He had gazed into the distance from mountaintops, but towards the end he shuffled along with his Zimmer to sit on a bench and stare at the Needles lighthouse. I'm sure he was studying the cliffs of Alum Bay, figuring out the best route to the top. I said *kwaheri* to him two days before he died.

'Mountains possess a power of taking a man by the hand, whatever his religion or calling, whatever his beliefs, whatever his sins or sorrows, and of leading him upwards to immeasurable happiness.'

Lord Chorley
1930 - 2016

With the death of Roger Chorley on 21 February 2016, the Alpine Club has lost one of the most distinguished, loyal and innovative members in its long history.

The son of Robert Chorley, first Baron Chorley, Roger was educated at Stowe School and at Gonville and Caius College, Cambridge. He became president of the Cambridge University Mountaineering Club and graduated in 1953. His parents' love of mountains was the inspiration for Roger's own passion for mountaineering and the environment. Roger's mother was a Hopkinson, that distinguished mountaineering family. She was a vice-president of the FRCC and went on to become president of the Ladies' Alpine Club in 1953. Roger's father was a president of the FRCC; he became vice-president of the AC in 1957. Roger's own name appears in lists of first ascents of some Welsh rock climbs. The happy conjunction of two strands of Roger's life as an accountant with a passion for mountaineering led him to become a very long-serving honorary treasurer of the Club. He was vice-president in 1975 and then president in 1983.

Always a true internationalist, Roger was much in demand by organisations as varied as the National Board for Prices and Incomes, the Royal Commission on the Press, the Ordnance Survey Review and the British Council. In the 1980s, Roger chaired the enquiry into the handling of geographic information and was a member of the National Environment Research Council. In 1987, he was made president of the Royal Geographical Society. Following reforms to the House of Lords, he was elected in

2001 as one of the hereditary peers to remain as a working peer, sitting as an independent on the cross-benches until his retirement in 2014. He became visiting professor at Imperial College in 1979 and received honorary degrees from several universities.

By far his most demanding and historically significant role arose when he took over the chair of the National Trust in 1991. Before that, Roger had chaired the Trust's finance committee for many years. Under his professional scrutiny, the National Trust policy on land and property acquisition was formalised in 1968 as the 'Chorley Formula', a calculation of endowment required; it is applied to most acquisitions, up to and including the present day.

Lord Chorley

Roger became a member of the Alpine Club in 1951. In 1952 he was invited to address the Club – at the age of 21, the youngest member to do so – and as a result of this intervention the Alpine Climbing Group came about. This 'ginger' group broke down class barriers and included women members from the outset.

In 1952, together with George Band, Roger undertook a glacier-tunnelling project on Monte Rosa for an American geologist millionaire. It was demanding, high-altitude work and of course he and George climbed together on their days off. This project was to have far-reaching consequences. They were paid in Swiss Francs when UK currency restrictions were still in force and could thus afford an extended Alpine season.

They were also fit, from all that tunnelling, allowing them to climb the *Cresta di Santa Caterina* on the Nordend. Later in the season, with Ted Wrangham, they completed the the Mer de Glace face of the Grépon via the Knubel Crack. Later still, with Arthur Dolphin and Ian McNaught-Davis, they made the first ascent of the north ridge of the Aiguille du Peigne and the south ridge of the Aiguille Noire de Peuterey. During the following spring, George Band was chosen as the youngest team member of the 1953 expedition to Mount Everest.

In 1954, the Cambridge University Mountaineering Club attempted the first ascent of the Karakoram peak Rakaposhi (7788m), a formidable challenge. Although the weather robbed them of their attempt on the summit, they achieved much and gave, in Eric Shipton's words, 'A fine example of what can be achieved by a privately conducted expedition on a high and difficult peak.'

In the company of Hamish Nicol, John Tyson, Dick Viney and Tom Bourdillon, Roger visited the Baltschiedertal hut in 1956. Bourdillon and Viney set off to attempt a nearby peak but did not return. Fearing the worst, Roger and John climbed up to the glacier at the foot of the Jägihorn and found them still roped together: they were dead. There is a view that their deaths ended a golden age of mountaineering.

Wilfred Noyce invited Roger early in 1957 to join an expedition to Machapuchare, then known as Fish Tail, in Nepal. This was to be Roger's last major mountain expedition; he developed polio at camp one. Noyce and David Cox climbed to within 150ft of the summit before being defeated by a blinding snowstorm. The after-effects of polio would restrict Roger throughout the rest of his life but by no means end climbing for him.

George Band introduced me to Roger after we climbed together on an AC 1991 expedition to the Bhutan Himalaya. At that time, I was living in the Lake District. In due course, Roger said to me: 'I live in London but my home is in the Lake District.' It was clear from then on that we shared a love of travel, mountains, architecture and photography, which soon became the foundation of our travels together.

In 1996, George Band, as president of the British Mountaineering Council, was charged with investigating the possibility of creating a museum of mountaineering to show how the sport had evolved. By 2001, the National Mountaineering Exhibition was completed and officially opened by Tony Blair. This led to the foundation of the Mountain Heritage Trust under the chair of Sir Chris Bonington, with Roger Chorley, George Band and others as trustees. Roger, once again, used his administrative skills to steer the trust through its formative years. Indeed, his final generous gesture was to give the MHT the Chorley Hopkinson Library of mountaineering books, now housed in the National Trust property Allan Bank in Grasmere.

Throughout this period, we travelled extensively, with our wives. The first of many journeys was through Central Asia into north-west China, then down the Karakoram Highway to the foothills of Rakaposhi. In matters of travel, Roger was a minimalist: the smallest suitcase possible always accompanied us, its contents closely guarded. We visited Chile to explore Patagonia and the Straits of Magellan, as well as Peru and Machu Picchu. In Europe, our pursuit of perfection in the art of the Baroque – always with a critical eye – led us to Bohemia, Bavaria and the Czech Republic. It soon became clear that Roger was in some ways a frustrated architect, full of appreciation and understanding of space, decoration, proportion and composition. His artistic talent was further evident in his outstanding photography. It was in mountains and architecture that he found beauty and inspiration, for he had an extraordinarily refined and acute instinct for mountain topography.

It was a privilege to have known Roger as friend and companion: a man of wisdom and wit. Life with him was fun. He will be greatly missed by all who share the activities that he graced. Our heartfelt sympathies go to Ann and her sons Nicholas and Robert, their families and the grandchildren.

John Innerdale

Steve Town writes: If, in the early 1980s, someone had asked, 'Why does the Alpine Club exist?' the best answer would probably have been, 'Because it's there.' It was the 'Temple of Mountaineering', in the words of a previous president, a wonderful repository of knowledge and experience. But it looked back, not forwards. Elected president for the years 1983-5, Roger applied his talents to developing a fresh approach to the role and function of the Club, with a look to the future.

Picking up on recent trends in mountaineering, Roger quickly realised that the focus was changing. His analysis of these changes is encapsulated in his valedictory address published in the 1986 edition of the *Journal*. The focus of mountain exploration and adventure that had led to the foundation of the Club over a hundred years earlier had moved from the Alps to the Himalaya and other high and remote mountain ranges; modern transport made such change possible for the mass of climbers, not just a monied and leisured elite.

Roger embarked on a programme both to re-invigorate the Club and focus interest on the Greater Ranges. Thus, in 1984, the Club hosted a symposium on lightweight expeditions to the Greater Ranges, the first in a series of symposia about mountain exploration that has continued for many years. He recognised the problems of getting information about such areas; his efforts in fundraising and planning led to the creation of the comprehensive, computerised Himalayan Index, which continues to be a major source of information about climbing in that part of the world. And he encouraged a series of initiatives to bring life into the Club, including an increased lecture programme, and more meets at home, in the Alps and further afield. The Alpine Climbing Group, of which Roger had been a founding member, was at risk of disintegrating; considerable effort was put into building a firmer relationship with the Club, while retaining the ACG's distinct identity.

Roger deployed his skills as an administrator to superb effect. His skills of leadership and diplomacy in public life are well recorded elsewhere. He was conscious of his wider standing, and knew how to use it to best advantage. Thus, the support and trust of a vocal dissident AC member with strong socialist affiliations was won over at a quiet lunch in the House of Lords dining room.

Although polio had sadly put an early end to his climbing career, he retained his deep interest and commitment. I recall an occasion when he dropped in at the Club's rooms for an informal meeting and happened upon a couple of young members who had recently done the *Peuterey Intégral*. Business was postponed while Roger, who with George Band had made possibly the first British ascent of the south ridge of the Aiguille Noire over thirty years earlier, enthusiastically exchanged memories with them. He remained, above all, part of the fellowship of mountaineers.

Richard Coatsworth writes: Roger was the best chair of any committee I have been on. He ensured that everyone spoke, and no one person held the stage. Committee meetings were well planned in advance and business was conducted so that decisions were made. Meetings were limited to one hour at a time. All officers were phoned every Sunday night so that Roger kept us all – sometimes somewhat ruefully – on our toes, and focused on the jobs to be done, to make sure we completed everything to his satisfaction. He went on from being president of the AC to that of the RGS, and was proud to have been the last unpaid chairman of the National Trust, seeing it through a difficult period with much time expended on debating deer-hunting on NT land.

Mike Baker writes: I got to know Roger well when I became the AC's hon secretary in 1972. By then, he was already distinguished in mountaineering circles as a member of the Alpine Climbing Group, an experienced Himalayan and Alpine climber, a member of the management committee of the MEF, and a former president of the CUMC and hon secretary of the Climbers' Club. He was also a long-established partner of the prestigious London accountants Cooper Brothers, as they then were, from 1967 to 1989. To me, a callow youth in his twenties, Roger was the embodiment of urbanity and sophistication though, on reflection and making a quick calculation, he was only a decade or so older than me. His friendship and support, however, were extended unconditionally and unstintingly as was his wise advice and assistance.

Two memories of Roger spring to mind. The first, illustrative of the negotiating skills his obituarists have noted, was the anxiety and the wholly benevolent and careful scheming which preceded his bearding of the Club's housekeeper, the formidable and cantankerous but fiercely loyal Mrs Lewis, with a view to getting her to accept retirement. To the surprise of all involved – perhaps not least herself – she accepted it like a lamb after an interview with Roger. The second memory is of his disarming wit. For some reason, some sections of the Club always wanted their sixpenny-worth at the Annual Meeting. At the AGM one year, Roger's hon treasurer's report to the assembled members consisted simply of the words, 'In the last twelve months we have made a profit. Are there any questions?' That silenced even the 'tribal chieftains', the likes of the late great Douglas Milner.

Of course, Roger's career became increasingly distinguished in later life after he succeeded his father in 1978. By no means his least contribution at this time was the leadership he gave as president of our own Club. He played a major role in the reintegration of the ACG into the main body of the Club; he led the move to merge the Club with the LAC when the issue of admitting women was raised; and, perhaps his greatest legacy, it was he who spearheaded the move to form the Library into a charitable trust, allowing us to preserve and nurture our greatest treasures.

Roger's love of mountains, and especially of the Lakeland hills, could be seen in the pictures throughout the Hawkshead house he and Ann cherished. Understated as he was, he ended his president's valedictory address with a quotation which reflects exactly that love, and which has a particular poignancy given his disability. He said: 'Perhaps the last word should be indeed on our own hills, from Geoffrey Young, in reflective mood at the end of a unique Alpine career, "For me, too, our own hills, within the measure of my walking, are as lovely and as full of surprises as they ever were."'

Jim Curran
1943 - 2016

Jim Curran in Tibet in 1997. *(John Porter)*

Alas, another of the climbing world's great characters, not to mention an author, film-maker and artist, has gone.

My first encounter with Jim took place at The Moon, a popular meeting pub for climbers in Stoney Middleton, Derbyshire in those far-off days of more relaxed drinking and driving laws. It was Paul Nunn who introduced me to his art lecturer companion, modishly rigged out, with flared jeans, long hair and drooping moustache. Happily, it was to be the first of many meetings, all of which were fun.

Jim's early life was spent in Ealing, London. It was while he was at school there that he made his first visit to southern sandstone in the rather unlikely and highly private Chiddingly Wood. It was a visit that changed his life and started his lifelong love affair with climbing.

Jim came from a cultured family. Both parents were musicians, as is his younger brother Phil. Jim's talent was for art: he started his artistic studies at Ealing Art School. His passion for climbing was at first satisfied by weekends on southern sandstone, which inevitably led to holidays in North Wales then further afield to the Pyrenees, Dolomites and Western Alps. His progress as a climber was slow but sure.

After his degree, Jim did his teacher training in Manchester where he met his first wife, Ali. He quickly decided to dodge the drudgery of school teaching and successfully applied for a lecturing post at Rotherham Art College. It was a happy move. He found a house in Sheffield, a city to which

Jim Curran, Brian Hall and Tony Riley at Pembroke in 1981. *(John Porter)*

he was to become closely attached and where he became the father of two lovely girls; his love of Derbyshire and its gritstone edges continued to grow.

In 1970, fearing that his Rotherham post was to be a victim of educational reforms, he applied to be a lecturer on the foundation course at Bristol Polytechnic. This marked the beginning of a long and rather unsettled time for Jim as he shuttled endlessly between Bristol and Sheffield. At first, he was not entirely happy in his new post; his marriage broke down. He entered a period of self-doubt and uneasy depression.

Life brightened when Jim took a postgraduate course in filmmaking in Sheffield; once again he had found an art form that excited him, a form of creativity that he could happily combine with his love of climbing. His first film, made with Tony Riley, was *A Great Effort*, a version of Menlove Edwards' classic essay. The film was well received. Jim and Tony then offered to make a film of our second and successful Trango expedition, joining Joe Brown, Mo Anthoine, Malcolm Howells and me. It was a joyful trip, with much laughter and good companionship.

It was a pity that the film, which could have been a minor classic, was largely ruined by fogging of so much of their crucial footage that it had to be abandoned. The film might have been spoiled but Jim made amends by demonstrating another of his great talents by writing *Trango: The Nameless Tower*. It was to be the first of several fluent and entertaining books.

For the next few years Jim concentrated his efforts on film and in 1979 made his first really significant film, *The Bat*, based on an article by Robin

Smith about a first ascent on Ben Nevis, once again made with Tony Riley, and with Brian Hall and Rab Carrington, respectively, acting as Smith and Dougal Haston. It was a satisfying and intense film, which premiered at the first Kendal Mountain Film Festival in 1980. Jim co-created the festival with Brian Hall and John Porter, an event that instantly achieved cult status. The story of the first attempt to screen the film – see below – is both funny and typical of the chaos that occasionally accompanied Jim's greatest successes.

A succession of expedition films followed; in 1981 he recorded the ascent of Kongur with Chris Bonington, Alan Rouse, Pete Boardman and Joe Tasker. His friendship with Alan Rouse led to his filming on K2 in the terrible season of 1986. After its sequence of disasters and death, Jim was persuaded to write *K2, Triumph and Tragedy*, which many consider his outstanding work. The tragedy was heartfelt, since it included the loss of one of his best friends, Al Rouse.

He followed this with a history, *K2: The Story of the Savage Mountain*, which won the non-fiction prize at Banff Mountain Festival, and *High Achiever*, a biography of his friend Chris Bonington. There was a collection of essays, *Suspended Sentences*, and an account of his epic cycle ride from Muckle Flugga to Land's End, *The Middle-Aged Mountaineer*. His last and in my opinion best book was *Here, There and Everywhere*, a memoir which gives an honest and, as ever, amusing account of his life, loves, tragedies and climbs.

Throughout his years of lecturing, filming, making elegant and witty after-dinner speeches and writing about climbing, it is a wonder that he had any time for recreational climbing, but Jim had a capacity for hard work when it was necessary. His film-making continued apace with trips to St Kilda and the Caucasus, where he climbed Elbrus. He filmed for TV and made an Emmy award-winning film of Catherine Destivelle soloing the Old Man of Hoy. He twice filmed on Everest, in the Andes, the Atlas and Tibet. He also filmed an Anglo-Indian expedition to Kinnaur with Chris Bonington, Paul Nunn and Jim Fotheringham, among others. His final two expeditions were to Sepu Kangri in Tibet with Chris Bonington.

Jim was proud of his achievements. Equally, he could be sensitive to sniping and unjust criticism. He was not unnaturally deeply hurt not to have won the Boardman Tasker prize despite being shortlisted no fewer than five times. With typically self-deprecating humour, he shrugged off his disappointment, which was only partly assuaged by receiving a Boardman Tasker lifetime award in 2014. He was less inclined to dismiss what he considered a damaging slight to his safety as a climber when Jim Perrin named him (perhaps light-heartedly, perhaps not) as one of his worst climbing partners. He was not alone in this category but it so happened that all the others were dead. There followed an unpleasant and protracted legal battle perhaps best forgotten.

Throughout Jim's many trips abroad he maintained his love of rock climbing. He was a safe and determined rock climber who never realized the dizzy heights of the highest standards, but that did not matter to him.

He was always a reliable second, ready to have a go, and he managed to climb many fine routes with a grace that belied his large size.

Size was to become a problem in later years as he began to suffer with his joints, in particular his knee. The lack of mobility led to an increase in weight and the end of his rock climbing. Following knee replacement he suffered all manner of distressing illnesses.

His demise as a rock climber was not all bad news, since it allowed him to revive his artistic talent. He had long yearned to return to his art; now he had the time to devote to it. The subjects of his paintings were largely the mountains and landscapes of his life. He produced a bold series of architectural works of Trango, Mount Kenya and notably the mountains around Sella in Spain. He exhibited his work in the Alpine Club in 2004 and finally in his Sheffield studio in 2014. For his last exhibition there, opened by Chris Bonington, he miraculously recovered sufficiently to leave his hospital bed to make his customary welcoming speech.

His last set of paintings was appropriately a homage to his first climbs on sandstone. He painted some large oils of High Rocks and a series of very good, delicate watercolours that capture the rocks to perfection.

Jim was always a delightful companion. He made many warm and lasting friendships and it is remarkable how long some of these go back, not least to the late Steve Durkin, his companion on his first climbs. He was perhaps less lucky with his romantic liaisons. His second marriage to Lorraine came to naught, but despite his chequered love life he always remained a devoted father to his daughters, Gemma and Becky.

Jim's last years were a torment of ill health and stays in hospital. We visited him several times there when he was at death's door. Amazingly, he would recover sufficiently to put aside his breathing mask and crack a joke so that one left with a smile. Jim never did give in easily; he was determined to die in his own home. Thankfully he did, peacefully, with his daughters at his side.

Jim may have considered himself a jack-of-all-trades but he was a man of enormous talent. His achievements will last. He will be much missed.

Martin Boysen

John Porter writes: It is difficult to know from the many stories about and by him, which best illustrates Jim's spirit, a kind of self-deprecating sarcasm. In perfect tune with this spirit, Maggie Body quipped: 'Jim would have been most impressed that Chris Bonington spent the second day of his honeymoon at his funeral.'

The story of the premiere of *The Bat* at the Kendal Film Festival has taken on the proportions of an epic for those of us who attended it. It was scheduled for a Saturday afternoon in October 1980 in the United Church just up from the Brewery Arts Centre. The church held around 400, the largest venue in Kendal in those days. First thing on Saturday morning, a team of local climbers clambered onto the roof to cover all the windows with sheets of black plastic while others fitted up the church balcony as the projection box. All worked very well during the morning programme. But unknown to us, including Jim, the church's usual vicar had not told his replacement that the church had been rented for the whole weekend. 'Vicar Two' arrived around 11.30am to prepare for a 12.30pm wedding and found a congregation of climbers occupying his church. Brian Hall and I told him: 'No problem, we'll sort it.' We didn't dare tell Jim.

At noon, the film programme finished. As the audience headed for the pub, we went into action. One team took down the black plastic, another picked up the empties from under the pews and others helped install the flowers. As the first of the wedding party arrived, everything looked just about normal. The wedding took place on schedule, and as the bride and groom left, up went the lads with the black plastic. By 2pm, the church was again full of climbers shuffling expectantly in anticipation of Jim's much-heralded new film. Ten minutes later, Jim arrived with his precious spool, which was taken up to the balcony where our half-blind projectionist was waiting to thread the film. Jim gave a very brief introduction, then shouted up: 'Roll 'em!'

The screen spluttered into life with the initial credits – but something was wrong: with only minutes to re-install the blackout plastic, some of the sheets were already slipping off and light was creeping onto the screen, which by now had begun to show the opening credits out of focus. Everyone remained silent, in the hope that the situation would sort itself out, when there was a mighty shout: 'Stop! That's enough!' Looking down from the balcony, I saw Jim emerge, arms waving in fury in all directions, but particularly towards us standing at the projector. 'This isn't good enough! This isn't good enough! My film is not being shown in f*****g abysmal conditions! That's the end of it!' Jim carried on for some time, lambasting the state of our world and everyone in it. There was a murmur of approval as the congregation took Jim's side.

'Okay, Jim!' Brian shouted down in his best Mr Fixit voice, 'we'll sort it and show the film this evening.' The drama ended and the congregation filed out, unexpectedly entertained by Jim rather than his film. We patched up the church blackout and managed to complete the screening of the afternoon film programme. At 7pm, the church was more than packed with a crowd wondering what might happen next. With a new projectionist, and extra care, the film was shown in focus, with audible gasps during the fall and cheers at the end. This film clearly added something completely new to the climbing-movie genre. At the close, Jim stood at the front of the church to take applause and cheers, a day none of us ever forgot, and a special moment for Jim.

John Disley CBE
1928 - 2016

John Disley is followed by Eric Langmuir during the 1969 attempt. Langmuir, then head of Glenmore Lodge, had laid on resupply at Dalwhinnie and Glenshee ski areas. *(John Cleare/ Mountain Camera Picture Library)*

John died on 8 February, at the age of 87. To the general public, he was a famous athlete from that bygone era when Olympians were amateurs. His event was the 3,000m steeplechase, for which he held the Commonwealth record in 1952 and the world record in 1955, only missing Olympic gold in Melbourne in 1956 because of a bout of pneumonia; in the event Chris Brasher won the gold.

But steeplechasing was not John Disley's only claim to fame, for he was already well known in climbing and mountaineering circles, especially in his native Wales. He was born in Corris, near Cadair Idris, and as a boy had run the three and a half miles to school every day because buses were infrequent and it seemed the obvious thing to do; he had not seen a running track until he went up to Loughborough to study PE.

In 1948 and 1949, before he was captured by competitive athletics, he was involved, with such celebrated rope-mates as Peter Harding and Tony Moulam, in a dozen or so first ascents of Llanberis Pass rock climbs, such as *Kaisergebirge Wall* and *Brant Direct*, these being among the harder routes at that time. He was elected to the Climbers' Club in 1949.

He was a fell-runner, too. In 1952, fit from the Olympics, he broke the existing Welsh 14 3,000ft peaks record by three minutes. This gruelling challenge covers a distance of over 22 miles linking all the 3,000ft summits from Snowdon to Foel Fras, with almost 10,000ft of ascent in the process. His time was 7h 24m.

John taught PE at Isleworth grammar school, which he joined in 1951. At that time, educationalists were starting to realise the value of outdoor pursuits and adventure training; in 1955, the Central Council for Physical Recreation, later the Sports Council, established Plas y Brenin at the former Royal Hotel in Capel Curig as an innovative, residential mountain centre. Sir John Hunt was its chairman of trustees. Disley, now an experienced PE teacher and seasoned mountaineer, was appointed chief instructor and

John Disley and Chris Brasher making a river crossing in the 1968 attempt to ski across Scotland somewhere up between the head of Glen Nevis and Loch Treig. Brasher has already crossed; Disley is crossing. The following year offered a better frost and the team were able to ski down one river for a while. *(John Cleare/Mountain Camera Picture Library)*

over three years was instrumental in developing a benchmark curriculum for training students in mountain skills: fell walking, rock climbing, navigation, kayaking and so on.

In 1957, John married Sylvia Cheeseman, herself a 1952 Olympian, and worked for some years in the 1960s as an inspector of education and organiser of outdoor education for Surrey. Intrigued by all things Scandinavian, it was Disley who brought orienteering to Britain about this time, and in partnership with Chris Brasher organised its establishment as a serious sport.

Fellow-Olympian Brasher was an old and stalwart friend; they had first met in a climbing hut when Brasher was holding forth on how to make porridge – but Disley knew better! Their friendly rivalry followed them all the way to Melbourne. They were natural partners: Chris ebullient and combative; John measured and practical. Later, in 1981, the two 'invented' and initially masterminded the London marathon, not without much opposition from various authorities and bureaucracies. It was a triumph of organisation and logistics.

John was an excellent all-round mountaineer. In earlier days, he climbed mainly from Zermatt, completing such ascents as the Matterhorn and the Breithorn, and Chamonix, where he ascended, as examples, the Tour Rouge, the Grépon and the Dent du Requin. Further afield, he traversed some of the hardest Tatras in 1965 with the Hunts, going on in the 1980s to make his way up Kilimanjaro and even reached Mount Kenya's Point Lenana when he was 65.

Disley, however, eschewed harder technical climbing challenges for adventures favouring endurance and stamina. He frequently swapped his running shoes for mountain or ski boots, often in company with Brasher. Nordic skiing was a particular favourite. Characteristic of their many adventures were two attempts to make the first ski crossing of Scotland from sea to sea. The distance from Fort William to Stonehaven is 125 miles as the crow flies, the route crossing the railway at Rannoch Summit and Dalwhinnie and the road at the Glenshee ski area, while traversing several groups of high mountains and fording numerous rivers – hopefully frozen.

A major logistic problem is that only rarely does snow reach sea level simultaneously on both coasts, so for a London-based party the planning was daunting. Nevertheless, in 1968 and 1969, with two companions and carrying food, bivouac gear and survival equipment – and just enough Talisker – for some seven days in the height of winter they twice reached the halfway mark before heavy rain turned the snow to slush. These were memorable adventures. I well remember the white-out descent from Ben Alder where the temperature-change every couple of hundred feet necessitated a different ski wax, and the night at McCook's Cottage where Eric Langmuir, in flickering candlelight, explained how it was the most haunted bothy in Scotland.

In 1983, Disley and Brasher founded Fleetfoot, based in Lancaster, as the UK distributor for Reebok, eventually becoming Reebok UK. Among their developments was the popular and innovative Brasher hillwalking boot, built on a curved shepherd's last. Disley was testing a prototype pair in Wales when his cottage in Llanrwst was burgled, the boots being among the loot. Sometime later, in the local supermarket, Disley spotted a yobbo flaunting his unmistakable footwear. When apprehended, the thief claimed he'd purchased the boots at a well-known mountain equipment store. He didn't fool the magistrate.

Tackle Climbing this Way (1968) is among the several instructional books John wrote on climbing and orienteering. He served as vice-chairman of the Sports Council for eight years from 1974, and in 1979 was awarded a CBE for services to outdoor education. In 1982 he established the spectacular Snowdonia marathon. He was a past president of the Snowdonia Society environmental charity, a member of the Alpine Club and an honorary member of the Climbers' Club.

John Cleare

Colin 'Dan' Drew
1936 - 2016

Colin Drew

In 1968, Dan and I were holed up in a barn near the village of Nesheim in Norway, approximately 20 kilometres north of Bergen. The land was covered by two metres of snow. In our party were two subalterns, one of whom came from a good boarding school and probably an even better regiment. After a few days, the subaltern complained about the lack of privacy for his morning ablutions and of having lost his toothbrush in the morning *mêlée*. Dan looked at the soldier in pity and said, 'I don't understand; I would lend anyone my toothbrush providing they were decent blokes.' It was typical of Dan, one of the most generous and charming people one could meet.

Our first encounter was probably in the late 1950s when he was a cadet at the Royal Air Force College at Cranwell. We climbed mainly in Derbyshire at that time. Dan's first trip to the higher mountains was skiing the Haute Route from Chamonix to Saas Fee, after which he joined whatever party came his way. His popularity was such that trips came along fairly frequently. In 1967, he joined wing commander Dicky Bird's expedition to Ellesmere Island, an expedition enthusiastically supported by Lord Shackleton, who had been there as a student. Ellesmere Island is the nearest land to the North Pole and has been the jumping-off point for many polar expeditions. Dan was part of the survey party; he and Phil Pinney completed the survey of the eastern part of the island, climbed three peaks, and were avalanched 1,000ft. Bruce Reid, a member of the team, recorded in his diary for 4 May 1967:

> *They were roped together but as one would reach terra firma the other dragged him back in and vice versa some several times. Both lost his axe and Phil also his goggles. It is miraculous how neither was hurt in the slightest degree. I can appreciate their incredulity in this matter for it is not a phenomenon in these regions for this kind of avalanche to occur. I guess it must have been a rather bad case of wind slab slipping.*

Dan's next expedition came in 1971 when he climbed in the Taurus in Turkey. In 1972 he skied with Alan Blackshaw and several other notable climbers along the length of the Alps. (See Peter Cliff's account below.)

Also during 1972, Dan climbed Mount Rainier and other peaks in the Cascades in Washington State with the RAF Leeming mountain rescue team. Two years later he was chosen as a member of the Joint Services trans-Greenland expedition, and then the Royal Air Force expedition to the Sierra Nevada de Santa Marta in Colombia.

The trans-Greenland expedition was led by Dan Gleed and planned to cross Greenland unsupported from Angmagssalik in the east to Sondrestrom in the west. Because of poor weather they had to reverse the direction of travel and man-haul 1,600lb of food and equipment into a headwind from east to west in poor snow. They ended up being rescued by local fishermen from an ice floe.

I was the leader on Dan's next expedition to Colombia. The Santa Marta range is snow capped, rising to about 19,000ft, and is situated in a national park, 10°N of the Equator. The park is home to a tribe called the Kogi who are xenophobic by nature. The Kogi believe they are born out of local lakes and their bodies reside in the Santa Marta after death. Consequently, it is extremely difficult to gain entry to the park. Dan was treasurer to the expedition and he soon proved adept at negotiating free airline seats and changing money in odd places.

The expedition found a note on an airline ticket in a tin on the summit of La Reina in the Santa Marta which read: *Pico Bolivar*[:] *Vin Hoeman arrived 8 Dec 1967 by terrible NE ridge. I thought that I was climbing C Colon,* [Pico Cristóbal Colón (5700m), local name Gonawindua] *beautiful place to die. Let them know I made it. Member of Mtrg Club of Alaska.*

Dan remembered the name Vin Hoeman and recalled he had been killed while climbing in the Himalaya. Hoeman had indeed died in an avalanche that overtook seven members of Boyd Everett's expedition to Dhaulagiri in 1969.

Dan's next venture was to join squadron leader Charlie Cartwright's expedition to south Greenland in 1975. The team explored and climbed in the Søndre Sermilik Fjord area. They had a fairly hairy trip through the sea ice in a fishing boat. The team climbed 20 peaks, some of which were previously unclimbed, in 17 days. Dan's final expedition was to Nepal, in 1985, where he climbed Kala Pattar and Island Peak (6189m), his highest altitude.

Born in Hythe, Kent, Dan was the son of an airfield engineer employed in the airfield construction branch of the Royal Air Force in Germany. He was educated in part at a service boarding school in Plön, near Kiel in Schleswig-Holstein, followed by the Royal Air Force College. His headmaster at Plön School was the redoubtable Freddie Spencer Chapman but I was never sure what effect this association had on Dan's subsequent love of the outdoors.

Dan had many climbing partners but often climbed with Bob Honey. They did many classic routes all over Britain, probably the best was *King Rat* on Creag an Dubh Loch in the Cairngorms. Such was his range of contacts that he was able to recommend a climbing partner for Bob when he was posted to Toronto.

Dan was father to two children, Miles and Zoe, from his first marriage to Joy. In 1976 he married Susie and they had two children, Becky and Greg. Dan and Susie had a long and happy marriage, climbing in Morocco, the Pyrenees and the Alps. A small place in Finestrat in Spain provided the outlets of renovation work, good rock-climbing and happy family holidays. When Dan retired from the Royal Air Force he was employed mainly in the oil industry, necessitating a family move to the north of Scotland. He suffered a severe fall on an oilrig that broke his neck and ended his working career. After some amazing surgical repair work, he resumed his outdoor activities at a lower and slower level, but he was left with some demons to fight as well as deteriorating health.

Among his many interests he counted film, traditional jazz, painting, running, cricket, football, squash and golf. He was also a fine linguist, with five languages at his command. There are few people of Dan's kindly, friendly and enthusiastic ilk. He will be sadly missed by his many friends. Our thoughts and condolences go out to Susie, his four children and seven grandchildren.

Norman Ridley

Peter Cliff writes: In 1972 Dan was a member of the British Alpine ski traverse, a group of eight amateurs led by Alan Blackshaw, who skied from Kaprun, just south of Salzburg, to Gap, between Nice and Grenoble. The straight-line distance was 400 miles, ten times that of the Haute Route, with an overall vertical height gain of 120,000ft. The party climbed various major peaks on the way, including the Rheinwaldhorn, Monte Rosa and Mont Blanc; the trip took 49 days.

They moved in three groups, the front three breaking trail and navigating, then two strong members in reserve, followed by three at the back, resting. Under Alan's direction the team regularly roped up with different partners, with the exception of Dan, who on the first day roped up with me, a partnership which proved so strong that we not only stayed together as a rope throughout the trip, but for most of it we were in either the front or second group.

I recall hours of skinning up to distant cols with the main topic of conversation being Dan's future direction in life, in particular whether he should become a monk. Dan himself felt it could be a fulfilling thing and that he was in many respects cut out for it, while I thought he needed to properly consider those aspects of life which he would be forsaking if he became a monk and in which he clearly not only had considerable experience, but which he might find difficult to give up. Dan maintained this interest in things metaphysical throughout his life.

His all-round strength as a mountaineer, his equable temperament and his great sense of humour contributed greatly to the success of this trip.

David Brett Duffield
1937 - 2015

Dave Duffield outside the Noire hut, across from the foot of the south ridge of the Noire de Peuterey. Dave is in front furthest from the camera in a dark grey shirt looking down. Ian Howell wears a spotty loose sweater. The other three, two young women and a young man were friends of Kurt Diemberger, who took the picture with Howell's camera. *(Ian Howell)*

David Duffield was born in Leeds. His father was a bookseller in York and his grandfather a lord mayor of Leeds. He went up to Oxford to read English but remained for only a year, rebelling against what he considered its oppressive sense of privilege. He joined the Royal Court Theatre then Nottingham Playhouse, where he was employed as stage-technician and carpenter, then production assistant and stage-manager. In 1964, he was appointed resident playwright in Nottingham. From there he became resident playwright at the Traverse Theatre, Edinburgh.

His life changed course after graduating from Leeds University in philosophy and history of art in 1976. He held a lecturing post at Bradford University then moved to Northern Ireland where he went on to become a reader at the University of Ulster. By the 1990s, he had formed his own production company. The bulk of his professional life was taken up writing and directing stage and radio plays and novels, and in commenting on the visual arts. He wrote several books, mostly on heritage and the decorative arts, and translated the writings of several major European authors.

Described as a 'steady' alpinist, David became a Full Member of the AC in 1968, but had been guideless climbing and ski touring – he was a competent skier – in the Pyrenees, Alps and Norway from a much earlier date, his first Alpine season having been in 1959. He spent the 1965 season winter trekking and climbing in West Virginia, while teaching history of architecture at the American University in Washington DC.

In the 1960s, he climbed with Ian Howell on such routes as the Noire de Peuterey, the *North Face* of the Bionnassay and the Petit Capucin. He was obliged, however, because of family commitments, to leave his Himalayan ambitions unfulfilled and had to withdraw from a Gauri Sankar expedition.

David had a penchant for high-level routes, in the 1970s taking 44 days to climb solo from La Bérarde in the Dauphiné to Heiligenblut at the foot of the Grossglockner, crossing over 30 passes on the way. In 1981, he claimed to be the first Briton to have traversed the Alps, described in his *High Level: The Alps from End to End* (Gollancz, London, 1983).

He was a quiet, sincere man, with a keen interest in local history. He was a more than competent linguist, being fluent in three languages apart from English and also speaking passable German. He died of a stroke not long after undergoing cancer surgery in September 2015. Surviving David are his wife, the distinguished artist Barbara Freeman, and their children Matthew and Sophie.

Catherine Moorehead with contributions from Dennis Gray and Ian Howell

J M C 'Chuck' Evans
1959 - 2016

Chuck Evans

Chuck Evans had mountaineering and sailing, which he took up in the latter part of his life, in his blood: his parents, Sir Charles and Lady Denise Evans, were both distinguished sailors. His mountaineering pedigree could hardly have been improved upon: Sir Charles was the deputy leader of Lord Hunt's 1953 Everest Expedition and leader of the 1955 expedition which made the first ascent of Kangchenjunga. He was a past president (1968-71) of the Alpine Club, while Lady Denise became the Club's first female president in 1986.

Chuck was educated at Eton, a contributory factor in forming his highly individualist character. Much of his formative life, however, was also spent in Snowdonia, particularly at his parents' house in Capel Curig and at the Pen-y-Gwryd. In later years, he contributed to Dr Rob Goodfellow's book *The Pen y Gwryd Hotel: Tales from the Smoke Room* (Gomer Press, pending), with reminiscences and anecdotes, particularly those relating to colourful local characters and the remnants of equipment which had somehow returned from the 1953 Everest expedition.

From Eton, Chuck went on to Magdalene College, Cambridge, to read engineering, although he could equally well have studied English or history. A further string to his bow was added when he took up employment with Coopers & Lybrand (as they then were), having passed their accountancy exams.

After a gap year in the Pyrenees with his family, he and Caroline were married in 1991, having met while ski touring, and Chuck returned to PricewaterhouseCoopers, as it became known. Here, his conventional career-path was interrupted in 1998 when, as something of a professional pioneer, he moved to Paris to take up the then new venture of corporate recovery, helping firms in trouble to prevent them from going under. He pursued this career until he developed the bowel cancer that led to his death earlier this year.

Caroline and Chuck had two children, Natasha, born in 1993, and Charlie, who arrived in 1994. Aged 11 and 9, their parents took them on a trek to northern India, starting at Manali, then crossing the Rohtang La into Spiti to emerge at Simla. Their enthusiasm for mountains continues. Caroline and Chuck later separated amicably.

Once described as something of a 'travelling wardrobe', Chuck was not interested in image, although later he became more stylish. Rather, he was quirky and individualistic. He could, for example, in full adulthood, be heard muttering extracts from Winnie-the-Pooh, oblivious to his surroundings. Many of the ascents on his AC application, such as the Vignemale by the Ossoue glacier or the Pic d'Aneto, were completed alone, a testimony to his enjoyment of being isolated in the mountains. Nonetheless, he and Caroline made many ascents together, such as the Zinal Rothorn, the Wellenkuppe and the Breithorn.

In 1988, he organised an expedition to Jaonli (6632m) in the Indian Himalaya. Accounts of Chuck's participation in this venture appear below. He also visited Churen Himal in mid-west Nepal and Saipal in north-west Nepal, and made a trip to Khumbu.

Chuck was very well liked: a sociable enthusiast who nonetheless much enjoyed his own distinctive company.

Caroline Purkhardt

Prof Andy Pollard writes: When I was a medical student at St Bartholomew's Hospital Medical College and chairman of Barts Alpine Club, I received a call out of the blue from Chuck Evans, inviting me to join him on an expedition to climb Jaonli, in the Garhwal, and to help him assemble a team. Although initially suspicious of this unknown caller who claimed to know something about climbing, I was excited by his careful and detailed strategy and infectious enthusiasm for the project. It was only some days later, after some detective work, that I discovered this man had such an amazing climbing pedigree.

To introduce me to the plans and to get to know each other, Chuck drove me (faster than I have ever experienced except in an aircraft) from London to his father's house in Capel Curig, from where we set off to climb the route *Avalanche* on the slimy rocks of Lliwedd. That evening, sitting with Chuck and Sir Charles, rather frail by then, but who seemed to remember every detail of the slippery route up Lliwedd, I listened to the Evans banter and absorbed the warmth and the kindness of the men in my company, and I knew that I was blessed with the opportunity to travel to Jaonli with Chuck.

Chuck led this first British ascent of Jaonli with his characteristic calmness and good nature. We stood atop our first Himalayan peak together. Apart from a dramatic avalanche during the descent which washed me into a crevasse, the climb was uneventful, but the journey was an important one for all of us and has framed much of what we have done and how we have been since. Thank you, Chuck.

Peter White writes: I was on the Jaonli Expedition in 1988, and struck up a friendship with Chuck while sharing a tent with him at base camp. We maintained our friendship. When my middle daughter, Catherine, was 11, Chuck and Caroline kindly took her into their home and helped to arrange for her to attend Natasha and Charlie's school in Maule for a month. During that time, I went to Paris to compete in a short triathlon along with Chuck and Caroline and was convincingly beaten by them. Following that we kept in touch through skiing, and offered each other reserved support as our respective marriages ran into difficulties. Having come across an exhibition about his father on Kangchenjunga at the Keswick Museum and having sent him some photos of his father's letters, I visited him during his final illness. I think our conversation reflected the basis of our friendship as we shared our thoughts about family, religion, relationships old and new, music, art, the classics, parents, adventure and – inevitably – his illness, hopes for recovery and feelings about death. He was a remarkable man who made me feel I had a special place in his life, a reflection I am sure of his own openness and warmth rather than anything to do with me.

Andrew Knight writes: I first met Chuck in 1987 when he was looking for climbing members for his Jaonli expedition. Several other junior doctors from Barts Hospital and I joined him. Chuck was a resolute and cheerful leader, useful qualities when walking in during the monsoon with very limited maps and information. We kept in touch for several years after that and climbed in the UK and skied with his in-laws in Vaujany.

My wife and I attended his wedding. He was kind enough to introduce us to his father who became patron of one of our later expeditions. I have very happy memories of Chuck at those times. He was a kind, gentle and resourceful man with a determined attitude to mountaineering and a love of wild places and adventure.

Alan Fisher
1939 - 2015

Alan Richmond Fisher was born in 1939 in Abingdon, Oxfordshire. His father was a GP and his mother a physiotherapist. Both were keen climbers. Alan's climbing began early, with his parents and elder brother. They regularly visited North Wales and the Lake District and, later, the Alps. His exceptional ability was illustrated when Alan's uncle Mike was asked to go to Wales to check that Alan and his brother Richard, camping alone, were all right. When Mike got back, he told his horrified wife that he'd climbed the Milestone Buttress but that it was okay: 'Alan was leading so it was perfectly safe.'

Alan Fisher

Alan's particular fondness for Skye began when he was 15. When his school climbing party from Sherborne failed to turn up, Alan, who had travelled up independently, went to the youth hostel at Glen Brittle and joined with another climber staying there. This started a passion for climbing in the Cuillin that lasted a lifetime. He traversed the Cuillin Ridge on several occasions and, as a student, would think nothing of walking the 16-mile round trip to Sligachan from the Coruisk hut to have a few pints, before returning in the dark to climb the next day. Others reported his nonchalance on the Cuillin's sharper ridges, where he would carry a rope for those who might be losing their nerve.

Another Sherborne climbing trip that proved inspirational was to Norway. Over 40 years later, Alan enjoyed sharing memories of climbs with one of his son's friends who was doing PhD work on the glaciers at Sydbreen and Jiehkkevárri and comparing photographs from the 1950s with the 1990s.

In 1957, after Swanbourne House and Sherborne, Alan chose to do his national service, although hopes of Norway with the Royal Marines were replaced by 18 months of what for him was the uncongenial sun and sand of Malta and North Africa. He did, however, make an ascent of Etna.

Alan then went on to study dentistry at Guy's Hospital in London. He joined the hospital's climbing club, serving as its secretary in 1961-2. The club tended to meet at weekends in North Wales, with longer holidays spent in the Cuillin, the Alps and the Dolomites. He also played rugby for Guy's first XV, as well as low-handicap golf.

Alan's early Alpine seasons centred on Arolla where he climbed the Pigne and the Aiguille de la Tsa. From Grindelwald he climbed the Rosenhorn, the Mönch and the Jungfrau. From Zermatt, he ascended the Matterhorn when he was 20, followed in the same season by the Breithorn, Monte Rosa and the Zinal Rothorn and followed this up with a traverse of the Matterhorn via the *Hörnli* and *Italian Ridge* the following year. In 1964, he enjoyed a successful season in the Dolomites with climbs on the First and Third Sella Towers and the *South-West Ridge* of the Torre del Lago.

He qualified in 1965 and was elected to the Alpine Club in 1966, his proposer being Dr Schweitzer of the Austrian Alpine Club. The following year, he married Meg, a qualified nurse at Westminster Hospital. In 1968 they moved from London to Dorchester-on-Thames after Alan became a partner at a dental surgery in Wallingford, Oxfordshire. They raised four children and have four grandchildren.

Alan passed on his love of the mountains to many of his family and friends: his enjoyment and sense of wonder were infectious. The higher, more remote and isolated he got, the happier he became. He also loved camping, mainly for its sense of freedom. He patiently passed on his knowledge of mountain-craft to his children, and was most often seen puffing on a cigar while he demonstrated how to run screes, avoid bogs or cut steps. A memorable family climb in this period was of Sgùrr nan Gillean under winter conditions. When not in Scotland, the family spent most of their holidays in the Alps or the Pyrenees, or in the Dolomites on via ferrata.

Another facet of his mountaineering interests was to try out new equipment. This was not always successful: once, a misguided test of a new karabiner and ropes on the side of his house resulted in an abseil through the dining-room windows. In retirement, Meg and Alan travelled and walked in the Pyrenees, Nepal, Patagonia, Peru, New Zealand and Tasmania. These trips were enjoyed enormously, before disability and illness intervened.

Alan pursued several interests other than climbing. He was a passionate golfer, of professional standard, the longest-ever playing member of the Frilford Heath club near Abingdon. More creatively, he enjoyed working with wood and, later, stone and gold jewellery. More challenging interests included opera choruses played loudly on hairpin mountain roads, and a passion for Norwegian goat's cheese.

Alan was a kind, gentle and thoughtful man – appropriate qualities for his profession. He was always helpful and involved, offering guidance or advice with a good measure of teasing, wit and kindness. He loved people: his parties, Sunday lunches and welcomes stretched from Skye to Oxfordshire. This extended to his local community, where he played for the village cricket team and golfing society, and helped with St Birinus Pilgrimage, a local ecumenical gathering and walk. Most of all, he enjoyed conversation, whether as devil's advocate, teasing or making sure that people felt at their ease. He was patient and loyal, a good-humoured friend who only ever spoke well of others.

Meg and Rachel Fisher

Robin Garton
1945 - 2015

Robin Garton was born in Oxfordshire and educated at Eton. He then went up to Oxford but left after a year. He enjoyed a distinguished career as an art dealer, taking early retirement at almost 60 in order to read physical geography at Southampton University. The course included much on glaciers, his passionate interest.

Robin Garton

When Robin went back to university he became, in his own words, 'radicalised'. He left Southampton with a burning desire to help in the battle against climate change and went on to found the Glacier Trust, to help communities at altitude adapt to and mitigate climate change. He worked unstintingly for the Trust until the time of his death. Even in his late 60s, he retained this ability to look at everything with a completely open mind.

Robin had known from an early age that he wanted to work in art. He started on Christie's front counter, where he learnt his trade in great depth and began to develop his passion and knowledge into specialist areas. A distinguished 40-year career followed.

Robin was hugely admired and respected for what he achieved, while being typically modest and self-deprecating. Colleagues have described him as one of the outstanding dealers in British art of his generation, with an instinctive understanding of artists. Forty years after he edited and published two books, *British Etchers* and *British Printmakers*, both remain the seminal texts on the subject. In the 1980s, he founded the International London Original Print Fair, which still flourishes today. A minute's silence was held in his honour at the recent New York International Print Fair; his contemporaries wished to remember a talented colleague and a wonderful friend.

It was only when already aged 55 that Robin began mountaineering, which led to an interest in glaciology. He was so inspired that by 60 he took early retirement and made the frankly brave decision to take a geography degree some 45 years after his last science lesson, having worked only in the arts in the intervening period. This was a challenge, even for an erudite man. The degree was difficult, but he loved it. He would stay up all night, learning about climate change, while also raising considerable amounts of money for organisations working to mitigate it, for example in supporting projects in remote parts of Bangladesh. Most of the Glacier Trust's work, however, is carried out in Nepal.

Although it is not known precisely what happened to Robin, it is believed he was lost on 25 September 2015, while traversing the Aonach Eagach ridge in Glen Coe, a route well within his abilities; he respected the mountains and was never complacent. After 2,500 hours of searching with dogs, drones, divers and helicopters, the Glencoe mountain rescue team volunteers say they are baffled at not having been able to find him.

Robin was the most devoted husband, father and grandfather. He was adored by his immediate family and much loved by a wide circle of friends and relatives. He was a most hospitable and considerate man; he would want to say sorry that his disappearance had occurred. He loved life, had many plans and much to live for.

It is said, and so it seems that, 'the mountains keep their favourite children.'

Lee, William and Francesca Garton

Paul Moores writes: As a mountain guide, I love the opportunity to meet and climb with new people. Late one evening a few years ago the telephone rang. It was Robin Garton: 'I want to climb the Matterhorn this summer.' I listened carefully to Robin's plan. Robin had been coming to the Alps for the past two summers and we had climbed many of the classic Alpine routes together in the Mont Blanc massif, but nothing quite as serious as the Matterhorn.

Clients tend to return to the same mountain guide, as Robin had done. After a few trips to the mountains we had got to know each other quite well. Robin discovered climbing later in life but soon he was totally smitten by the climbing world. I felt he had the ability and the drive to make an ascent of the Matterhorn, and we did it! This was a fantastic achievement for Robin, particularly as he had not been climbing for very long. In the process, he had raised a lot of money for charity. We went on to climb such classics as Mont Blanc du Tacul, the Petite Aiguille Verte and the Aiguilles Crochues.

With his drive and desire to climb better and harder routes, he teamed up with Jon Bracey and Matt Helliker to make more Alpine ascents, as well as with others, such as Yannick Pralong, to climb for example the Dent Blanche and the Grand Cornier. He also spent a season in Peru where he topped 6,000m on a couple of occasions: Tocallaraju and Chopicalqui lower summit, both with Oscar Negreiros Cerna. These cherished friendships helped Robin to develop his ideas for various charity projects, which have helped so many people. Robin will be remembered for his enthusiastic passion for the mountains, his determination to be in and around the mountains and his love and help for those people who work and live among them.

Jamie Forsyth, from the Glacier Trust, writes: Robin Garton's generous, principled and timely work in establishing the Glacier Trust, which he founded in 2008 at the age of 61, was no mean feat. It stemmed from a fascination with mountain environments and, in particular, certain types of natural disaster prevalent in the Nepali Himalaya known as glacial lake outburst floods (GLOFs).

Originally, Robin had intended to help communities devastated by these extremely powerful floods in the high Himalaya. However, after having visited Nepal, he soon learned of a more immediate and widespread problem that was affecting the whole country: climate change. He found that many upland, remote, rural communities, whose whole livelihoods depended on the success of the next crop cycle, were and still are extremely vulnerable to climate change through lacking the capacity to adapt to the environmental changes that are reducing their crop yields.

After many discussions with international and local nongovernmental organisations, Robin found that small-scale interventions were the way forward, because topography and climate differed so markedly across such small distances: small, bespoke projects for individual communities were needed. *Small is beautiful* became Robin's tag line. After eight years, the Glacier Trust is now known and respected by many; it has supported numerous mountain communities of Nepal in adapting to their changing environment. It is enabling communities, which would otherwise have struggled badly, to adapt to climate change.

Robin gave all he had to give in bringing this charity to where it is now, and he would be so pleased to know that the Glacier Trust is continuing in his absence. This is his legacy, but more importantly the work Robin saw as so vital and life changing for many vulnerable Nepali communities will continue. To support the Glacier Trust, please go to: www.theglaciertrust.org/donate.

Terence Goodfellow
1938 - 2015

Terence Goodfellow

Terence was the son of the well-known mountaineer and mountain photographer, Basil Goodfellow. After his education at Clifton College and Cambridge, where he read history, Terry went on to teach English before joining ICI in an administrative post, a role that did not suit him. After a short period there, he 'took off' for a couple of years and became a climbing instructor in Snowdonia, an early sign of his passion for climbing which came with the realisation that it could not be a long-term career.

In the late 1960s, Terry moved to London, where he spent the 1967-8 academic year at London University's Institute of Education. He then taught in schools in Shoreditch and at the Isaac Newton school, North Kensington, for six years before becoming director of Hoxton Hall community centre and theatre. After much fundraising, he and a colleague set up the Hoxton Theatre and Education Project. He worked there for about 15 years, during which time he became deeply involved with the work of the Anthroposophical Society, the UK base for the Rudolf Steiner movement. Terry became house manager of the society headquarters at Rudolf Steiner House, Baker Street. He remained there for the rest of his career, indeed remained closely associated with many of the activities of Rudolf Steiner House for the rest of his life.

Liz Goodfellow

Peter Bell writes: Terence was introduced to climbing at an early age. I was invited, as a teenager, to join his first trip to the Alps with the adults, venerable men such as John Lloyd and Michael Wilson. We met as a party in Arolla and, never having climbed before, immediately set out for a hut before traversing the Aiguilles Rouges. We met after that at every opportunity, to join the grown-ups at Pen y Gwryd or go on our own to climb in the Pass. Terence was an indomitable character, always good-humoured and great fun to be with.

At Cambridge, Terence introduced me to night climbing with too much alcohol and a scant regard for safety. But we survived – not that we deserved to! He became a staunch member of the Cambridge Climbing Club and participated in the club's two-month 1961 expedition to Cumberland Peninsula, Baffin Island. After leaving university, Terence also climbed with his father in the Vanoise and Zermatt areas, on such peaks as the Grande Casse and the north face of the Breithorn, as well as in the Brenta Dolomites and the Ortler Alps.

At that time, we would travel together on my old Triumph motorcycle to climb in the Alps, revisiting Arolla in particular. But we also went off the beaten track, to such places as the Englehörner, climbing freely and quickly on such routes as the *Macdonald-Kamine* on the Grosser Simelistock.

At weekends, we would go to Wales or Swanage, where we opened up the climbing, particularly on the Boulder Ruckle; it had hardly been climbed at that time. It was exhilarating stuff, abseiling off an old fence-post onto rocks in the sea and then climbing vertically back up some hundred feet, with steep grass to finish. Terence was the perfect companion, bubbling with enthusiasm in the sun, the wind and the waves.

We introduced Gunn Clarke, Ian McNaught-Davis and Chris Jones to this area and put up many climbs together with them. For ten years or so we were very close but after that only met through mutual friends.

David Lea writes: I first met Terence at least 60 years ago when we found ourselves at Clifton College in Bristol, though we were in different houses. He and a mutual friend, Peter Worsley, shared an anarchic attitude to public school life, though Terence was more skilful than Peter at avoiding retribution.

Terence had wide interests, including painting and singing, and he was a reasonable rugby player, but what really interested him were the college buildings. He could never resist a wall, natural or man-made, though he preferred good vertical rock. The neo-Gothic buildings of Clifton provided a dramatic setting for his first urban climbing exploits. Later, I discovered that he was the first House Sixth to refuse to use the cane in punishment. This independence of spirit required considerable courage at that time.

His years at Cambridge gave him the opportunity and impetus for ambitious expeditions to Baffin Island, Afghanistan and Kashmir. I was not part of these, but joined him one summer to go to Greece. Preparations involved frequent visits to his home, with the quintessentially English name of Parsonage House, at Helions Bumpstead in Essex.

His father, Basil, gave us the family's old A30 van for our Greece expedition. There was no continuous road down the Yugoslavian coast at that time so we drove on rough tracks along the beach. It was a wonderful, carefree trip and I remember that we sang a lot. People found it hard to believe we were English – maybe Canadian?

Although Terence was supposed to follow Basil into ICI for a secure future, he felt increasingly unhappy with this and cast around for a change in direction. For some months, he hung about learning the guitar, singing French songs and perfecting the way a Gauloise might hang from the corner of his mouth. He decided to take up teaching and moved to London. Here, he met a group of kindred spirits who shared his love of the theatre and who saw its potential for education. They named themselves 'Nevern Square'. It became a close-knit cast of friends who have held together throughout their working lives, as colleagues and audience. Terence's own inspiration was Michael Wilson, a saintly friend of his father who had given up life as a successful musician to run a home for children with disabilities. Michael based his work on the ideas of Rudolf Steiner; Terence shared this interest.

I was also in London at the time so we looked for and then renovated a house to share. When he became director of Hoxton Hall he quickly brought most of Nevern Square in to run a variety of courses and theatrical events. The Christmas pantomimes were fabulously and memorably funny. Hoxton rapidly became the focus of his working life.

Having set all this up, he then embarked on the search for a wife. In discussing these matters he would say, 'You feel it in your bones,' with his inimitable emphasis on 'bones'. Before long, he and Liz were married. They shared a positive, active outlook on life and Liz became a rock of support when Terence was struck down by illness.

After seven years in London I moved to Ogoronwy, a smallholding on the south-western edge of Snowdonia. We had imagined a rural base for visiting Hoxtonians; Ogoronwy was ideal, being set in a wild landscape of rocks, crags, trees and streams, close to the mountains that Terence loved. Over many years I would look forward to the Hoxton visits, with their entirely different dynamics, which turned my normal existence upside-down.

Terence threw the Hoxton children in at the deep end, teaching them rope-work on the crags around my home, leading them on wild walks through Snowdonia in all weathers, sometimes in darkest night. In time, a core group settled down to two visits a year and a few of them continued to visit Snowdonia on their own, even after Terence had left Hoxton.

At that time, he seemed tough, strong and indestructible. Peter Bell said, 'Terence will be tramping the hills long after you and I have hung up our boots.'

As we grew older, part of Nevern Square morphed into the 'Crusty Climbing Club', mythically established by one Dame Emmeline Cranston, a spoof organization established to record for posterity our holidays in the mountains of Europe and the Crusties' love of tricks and teasing. Since I was kept in the loop by e-mail I watched in some disbelief the extraordinary lengths to which the Crusties would go in arranging their affairs, but it was clear that the opinions of Sir Arcane, as Terence was called, were held in very high regard.

Terence was the most unflappable, imperturbable man I have known. He was at the same time very traditional, very 'English', but also an independent spirit who found his own way. He was very kind to everyone, accepting people in a democratic way. He kept his own counsel and wouldn't condemn others, though sometimes he allowed an amused exasperation to show.

Terence was quite suddenly struck down in the autumn of 1999 with what was eventually diagnosed as rheumatoid arthritis. I think of his courage and his positive spirit shining brightly in the face of this crippling disability which shrank his body and made walking a torture.

About a year ago he spoke to me of the silver lining in this experience. This reminded me of when we were once travelling up to Wales late one night and had stopped at a service station on the M1. We felt blasted by cars, noise and speed. 'We forget about death,' Terence said. This seemed true at the time, and I feel it still, a profound truth. He was a very lovable person and a very lovable friend.

Terence is survived by his wife Liz, and their children, Lucy and Thomas.

Denis Greenald
1925 - 2016

Denis Greenald

Denis was born in Bradford; his father was a travelling salesman for the Elgic Tea Company while his mother hailed from farming stock near Halifax. His father also played the piano for silent films, a talent Denis inherited. During the war, Denis and his sister Sylvia were evacuated for three months to stay with the Wilson family on the moor near Howarth, a formative experience in his passion for the outdoor life.

After leaving school, Denis enrolled as an engineering cadet until he was called up for national service. He joined the Fleet Air Arm and was stationed near Portsmouth. After demob, Denis was accepted on a course at the London School of Economics. Here, he met his future wife, Gwen. They enjoyed a fabulous few years, climbing mountains in the UK and the Alps. Denis graduated with a BSc in economics but admitted that he had spent more time climbing than studying. He then taught in a secondary school for a year before embarking on a career change into educational psychology.

He was, however, looking for greater challenges and adventures: along with Edward Williams and Jim Durbin they planned an expedition to the Himalaya. In 1956 they travelled to Baltistan to climb Lukpe Lawo Brak (6593m), the Snow Lake Peak, a then unclimbed mountain in a remote part of the Karakoram. In addition to carrying their own hefty rucksacks, they employed forty porters and two high-altitude Sherpas to move a ton of gear along the 100-mile approach march. With the summit in sight, severe weather caused them to abandon the climb. A successful descent was achieved despite Denis losing his ice axe. He was amazed, 33 years later, when the Metropolitan Police returned his axe to him. They had found it while making the first ascent of the same mountain; it was, they said, the most unusual case of lost property they had ever known.

A few days after their abortive attempt, the team had to content themselves with a lower mountain they named Cornice Peak. This expedition was a major event for Denis, and he replayed it regularly, thanks to the fine photos he took, right up to his last weeks of life.

Back in the UK, Denis settled into work as an educational psychologist at Southampton, and started a family. Steve was born in 1958 and David two years later. Alison was born shortly after, just after a move to Chester for a new job with the education department of Cheshire County Council. Later, Denis and Gwen became foster-parents to Nicola, the daughter of a friend who had died.

Denis and Gwen teamed up with friends, the Tombs and the Brownsorts, and bought a near-derelict cottage in Snowdonia. The idea was for two couples to go climbing while the other couple looked after the children. The reality was that the cottage needed so much work that for the next few years they rarely ventured onto the hill. When the children were older, Denis and Gwen introduced them to mountain-craft and led them on many classic climbs in North Wales, Skye and the Alps. Such excursions were not always plain sailing, however: although generally an enthusiastic leader, Denis had a habit of turning some outings into an epic, thanks to some precarious climbing and long marches through treacherous terrain.

Denis and Gwen loved the Alps and managed to buy a small house in Chamonix. After the children had left home, they skied and climbed there, during the holidays, for about 15 years. As they became less active, they sold the house in Chamonix and bought another in the south of France. There, they enjoyed a few happy years of long holidays but had to sell up as their health declined.

Aside from climbing, Denis's other passion was music. He played the piano and tried his hand at the clarinet and trumpet. He also shared Gwen's enthusiasm for knowledge. They took an O-level course in Italian and translated a book into French for a friend. If he had had another lifetime, he would have been a politician or a product designer – along with a few other careers he had in mind. His later years were spent playing music, campaigning for various causes and being a thorn in the side of any bureaucracy that he did not agree with.

Denis was over 80 when he acquired his first laptop and had started an online petition a few days before he had the stroke that took away his independence; he thought he would live forever, as he was always on a mission. As his daughter Alison remarked: if there is a life after death, Denis would be busy redesigning it, battling with the hierarchy to sort out the beyond, and climbing mountains in the sky.

Steve Greenald

Malcolm Eldridge writes: In the course of his presidential speech at the 2009 dinner, Tut Braithwaite announced that it was the 60th anniversary of the first dinner attended by one member present, Denis Greenald. The membership handbook shows this: Denis Greenald ACG 1953, AC 1977. And next is Gwen Greenald ACG 1953, AC 1977. There must be two good stories here.

Denis, with his cousin Johnny Lees, started his teenage mountaineering in the early 1940s in a modest way, escaping from urban Yorkshire for the freedom of moors and hills through walking and scrambling. While at the LSE, where he came under the influence of Peter Dietz and Geoff Millward, he was selected for the AC training meet at Kleine Scheidegg in 1948. A year later, Denis went with Geoff to Courmayeur, where Toni Gobbi took them under his wing, initially allowing them to follow him and his clients, but later guiding them on the Rochefort Ridge and the Arête des Hirondelles on the Grandes Jorasses. Back at LSE, Alexander Carr-Saunders, the director, told T Graham Brown about these climbs. Brown then submitted a note of their exploits to the *AJ* and invited Denis to the AC dinner in 1949.

In 1950, Denis went to the Alps with his new climbing partner, Gwen. They climbed and gained experience in the Gran Paradiso and then the Chamonix Aiguilles, including the traverse of the Grépon. After returning home, Gobbi proposed that they might attempt the *South Ridge* of the Aiguille Noire – he having completed the first winter ascent. In 1951, now married, they enjoyed a good season in Chamonix and then the Valais, though bad weather frustrated their most ambitious plans. In 1952, they might have fulfilled Gobbi's proposal but, after carrying a 200ft hemp rope around the Alps for the abseils on the Noire, they were again frustrated by the weather.

In 1953, things finally fell into place and they arrived at the Noire hut with a distinguished cast, including Pat Vaughan, Alan Blackshaw and Hamish Nicol. Three parties of two climbed the ridge. George Band, Roger Chorley, Ted Wrangham and 'Goff' Francis had made the first British ascent in 1952, but it was a sufficiently prestigious route for entry into the recently formed Alpine Climbing Group. Denis might have joined the AC at that time but refused to join a club that would exclude his climbing partner and wife. This partnership lasted a further 50 years, including a small expedition to the Karakoram in 1956. After a break for raising a family, Denis and Gwen returned to the Alps, climbing with their teenage children until 1975. It was not until 1977 that they both joined the Alpine Club.

There are other couples in the AC who have been members for longer but the very early inclusion of Denis and Gwen in the ACG gives them a unique place in the history of British climbing. They celebrated their 60th wedding anniversary in December 2010.

Dr A S G Jones MBE
1933 - 2016

Dr Tony Jones

Dr Tony Jones died on 6 May 2016, after suffering a degenerative illness. He had been a major influence on mountain rescue in the UK and around the world since the mid 1960s.

Tony was born in India, the son of an officer in the British Indian Army. As a young boy, he moved to his mother's home country of South Africa. Having suffered at an early age from polio, which left him with a weak leg, his first choice of sport was diving. Growing up in the shadow of Table Mountain, however, and as a student of geology, he soon took an interest in the mountains and became a member of the Mountaineering Club of South Africa, a membership he retained for 60 years.

It was through the MCSA that he first became involved with mountain rescue. Having graduated in marine geology, he moved to the UK in 1963 to further his studies at Aberystwyth University. He joined the university mountaineering club, which held regular meets in Snowdonia, especially in the Ogwen valley. In 1965, when the Ogwen Valley Mountain Rescue Organisation (OVMRO) was inaugurated, it depended upon known and trusted groups of mountaineers to staff the rescue team, particularly at weekends. Aberystwyth University became one of those groups, thus beginning Tony's role in UK mountain rescue.

Having gained his PhD, Tony moved to Bangor to lecture in marine geology at the University College of Wales. In 1966, he became a full member of OVMRO. Shortly afterwards, he was appointed one of the team leaders, an office he held until 1998. In 1969 he was elected as chair of OVMRO, a position he held for 21 years.

Being a single man and living in university halls, where he was a warden, he could devote his free time to the study of mountain rescue. He became chair of the North Wales Mountain Rescue Association, the regional body.

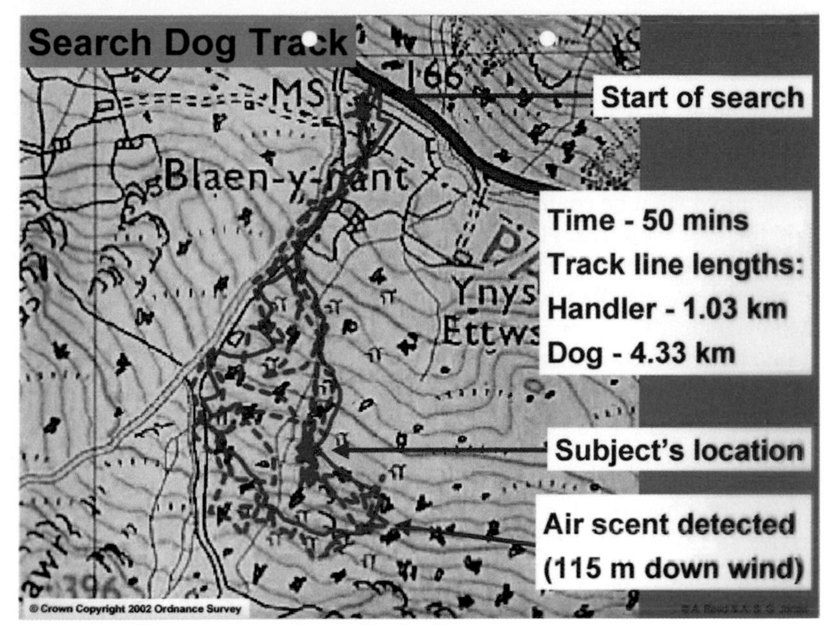

It's a dog's life. A GPS track recorded by Tony Jones of his own walk in Snowdonia and that of a search and rescue dog, in red.

He held this post for 40 years. In addition, he became involved with the national body, the Mountain Rescue Committee, later Council, later still Mountain Rescue England & Wales (MREW). Tony was involved for over 30 years with several sub-committees including communications. He held the post of vice-chairman for several years and later became a trustee.

Tony encouraged innovation. In his early days, his good friend, Dr Ieuan Jones, casualty doctor at Bangor's accident and emergency department, realised that the better first aid at the accident site, the better the outcome for the casualty. He devised a series of first aid courses for mountain rescue that were taught to RAF and civilian teams. Tony embraced this training and was soon teaching courses to MRT members around the country.

Following a visit to the USA, Tony and a couple of others involved with mountain rescue brought the American style of search management back to the UK. Soon he was organising and delivering these courses to mountain rescue team-members and members of the police. He took these courses around the world, including Hong Kong, Iceland and New Zealand.

Through his contacts in the USA, Tony established close contact with the USAF Pararescue, known as PJs, stationed in the south-east of England. They came to Snowdonia to train, and also to climb and socialise with members of OVMRO. Tony became an honorary member of the PJs and was proud to have their motif of a pair of green feet tattooed on his buttocks.

In 1992, Tony's contribution to mountain rescue was recognised nationally when he starred in the TV programme 'This Is Your Life'. Being a man who did not enjoy publicity and not owning a television, when the Wessex helicopter landed and Michael Aspel jumped out with his famous red book, there was some trepidation from the three Ogwen mountain-rescue members who had organised it all. Michael walked up to Tony and said, 'Dr Tony Jones, this is your life.' Fortunately, there were enough good friends around him to make sure there were no expletives. Mr Aspel was not told what he could do with his red book.

In the 1995 New Year Honours, Tony was awarded the MBE, thoroughly deserved recognition for years of dedication to mountain rescue. And when he resigned as a member of OVMRO in 1999, he was appointed to honorary membership.

In addition to his membership of the Alpine Club, MCSA and OVMRO, Tony was a member of the Climbers' Club. For many years he was warden of the hut at Helyg, in the Ogwen Valley. Despite his weakened leg, he climbed Mont Blanc, Kilimanjaro and Mount Kenya. He also climbed and walked extensively in the Drakensberg, the Dauphiné and Stubai Alps, and Norway.

Soon after his arrival in Bangor, North Wales, Tony joined the local fire service. In 1970 he was able to put this experience to good use when the drying room of the Clachaig Inn, Glencoe, caught fire. When the fire engine arrived, he volunteered his expertise, using the hose to save the fine selection of malt whisky displayed behind the bar.

Tony's funeral was held in the cathedral at Bangor. It was filled with members of several mountain rescue teams from North Wales and members of MREW. There were several representatives from RAF mountain rescue and of 22 Squadron, search and rescue helicopters. Tony became well known to many members of the RAF mountain rescue as they served at RAF Valley on Anglesey. He kept up the friendships that he made. Brian Canfer of the RAF Mountain Rescue Association spoke forcefully about this strong relationship.

The Maritime and Coastguard Agency (MCA) and RNLI were also represented as well as North Wales Police and other forces. The deputy chief constable for North Wales, Gareth Pritchard, spoke about Tony's wealth of knowledge and the great respect that he held in such circles. Bill Dean, who met this forthright South African when Tony arrived at Aberystwyth in 1963, recalled introducing him to the university club and then to OVMRO. Alistair Read spoke on behalf of MREW as national training officer. In the early days of civilian mountain rescue in North Wales, RAF mountain rescue was closely involved in its development.

Rick La Valla and Don Cooper, instructors on the annual search management courses held by MREW and run by Tony at Bangor University, flew from the USA to speak at the service. Finally, Peter Price, who had known Tony through membership of OVMRO since the late 1960s and had been a close friend and a loyal support to Tony in his latter years, recalled their friendship with passion. The service ended with a small local choir singing a stirring rendition of 'Nkosi Sikele Afrika', the national anthem of South Africa.

A book should be written about this unusual and remarkable man, born in India, brought up in South Africa, with the Welsh surname of Jones and who wore a kilt of Scottish tartan. He led with single-minded authority. He was a generous man, always willing to help fledgling team members with his vast knowledge of mountain rescue. He was respected for that authoritative knowledge gained by thorough research and the university of life. For those who knew him and worked with him, they will have understood what a privilege it was to have known him.

Chris Lloyd, OVMRO

Dr Paul R T Newby writes: Years ago, Tony gave me this interesting example of a practical application for combining digital geographical information from different sources in a mountain rescue context. You will recognise the impression we all have that dogs cover at least three times as much ground as their masters when out for a walk. Tony put this perception to the test with his search and rescue dogs. On an exercise in Cwm Glas on Snowdon, he equipped both himself and his dog with a continuously recording GPS receiver. The result (see picture) shows that the dog actually covered more than four times Tony's distance, and detected the missing person at a range of 115m. It's a nice illustration of how Tony brought his professional expertise – and modern technology – to bear on developing the process of mountain rescue in Snowdonia.

Helge J Kolrud
1938 - 2016

Helge Kolrud was born in the Bergen district of Fana in 1938 and graduated from school there in 1957. Thereafter, he lived in Oslo. He qualified as a lawyer in 1965, and went on to become a judge and attorney. He was a partner in the law firm Vislie, Ødegaard & Kolrud, and later at Haavind.

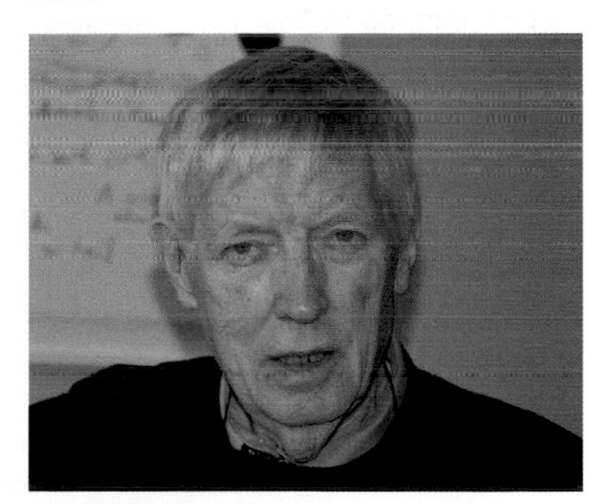

Helge Kolrud

His father was a teacher and school inspector, and was politically active in the Norwegian Labour movement. His mother's background was conservative. Helge inherited his father's teaching talents and attributed his finicky interest in language to him. While at university, he was much influenced by the philosopher, historian and writer Arild Haaland.

Helge was evacuated from home at the outbreak of war. When not quite six years old, he witnessed, unforgettably, the terrible accidental explosion at the port of Bergen on 20 April 1944, when a Dutch cargo ship with hundreds of tons of TNT exploded outside Haakon's Hall. Five thousand people were injured; 300 died.

Helge's membership of the Norwegian Alpine Club, which he much enjoyed, stretched over 25 years. He had, however, always loved mountains and mountaineering and climbed Store Skagastølstind, Norway's third-highest peak, for the first time in 1972. He often visited Turtagrø in the Jotunheim, central Norway, particularly to climb in the jagged massif of Hurrungane, one of Norway's most alpine areas. On the Norwegian climbing difficulty ranking of 1 to 9 he claimed, with his customary modesty, to have been generally restricted to level 3 and sometimes 4 – equivalent to Severe.

He was recognised at home and abroad for his very extensive technical and organisational abilities. He was author of several legal works and also known as a university lecturer. He was, furthermore, a highly regarded committee legislator and sought-after arbitrator. As well as being chairman of the Norwegian Bar Association, he represented over 700,000 lawyers through his presidency of the Council of Bars and Law Societies of Europe (CCBE).

One might have thought him too busy and inclined to spend too little time on each of his many activities. In fact, he was known for his accessibility and efficiency and for ensuring he spent long holidays with family and friends, particularly at his beloved Kursen, in southern Norway, to which many friends were invited over the decades. In later years, he was beset by several illnesses, but was never heard to complain.

He claimed to be happiest when net fishing at Tvedestrand, a picturesque coastal village in southern Norway. There, he was out of reach of his mobile and was happy performing simple tasks like repairing his nets.

In 1968 he married Anne Johanne, known as Hanne; they had two children.

Translations and compilation by Catherine Moorehead

Hasse Eriksen writes: Helge J Kolrud was by profession a supreme court lawyer; he was chairman of the Norwegian Bar Association from 1991 to 1994 and chairman of the European Lawyers Union from 2003 to 2005. During his time as the Tine (Norwegian Association of Dairy Farmers) 'house attorney' he secured the 1994 agreement with the Mountain Mus eum in Lom for a permanent place for the Club's W C Slingsby heirlooms.

His professional and international background also came in handy when, as the Club's representative within the UIAA organization committee, from 2006, he secured its position as a member of this important organization.

He joined the NAC as a 45-year-old after a long career as a rock climber and high-mountain skier with a consuming interest in and knowledge of Norwegian and foreign climbing history. This made him an obvious choice as a member of the book committee appointed to oversee the release of the NAC's 100th anniversary book '200 years of Norwegian Mountaineering'. As one of the book's main authors, he was generously praised for his detailed knowledge of mountaineering history.

Reproduced in translation by kind permission of Hasse Eriksen and the Norwegian Alpine Club

Donald Lee
1933 - 2016

Donald Lee

The mountains and mountain activities played a large part in the life of my husband, Don Lee. But despite many years of Alpine holidays he felt that his achievements, while giving him great pleasure and satisfaction, were too modest for full membership of the Alpine Club: he thus became an Associate Member in 2007. This gave him the opportunity to take part in social events and to keep in touch with Club members and their activities. He would look back with particular pleasure to the Club's 150th anniversary celebrations in Zermatt and to the Lincoln's Inn dinner later that year.

Born in Manchester, Don grew up in Wallasey where he attended Wallasey Grammar School. Afterwards he worked for a short time with a small local firm then became a National Westminster Bank, as it then was, employee, working in branches in the Liverpool area, in Cumbria and eventually in the Manchester area until his retirement.

Don was, however, happiest when involved in something active or practical. He played rugby for New Brighton, was a very strong swimmer and, during his national service in Germany he seemed to spend much time running in the local forests while learning how to throw the javelin. But his main love was for the mountains: on Friday night, he used to drive on his Vincent motorbike from Wallasey to North Wales, to return on Monday morning in time for work. He loved to tinker with his beloved Vincent and, later, his cars. His meticulous practical skills revealed themselves in later years when he converted two small adjacent terraced houses at Tintwistle, near Glossop, into a lovely country cottage.

He was a competent and very safe climber and became a mountaineering instructor for the Mountaineering Association. He was chosen to join an expedition to the Himalaya but was not allowed the time off work: he was told to choose between being a mountaineer or a banker, a response that rankled with him for many years.

Don was already a member of the Wayfarers when we met. (Together, we later joined the Fell and Rock.) Our first meeting took place on Boxing Day 1966 at the Old Dungeon Ghyll in Langdale. Here, I was introduced to him and to his red Triumph Spitfire sports car. We made no arrangements to keep in touch but a few weeks later he contacted me by writing to my Education offices in Manchester with a forwarding letter in which he invited me to go to Skye with him at Easter. The lure of the Cuillin and the Triumph Spitfire was too good to miss and I accepted. So began 50 years of friendship and companionship, leading to our eventual marriage.

Don was a kind, quiet, modest person who never sought the limelight but whose support and inner strength were invaluable. He loved music and was a competent pianist although he seldom played. And he loved our many visits to our friend in Vienna where he enjoyed the tranquillity of her home in the Vienna woods, as well as the culture and the music.

Our great love for the outdoors, warm sunshine and the mountains led us to spend many happy and rewarding summer weeks in various parts of the Swiss and French Alps, in the Pyrenees and Picos de Europa, in the Maritime Alps, the Julian Alps and the Gran Paradiso. Don had a special affection for Corsica, which we visited nine times. In particular he liked to recall our following the GR20 before there was a series of huts or any provision points *en route*. We carried only a tiny tent and enough food to last for a frugal ten days. We saw only three other people during the whole trip and we both lost much weight. Later, Don loved driving with a motor-home over some very challenging roads and passes to the south of France or across to Chamonix or Zermatt.

During the winter months there was plenty to keep us occupied in the Lakes or in Scotland. We would visit the Cairngorms, Ben Nevis and Glencoe, while other trips would start on the north coast and gradually move down through the north-west Highlands while climbing as much as possible *en route*.

Don had always enjoyed good health, so it was a great shock early in the New Year for him to be diagnosed with bowel cancer. The subsequent operation was completely successful and all seemed well until he contracted an infection from which he did not recover. Don was a man of integrity, kindness and high principles and was spoken of as a true gentleman. The many messages of condolence and the outstanding attendance at his funeral showed that he was held in very high regard. He has left behind many happy memories and will be sadly missed, especially by me.

Maureen Linton-Lee

Ralph Villiger
1975 - 2015

One day, Ralph came to my office saying, 'Will you take care of my business for a while? I leave in three days for a true adventure.' I couldn't work out what was crazier: leaving his business to someone else, or going off on the trip he was planning. But this became a habit: Ralph was a hero of his kind with a remarkable ability to believe in others and fulfil extraordinary adventures with the utmost straightforwardness.

Swiss born, located in Basel, already globally-renowned as a thought-leader in intellectual property valuation in life sciences, entrepreneur, wine aficionado to the extent of opening a wine-bar in Zürich, Ralph wanted to broaden his horizons and explore new heights, with what he called 'true adventure'.

Ralph was not chasing famous records like the 8,000m summits, or extreme solos. Being inspired by pioneers in sailing, hiking and climbing,

Ralph Villiger

his enjoyment came from designing and running multi-disciplined, original expeditions in remote areas, choosing paths open only for a very few days in the year. Guided by a remarkably gifted mind and a limitless passion for discovering the unknown, Ralph succeeded.

He thus put his work aside to run the OSTAR 2013 singlehanded race across the Atlantic Ocean, to then sail north to America, reach Greenland and climb where none had climbed before. On the way back he wintered his boat *Ntombifuti* in Iceland, to prepare for the next dream he wanted to fulfil.

As a child, he did a lot of hiking with his brother and parents in the Appenzell area of Switzerland. After he had finished his studies in mathematical engineering from the Swiss Federal Institute of Technology Lausanne, the Technical University of Catalonia, Barcelona and the St Petersburg State University, Russia, as well as an MSc in mathematical finance from the University of Oxford, he became more and more interested in climbing and completed many routes in the Alpstein massif, many of them solo. It was not the difficulties he was thinking about: he just enjoyed being out there on his own, doing all this by himself. It was not about being the strongest, just about daring and doing.

On a family trip to Antarctica he was inspired by the ice and its tough and wild conditions. He began planning to explore the Polar regions on his own and with very little support from outside. This dream came true in 2013.

I got to know Ralph in 2006 during a guided tour in Chamonix. At this time he was a mountaineer, with average climbing skills. I was impressed most by his stamina: he never thought about giving up. I think he never really became aware of being wet or cold. Almost always wearing the same layers, whether it was cold or mild, he just said, 'No problem, I think we will make it.' In the beginning, our climbing partnership started as a classic guide-client tandem but it quickly turned into a deep friendship.

One of his big dreams was climbing the Eiger *North Face*. After a few years of training we finally realized this in 2014. During this training, we completed a lot of other routes in the Alps, from Chamonix to the Dolomites: the *Supercouloir* on Mont Blanc du Tacul, the Eiger's *South Face*, Cima Grande's *North Face*, the Piz Badile and Dachstein were just some of them.

In 2012, we discussed a combination of sailing and climbing in very remote areas. Ralph was lucky to own a sailing boat, which was perfectly suited to our plans. We wanted to go to as far north as possible, just the two of us, no other climbers, no skipper. (Ralph was a skipper in his own right, having successfully completed the AZAB 2011 before the OSTAR 2013 courses.)

We visited Greenland's east coast twice, once in 2013 and then in 2014, followed by dolphins when sailing, and sometimes polar bears, one of which even considered us as a good snack. The main problems were the navigation through the icebergs and not knowing anything about where we would find anchorages to keep the boat safe while we were climbing. Each time we were away for four or five weeks, living on the boat. We were able to make a few first ascents during these two trips, the most important one being that of Kirken (1209m), in Liverpool Land in 2014. (See the 2015 *AAJ*.)

For this ascent, we won Adventurer of the Year from the German-speaking climbing community. Apparently, we were not the only ones inspired by this expedition. The award, however, arrived in October 2015, too late for Ralph, but I can still feel the emotion it would have raised in him.

As soon as one project was completed, and before he was even off the peak, Ralph, in his unique way, had already started thinking about the next one. While we had so much time on our expeditions, it was easy to think about new projects, but the big difference between the two of us was that I was thinking and dreaming while Ralph was already planning everything in detail, selecting the next fascinating challenges and routes to make it unique. He made everything concerning planning look so easy. Within a few days he could find out about the remotest areas, name a handful of unclimbed peaks there and get in touch with the very few people who might have at one time approached or thought about the area. This I will miss a lot.

When coming back in August 2014 we decided to go to Patagonia to have a try at Mount FitzRoy. Unfortunately, bad weather conditions forced us to turn back 10 pitches below the summit. Disappointed but motivated to come back in 2016, we left Patagonia after four weeks.

Our last trip together brought us to the Caucasus in July 2015, where we climbed South Ushba. We did it in the most uncommon way, via the ice face, which offers only very few windows for climbing each year, and has to be done in the early morning and quickly enough in order not to be trapped by rising temperatures.

A few days after coming back from Ushba, our next trip to Patagonia to finally climb FitzRoy had been decided. Ralph wanted to train on the normal route of the Gspaltenhorn. He told us he wanted to spend some time as well in 'his' mountains, the Swiss ones. He talked about it many times; it must have been something special for him.

To all of us, it was always obvious that Ralph would make it back from everything. Nothing could resist his beautiful mind in planning or his stamina in action. On the way down from the summit, he slipped on a slab and never came back. He had not turned 40, yet had led a life as full as someone twice that age.

His father gave him the taste for mountain and polar expeditions. Each time Ralph used to speak about what a pioneer did or what he planned to do, his father, fuelled by the same excitement as his son, had already found all historical data on the topic by the following day. Ralph always said that his parents were the most supportive ever. He was keen on living what his father dreamt of and always texted his parents at the summit of every peak he reached, simply to express how wonderful life can be.

Ralph still had many ideas and adventures planned on all horizons of his life… He wanted to create new seasonal batches of his gin brand *N-Ginious*, to save lives from cancer or multi-resistant bacteria strains. We truly hope that some day these may still become reality and we strive for that. The lesson in life he left us is to never stop dreaming, always live to turn ideas into adventure, and fulfil them with passion.

His does not only leave our two hearts full of inspiration, but the heart and mind of many, all those he met along the way, from life sciences to wine tasting to sailing, climbing and those he loved.

Harald Fichtinger and Marie Petit

Professor Edward Sydney Williams PhD, FRCP, FRCR 1923 - 2015

Edward Williams was born and brought up in a very rural part of Shropshire near the Long Mountain, close to the Welsh border. His mother was a local schoolteacher; his father spent most of the First World War on the Western Front after which he became a gardener. Edward's home was so remote that the family could only get to church about twice a month, when a service was held at a chapel about one and a half miles away across fields. However, he developed a strong faith and in retirement he took the required training to become ordained as a part-time priest.

Prof Edward S Williams

He attended the primary school where his mother taught. He went on at 14 to the Technical College in Shrewsbury. He did well in both academic and practical courses and became an apprentice to an electrical construction company before moving to the West Midlands Joint Electricity Authority as a draftsman. In 1940, aged 16, he joined the LDV (later the Home Guard).

At 18 he was called up and entered the navy as an electrical midshipman, RNVR. He found himself working with university graduates. However, he must have impressed his seniors because he soon became the leader of a team working directly under the Admiralty, visiting ships in various UK ports, sorting out problems in relation to the new devices of RADAR and ASDIC and interference by power cables and wireless.

After D-Day, he was posted to Colombo and the naval base at Trincomalee. The war soon ended and there was not a lot to do. He climbed Pidurutalagala (2524m) and lectured on mathematics while continuing to self-study to compensate for his lack of formal education. He also enjoyed swimming, sailing, walking and fishing.

After leaving the navy he was successful in gaining entry to King's College, London, to follow a special honours course in physics. A fellow student was Peter Higgs of 'Higgs Boson' fame. After graduating in physics, he decided he wanted to work in the new field of nuclear physics applied to medicine, so he embarked on a medical course at the Middlesex Hospital, London. There he joined the Middlesex Mountaineering Club. As a boy he had been accustomed to long walks in the country near his home. Now, he added hill walking and rock climbing in North Wales and the Lakes. He got to know Peter Harding, one of the leading rock climbers in the 1940s and did a number of hard routes with him at Helsby, on Derbyshire grit, as well as in North Wales. He joined the Climbers' Club in 1948. He made a number of trips to the Alps from 1950 to 1956, climbing with Denis Greenald out of Chamonix and Val d'Isère, and in the Dauphiné.

In 1956 Edward, with Denis and Gwen Greenald and Jim Durbin, made an expedition to the Karakoram, at a time when such trips were few. They attempted three peaks in the 6,000m range. They succeeded on two of them: Brandu Brakk (6285m) and Lukpe Barak, a bit lower, and failed on the third because of very bad weather. From this trip he brought back samples of saliva, from which the sodium-potassium ratio allowed him to predict the changes, due to altitude, in the level of the hormone aldosterone. This had only just been discovered at the Middlesex Hospital by James Tate. (It regulates sodium excretion by the kidneys.)

Edward qualified in 1958 and married Wendy. They honeymooned in Scotland where he introduced his bride to the joys of Scottish winter mountaineering.

After junior hospital jobs he naturally started to specialise in the new discipline of nuclear medicine. The Middlesex Hospital was fortunate in 1961 to get a generous grant from the Nuffield Foundation with which to build a new four-storey Institute of Nuclear Medicine. Edward was the obvious choice as its first director; though rather young for such a role, he was appointed in 1964 and helped to design the building. This was opened in 1969. He was appointed the first professor of nuclear medicine in the UK in 1971. He soon started an MSc course in the subject; it attracted a worldwide group of students. Besides running this institute and carrying out clinical work with hospital patients, he was in demand for numerous committees, in this country and in Europe: these were involved with regulating this new field of medicine, with its inherent dangers.

In 1960 Edward led a 15-day expedition to the Vallot refuge on Mont Blanc to study the effect of altitude again on kidney function and aldosterone. Conditions were quite austere, to put it mildly. Among the members of this party was his new bride, Wendy, a nurse from the Middlesex Hospital. Two years later he led another similar expedition, this time to the Plateau Rosa, camping in the cable-car station on the Theodul Pass at just on 3,500m.

I came to know Edward via Mike Ward around 1976. Soon after this, we started a series of field studies in the hills of this country and later in the Alps. The object was to try to work out what the effect of mountaineering-type exercise was on fluid and salt balance in the body. The exercise we were interested in was of long duration, eight hours or so, and sustained for some days, as mountaineers do. Any previous work in this field had been on once-only exercise of 15-30 minutes duration. Our interest was stimulated by stories about high-altitude pulmonary oedema, often with a history of considerable exertion before onset. We collected a group of five or six friends for these studies which we held first in North Wales, later in the Lake District and finally in the Alps, in the Kulm Hotel on the Gornergrat. Each study had a four-day period at rest, a five-day exercise period, where each day included eight hours of vigorous hill walking, and then four days at rest. We needed to be on a strictly regulated diet, all eating the same food with the same diet each day. We measured all fluid in and out and took blood samples each day. In this way we were able to show that this form of exercise caused us to retain some water, a considerable amount of sodium and to shift water from inside to outside our cells, into the blood and extra-cellular fluid. In the later studies we showed which hormones were responsible for these changes. Finally in the Swiss study we showed that the addition of altitude to the exercise had only a small effect. All these studies resulted in papers in physiological journals.

In 1981 Edward was a member of the science team on Ward and Bonington's successful Kongur expedition. At 7,749m it was one of highest unclimbed peaks and, being situated in Xinjiang, north of Tibet, it was quite a coup for Mike Ward to get permission to explore the approaches and then to attempt the peak the following year. Kongur is in fact a whole range of peaks with Kongur itself in the middle; the route was not at all obvious. Mike, Chris and Alan Rouse made the reconnaissance in 1980. The team of ten members flew out to Kashgar in spring 1981. There were four climbers: Chris, Alan, Peter Boardman and Joe Tasker. The scientific team consisted of Mike, Edward, Charles Clarke and myself. Jim Curran was our journalist and cameraman, and David Wilson, with experience in the diplomatic service and fluency in Chinese, came as liaison officer. The peak proved quite a hard nut to crack but the four climbers were, eventually, successful. We studied the differences between us scientists, more or less normal subjects, and the four elite mountaineers, with respect to our physiological response to exercise at altitude. While the climbers were doing their stuff high on the mountain, we had time to climb a few modest peaks within range of base camp.

In retirement, as well as working as a priest, he wrote and published a slim volume of verse. He continued hill walking, especially in the South Downs near his home in Surrey and made a solo walk from the sea in South Wales to the North Wales coast. His eldest son, David, said in his funeral oration, 'He stayed with mountaineering his whole life and even a passing reading of his writings shows that it was the greatest passion he had. Many of his longest friendships were made through climbing, his greatest happiness being in the mountains.'

Despite his considerable achievements, he was always modest and unassuming. He was a delightful climbing, walking or expedition companion. He leaves a wife, three sons and many colleagues and friends.

Jim Milledge

OFFICERS AND COMMITTEE FOR 2016

President .... Lindsay Griffin
Vice Presidents .... Sandy Allan, Malcolm Bass
Honorary Secretary .... Anna Lawford
Honorary Treasurer .... John Dempster
Honorary Editor of the *Alpine Journal* .... Ed Douglas
Honorary Librarian .... Jerry Lovatt
Chairs of Sub-Committees:
Climbing & Events .... Jonathan White
Finance .... Kimball Morrison
Marketing, Membership & Recruitment .... Tony Westcott
Property .... Victor Saunders
Chair of the Alpine Club Library Council .... Hywel Lloyd
Committee, *elected* .... Charlie Burbridge, Susan Jensen, Neil Pitts
Committee, *co-opted* .... Hugh Alexander

OFFICE BEARERS

London Lecture Organiser .... Derek Buckle
South-west Lecture Organisers .... Tony Westcott, Chris Storie
Peak Lecture Organiser .... Martin Wragg
Lakes Lecture Organiser .... Laetitia Sterling
Edinburgh Lecture Organiser .... Des Rubens
Winter Dinner Convenor .... William Newsom
BMC Liaison Officer .... Alison Stockwell
Meets Officer .... Kate Ross
Chair of the Climbing Fund Sub-Committee .... Malcolm Bass
Chair of the Membership Applications Sub-Committee .. Richard Nadin
Chair of the IT Sub-Committee .... David Lund
IT Sub-Committee Secretary .... Jeremy Gould
Membership Secretary .... Sherry Macliver
Student Liaison Officer .... Sherry Macliver
UIAA Representative .... Steve Goodwin
Chair of the International Panel .... Malcolm Bass
Honorary Archivist .... Glyn Hughes
Honorary Keeper of the Club's Artefacts .... Jerry Lovatt
Honorary Keeper of the Club's Monuments .... Charlie Burbridge
Honorary Keeper of the Club's Paintings .... John Fairley
Honorary Keeper Emeritus of the Club's Paintings .... Peter Mallalieu
Honorary Keeper of the Club's Photographs .... Peter Rowland
AJ Advertising Officer .... Ursula Haeberli
Assistant Editor of the *Alpine Journal* (obituaries) Catherine Moorehead
Newsletter Editor .... Adele Long
Website Editors .... David Baldock, Jeremy Gould
Honorary Solicitor .... Rhys Williams
Trustees .... Michael Baker, Adam Roberts, Philip Sanders
General Manager .... Ursula Haeberli
Administrator .... Iwonna Hudowska
Librarian .... Tadeusz Hudowski

Alpine Club Notes

Illustration for *An Olympus in the Dream*, a bookwork which has taken 15 years to put together and is a deeply multi-layered piece of work using text, images, cut-outs, rubber stamps and music. It exists in an edition of 14 and while the text in each, telling a strange autobiographical story, remains the same, the illustrations, numbering over 200, are all hand-finished and provide a varied counterpoint. Each copy therefore is a form of variation on an original theme.

Rob Fairley, 2006. (Ink, watercolour, gold leaf and digital photographs. 24.5cm x 17cm. Two copies in the National Library for Scotland (HB6.215.4.9 and HB6.215.3.58), six in private collections, six still available.)

Rob Fairley: Renaissance Man of Moidart

This year's section pages are illustrated with works by Rob Fairley. Rob joined the Club in 1991 as a result of an encounter with George Band on Roisbheinn a few years before, when Band was president. A stag was the target, Band was the gun, and Fairley, who keeps a croft at the foot of the hill, was employed as the stalker. The pair found no stag, perhaps because they spent the day discovering their mutual acquaintance with various giants of Nepal. A presidential command to join the Club followed shortly.

There are five distinct strands in the rope of Fairley's life: artist, crofter, educator[1], mountaineer and writer[2]. He was a pupil at George Watson's School in Edinburgh in the 1960s where his interest in mountains was fostered by Archie Hendry, who taught languages there and who also influenced Robin Smith and Mal Duff, Fairley's exact contemporary. Fairley's early mastery of mountain landscape drawing is evident in the Eiger drawing in 'John Harlin', painted while still a schoolboy. After graduating from Edinburgh College of Art in 1975, he moved to Mallaig briefly before becoming the sole human inhabitant of the tidal island Shona Beag in Loch Moidart until 1979 when he moved to a croft at Alisary on Loch Ailort. During this period, besides regular landscape work, Fairley practised a form of ephemeral shamanistic 'land art', occasionally recorded by drawing or by pinhole photography from cameras constructed from animal carcases, stone enclosures, etc. To some degree 'A Line Made by Red Deer', and 'A Line of Fox Bones' reflect these early interests[3]. At the same time, he did not neglect mountaineering, climbing regularly at a high level in winter and summer, usually solo except for the company of his intrepid collie Jinny, who dodged the cruxes but never failed to greet him at the top of the routes. The two huge pencil drawings of Ben Nevis, 'Building in a Landscape' and 'Figure in a Landscape' date from late in this period. According to Fairley, they were done in his croft/studio by the light of oil and Tilley lamps, working more or less naked because of the extreme heat they generated. These are extraordinary works, perhaps the most impressive mountain drawings in pencil since Edward Lear's Lake District drawings in 1836[4].

In the mid 1980s, Fairley resumed acquaintance with Mal Duff. Duff had taken two poets, Andrew Greig and Kathleen Jamie, to the Muztagh Tower and had the idea of taking an artist along to illustrate his expeditions. In Fairley, he found an artist who could climb as well. As well as going

1. Fairley was involved from the beginning in the extraordinary Room 13 experiment at Caol Primary School, Fort William, in which children pursued art and photography projects of their own devising, lightly advised by Fairley, and managed grant-getting, exhibitions and sales of their work, etc. The initial project was expanded to other Lochaber schools and then around the world. See room13international.org for more information.

2. Roshven House on Lochailort, close to Fairley's croft, is the repository of the archives of Jemima Blackburn *née* Wedderburn (1823-1909). Blackburn was an able amateur artist and a cousin and contemporary of James Clerk Maxwell. Her work consisted of lively watercolour sketches of family life, and more detailed drawings of birds. Fairley has written two beautifully illustrated books about Blackburn's life and work: *Jemima – the Paintings and Memoirs of a Victorian Lady* (Canongate, 1988 & 1998), and *Blackburn's Birds* (Canongate, 1993).

3. *Rob Fairley – The Early Works* (Resipole Studios, 2011) contains three fascinating essays describing his life and art in this period.

4. See Charles Nugent, *Edward Lear the Landscape Artist: Tours of Ireland and the English Lakes, 1835 & 1836*, Wordsworth Trust, 2009.

Sketchbook portrait of a Nepalese girl.

to the Himalaya with Duff, he was also recruited by Henry Todd, and in his own words worked as a 'climbing mercenary' there for many years, during which he visited Annapurna, Annapurna III, Kusum Kanguru, Ama Dablam and Tawoche besides many trekking peaks. Numerous wonderful watercolour landscapes from this period survive – Fairley is notorious for destroying his own work – and are represented here by 'Everest from Rongbuk Glacier', 'Andy Perkins & Andy Cave at Annapurna III Advanced Base Camp', 'Annapurna Camp One', and 'Breakfast with Henry'.

Fairley became fascinated by Nepal's culture and people, and grasped every opportunity to record this in his sketchbooks and in watercolour work finished at home. His sketching method (illustrated below) used a tube of watercolour, whatever sort of water was to hand, his unused hand as palette, and many such sketches were executed in a very few minutes.

While all of this portrait work is remarkable, it is perhaps his pure watercolour portraits that deserve most respect. These are in the tradition of the likes of George Richmond or James Guthrie, but the technique is purer. This work is represented here by 'Tibetan Trader', 'Tsering' and 'Quin Ego Hoc Rogem'. The latter is in egg tempera colours, not watercolour, but this medium has the same qualities of flatness and transparency, and will last 1,000 years or more.

I am delighted to have had this opportunity to present Fairley's work in the *Journal*, and I commend him to readers as a mountaineer-artist of the first quality, to my mind to be ranked alongside such distinguished predecessors as Edward Compton and Ernst Platz, but undoubtedly with greater range.

Robin Campbell

Fifty years of the Troll Wall

If you were into new routes and big walls in the 1960s you would have known about a monster in Norway about which ominous stories circulated that can be summed up in one word: 'unclimbable'. The Troll Wall was also known as 'the vertical mile', and described as 'the largest overhanging wall in Europe'. It was reputed to be smooth and holdless for 5,000ft, and impossible without the aid of bolts. It also faces north and is as far north as Alaska's Denali. Quite a proposition!

Strange then that none of the 'big boys' went for it. Instead a team from a small Peak District club called the Rimmon decided it was worth a go and in July 1965 despite everyone's doubts and some horrendous weather actually climbed it. Apart from me, the team were Tony 'Nick' Nicholls, Bill Tweedale, John Amatt, Rob Holt, Jeff Heath and Margaret Woodcock.

The six lads spent numerous days in bad weather on rain-soaked rock establishing a bivy at the foot of the face above the introductory slabs. The first attempt by Bill, Nick, John and me failed after five days, once again in atrocious weather, Nick getting us off the wall and trashing his hands in the process. Bill, John and I returned a couple of days later and succeeded in five and a half days, reaching the top just before another storm broke.

Following the ascent, one well-known British climber who was very familiar with Norway actually wrote to J E B Wright, then the editor of *Mountain Craft*, implying that we must have found a way to sneak up the back without being noticed; in the end the letter wasn't published. On the other hand, Joe Brown said: 'The ascent must rank as one of the greatest ever achievements by British rock climbers,' and Aslak Aastorp, a top Norwegian climber, described the route as 'a masterpiece of route-finding at the highest free and aid standards of the day.' I think his grade comments were over-enthusiastic, but I liked the route-finding bit; finding what proved to be the best natural line up the wall was something I was always pleased about.

Perhaps the most unusual thing about the ascent was that a team of Norwegian climbers arrived in Romsdal a day or two before us and by the time we arrived they already had a rope fixed on the wall. They had claimed their route. To our great relief it wasn't the route we had planned. To this day I'm not sure if it was a coincidence or whether Arne Randers Heen, Norway's elder statesman of climbing with whom I had been corresponding, had tipped them off.

The presence of two teams on the face was tailor-made for a press field day. 'The competition' was in the news every day both in Norway and the UK – though it never was a competition. The Norwegians, Leif Norman Pattersen, Odd Eliassen, Ole Daniel Enersen, Jon Teigland and girlfriends were camped not far from us. Leif Norman and Jon had both climbed in the Himalaya, whilst Ole Daniel and Odd were also amongst Norway's top climbers.

Unlike us they were armed with an impressive collection of American hardware including jumars and chrome-moly pegs brought out from the States by Leif. It was all brand new on the market and totally unavailable in Europe. We, on the other hand, were stuck with Hiebler ascenders that were untrustworthy and our soft steel European pegs that crumpled at the first obstacle. Descenders were still to be invented, as were sit harnesses. The Norwegians had chest harnesses. We had a waist belt of my design, which could be made into a sit harness for abseiling and climbing roofs by the addition of a sit sling. It later became the Troll Mark 2, which led to the design of the Whillans harness, then the Troll Mark 5, on which almost all modern sit harness designs are now based. Our Troll Wall ascent was probably the last of the world's big walls to be climbed in the old style with 'old gear': no sit harnesses, no reliable ascenders, no descenders, no modern range of nuts, and bivy gear and waterproofs so bad we almost died.

But I digress. When we retreated on our first attempt, the Norwegians were in a better situation and survived the storm. As soon as the weath-

Above: Stein P Aasheim interviewing Ole Daniel Enersen, Odd Eliassen, Jon Teigland, Tony Howard and Rob Holt at the 2015 Romsdal Fjellfestival. The two main headlines of the 1965 newspapers on screen read: 'Norwegians 150 metres higher than the British' and 'Norwegians and English race to be first up Troll Wall'. *(Di Taylor)*

Left: Tony Howard and Rob Holt below the Troll Wall 50 years after the first ascent. *(Di Taylor)*

er improved they continued with their route and topped out a day before us after 11 days on the face, much to the jubilation of the Norwegian press. Of course Bill, John and I were unaware until we came down after completing our route the following morning to be met by the press and members of both teams armed with copious amounts of celebratory beer before we were all feted in the Grand Hotel. It was reported in the Norwegian press that the Norwegian team 'thought our achievement on the Troll Wall put theirs in the shade', which was over-kind of them and far too modest.

In 2015, on the 50th anniversary of the climbs, both teams were invited to Romsdal for a celebratory reunion at the annual mountain festival in July. Arne Larsen wrote an article in the Norwegian magazine *Klatring* about the leader of the Norwegian team, Leif Norman Patterson. The story, which was later translated to English by Anders I Ourom, says of Leif that he 'was, by far, the most experienced of the four-man team. By 1965 he had nearly ten years' experience on the hills, and was well known in the USA for his many challenging winter climbs. In addition he also brought much newly designed climbing equipment to Norway – hard steel pitons, several hundred metres of first-class ropes and slings, and jumar rope-clamps which would be indispensable on the wall. It isn't overstating the case to say that without Leif Norman Patterson's initiative there probably wouldn't be a *Norwegian Route* on the Troll Wall, and the British team would not have had to share with others the honour of the first ascent of North Europe's highest and steepest mountain wall.' Which overlooks the undoubted ability and commitment of the rest of the team who, I'm sure were quite capable of overcoming any obstacle met on their route even without their new American gear and Leif's undoubtedly inspirational leadership.

Rob Holt and I were the only two Brits who were able to make it to the 50th reunion. Though he was not on the actual ascent, Rob, who was only 18 at the time, had provided unselfish back up for our climb getting gear up to and down from our first bivy. In 1967 he did the third ascent with John Finnigan, another Rimmon lad, soon after Pete Livesey and John Stanger did the second. Jon, Ole and Odd represented the Norwegian team, Leif Norman having been killed in the Himalaya. The five of us were together on stage reminiscing about our ascents, taking questions from the audience and later being interviewed by the press and Norwegian TV. None of us had expected the fame and limelight created 50 years ago by the press in their concocted stories of 'Climbers Compete on the Troll Wall', so it was a perfect opportunity to dispel the myth.

In the intervening years the *Norwegian Route* has only had about ten repeat ascents. I still think it was technically the more difficult of the two although the *Rimmon Route* became the most popular climb on the face until 1998 when a huge section of the wall collapsed. Rumours of subsequent ascents have never been verified. I'm happy to say that both the first ascents – if I may call our route that, since actually we were second – were the epitome of good old-fashioned adventure climbing, poking the dragon to see what happened. How good it was to get together with the Norwegian lads once again after all those years.

Tony Howard

Editor's note: Troll Wall, the story of the British first ascent of Europe's tallest rock face, was written immediately after the climb and published in 2011 by Vertebrate Publishing. The book was given a 'Special Award for Norwegian Mountain Literature' at the Romsdal Fjellfestival in July 2011. The Italian translation published by Versante Sud won the ITAS 2013 Mountain Book Award in Trento and the 2014 Leggimontagna Literary Award in Tolmezzo. The book was reviewed in *AJ* 2012. Tony Howard's website is: www.nomadstravel.co.uk

The 2016 Piolets d'Or

In keeping with the drive to develop the Piolets d'Or into a celebration of all that is great and good about progressive modern alpinism, the 2016 event was moved from Chamonix and Courmayeur to the somewhat sleepy hamlet of La Grave at the foot of the Meije. The result was deemed to be the most successful Piolets d'Or in recent years.

The informality of the event attracted a surprisingly huge and enthusiastic audience, especially given that the access road from Grenoble was still officially closed, and the télépherique above the village, which gives access to world-class off-piste skiing, inoperative on key days due to high winds or poor visibility.

Alpinism is not an Olympic sport, so trying to compare one fine ascent with another is futile. The ethics of the Piolets d'Or are about doing more with less, about bringing together a group of like-minded alpinists, about

No podiums, just a lot of talented alpinists. Nominated ascent teams, organisers and participants at the 2016 Piolets d'Or held in the Écrins, outside the legendary hotel and restaurant La Cordée in St-Christophe-en-Oisans. Standing, from left: AC president Lindsay Griffin, former AC president Mick Fowler, honorary AC members Marko Prezelj and Voytek Kurtyka, who accepted the lifetime achievement award having previously turned it down, La Cordée's well-known proprietor Marie-Claude Turc, the artist and alpinist Andy Parkin and the celebrated Austrian climber Robert Schauer. Middle row, seated: Urban Novak, Nikita Balabanov, Piolets organiser Christian Tromsdorff, Victor Saunders, Lise Billon, Mikhail Formin, Hayden Kennedy, Jerome Sullivan and Manu Pellissier. Front row seated: Paul Ramsden, Antoine Moineville and Diego Simari. *(Piotr Drozdz/Piolets d'Or)*

inspiring future generations, about trying to maintain that wonderful spirit of adventure that is maybe declining in normal society – and then trying to share that spirit with the general public. The organizing team tries to bring to the "stage" a superb representation from the previous year of bold, innovative, imaginative climbing, executed in what is felt to be the best possible style. Awards are not made to the alpinists, but to the route, the legacy. There is also the question of commitment, and it is notable that the parties involved with each of the four representative ascents awarded a 2016 Piolet d'Or went over the summit, descending by a different route, in many cases on completely unexplored ground.

In addition, there is the Piolet d'Or Carrière, the lifetime achievements award, which this year was bestowed on the Club's honorary member Voytek Kurtyka. This was the eighth occasion when this accolade was awarded, and the seventh to an honorary member of the Alpine Club.

Honorary AC member and publisher Catherine Destivelle sits between two of her authors, Victor Saunders and Mick Fowler. In a smart piece of publishing, Destivelle combined the works of these two in one volume, *Les Tribulations des Mick et Vic*. For further 'tribulations des Mick et Vic', see Saunders' account in this volume of trying to punch Fowler. *(Piotr Drozdz/Piolets d'Or)*

This year the awards were different; the characteristic gold-painted ice axe was replaced by individual sculptures courtesy of Andy Parkin. Thirteen members of the AC took part in the event, either as speakers, recipients of awards or in organisational capacity. Apart from Voytek Kurtyka, those whose routes were celebrated were: AC members Mick Fowler and Paul Ramsden for their first ascent of Gave Ding, Nepal; Nikita Balabanov and Mikhail Formin from the Ukraine for their new route on Talung, Nepal; Hayden Kennedy (USA), Urban Novak (Slovenia), Manu Pellissier (France) and AC honorary member Marko Prezelj (Slovenia) for their ascent of a new route on Cerro Kishtwar, India; and Lise Billon, Antoine Moineville, Jerome Sullivan (all France), and Diego Simari (Argentina) for their new route on Cerro Riso Patron Central, Patagonia. Twenty-seven-year-old aspirant guide Lise Billon is the only living female, and only the second female overall, to have received a Piolet d'Or.

Lindsay Griffin

Boardman Tasker Award 2015

The 2015 Boardman Tasker event, featuring short-listed authors and the presentation of the award, was a great success. Held in November at the Kendal Mountain Festival, there was as usual a big demand for tickets.

Four of the five short listed authors were able to attend. Martin Wragg, the chair of the Boardman Tasker Trust, welcomed everyone and introduced Stephen Venables, who interviewed the authors.

Stephen began by talking with Sandy Allan, whose book *In Some Lost Place* is a truly gripping account of the traverse of the *Mazeno Ridge* on Nanga Parbat, and then a bold attempt to reach the summit and descend the *Kinshofer* route. This represented one of the greatest achievements in the history of modern high-altitude climbing and Sandy's low-key comments drew much admiration from the audience.

Next up was American author David Pagel, whose *Cold Feet: Stories of a Middling Climber* is a fascinating account laced with a wonderful level of humour, of a mountaineering life in the middle lane. A book very much in the tradition of Tom Patey's *One Man's Mountains*, David emerged as a very capable mountaineer with a wonderful self-deprecating humour and sense of the absurd. Stephen's interview with him produced a great deal of laughter in the audience and he was very warmly received.

The third author on stage was Canadian master mountaineer Barry Blanchard to talk about his book *The Calling*. Barry came across as a humorous low-key dude, but his book is full of action, high drama and many descriptions of the fearful visceral sensations of alpinism at the highest level. Barry has a good turn of humour and humanity in the stories he tells, but the book contains plenty of fear and deep uncertainty and leaves the reader in no doubt of the nature of mountaineering at this level, the deep commitment required and the consequent impact on body and mind.

Daniel Arnold, who was unable to come over from the USA, had sent a short film. His strange book of mountain fiction *Snowblind: Stories of Alpine Obsession* greatly impressed the judges, with its gothic overtones and intensity of narrative.

The final author Stephen interviewed was John Porter. His book *One Day as a Tiger: Alex MacIntyre and the Birth of Light and Fast Alpinism* describes the life of Alex MacIntyre and the very rapid developments in high-altitude climbing in the 1980s and the consequent heavy death toll among activists. John's book illustrates the hard struggle of talented activists to push the boundaries in this most extreme form of mountaineering, and the key role Alex played. It is a very fine account of a crucial period in the history of mountaineering and makes clear the deep cost of such dangerous activity in the world's highest mountains, both to the climbers themselves and their loved ones.

After a short break Martin Wragg made the presentation of only the second Boardman Tasker lifetime achievement award to Ken Wilson. Martin outlined Ken's huge contribution to mountain writing over almost 50 years and acknowledged the great support he had always given the BT Award itself. Ken had suffered with ill health in recent years and the award was received on his behalf by Richard Hale, who made an excellent acceptance speech.

The chair of the judges for 2015 was Robin Campbell and his speech was greatly anticipated. He did not disappoint, having the audience in stitches as he set himself up as something of a curmudgeon viewing the submitted books with a genial albeit cynical eye. In the end he brought the house down; in the view of this writer, it was the best chairman's speech we have had. The 2015 Boardman Tasker award for mountain literature went to Barry Blanchard, for *The Calling*. To quote Robin: 'it is a proper history. Barry writes with tremendous intensity and pace, communicating his startling experiences well.' It was a hugely popular winner and is a book likely to inspire the next generation, being one of the finest mountaineering books of the modern era.

There was a general view in the room that this was the best Boardman Tasker event ever, culminating in a truly outstanding winning book. The 2016 event is on Friday 18 November 2016; tickets go on sale in September. Please see the BT's new website, www.boardmantasker.com, for images from the event and for the complete text of Robin Campbell's speech. The other judges were Terry Gifford and Graham Desroy, chair for 2016.

Steve Dean
Boardman Tasker Charitable Trust

Alpine Club Library 2015

We have in the Alpine Club collection of paintings a splendid scene of 'Les Grandes Jorasses' by E T Compton. This year, it has been the iconic image for posters for our exhibition 'Les Trésors de l'Alpine Club et l'Alpinisme' held at the Musée Alpin in Chamonix, a French national museum. Edward Theodore Compton, 1849-1921, was a keen artist and mountaineer, elected to the AC in 1880.

The exhibition celebrated 150 years since the Golden Age of Alpinism, a time when British climbers and their local guides made a very large number of Alpine first ascents. 'Les Trésors de l'Alpine Club et l'Alpinisme' was created through a collaboration between the Chamonix tourist office, the curator for the Musée Alpin, and the Alpine Club Library team. Around 100 items were loaned from the AC collections; these were augmented with items from the Chamonix museum and other private collectors. The exhibition ran from July 2015 until April 2016 and had over 20,000 visitors, including many AC members who visited Chamonix during this period.

Displayed in the spacious rooms of the Musée, the AC exhibits included many paintings and engravings, important historic books, including *Führerbücher* of leading guides of the day, special artefacts such as Whymper's

'Les Grandes Jorasses', 1911, by E T Compton (1849-1921), elected AC member 1880. The Grandes Jorasses was first climbed by Horace Walker with local guides in 1868.

ice axe, and over 300 scans of our historic photographs, all were extremely well presented. It was essential to organise the robust packing, secure transport, and insurance of all these items. They were all scanned or photographed at high resolution before they left Charlotte Road, and the watercolour paintings were on show by rotation to limit their exposure to light (see also notes in *AJ* 2015, p454).

A double page spread from the survey notebook of Anthony Adams Reilly (1836-1885), elected in 1862. Adams Reilly compiled the first map of the massif 'The Chain of Mont Blanc' in 1865, climbing it by seven different routes. He also made ascents with Whymper.

'Grütli, Uri Rostock from Lake Lucerne', late 1850s, by John Ruskin (1819-1900). Ruskin was elected to the AC in 1869 with the citation 'literary, artistic and scientific contributions towards our appreciation of the Alpine scene'.

On 11 July, ten of us attended the opening ceremonies, listening to many speeches in French. The Chamonix tourist office team presented us to a large gathering of well-wishers. The mayor of Chamonix opened the exhibition, and gave the Library a magnificent book of engravings of early Mont Blanc history and ascents. Jerry Lovatt, our honorary librarian, presented Chamonix with an item from his private collection, an early original *Führerbuch* of Chamonix guides, the brothers Jean and François Simon. We presented special engraved souvenirs to Eric Fournier, the mayor,

Claude Marin, the curator of the exhibition and a Chamonix guide, and Claire Burnet, organiser at the tourist office.

In Chamonix, there has been considerable praise for the exhibition by many visitors. The tourist office has been delighted with visitor numbers, and we received an official letter from the mayor, appreciating all our help. Apart from the kudos of the event and promotion of the AC, there is a further legacy: the scanning or photographing of all the exhibits means that future researchers can refer to high-quality digital images and this will minimise the handling of originals. This also safeguards images of the AC collections and contributes to the range of scans we can offer to publishers to gain one-time reproduction fees that help finance the Library.

To conclude, congratulations and thanks are due to everyone in the Library team for providing so much expertise and hard effort, often under considerable time pressure as things developed. Next, we plan follow-up exhibitions in the UK.

Hywel Lloyd

Contributors

DEREK BUCKLE is a retired medicinal chemist now acting part-time as a consultant to the pharmaceutical industry. With plenty of free time, he spends much of it rock climbing, ski touring and mountaineering in various parts of the world. Besides climbing, his greatest challenges are finding time to accompany his wife on more traditional holidays and the filling of his passport with exotic and expensive visas.

ROBIN CAMPBELL has held every office in the Scottish Mountaineering Club for which administrative competence is not required, including a long stint as Editor in the 1960s and 70s, and as Archivist since 1997. Retired from a desultory career as an academic child psychologist, he now wastes his time and money in collecting and studying old drawings and water-colours, particularly those depicting mountains before they were trampled into familiarity by the boots of mountaineers.

GEORGE CAVE works for much of the year as a design engineer in Warwick. In search of more adventurous peaks he developed in interest in planning expeditions abroad, particularly to central Asia. In recent years he has climbed or skied in Kyrgyzstan, Iran, Morocco and Russia, using his background in engineering and technology to take advantage of the latest digital mapping tools when planning ascents of unclimbed peaks.

JOHN CLEARE has been a freelance professional photographer for over 50 years but a climber for rather longer. Business and many expeditions have taken him all over the world, while he has several dozen books, several films and live TV broadcasts, more than a few new routes and several virgin summits to his credit. An ex-vice president of the AC and an ex-president of the Alpine Ski Club, he lives in remote Wiltshire.

MICK FOWLER works for Her Majesty's Revenue and Customs and, by way of contrast, likes to inject as much memorable adventure and excitement into his climbing ventures. He has climbed extensively in the UK and has regularly led expeditions to the greater ranges for more than 27 years. He has written two books, *Vertical Pleasure* (1995) and *On Thin Ice* (2005). Mick served as president of the Alpine Club from 2010.

DR ABBIE GARRINGTON is senior lecturer in modern and contemporary literature at Durham University, and is currently writing *High Modernism: A Literary History of Mountaineering, 1890-1945*. She brings literary perspectives to the history of British mountaineering, and co-curated this year's exhibition 'Savage Arena: The Legacy of Joe Tasker' with the Mountain Heritage Trust and Ushaw College. She is a former expedition leader with British Exploring and a fellow of the Royal Geographical Society.

TERRY GIFFORD was director of the annual International Festival of Mountaineering Literature for 21 years. Former chair of the Mountain Heritage Trust, he is the author of *The Joy of Climbing* (Whittles, 2004) and *Al Otro Lado del Aguilar* (Oversteps Books, 2011). Visiting professor at Bath Spa University's Centre for Writing and Environment and *profesor honorífico* at the University of Alicante, he recently celebrated his 70th birthday appropriately on *Wreckers' Slab*.

JIM GREGSON has climbed widely in the Alps since 1972. He is also a telemark ski mountaineer who makes regular trips to Norway. He first visited the Arctic in 1991 and has returned many times, often as an expedition leader, and is one of Britain's leading Arctic mountaineers. His book *Exploring Greenland* documents many of his trips and showcases his photography. He hopes to return to Greenland again and again…

LINDSAY GRIFFIN lives in North Wales, from where he continues to report on the developments in world mountaineering. An enthusiastic mind still tries to coax a less than enthusiastic body up pleasant bits of rock and ice, both at home and abroad. He is currently serving as AC President.

ANDY HOUSEMAN is based near Harrogate, Yorkshire where he works in the family haulage business. He has climbed extensively in the European Alps as well as many expeditions to the Greater Ranges with significant repeats and new routes in Alaska, Nepal and Pakistan, but is just as happy spending his time cycling, running and climbing in the local Yorkshire Dales.

GLYN HUGHES is a some-time hon secretary of the Alpine Club, but now carries out the equally important roles of hon archivist and barman – or as the AC quaintly puts it, 'Chairman of the Wine Committee'. In 2014 he took on the near-impossible task of following Bill Ruthven as hon secretary of the Mount Everest Foundation.

SUSAN JENSEN grew up in Anchorage, Alaska, and started climbing some time shortly after the millennium while living in Surrey. Now in Scotland, she has a day job doing statistics for NHS Scotland and also works with the Scottish Mountaineering Trust publications on the climbers' guides. These are fitted in around summer and winter climbing, expeditions, sleep and cakes.

MARC KÖNIG was born in Germany and is an associate member. He works as an urologist in private practice. Besides mountaineering for a long time in the Himalaya, Africa and Laponia his interest is in research in mountaineering medicine and especially the development of mountaineering boots over time.

EUAN MEARNS has BSc and PhD degrees in geology from the University of Aberdeen. He is an avid hill walker and nordic skier. He has been blogging on energy and climate change issues for ten years. He passionately believes that the fossil fuel plus CO_2 is bad and renewable energy is good meme is over simplified and threatens to undermine the fabric of modern society and science.

JIM MILLEDGE began rock climbing as a medical student in Birmingham. After service in the RAF as a medical officer, he specialised in chest medicine and was a member of the 1960-61 Silver Hut Expedition leading to a lifelong interest in mountain medicine. He has been on numerous expeditions, some with scientific aims, some for fun, and is co-author of the textbook *High Altitude Medicine & Physiology*.

ALEX MILNE is a petroleum geologist based in Aviemore. He has climbed, skied and trekked extensively in the Alps, Africa, the Karakoram, the Himalaya and his native Scotland. He specializes in mountain photography and is never happier than to be out in the mountains exploring photographic opportunities.

CATHERINE MOOREHEAD recently retired from being Mistress of Scholars at the Royal Grammar School, Guildford. She became a 'Compleat Munroist' in 1996, and has led expeditions to the Mongolian Altai, Kazakhstan, Zanskar, Xinjiang, Tibet and Bhutan. In 2013, she published *The K2 Man*, the biography of Godwin-Austen.

TED NORRISH read classics at Brasenose College, Oxford, where he enjoyed three Alpine seasons, an expedition to Arctic Norway in 1955, and, in 1958, organised and partly led the Oxford Chitral expedition described in this volume. A classics master at King Henry VIII school in Coventry for 30 years, Ted has climbed in the Taurus, Carpathians, Elbruz and Hindu Kush and spent time as a volunteer ranger in four US national parks, including the Grand Canyon.

WALTER POLIDORI lives in the north of Italy and has been mountaineering for over 20 years. He is a national mountaineering instructor at the School of Mountaineering and Ski Mountaineering Guido della Torre and a member of the Italian Alpine Club's Legnano section. He loves climbing on rock, ice and mixed and has opened new routes on rock walls, usually in traditional style. He frequently writes about his new routes.

SIMON RICHARDSON lives in Aberdeen. Experience gained in the Alps, Andes, Patagonia, Canada, the Himalaya, Caucasus, Alaska and the Yukon is put to good use most winter weekends whilst exploring and climbing in the Scottish Highlands.

C A RUSSELL, who formerly worked with a City bank, devotes much of his time to mountaineering and related activities. He has climbed in many regions of the Alps, in the Pyrenees, East Africa, North America and the Himalaya.

VICTOR SAUNDERS was born in Lossiemouth and grew up in Peninsular Malaysia. He began climbing in the Alps in 1978 and has since climbed in the Andes, Antarctica, Papua, Rockies, Caucasus and across the Himalaya and Karakoram. Formerly a London-based architect, he is now an IFMGA guide based in Chamonix. His first book, *Elusive Summits*, won the Boardman Tasker Prize. In 2007 he received an honorary MA from the University of Stirling for services to Scottish mountaineering.

MARCELO SCANU is an Argentine climber who lives in Buenos Aires. He specialises in ascending virgin mountains and volcanoes in the Central Andes. His articles and photographs about alpinism, trekking, and mountain history, archaeology and ecology appear in prominent magazines in Europe and America. When not climbing, he works for a workers' union.

BOB SHEPTON was fortunate enough to find the cliffs of Lulworth and Portland unclimbed in the 1960s and 1970s and set about steadily developing them. In latter years he has led Tilman-type expeditions to the west coast of Greenland and arctic Canada, sailing and climbing new routes from his boat, culminating in the 'Big Walls' expedition awarded a Piolet d'Or in 2011.

BEN SILVESTRE is a North Yorkshire-born climber, now based in Sheffield. Working as an industrial abseiler allows him a lot of freedom for going climbing, and although he loves the small Peak District outcrops, he tries to spend as much time travelling to, and climbing in new and adventurous locations, whether that means British sea cliffs, or distant mountains.

DR NATHAN SMITH is a lecturer and researcher in sport psychology at the University of Northampton. His research is broadly related to health and wellbeing in physical settings, with a particular interest in psychological processes in extreme environments. Over the past few years, Nathan has conducted studies with polar and desert expeditions, mountaineers, Antarctic over-winterers and participants involved in Mars simulation studies. Nathan's extreme environment research focuses on issues related to selection and preparation, stress-resiliency and coping, and post-expedition adjustment and growth.

KIM SOMMERSCHIELD credits his love of mountains to his father's native Norway. His mother was an amateur painter whose invitation to try oils he refused, stubbornly persisting with watercolour in the vain hope he would one day master the technique. He's a member of the Italian Watercolour Society, holds a postgraduate degree in musicology and his many vices include fly-fishing and the Scottish smallpipes.

TOM RICHARDSON first visited the Himalaya in 1979 and has returned frequently to them and other Greater Ranges ever since, leading commercial groups for KE Adventure Travel and doing his own thing. Until retirement in 2016 he was a long-serving gear editor for *Climb* magazine and represented the Alpine Club on the Steering Committee of the Mount Everest Foundation. His autobiographical book is *Judgement Days in a Mountaineering Life*.

WILL SIM is a climber and mountain guide from west Cumbria now living in the French Alps. Will regularly seeks out adventurous missions on remote mountains all around the world as well as climbing and skiing in the Alps most days of the year for work and play. He likes crimping just as much as sitting on icy ledges, and will never be able to choose one above the other.

ERIC VOLA is a French climber who lives in Chamonix and Marseille. He spent three years at University College, London, and climbed in the early 1960s with Chris Bonington, Nick Estcourt, Don Whillans and other Brits. In recent years he has translated British mountaineering books, including a selection of Chris Bonington's best stories and Andy Cave's *Learning to Breathe*.

IAN WALL worked at Plas y Brenin in the 1960s. Since then he has climbed extensively throughout the UK, the Alps and in Norway. He was involved with the first round of the Kendal Mountain Film Festival in 1980. He has led treks in Africa, Ladakh, Tibet and Nepal, where he now lives and acts as an advisor to the Kathmandu International Mountain Film Festival, Kathmandu Environmental Education Project and in developing and training the Nepal Mountain Leader programme working closely with the Nepal Mountaineering Association.

NOTES FOR CONTRIBUTORS

The *Alpine Journal* records all aspects of mountains and mountaineering, including expeditions, adventure, art, literature, geography, history, geology, medicine, ethics and the mountain environment.

Articles Contributions in English are invited. They should be sent to the Hon Editor *The Alpine Journal*, Alpine Club, 55 Charlotte Road, London EC2A 3QF, UK. (**journal.editor@alpine-club.org.uk**) Articles, including images, should be sent on a disk or memory stick (with accompanying hard copy as appropriate, e.g. sketch maps) or as an email attachment. With files created in Microsoft Word please confine any extra formatting to italics and bold and set the language to English UK. Length should not exceed 3000 words without prior approval of the editor **and may be edited or shortened at their discretion**.

It is regretted that the *Alpine Journal* is unable to offer a fee for articles published, but authors who are not AC members receive a complimentary copy of the issue of the *Journal* in which their article appears.

Preferably, articles and book reviews should not have been published in substantially the same form by any other publication.

Maps and diagrams These should be well researched, accurate, and show the most important place-names mentioned in the text. It is the author's responsibility to get their maps redrawn if necessary. If submitted electronically, maps and route diagrams should be originated as CMYK .eps files in Adobe Illustrator, Freehand or similar ensuring any embedded images are at 300dpi resolution and CMYK. Hard copy should be scanned as a Photoshop compatible 300dpi tiff at A4 finished size. This can be arranged through the production editor if required.

Photographs Colour transparencies should be originals (not copies) in 35mm format or larger. Prints (any size) should be numbered (in pencil) on the back and accompanied by a separate list of captions (see below). Pre-scanned images should be **300dpi** Greyscale or RGB, tiffs or Maximum Quality jpegs at A4 final size or larger. **Images from digital cameras** should be submitted at the largest file size (quality) the camera can produce, e.g. 'Large' jpegs, tiffs or RAW files. Image files should have **short**, unique names/serial numbers **that correspond to the list of captions** appended to your article, as a separate word processing document, or in an email. Captions should be reasonably detailed and include the photographer's name. Captions must be provided for all images, including any slides and prints.

Copyright It is the author's responsibility to obtain copyright clearance for text, photographs, digital images and maps, to pay any fees involved and to ensure that acknowledgements are in the form required by the copyright owner.

Summaries A brief summary, listing dates, team members, objectives attempted and/or achieved, should be included at the end of articles where appropriate.

Biographies Authors are asked to provide a short biography, in about 50 words, listing the most noteworthy items in their climbing career and anything else they wish to mention.

Deadline Copy and photographs should reach the editor by 1 February of the year of publication.

Index 2016

D

H

I

J

K

L

M

O

P

Q

R

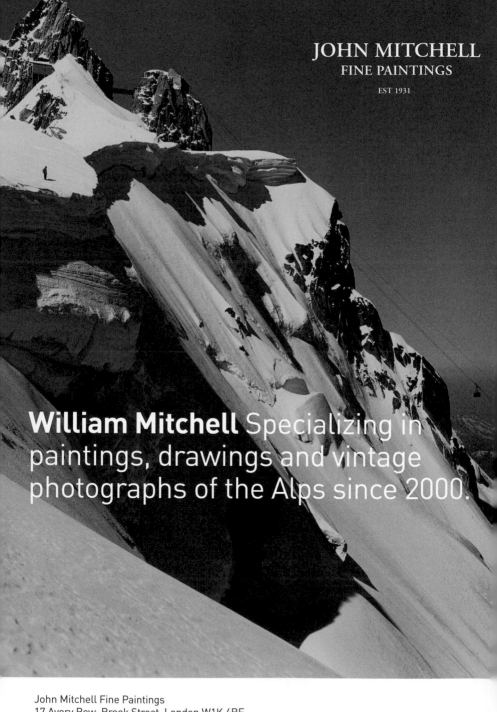

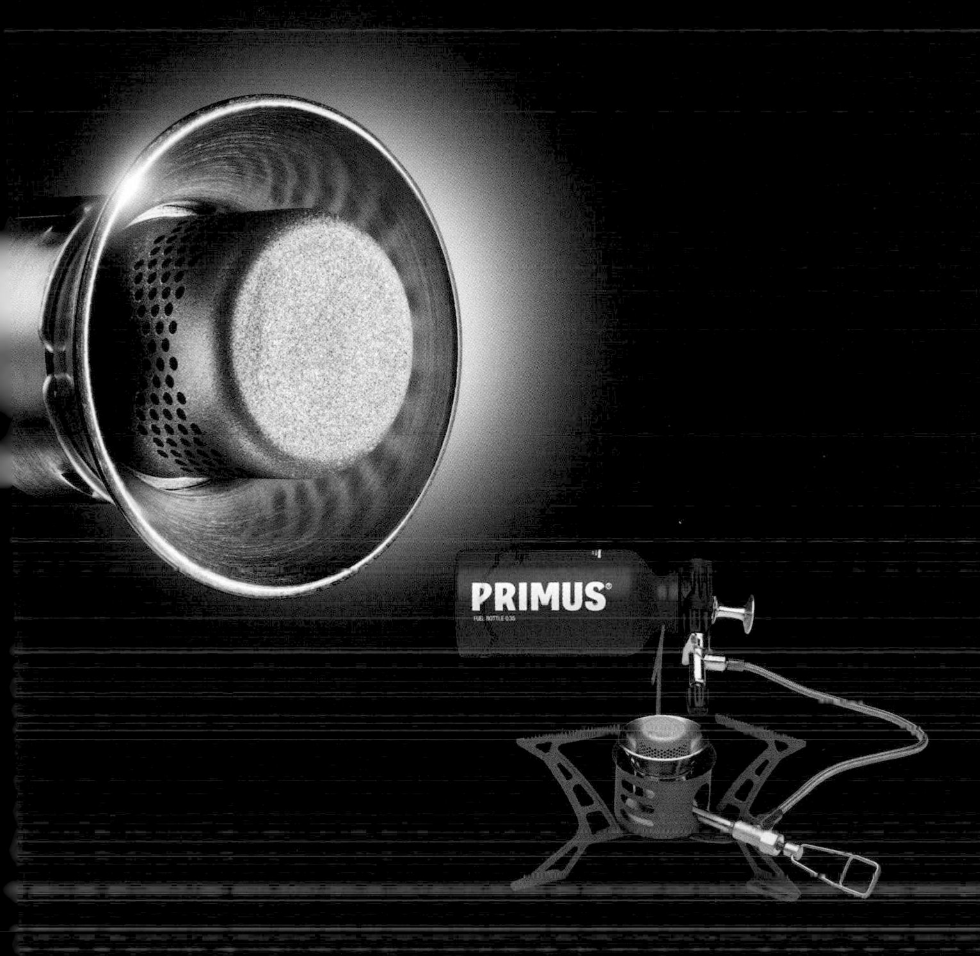
PRIMUS

SWE
PRIMUS

COLD MOUNTAIN KIT

In the bleakest
of walls, see
beautiful lines.
#TestYourExtrem

EXTREM
berghaus
AVAILABLE AT BERGHAUS.COM